BRAHMS

HIS LIFE AND WORK

BRAHMS

HIS LIFE AND WORK

KARL GEIRINGER

IN COLLABORATION WITH
IRENE GEIRINGER

Third Edition, Revised and Enlarged,
WITH
A New Appendix:
"Brahms as a Reader and Collector"

A DA CAPO PAPERBACK

Library of Congress Cataloging in Publication Data

Geiringer, Karl, 1899–
  Brahms, his life and work.

  Previously published: London: Oxford University
Press, 1947.
  Bibliography: p.
  Includes index.
  "A Da Capo Paperback."
  1. Brahms, Johannes, 1833–1897. 2. Composers —
Germany — Biography. I. Geiringer, Irene. II. Title.
ML410.B8G42   1984   780′.92′4 [B]   84-11401
ISBN 0-306-80223-6

Published by Da Capo Press, Inc.
A Subsidiary of Plenum Publishing Corporation
233 Spring Street, New York, N.Y. 10013

TO
THE MEMORY
OF
MY MOTHER

PREFACE TO THE FIRST EDITION

Is a new biography of Brahms really necessary? Have not enough books been written on the master's life? These questions will be asked by many who hear of this new publication. The answer can only be: Undoubtedly, the number of first-rate books on Brahms is considerable; but so many hitherto unknown documents relating to Brahms, as man and as artist, have recently come to light, that a new work seems not only justified, but really essential.

A unique body of material, until now inaccessible to other investigators, has been placed at my disposal. It consists of over a thousand letters received by Brahms from all sorts of correspondents. In accordance with an agreement between Brahms's heirs, they were handed over to the 'Gesellschaft der Musikfreunde' in Vienna, and there kept under official seal. As Custodian of this collection, I was authorized to be the first to read and use them for the purpose of my book. The bulk of the letters are from Brahms's mother, father, brother, and sister. They are supplemented by letters from a large number of eminent persons, among them some of Brahms's intimate friends; for example: Eugen d'Albert, Adolf Brodsky, Daniela von Bülow, Friedrich Chrysander, Peter Cornelius, Anton Dvořák, John Farmer, Benjamin Godard, Edvard Grieg, Sir George Grove, Sir George Henschel, Ferdinand Hiller, Hermann Kretzschmar, Franz Liszt, Adolf Menzel, Arthur Nikisch, Gustav Nottebohm, C. F. Pohl, Anton Rubinstein, Robert Schumann, Richard Strauss, Karl Tausig, Mathilde Wesendonck. From this valuable source new and interesting documents are available for almost every period of the master's life. Important supplements to these are: the letters from Clara Schumann and Joseph Joachim to Brahms's parents; a particularly interesting letter from Brahms to Amalie Joachim; numerous letters from Brahms to Hans von Bülow; and Brahms's correspondence with J. Allgeyer, which is in the possession of the Viennese Municipal Library. Unknown as yet in the English Brahms literature is the correspondence between Brahms and Eusebius Mandyczewski, the former librarian of the 'Gesellschaft der Musikfreunde,' Brahms's correspondence with Theodor Billroth, and also the master's letters to his Hamburg relatives.

With reference to the master's works, I was once more enabled to draw upon extensive material, which, though of the highest importance, had remained almost unnoticed in former biographies of Brahms. This material consists of the composer's sketches, also preserved by the 'Gesellschaft der Musikfreunde' (the heir to his artistic legacy), which are exceptionally rare, as he generally destroyed all his first drafts. In addition to this there are the manuscripts, which were thoroughly studied, as they give valuable indications of the changes which many compositions underwent between their first conception and their publication. The 'Gesellschaft der Musikfreunde' possessed also Brahms's own collection of single copies of each of his published compositions, in which he noted corrections and alterations for possible further editions, throwing light on his later attitude to his works. Taken 'as a whole, this material illustrates the different phases in the process of composition and gives one a profound insight into the master's mode of working.

I should be reluctant to close this Preface without thanking all those who have helped me in my work. In the first place, I wish gratefully to acknowledge the assistance which the directors of the 'Gesellschaft der Musikfreunde' have granted me, by removing all restrictions to the use of the Brahms legacy for the purposes of this work. Again, my sincerest thanks are due also to Mrs. Lisbe Leacock and Mrs. Helen

PREFACE TO THE FIRST EDITION

Perkin-Adie for their most valuable and untiring assistance in preparing the English version of this book. Further, I have to thank, for interesting new material or other important help, Mmes. Ottilie von Balassa, Olga and Else Lewinsky, Alice von Meyszner-Strauss, Mici Popper, Henriette Ribartz-Hemala, and MM. Dan Booth, Robert Caillet, Bronislaw Huberman, Professor Dr. Josef Hupka, President Director Wilhelm Kux, Eugen von Miller, and Professor Paul Wittgenstein.

KARL GEIRINGER

PREFACE TO THE SECOND EDITION

THIS new edition, the publication of which has been greatly delayed by the Second World War, discusses various compositions of Brahms that were discovered after the book was first printed. The main addition consists, however, in a number of letters by the composer that were previously not available to the English reader. A few are incorporated in the text of the biography, while most of them are to be found in an Appendix at the end of the book. It is hoped that they will contribute to a better understanding of the strange personality of a man who, in spite of his forbidding and often rude manners, had quite an unusual gift for making faithful friends.

The author is indebted to Mr. Henry S. Drinker of Philadelphia, who performed the most important task of newly translating the complete vocal work of Johannes Brahms into English. These excellent translations are used whenever reference is made to compositions for voice. Sincere thanks are also offered to the editorial staff of the Oxford University Press, New York, for its cooperative and understanding attitude, and to Mr. Walter F. H. Blandford, London, who, as in previous cases, completely revised the English text of this book.

K.G.

Boston, August 1947

PREFACE TO THE THIRD EDITION

THE selected Bibliography has been updated for this edition. Moreover, a new chapter has been added to the Appendix, dealing with Brahms's unusually strong literary and scholarly interests. Special thanks go to the *Musical Quarterly* and its Editor, Joan Peyser, for granting permission to use here large sections of an article I previously wrote for the periodical.

KARL GEIRINGER
Professor
University of California
Santa Barbara, September 1980

CONTENTS

I *His Life*

II *His Work*

CONTENTS

LIST OF ILLUSTRATIONS

PART ONE
HIS LIFE

FATHER AND MOTHER

THE Hamburg Pastor von Ahlsen must have thought the two people whom he married on 9 June 1830 an odd couple. The man, dressed in the becoming uniform of the Hamburg militia, was young, healthy, and good-looking; the woman, on the contrary, was frail and elderly, with one leg shorter than the other, her only attractive feature being her beautiful blue eyes. The first impression of a great difference in age was confirmed by the documents, for the bridegroom, Johann Jakob Brahms, was twenty-four years old, whereas his bride, Johanna Henrike Christiane Nissen, had already completed her forty-first year. It was not without some scruples that the pastor joined this ill-assorted pair, and he may have thought it advisable to keep an eye on the Brahms family. At first the newly married couple lived much as poor people do; that is, from hand to mouth, and often moving from place to place. According to the fluctuations of their income, they changed from poor rooms to even poorer ones, and then back again into roomier quarters if the coming of another child made this inevitable. A family soon began to arrive: first a daughter, who was christened, by Pastor von Ahlsen, Elisabeth Wilhelmine Luise. After this, on 7 May 1833, a son was born, who received the name of Johannes, and on 26 March 1835 a second son, Fritz Friedrich. In spite of heavy financial worries, Brahms and his wife appeared happy and contented, and it seemed that Johann Jakob had made a fortunate, if somewhat inexplicable, choice. What could have induced him to make it—love or reason? To answer this question it is necessary to learn more of the history of these two people.

Johann Jakob was born in the small village of Heide in Holstein, where his father kept an inn and a provision store. The elder brother, Peter Hoeft, inherited the father's business, and became, in addition, a pawnbroker and a dealer in second-hand goods. He soon grew so attached to his acquired treasures that he was loth to sell a single article, and we shall see a corresponding trait in his nephew's character. Johann Jakob had very different ideas, and to the horror of his family, who had always lived by trades and handicrafts, the boy declared his intention of becoming a musician. With the tenacity of the Holsteiner, who is accustomed to work under the most difficult conditions, he finally overcame all opposition. After he had run away from home several times, his parents at last allowed him to take lessons from a local musician, with whom he studied until 1825. This was all the family could do for their unruly son, and now he had to fend for himself. Johann Jakob did not stay long in the little provincial town, for he felt that a magnificent destiny awaited him in Hamburg. His worldly possessions were small, but he had the greatest confidence in the future.

Before long the youth of nineteen was to find that it was by no means easy to live in the capital on his earnings as a musician. Although he had learned to play all the stringed instruments, the flute, and the French horn moderately well, this versatility did not help him very much. There was nothing left for him but to clench his teeth and make the best of things; and the dockside district swallowed him up. Here, in the meanest taverns, he played dance music; here, too, he found the squalid lodgings, which were all he could afford. But all the dirt and ugliness that Johann Jakob had to endure in those first years in Hamburg were powerless to shake him in his purpose. He did his job as musician as thoroughly and conscientiously as his forebears had worked at the carpenter's bench and the counter. Shrewdly realizing his musical limitations, he played mainly the double bass, which offered few difficulties, and was indispensable in an *ensemble* of any size. And so, what with hard work, and some ability, he slowly succeeded in obtaining engagements at the better places of amusement, and in the end he became first an occasional and then a permanent member of a well-known sextet in the fashionable 'Alster-Pavilion,' where the best society assembled. Even before this, his horn-playing had won him an appointment in the Hamburg militia, and the assured, though very small, income on which he could now count encouraged him to consider a complete change in his hitherto unsettled existence.

It is best to let Christiane Nissen herself tell of what followed, for she describes her life before her marriage, with touching simplicity, in a letter [1] to her famous son, written shortly before her death.

Auntie and I ['Auntie' was her sister, married to a workingman, Philip Detmering] grew up very simply. I was thirteen when I started going out to sew. In the evenings I came home at six o'clock, then I liked to give mother a hand, and sometimes I sewed until midnight. Six years I went on like that. Then I worked for ten years with very respectable employers as general servant. Then again I went out sewing. . . Then Auntie married, and I lived with her, helped in the shop [a hardware shop] and earned what I could by sewing. Father [Johann Jakob Brahms] took a room with us, and so we got acquainted. He had only been living with us for a week when he wanted me to become his wife. I could hardly believe it, because our ages were so different. Uncle spoke of it again and again, and so I felt it was intended.

If one can believe the old lady's recollections, and there is every reason to do so, for Frau Brahms is said to have had a remarkable memory, Johann Jakob Brahms made this important decision with surprising promptitude. All Brahms's biographers are agreed that Christiane's excellent qualities as a housewife obscured the obvious disadvantages of the match in the eyes of the young musician, who had lived for years under the most unsettled and squalid conditions. There

[5]

may be some truth in this, but her domestic virtues cannot have been wholly responsible for his choice since capable housewives were not rare in those days. From the same letter we learn that shortly before he met Christiane he had been greatly attracted by a pretty girl of seventeen. There must have been some profounder reason why the robust and vivacious young man preferred the fragile spinster of forty-one. As a matter of fact, the personality of Christiane Nissen—strange as it may seem—appealed to one prominent trait in Johann Jakob's character: his ambition to rise in the world. This ambition had led him from the country to the capital, from the lowest social rank to a respectable middle-class existence. The undersized little seamstress, who had earned her living since her thirteenth year, was in many respects the young musician's superior, and Johann Jakob must vaguely have felt that she was the right companion for him, as she would do her utmost to help her husband realize his ambitions. The stock from which she came was much higher in the social scale and far more respected than his own. In the *Ahnentafel berühmter Deutscher* (Genealogy of Famous Germans), published in 1929, we read that Christiane Nissen's mother (A. Margarete von Bergen) was of gentle birth, and that her father's family can be traced back as far as the fourteenth century. Among his forefathers were ecclesiastical administrators, councillors, burgomasters, and clergymen, and although the family gradually lost their prominent position in society, Christiane's great-grandfather and grand-- father were both members of a learned profession. They were schoolmasters, whereas her father was merely a tailor. It was probably to him that she owed her great manual dexterity. But it was from her remote forebears that she inherited the notably keen mind which must have impressed the rather slow-witted Johann Jakob.

Concerning Johannes Brahms's mother, research has hitherto yielded very little exact information. But now, thanks to the letters that have recently become accessible, I am

[6]

able to remedy this. The 120 letters written by Christiane
to her son Johannes, supplemented by those of his brother
and sister, paint such a living portrait of this admirable
woman that I feel I must speak of her more particularly.

No one, on reading Christiane's letters, can fail to be
deeply impressed. This simple woman, whose limited education is betrayed by her faulty spelling and phrasing, was
able to express herself so vividly in her correspondence that
one can almost hear her speaking. She is the only member
of the family who seems not to have been embarrassed by
the act of writing, and on the rare occasions when the
busy woman found a little leisure in the evening there was
nothing she enjoyed more than writing to tell Johannes all
that had been happening. The free and natural style, so rare
in people of little education, is but seldom to be found in
the letters of her other two children, and—with one significant exception (see page 95)—it is entirely lacking in those
of Jakob Brahms. During Christiane's lifetime he could not
be persuaded to write even a single line to his son. After
her death every one of his short reports to Johannes began
with an excuse, such as 'I hardly have anything to write
about,' [2] or 'I am afraid I have always avoided writing letters, which I suppose is why I find it so difficult.' [3]

Besides showing a certain unsophisticated pleasure in nar-
ration, Frau Brahms's letters give a strong impression of her
clear common sense and her great kindheartedness. In these
long letters, in which the mother tells her son all the interesting news from Hamburg, she hardly once speaks ill of anybody, and she even finds excuses for people of whom her beloved Johannes has reason to complain. When the violinist
Reményi, after a short joint concert tour, unexpectedly severed his connection with Brahms, thereby leaving the inexperienced and impecunious youth of twenty in a distant part of Germany and dependent on his own resources
(see page 31), Christiane wrote the following words, which
furnish evidence not only of her unwavering belief in her

son's capacities, and this long before he had become famous, but also of her kindness of heart.[4] 'I hope you have parted friends. After all one can't be angry with him. He probably thinks he is better off on his own . . . with you he may make a good impression at the moment, but not in the long run.' As for her boy's friends, nothing that she could do was good enough for them. She often reminded him to write to them, knowing his reluctance to do so, and although she counted the hours until the arrival of his next letter, she would ask him to write to his friends first, lest they should feel neglected.[5]

It always made her happy to help others. 'After all, what can give me greater joy than to help and serve my fellow creatures as far as lies in my power. People who live only for themselves and not for others are only half alive.'[6] A certain bitterness creeps into her letters only when she complains of being unable to help others. For example, she writes: 'We poor people haven't the means to help; we can only feel for others, and those who have the means don't help because they don't feel; they console people with fine phrases.'[7] When her daughter Elise received a present from Clara Schumann, Christiane wrote as though just a little envious to think that Clara should be well enough off to give pleasure to others.[8] Her kindness went hand in hand with a great delicacy of feeling. A charming little episode confirms this. When she once had to reproach Johannes for a thoughtless action, knowing that her son kept all her letters, she wrote the reproachful words on a separate piece of paper, so that 'You can burn it, and then you won't see it again afterwards.'[9] One consequence of this delicacy of feeling in all matters relating to her son is a certain hypersensibility. 'This morning, when I got up,' she wrote,[10] 'I felt your dear letter was coming. You are always my first thought, and I seemed to hear you say: "Today, Mother, you will get a letter from me." ' Such a woman must naturally be highly receptive to religious ideas, and in difficult situations she had implicit trust in God. When in 1854, to her intense dismay, **Fritz** Brahms lost an excellent post, she wrote: [11] 'Fritz must put his trust in God, who guides all human destinies. He will lead him out of this darkness.' It goes without saying that his mother never forgot to include Johannes in her prayers.[12] Yet she did not remember him alone; a true mother, she gave the other two less successful children the same loving care and forethought as Johannes who was the pride of her life. She always tried anxiously to keep the bond between the three as close as possible; she would remind Johannes not to forget their birthdays, or any present that he had promised them, so that Elise and Fritz should not feel hurt.

Whether her literary tastes were really as pronounced as all the biographers have imagined (according to Kalbeck she was supposed to know the whole of Schiller by heart) I am inclined to doubt after reading the letters of this much-harassed woman. In all this correspondence she only once mentions the name of a poet, Klopstock; and then she does not say that she has read his poems, but only that she has visited his grave on an excursion to Neumühlen.[13] On the other hand, there is every reason to cherish the highest opinions of her domestic virtues, for she was an excellent needle-woman and a remarkably good cook. Not only Johannes but even pampered artists like Clara Schumann and Joachim, who were accustomed to luxury, praised her culinary achievements, and particularly her famous bilberry fritters. In money matters she was extremely punctilious. 'You know your mother can't sleep if she owes a penny. Earn money wherever you can, but for heaven's sake no borrowing!' she exclaimed.[14] She held all the more firmly to this principle inasmuch as her restless husband was always seeking new— and sometimes very expensive—ways of getting on in the world. At first he tried his luck in the lottery, thereby losing part of his hard-earned savings. Then he persuaded her to open a small shop, like that she had run with her sister Detmering, but from the first it was clear that this venture had little chance of success, as Frau Brahms found it difficult to cope with the additional work. Later on he wanted to emigrate to America (see page 17), and the shop was sold, hurriedly, and, of course, at a loss. Considering that the Brahms household also tried their luck, at different times, with the rearing of chickens, pigeons, and rabbits,[15] we can understand that Frau Brahms's life as housewife was not exactly an easy one.

In Christiane, then, Johann Jakob had made a really good choice of a wife, and their life together was as happy as it could be under such trying material conditions. Under the circumstances, then, I do not think one is justified in speaking of 'a by no means harmonious marriage,' as most biographers have done. Doubtless they have had in mind the disagreements between husband and wife that arose during the last years of Frau Brahms's life, and which were naturally aggravated by the great difference in their ages. At that time Frau Brahms was a very old woman, worn out by a life of care and hardship, whereas her husband was only in the fifties, in the prime of life, and full of energy. During the greater part of their married life, which lasted for thirty-four years, there is no sign of any disharmony, if one may judge by the letters which have been preserved. Generally speaking, peace and cheerfulness prevailed in the Brahms household.

Both the father and the mother were artists in living, who knew the secret of enjoying the simplest pleasures with all their hearts. For example, they developed a particular ritual for birthdays, when all the pictures were hung with garlands, and in the evening toasts were drunk in egg-nog, a beverage beloved by all the family, including Johannes. This egg-nog is so often mentioned in the family correspondence that we are pleased to find the recipe,[16] which was written down for Clara Schumann by Elise Brahms: 1 bottle of rum, 12 eggs, 4 lemons, and 1½ lb. of sugar. This egg-nog festivity always created a very jolly atmosphere, remembered gratefully long

[10]

after the occasion; and once when Johannes wrote in praise of another kind of punch, his mother indignantly replied: 'I can't believe that pineapple-cup tastes better than egg-nog. I am so looking forward to the egg-nog when you come.' [17] Another family tradition was the Christmas goose. Johannes, at a time when his income was still very inadequate, once sent two thalers home to his parents, who were at that time very badly off, so that they should not be deprived of this pleasure.

The wretched apartments in which the family lived for many years were a source of misery to Christiane, and perhaps even more to her husband. For him, nothing could be good enough when his friends came to visit them.[18] Both were always eager to add to the comfort of their home as far as lay in their power. In her old age, Lieschen Giesemann, an old playmate of Johannes's (see page 20), refers repeatedly to the charming pastel portrait of Christiane Brahms as a young girl, in a red dress with tight bodice and short sleeves, which was hung in the place of honor over the piano in every home they had.[19] They were always fond of keeping song birds—once there is even mention of a nightingale—and whenever possible the room was adorned with flowering plants, in whose welfare the whole family took the liveliest interest. The delight these people took in all natural beauty is touching, compelled as they were to live in the ugliest parts of the town. When, in 1858, a better home was secured with an outlook over a garden, they rejoiced 'in the fresh air, as though we were sitting in a garden.' [20] Every phase of the growth of the wild vine that surrounded the window was reported to Johannes; and when the first snow fell Frau Brahms wrote with enthusiasm: 'How lovely it looks, as though every tree were covered with blossom! [21] The father, too, felt as happy in the country, with the forest almost at the door 'as though he had been in Paradise.' [22] Even as an old man, shortly before his death, when he was seriously ill, he could not resist making long excursions outside the town, and he enjoyed the beauties of his native land with unfailing appreciation.

Many of these traits can easily be traced in Johannes Brahms's character. From his father he inherited three characteristics: splendid health (Johann Jakob Brahms, in his late sixties, could dance all night through without getting tired), a determination to rise in the world, and his musical talent. However, there was an essential difference in the abilities of the father and the son. The father's musical talent was just great enough to enable him to rise from the status of street musician to that of contrabass player in a fashionable sextet, and later on to the position of member of the Hamburg Philharmonic Orchestra. Also, his musical versatility is deserving of mention; he not only played the double bass and horn, but was also an excellent flautist, who was praised, even at the age of sixty, by a new conductor.[23] When, in his declining years, the ailing man was free from financial cares, thanks to the munificence of his son, he played the first violin as a pastime in various private string quartets, and also kept up his practice of the flute.[24] Thus the father was certainly more than the indifferent bandsman that many of the biographers see in him, but his talent, nevertheless, lacked artistic inspiration; and although his progress as a musician was excellent, he always remained a journeyman. How the son's creative genius resulted from the father's mediocre musical talent is beyond understanding; but there is reason to believe that those spiritual and mental qualities that transform a reproductive into a creative talent came from the mother.

Apart from music pure and simple, the master certainly owed his intellectual versatility to the Nissen family. From his mother, too, he inherited his great kindness and helpfulness, traits which we shall meet again and again in the course of this book. In common with his father and mother he had a deep love of Nature, and an appreciation of the small joys of life. These had made his parents happy, in spite of cares and difficulties. That it was otherwise with their son, that in spite of such magnificent gifts he was not after all a happy man, is to be explained by the fundamental nature of creative genius. In Brahms's case, however, it was also due to a peculiar inner development.

UNPUBLISHED LETTERS REFERRED TO:

1. Letter from Christiane Brahms, 6 January 1865.
2. Letter from Johann Jakob Brahms, 23 August 1866.
3. Letter from Johann Jakob Brahms, 7 March 1865.
4. Letter from Christiane Brahms, 10 July 1853.
5. Letter from Christiane Brahms, Autumn 1862
6. Letter from Christiane Brahms, 4 October 1854.
7. Letter from Christiane Brahms, 11 July 1855.
8. Letter from Christiane Brahms, 14 February 1855.
9. Letter from Christiane Brahms, 23 July 1854.
10. Letter from Christiane Brahms, 16 September 1853.
11. Letter from Christiane Brahms, 15 May 1854.
12. Letter from Christiane Brahms, 3 September 1853.
13. Letter from Christiane Brahms, 12 June 1855.
14. Letter from Christiane Brahms, 20 March 1855.
15. Letter from Christiane Brahms, 6 January 1865.
16. Letter from Elise Brahms, 30 September 1856.
17. Letter from Christiane Brahms, 25 November 1857.
18. Letter from Christiane Brahms, 6 January 1865.
19. Letter from Elise Denninghoff, 25 September 1889.
20. Letter from Christiane Brahms, August 1858.
21. Letter from Christiane Brahms, 12 November 1858.
22. Letter from Johann Jakob Brahms, 8 August 1871.
23. Letter from Johann Jakob Brahms, 26 March 1867.
24. Letter from Johann Jakob Brahms, 16 December 1870.

II

CHILDHOOD AND YOUTH

(1833-1853)

O NE cannot paint too sordid a picture of the poverty-stricken surroundings in which Johannes Brahms grew up. Narrow crooked streets, dilapidated, age-blackened 'frame' houses, made up the so-called *Gängeviertel* in which he spent his childhood and youth. Dirt and disease were here matters of course, and—as the little Brahms was to learn—if fire broke out, its effects in the close-packed, overcrowded houses, which were largely built of wood, were devastating.

Although the atmosphere of the slums was certainly not favorable to the development of a growing child, Brahms's parents did their best to make their home an oasis of peaceful though humble security. In spite of material difficulties and worries, Johannes and his brother and sister spent a comparatively sheltered childhood, and their natural talents were fostered with understanding.

Little Johannes loved best to play with lead soldiers, never tiring of setting them up in new formations. It is curious to find the quiet, sensitive boy, who commonly avoided the noisy games of his contemporaries, occupied with so martial a hobby. But in reality the setting out of these lead soldiers —in which he indulged even as an adult, and which is said to have inspired him to creative work—had little in common with the usual boyish delight in warlike games. The arrangement of the little lead figures in varying formations gave him the same sort of pleasure he derived in later years from the writing of variations on a theme; for in both cases he was impelled by the urge to remodel a given material with the aid of imagination.

Soon, however, play had to give way to work; a school had to be found. Both parents agreed that no sacrifice should be spared to give the children a sound education. In Elise's case, unfortunately, this was out of the question; the poor girl suffered from such terrible headaches that study was impossible. But Johannes and Fritz were to enjoy a better education than their parents. Johannes was accordingly sent at the age of six to the private school of Herr Heinrich Voss, which he left in his eleventh year for the school of Johann Friedrich Hoffmann. The generally accepted story of Johannes' wretched education, told in most of the Brahms biographies, is not confirmed by recent research; both schools were good, and the boy learned as much as was possible under the standards of education then obtaining. Herr Hoffmann's school was even famous for its advanced methods. Besides teaching Latin, French, and English, it specialized in mathematics and natural history; and it possessed gymnastic appliances, which were not introduced into the State schools until many years later. The headmaster, described as 'kind-hearted, and full of imagination and energy,' would assuredly not have ill-treated the boy. This is evident from the fact that Johannes after thirty years still cherished kindly recollections of his teacher; and on the fiftieth anniversary of the school he not only subscribed substantially to a presentation,[1] but also sent his portrait to Herr Hoffmann.

Before long the importance of his school work receded into the background, both for the parents and for Johannes himself. That which could already be foreseen in the small child become more evident from day to day; the boy's irresistible inclination towards music. 'Very well,' said Jakob, 'let 'Hannes become an orchestra player like myself'; and he began to initiate the child into the mysteries of the stringed instruments. 'Hannes, however, was the true son of his father; he knew his own mind. The stringed instruments did not satisfy him, and just as young Johann Jakob forced his parents to make him a musician, so Johannes insisted that he wanted to be taught the piano, and at the age of seven his lessons began. Herr Brahms showed his sound sense in choosing a teacher, Friedrich Wilhelm Cossel, who was an excellent pianist and a true musician, a pupil of a highly respected Hamburg composer and teacher, Eduard Marxsen. In his teaching he combined the development of technical ability with a loving understanding of the inner content of a composition. He was never satisfied with mere brilliance of execution; every little phrase had to express an inward experience. This attitude, by no means usual in the days of Kalkbrenner, Herz, Moscheles, and others, had the greatest influence on the child's development. On the purely musical side it was important for Johannes that he should not be guided into the paths of the fashionable virtuoso; and even more valuable was the human gain. In Cossel the child saw a musician who regarded his profession in a very different light from his father and his father's colleagues; for to his teacher every work of art was sacred, and might be approached only with reverence.

Before long Cossel realized that Johannes was not only unusually gifted, but that he had in him all the makings of a remarkable musician, and a close relationship between teacher and pupil developed. To avoid wasting time in coming and going, the boy spent whole days in Cossel's house, and in the end the teacher decided to move nearer to Johannes' home. The neighboring families now became close friends, and helped each other in every way. In 1857 Johannes became godfather to one of his teacher's daughters,[2] and after the death of Frau Brahms, the lonely Elise was affectionately welcomed by the Cossels.[3] Only too soon she was able to show her gratitude, when Friedrich Cossel was taken from his family, and she looked after his children while the widow went out to earn her living.[4]

Under this excellent teacher's guidance 'Hannes' playing

BRAHMS'S BIRTHPLACE IN HAMBURG

made extraordinary progress. At the age of ten he played at a concert, arranged by his father, in the Beethoven quintet, Op. 16, and in a piano quartet of Mozart's. By chance there was in the audience a certain impresario, who promised Johann Jakob Brahms unbelievable wealth if he would emigrate to America with the young Johannes. This wonderful prospect intoxicated the poor Hamburgers; they agreed, and hastened to tell Cossel of this stroke of good fortune. The teacher, however, was of a wholly different opinion, knowing that a concert tour at this immature stage would be the ruin of this rare human prodigy. As all his arguments were of no avail, he decided to make a great sacrifice: he handed over his beloved pupil to Eduard Marxsen, one of Hamburg's most eminent teachers of music, in the hope that he would have more influence with the parents. Cossel begged him to teach the gifted boy, as he himself had nothing more to give, and when, after some hesitation, the famous teacher assented, the parents' pride and enthusiasm were so great that they followed the advice of both masters, and gave up the idea of going to America.

The year 1843, therefore, brought a decisive change in Johannes' musical life. At first Eduard Marxsen co-operated with Cossel in teaching the boy, but after a year or two he took entire charge of him. Cossel had provided Johannes with a solid technical and musical foundation to his playing; Marxsen now supervised his progress until his maturity as a pianist. He laid the greatest stress on two things, if we may judge by his own compositions: on the development of the left hand, and on precision in the playing of dissimilar and difficult rhythms. His method differed essentially from Cossel's in one important respect. While Cossel held that young Brahms would become a good pianist only if he gave up writing music, Marxsen did not hesitate to encourage his passion for composition. He recognized with delight Johannes' 'acute and profoundly thoughtful mind,' and gave him regular lessons in the theory of music and composition.

Marxsen himself had studied with Mozart's pupil, Seyfried, and with Bocklet, a friend of Beethoven's and Schubert's, and it was thus only natural that he should first of all introduce Brahms to the music of the classical and early romantic schools.

It is, however, unjust to speak—as is often done—of Marxsen's manifest hostility to the art of his time. His *Three Romances* record a certain familiarity with the works of Chopin, and Fritz Brahms, who, like his brother, was taught by Marxsen, studied Chopin's A flat major Polonaise with him in 1853.[5] In important principles Marxsen was entirely in agreement with his eminent pupil. The preference for the popular art of different countries, so characteristic of Brahms, and particularly his love of the German folk songs, as well as his delight in the art of variation, are prefigured in the teacher's compositions. And in certain passages of Brahms's early works we find echoes of Marxsen's idiom. If we consider the theme of Marxsen's *Characteristic Variations on a Peasant Dance*, Op. 67/1, we shall be surprised to see how closely this popular tune, with its continual alternative of ¾ and 4/4 time, resembles the theme of Brahms's earliest variations, Op. 21/2. And also in the course of Marxsen's *Variations on a Finnish Folk Song*, Op. 67/2, there are sections (Nos. 8 and 10) that sound like foreshadowings of Brahms's pianoforte variations.

In his character too, Marxsen differed widely from Cossel. He was reserved, harsh, witty, and shrewd; as an old man he still wrote to his famous pupil malicious and amusing accounts of the musical life at Hamburg. Despite his outward severity, he was, like many of his countrymen, and not least his pupil himself, inwardly very soft-hearted. When his old blind dog died, he and his family were for three days too miserable to touch any food.[6] The Brahms family, especially, could always be sure of his generosity. He accepted no remuneration whatever for his teaching, and in difficult periods was a wise and helpful friend, whose advice was accepted as an oracle.

Johannes was in the happy position of being able to give when he was at the height of his fame, proof of his heartfelt gratitude to Marxsen. He kept up a correspondence with him, and sent him every new work (sometimes, as in the case of the *Requiem,* in manuscript, with a request for corrections), and in 1882 he dedicated the *Piano Concerto in B flat major* to him. On Marxsen's 'fiftieth jubilee as an artist, in 1883, Brahms conceived the graceful idea of having printed at his own expense his teacher's *One Hundred Variations on a Folk Song.* Here is the old man's reply—he was then in his seventy-seventh year: [7]

What a surprise, what a great pleasure you have given me! In my old age it has been granted to me to see a second day of triumph in my artistic career. The first, of course, was when Seyfried, on account of my first symphony, called me 'his son.' The second is evoked by my faithful pupils, headed by you, the pride of my life and professional career. I want to clasp you to my heart, the loyal friend, who has employed his heavenly gifts for the true welfare of Art. May the Lord continue to protect you, may He lavish His love upon you, to the joy of all those who render homage to what is lofty and noble in Art. . . Your enraptured

MARXSEN

It seems as though fate had endeavored to atone for the trying conditions in which Johannes spent his youth by allowing him two such splendid teachers. His childhood, indeed, though not without joy, since humor and courage were never lacking in the Brahms household, was certainly not carefree. The amount that Herr Brahms was able to earn for his family of five was extremely small, so that the children had to turn to and help, and especially so gifted a boy as Johannes. Accordingly, he began at the age of thirteen to play in taverns and restaurants, and the fame of the young pianist soon spread among the proprietors of places of amusement. He would often be called away from home late at night to play at dances, receiving little pay, but allowed as much drink as he wanted. Obviously, these were dangerous surroundings for the boy, and one wonders that Frau Brahms gave her consent to this kind of work. Is it quite consistent with the impression of the loving mother that we have so far received? To answer this question, we must realize that Frau Brahms herself had begun to work at the age of thirteen and that it had always been her maxim that honest work could do no harm. Above all, she realized the importance of home influence for the formation of character, and at home Johannes lived in a thoroughly healthy atmosphere. Accordingly the mother was content, only trying, whenever an opportunity offered, to urge her son to lead a regular life. Even as late as 1853 she exhorted him [8] at the time of his quarrel with Reményi: 'keep in good health and *morally good,* then this disagreeable period will pass.'

Such a double life, however, could not fail to have a bad physical and psychological influence on the delicate boy. After a time Johannes began to feel the twofold strain of perfecting himself as a virtuoso under Marxsen's strict guidance, and of playing dance music for hours in a vitiated, smoke-laden atmosphere. He became so anemic and nervous that, as he afterwards told his friend, Klaus Groth, 'he could only walk along an avenue by staggering from tree to tree, otherwise he would have fallen.'

A stroke of luck helped him to get over this bad period. His father made the acquaintance of one Adolf Giesemann, from the village of Winsen on the Luhe, the owner of a paper mill, who invited the boy to stay with him for the summer so that he might teach the piano to his daughter Lieschen, and at the same time enjoy a change of air. Johannes spent the summers of 1847 and 1848 in this pleasant village, and without a doubt these carefree months were among the happiest memories of his childhood. 'Uncle' and 'Auntie' Giesemann pampered the pale town-bred boy, and Lieschen was an amiable playmate, always ready to read his beloved books with him. And here for the first time the young artist found an admiring musical community. He conducted the male choir of the village, for which he transposed folk songs and wrote original choral compositions. His happiness in having escaped from the city found expression in a spate of creative work. In fact, in a letter [9] written many years later, Lieschen Giesemann bitterly complained that the many manuscripts dedicated to her father, which had always been held sacred, had to be returned, in the 'sixties, at Brahms's request (probably for destruction). His relations with the Giesemanns were maintained for some time, and during Johannes's first concert tour all his letters to his parents had to be shown to these friends, who could never read them without being moved to tears.[10] Lieschen then married and went to live in Wilhelmshaven, and they lost sight of each other, but many years later, in 1888, when Lieschen's daughter, Agnes, was studying at the *Hochschule für Musik* in Berlin, the impoverished widow begged the famous friend of her youth to obtain a scholarship for the girl.[11] Brahms, only too happy to be able to help, of course fulfilled her wish. He immediately communicated with Joachim, the director of the Academy, and instructed him that he would secretly pay for the girl's tuition himself, should a scholarship be impossible. He explained his attitude with these words: 'I am indebted to the family of the girl for much love and friendship, and my memory of her grandfather is of the most beautiful kind that the human heart can treasure.'

When in the autumn of 1848 Johannes returned from Winsen to Hamburg, the delicate boy had developed into a sturdy youth, whose splendid health was never to fail him throughout his life. There was soon occasion to prove his new-found strength. On 21 September 1848, young Brahms, having previously taken part in various public engagements, gave his first recital. A fugue by J. S. Bach struck a peculiar note among the customary virtuoso pieces. In the spring of

[21]

1849 a second concert followed, in which he ventured to play Beethoven's *Waldstein Sonata,* and also a composition of his own—a fantasy on a popular waltz. Here, for various reasons, his career as a virtuoso ended for the time being. His success was not too great, either with his audience or with the critics; there was already a sufficient number of first-class pianists, such as Goldschmidt, Tedesco, in Hamburg, who could perfectly well compete with the sixteen-year-old Brahms, to say nothing of the many famous international stars who came to the city. Moreover, it became more and more repugnant to him to pay homage to the fashion of the time whereas he could have hardly filled a concert hall with a program of his own choice. Above all, as he approached maturity, he clearly realized the path which he ought to follow in his art; he knew that it was not as a pianist but as a composer that he could give his best. The creative tide flowed irresistibly within him, and the youth wrote compositions of such daring invention and persuasive rhythm that even at the height of his career he had no reason to be ashamed of them. In 1851 he wrote the *Scherzo in E flat minor,* Op. 4, and in November 1852 the *Piano Sonata in F sharp minor.* The same year witnessed the beginning of the *Sonata in C major,* Op. 1, which was completed in January 1853. He wrote, besides, a large number of songs, including the famous *Liebestreu.* These are only a few of the compositions he produced at this time, most of which, including some string quartets and possibly also a trio (compare p. 224), the master destroyed in his ruthless self-criticism.

This creative outburst was accompanied by a widening and deepening of his spiritual horizon. He devoured every book he could get hold of, and after contributing his share to the expenses of the household he spent every penny he had left on books, thereby laying the foundation of an imposing library. Among these books we find the *Generalbass Schule* of the Hamburger David Kellner (published in 1742), with the entry 'Johannes Brahms, 1848.' This choice is significant of the seriousness of Brahms at fifteen, and it also reveals his antiquarian interest, which was inherited from his uncle, and was directed particularly to the city of Hamburg. To counterbalance the dry theory of music, the youth became deeply engrossed in the world of romantic poetry, wherein he found, differently expressed, the spirit to which his own creations had given life. To announce his alliance with this romantic spirit he called himself 'Johannes Kreisler, junior,' after the principal character of his favorite novel, *Kater Murr* by the poet-musician E. T. A. Hoffmann. He began to copy the finest passages from his favorite authors into a number of little books which he called *Schatzkästlein des jungen Kreisler* (Young Kreisler's Treasury). The varying interests of these pieces give one a vivid impression of young Brahms's understanding of essential values, and reveal his intellectual versatility.

No one in Hamburg had the faintest notion of all this, for the reticent youth had hardly any friends, and felt quite a stranger even in his own family. To his mother, however, he was attached with all the fervor of his affectionate nature, and he knew that she would follow his ideas with her mother's instinct, even beyond the limits of her own understanding. It was, therefore, with his mother that he passed most of his free time, and in later years she delighted in recalling the happy evenings they spent together. In reference to one New Year's Eve she writes: [12] 'I still remember how we two, you and I [Father Brahms had an engagement], had such a happy time, don't you remember, it is many years ago, but it seems to me like yesterday. I've never seen you so merry since.' His father, too, he loved with all his heart, but he knew that he could not discuss spiritual problems with him, although they continually filled his thoughts. Above all, a young man must have sympathetic friends of his own age. Such friends his brother and sister were not. Elise's intentions were of the best, but she was a difficult companion.

She was highly emotional (she once spoke of Johannes' 'lovely, divine, heavenly letters') [13] which could not please her reserved brother. Then her terrible headaches would make her indifferent to her surroundings for days on end. But even when in good health she was capable only of discussing everyday affairs with Johannes, and her main concern was to prepare his favorite dishes to his liking. There may, however, have been in her also a spark of Frau Brahms's intellect, for it is surprising to find what excellent books she took from her brother's library when moving house after their mother's death. Besides Bürger's poetical works and *Paul and Virginia* we find Goethe's correspondence with Schiller, Mozart's biography by Otto Jahn, and an edition of Schumann's writings.[14] The world of literature was, however, revealed to her only at a later date, by her brother and possibly also by Clara Schumann (see p. 50); at the time of Johannes's spiritual growth his sister apparently could not follow the trend of his thoughts.

It would have been natural for him to associate more closely with his brother Fritz, who had enjoyed the same education and had likewise chosen music as his profession. Here, however, essential obstacles existed; Fritz's character was in some respects opposed to that of his brother; he was livelier, and he was given to fine words and promises which meant but little. A typical scene is recounted by Elise.[15] The mother was often deeply concerned about the future of her delicate daughter; but Fritz always declared, in an emotional manner, that he would, of course, watch over his sister with the most loving care. Johannes, on the contrary, listened in silence, yet when his sister was left alone in the world it was he, who had never made any promises, who devoted himself to her welfare (see p. 88), while the boastful Fritz never made the slightest effort to help her. In art, too, Fritz lacked his brother's ideals and his steady pursuit of his aims; and this divergence of character emphasized a rivalry resulting from the similarity of their occupation. Fritz naturally had to compare himself with his brother, and felt deeply wronged by nature and destiny. (It can well be imagined how hurt he must have been when he was given the nickname, in Hamburg, of 'the wrong Brahms.') The elder suspected this sense of wrong, and covered his own sense of guilt by wrangling. Frau Brahms, too, realized what was troubling her boys and she once wrote of Fritz: [16] 'The poor boy! Father often thought that Fritz had been neglected; so he wanted him to learn the fiddle, for he always thought he could get somewhere with it. Oh, what Fritz could have learned from you, had you behaved like real brothers!'

So we see that the young Johannes led a solitary life, and his work, too, was done in secret, hidden from the public gaze. Once only he took the initiative, sending his compositions to Robert Schumann, who was at the time giving concerts in Hamburg. But the master, who had much to do, returned them unopened, and the bitterly disappointed youth retired still further into himself. To the world Johannes Brahms was no more than a hard-working journeyman. He taught the piano, played accompaniments at the theatre, arranged music for the publisher Cranz, and even wrote popular drawing-room pieces for him, which, however, he did not publish under his own name.

The nature of these works is wrapped in mystery. Kalbeck states, though without giving his reasons, that these pieces were published under the pseudonym of G. W. Marks. It has been shown, however, that G. W. Marks figures as the author of works produced by other publishers such as Peters, Hofmeister, Bote & Bock, and it is out of the question that these could have been by Brahms's hand. Müller-Blattau believes that the name of Marks may have been a collective pseudonym of various authors; such pseudonyms were common at the time, and it is quite likely that Brahms belonged to this group of authors. That the *Souvenir de Russie*, by G. W. Marks, given as an example of Brahms's work by Kalbeck, can really have been his is highly improbable because of its extreme superficiality. We know for certain only that Brahms was continually preparing music for Cranz, 'for which,' as his mother writes,[17] he 'got quite a large amount of money.' No doubt, too, he also received such commissions from his publisher after his departure from Hamburg.

All this work was likely neither to bring him honor nor to help him towards a satisfactory position. His father, therefore, not unnaturally became impatient.[18] If this was all he could do, Johannes need not have learned so much! The boy, he thought, should be sent away from home; entirely dependent on himself, then he would be able to prove his worth. Johannes, too, no longer felt happy at home, and longed with all his heart to find an opportunity of leaving it and seeing the world. At last this possibility presented itself. The talented Hungarian violinist, Eduard Reményi, who had been forced to leave his country in 1848, owing to his political activities, and who met with great success in Hamburg, became interested in the young pianist. He invited him to join him in a concert tour, and Brahms enthusiastically accepted this offer.

On 19 April 1853, the crucial turning point of Johannes Brahms's life arrived. The unknown musician of twenty left his home, to return only a few months later—a famous artist.

UNPUBLISHED LETTERS REFERRED TO:

1. Letter from Fritz Brahms, 1874.
2. Letter from Elise Brahms, 27 April (1857).
3. Letter from Elise Brahms, 24 February 1865.
4. Letter from Elise Brahms, 2 September 1865.
5. Letter from Fritz Brahms, 1853.
6. Letter from Elise Brahms, 14 February 1863.
7. Letter from Eduard Marxsen, 29 November 1883.
8. Letter from Christiane Brahms, 10 July 1853.
9. Letter from Elise Denninghoff, 16 October 1880.
10. Letter from Elise Brahms, 9 September 1853.

11. Letter from Elise Denninghoff, 25 September 1889.
12. Letter from Christiane Brahms, 4 January 1855.
13. Letter from Elise Brahms, 9 September 1853.
14. Letter from Elise Brahms, 1865.
15. Letter from Elise Brahms, undated.
16. Letter from Christiane Brahms, 27 April 1859.
17. Letter from Christiane Brahms, 10 July 1853.
18. Letter from Christiane Brahms, 6 January 1865.

III

SEVEN EVENTFUL MONTHS

O<small>N</small> one of the last days of May 1853, visitors were announced by the servant of the King of Hanover's *Konzertmeister*, Joseph Joachim. Two young men entered the room, one of them dark and fiery, clearly a foreigner by his manner; the other shy and unpretentious, with clear-cut, handsome features, and long, fair hair. The foreigner embraced Joachim impetuously, and made himself known as Eduard Reményi, a former fellow pupil at the Viennese Conservatoire. Joachim now remembered the high-spirited Hungarian, and, full of interest, questioned him in regard to the vicissitudes of his life. Reményi could not tell his famous colleague, who had risen far above him, enough of his own successes, and of the triumphs he had won. The present little concert tour had been highly satisfactory also; so far, however, they had played only in small towns such as Winsen, Lüneburg, and Celle, but everywhere the results had been excellent, and there were prospects of giving concerts in Hanover and other large towns.

While the Hungarian brought all this out in the first few minutes of their interview, Joachim's eyes rested more and more frequently on Reményi's companion. Something in the stranger's absorbed expression attracted him strangely, and he tried to draw him into the conversation. Johannes Brahms was at first painfully embarrassed, having never before encountered an artist of international fame, as this young man of twenty-two already was. Moreover, this was Joachim, whose inspired rendering of Beethoven's violin concerto in Hamburg had filled the fifteen-year-old Johannes with ecstasy! Soon, however, he felt that he was facing an artist profoundly congenial in musicianship and ideas. His innate reserve left him, he talked of his aims and struggles, and before he realized it he had sat down at the piano and was playing his own compositions to Joachim. The impression he created was far stronger than he, with his modesty, could ever have imagined. The famous violinist was enraptured by the originality and the power of these compositions, and not less by Brahms's execution of them.

A few days sufficed to form a lifelong bond of friendship between the two artists, and Johannes experienced, for the first time, the supreme joy of finding perfect understanding. This happy period, however, had to come to an abrupt end for the time being. Reményi and he had hardly appeared at Court when the police discovered that a notorious Hungarian revolutionary had dared to play before the king. Reményi was subjected to a severe cross-examination, which ended with the immediate expulsion of both the violinist and his accompanist. Brahms sadly took leave of his friend, but was slightly consoled by an invitation from Joachim to come to him immediately if further co-operation with Reményi should become impossible. This first experience of freedom, success, and, above all, friendship with so noble an artist must have been an intoxicating experience for young Brahms. Unfortunately, he himself destroyed the detailed accounts which he sent to his parents, but some light is thrown upon them by his mother's answer: [1]

Your letter surprised and moved us so much that we could hardly read it, and when we came to the end, we said: happy Johannes, and we his happy parents. Surely, yes, this exquisite feeling, not for all the treasures of earth would we miss it. Now, Johannes dear, your life really begins, now you will reap what you have sown with toil and diligence here. Your great hour has come. You must thank Divine Providence which sent an angel to lead you out of the darkness into the world where there are human beings who appreciate your worth and the value of what you have learned. How much we should love to be with you a few hours, to see your happy face, and tell each other how happy we are. Alas, it is impossible. We will pray to God for your health, which, however, you must not overtax, and you must not stay up too late at night. . .

The next halt on the journey was at Weimar. Here, on the Altenburg, Franz Liszt reigned supreme over an enthusiastic following of pianists and composers. Joachim, knowing Liszt's extraordinary kindness and helpfulness towards young artists, had warmly recommended his new friend to him. The visit to the Weimar prince of music did not, however, pass off as expected. Liszt, who could well appreciate the individuality of an alien temperament, was very favorably impressed by the young Hamburger's compositions; he was quite willing to smooth the way to publicity for Brahms, if the youth would comply with certain conditions: he must adhere to the artistic standards of Liszt and his circle. The famous pianist realized that a vigorous and gifted nature like that of Johannes Brahms would be of the greatest assistance towards the victory of the so-called 'new German' school of music of which Liszt was the head. This new school, which derived from the works of Berlioz, tended towards a certain loosening of the fetters of tonality, and demanded, in particular, that the musical form be dictated by the content of poetic ideas. Brahms, however, did not find it possible to become a disciple. The 'new German' music, as he found it in Liszt's compositions, seemed to him empty and worthless, and the pupil of Marxsen firmly rejected an artistic conception that was in some degree derived from an extra-musical point of view. Moreover, for him, the whole mode of life on the Altenburg, where everything revolved round the idolized Liszt, went sorely against the grain. There was a wide gulf between him and these people, and he made no attempt to bridge it. This was characteristic of the man and the artist. Although he was aware that he urgently needed a patron, and that he was losing the good will of the most influential musician in Germany, he was not able to compromise, and it did not escape Liszt how little young Brahms admired his compositions. A whole legend has been woven around the meeting of these two artists on the Altenburg, and it has even been said that Brahms dozed off while Liszt was playing his own compositions. Even though this story is far from convincing (as Ehrmann tells us, Mason, the only authority on this episode, had not himself seen Brahms asleep, but had only heard of the incident from the absolutely unreliable Reményi), one thing is certain: Brahms offended the older master by his indifference to his creative work and lost what he might have gained by Liszt's further interest in him.

This incautious behavior had one result which Brahms certainly cannot have foreseen. Reményi became indignant. His fellow artist's behavior seemed to him the height of stupidity. Liszt's favor was of extreme importance to him, and he had, therefore, to do his utmost to avert the faintest suspicion that he shared Brahms's views. Moreover, for some time past his accompanist, who could not be kept in the background, had stood in his way. So he was glad of the opportunity, and refused to go on playing with Brahms.

Now the young man was indeed in an awkward position. Without substantial means (for so far his earnings must have been swallowed up by his traveling expenses), he found himself alone in an alien world. Whither should he turn? As to that there was no doubt whatever in his mind. Had he not a friend, Joseph Joachim? He wrote him a letter not only important in respect to its contents, but also characteristic of the romantic style of the young Brahms.

DEAR HERR JOACHIM, [Weimar, 29 June 1853.]
If I were not named 'Kreisler,' I should now have well-founded reasons to be somewhat dispirited, to curse my art and my enthusiasm, and to retire as an eremite (clerk?) into solitude (an office). . . Reményi is leaving Weimar without me. It is *his* wish, for my manner could not have given him the slightest pretext for doing so. I really did not need such another bitter

[31]

experience; in this respect I had already quite enough material for a poet and composer.

I cannot return to Hamburg without anything to show, although there I should feel happiest with my heart tuned in C-G sharp. I must at least see two or three of my compositions in print, so that I can cheerfully look my parents in the face. Will you write to me soon, if you are going to be at G[öttingen] in the next few days; this would make me inexpressibly happy, and if so, may I visit you there? Perhaps I am presumptuous, but my position and my dejection force me to it. . .

Joachim, of course, allowed young Brahms to visit him at Göttingen, where he was spending his vacation for the purpose of attending the philosophical and historical lectures at the university. Enchanted weeks, spent in music, reading, debates, and walks, were to follow, and each was constantly discovering some fresh aspect of the other's character. Joachim was not only a virtuoso of genius; he was at this time far more interested in composition than in execution. (This was not so in later years, owing to his enormous activity as a performer and teacher.) Young Joachim's compositions were highly appreciated by such authoritative artists as Schumann and Liszt. Brahms, too, thought that 'there was more in Joachim than in all the other young composers put together,' including himself. He devoted himself to the study of Joachim's compositions with such enthusiasm that solely for his private pleasure, without a word to the author, he arranged two overtures of Joachim's for the piano. Together the artists worked at each other's compositions, and their mutual affection spurred them on to do their utmost in helping each other to attain the greatest perfection. This intimate co-operation, and the similarity of their modes of thought, found a characteristic outward expression, for the manuscript notation of both young men acquired a striking resemblance. If, for example, the original manuscript of Joachim's *Demetrius Overture* is compared with Brahms's adaptation of it as a piano duet, anyone unacquainted with facts will find it difficult to conclude which copy was written by Brahms, and which by his friend.

Their relationship had now become so intimate that Brahms made no difficulty about prolonging his stay in Göttingen with his friend 'Jussuf' (as Joachim liked to be called). His parents, however, were of a different opinion. After the brilliant opening of the concert tour with Reményi, its sudden conclusion was a great shock to them. They could not understand why Johannes should retire to a small town like Göttingen, where he could not possibly achieve anything, and the sudden friendship with Joachim seemed rather strange to them. The family was ready to sacrifice everything to enable Johannes to continue his tour. They offered him his brother Fritz's savings, and when he refused them, saying that he needed no assistance, his mother replied in astonishment: [2]

You have not written plainly enough about your circumstances. For example, you need no money. Even if you have free lodging, food, and drink, you must have clean linen, your boots wear out, and, after all, how can you live away from home without money? If you have to get every little thing from Joachim, you will be under too great an obligation to the gentleman. You had better write to Herr Marxsen. He can advise you in everything. But you must write the exact truth, otherwise the same thing will happen as with Reményi. You understand people too little and trust them too much.

Joachim now wrote himself and reassured the anxious parents. His letter is one of the most precious documentary proofs of the unselfish love which united these two artists, and it is no less creditable to Brahms than to the writer himself. Among the letters kept by Brahms this, too, has been preserved, and is here reproduced for the first time:

Göttingen, 25 July 1853.

Allow me, although I am unknown to you, to write and tell you how infinitely blest I feel in the companionship of your Johannes; for who better than his parents know the joy which their son can give. Your Johannes has stimulated my work as an artist to an extent beyond my hopes. To strive with him for a mutual goal is a fresh spur for me on the thorny path that we musicians have to tread through life. His purity, his independence, young though he is, and the singular wealth of his heart and intellect find sympathetic utterance in his music, just as his whole nature will bring joy to all who come into spiritual contact with him. How splendid it will be when his artistic powers are revealed in a work accessible to all! And with his ardent desire for perfection nothing else is possible. You will understand my wish to have him near me as long as his presence does not interfere with his duty to himself. I believe, moreover, that Johannes too must find it pleasant to live undisturbed in quiet Göttingen, where he is sure of finding, in Musikdirektor Wehner and myself, two men who are glad to follow his idiosyncrasies in life and art. How glad I should be if I could ever render my friend Johannes a real service, for it goes without saying that my friendship is always at his disposal. I can only hope that our new bond will find the blessing of your approval.

Truly yours,

JOSEPH JOACHIM

The effect of the famous artist's letter on the parents, who, so far, had not been spoiled by too much praise of their son, can well be imagined. Proudly they showed it to all their friends, and naturally also it accompanied them to Winsen. Elise Brahms wrote: [3] 'I read this dear letter of Herr Joachim's to the Giesemanns, too, and Lieschen had to copy it on the spot. . . They were immeasurably glad that you have found·a friend who is able properly to appreciate your true art and your magnanimous character.'

Johannes himself, however, felt that he ought not to stay too long in Göttingen, since he had not yet achieved the task which he had set himself. He had to see some of his work in print, and to seek further connections in musical circles. So he decided for once to visit the west of Germany, not least in order to fulfil an old dream of wandering along the Rhine. The proceeds of a concert given with Joachim made this journey possible, and he set out in August. The impression he received of the beautiful countryside was extraordinarily vivid. The 'Loreley rocks' and the romantic and overhanging banks of the mighty river seemed to the Hamburger like real mountains, for which, although he was a native of the plains, he had far more feeling than for the poetry of the sea. We must once more be content, in the absence of direct accounts, to hear the echo of his descriptions from Frau Brahms's replies. The naive manner in which the mother's anxious heart reacted to the boy's exuberant pictures of Nature is as touching as it is amusing:

It is a lovely trip you are making, but surely sometimes very dangerous. I do beg you, over such steep rocks! How easily you could fall there! I tremble when I think of it. And your chest is strong of course, but one can overdo things with too much climbing. Nestler's daughter, a woman of twenty-five, also made a pleasure trip into mountainous country and soon after she came back she died of hemorrhage. Therefore, Johannes dear, please take care of yourself, and for heaven's sake don't go out in a thunderstorm. Malwine Erk was killed in Heligoland by lightning. For today enough of all these terrors, I can no longer think of them. . .

The journey was in all respects most satisfactory. In Bonn Brahms made the acquaintance of the conductor Wasielewski, who begged him to visit his friend Robert Schumann in Düsseldorf. Joachim had made the same suggestion, but Brahms had declined, finding it impossible to forget the imagined injury which Schumann had done him in returning his manuscripts unopened. Through Wasielewski he was introduced to the music-loving patrician family of Deichmann in Mehlem. In their hospitable house he was received most kindly, his compositions won new friends for him, and he formed connections with such eminent musicians as Franz Wüllner, Ferdinand Hiller, Carl Reinecke, and others. But all these events were presently to fade into the background in the light of the great experience which was coming to him. At the Deichmanns' he was persuaded to study

Schumann's works in detail, most of which he had never seen before. His astonishment and delight were profound; here a composer of genius had built up a world in music which 'young Kreisler' felt to be his own spiritual home. All recollections of the slight he had received vanished in an instant, and he was possessed by a fervent desire to make the personal acquaintance of this great master. He therefore decided to go to Düsseldorf, and on 30 September he first visited Schumann's home. Here he at once found himself in an atmosphere totally different from that of the Altenburg.

A little girl, the eldest of the master's six children, opened the door to him. The house was (as Clara Schumann states in her diary) 'agreeably and quietly situated,' but there was none of the luxurious splendor of Liszt's mansion. The master, too, was not surrounded by a crowd of disciples. When he asked Brahms to play to him, only one other listener was in the room: that exquisite musician, his wife Clara. Young Brahms's natural reserve melted away in this warm congenial atmosphere, and he who had found it impossible to perform his own compositions to Liszt now played them to the Schumanns, summoning up all the utmost powers of his art. The impression made on Joachim was repeated in the case of Schumann. He, too, was deeply moved, and instantly perceived that here was a great and rare talent. Already he seemed to hear the voices of a whole orchestra in the piano setting of the Sonatas, and he foresaw to what magnificent heights Brahms might soar 'if he would wave his magic wand where the power of great orchestral and choral masses could help him.' Robert and Clara Schumann's diaries are filled from cover to cover with accounts of Brahms; hardly a day passed on which his playing or his work was not mentioned in words of the highest praise. Moreover, a great friendship developed between the Schumanns and the much younger Brahms. Robert's profound and comprehen-

sive mind exercised the greatest influence over the eagerly receptive Johannes, whose innate North German reserve, intensified by a hard childhood, at the same time yielded to
Clara's refined, affectionate, and sympathetic manner. Happiness made him, as Joachim wrote, who joined the group in
the middle of the month, 'a better and a nobler man.' He
became communicative, often bubbling over with mirth, and
from day to day he felt surer of himself as he became accustomed to these new surroundings, so different from his
home. He became acquainted also with Schumann's circle,
the professors of the Düsseldorf academy of painting, and
Albert Dietrich, the master's pupil, who numbered for the
rest of his life among Brahms's most intimate friends.

Schumann, however, did not confine himself to extending
a most friendly welcome to the young musician. With all
the magnificent energy of his combative nature, he strove to
help the 'young eagle' by recommending him to Breitkopf &
Härtel, with such insistence that the big Leipzig publishers
were forced to take an interest in him. Above all, he longed
to tell the world of the young genius who had appeared like
a comet on the horizon, and to prophesy for him a splendid
career. Hardly a fortnight after Schumann first saw Brahms
he wrote the famous essay *Neue Bahnen,* in which he tells of
the artist 'at whose cradle graces and heroes mounted guard,'
who in Hamburg 'had created in obscurity and silence his
first compositions,' and who 'was called forth to give us the
highest ideal expression of our time.' This essay appeared on
28 October, in the *Neue Zeitschrift für Musik,* founded by
Schumann himself, and the words of this champion of romantic art, who for years had published nothing in this
periodical, found ready listeners everywhere. Instantly the
name of Brahms became known far beyond the limits of
musical circles, and the publication of his works was eagerly
awaited. One thing already seemed clear: it was not going
to be plain sailing for the young composer. The public and

the critics expected the very best after this sensational introduction.

Johannes himself read Schumann's article in Hanover, whither he had gone early in November to undertake a final revision of his works in the congenial atmosphere of his friend Jussuf's home, before sending them to the publishers. The young man was so disconcerted by this enthusiastic praise of his compositions that his delight alternated with dread of the too great responsibility laid upon him. Not until the middle of November did he feel that he could thank Schumann. With relentless self-criticism he completed the revision of his works, and following Schumann's emphatic advice, he went to Leipzig to play in person to the publishers.

Here he was received with some misgivings. The *Neue Bahnen* had done almost more harm than good, and the musical circles of Leipzig intended to form an independent judgment of the new genius. Again, however, the young man's genuine art and his simple and unaffected manner overcame all prejudice. This is charmingly expressed in the diary of Hedwig Salomon, to whose salon Brahms was introduced:

There he sat before me, Schumann's young Messiah, fair and delicate; though only in his twentieth year, his face showed the triumph of his spirit. Purity, innocence, naturalness, power, and depth—this describes his character. Schumann's prophecy tempts one perhaps to find him rather absurd, and to be severe with him, but one forgets everything, and loves and admires him without restraint.

Brahms played his works with considerable success, not only in the aristocratic houses of Leipzig, but also publicly at a David Quartet evening. Meanwhile he made many valuable personal connections, especially with the musician Julius Otto Grimm, who remained his lifelong friend. A satisfactory arrangement was made with Breitkopf & Härtel, and he received his first publishers' fee with ineffable pride. This he sent home,[5] as he afterwards sent the more considerable proceeds of his later works. Indeed, in the midst of all these exciting events, Johannes had never ceased to think of his humble family. He gave them detailed accounts of his doings, and when he was introduced to the Countess Ida von Hohenthal he succeeded in securing for his brother Fritz a position as her children's music teacher in the place of Grimm, who was leaving Leipzig.[6] As a token of gratitude he dedicated his Sonata, Op. 5, to the Countess, a fact which has hitherto puzzled his biographers, who were ignorant of Fritz's appointment in the Hohenthal family.

Christmas was drawing near, and Johannes' parents now saw their greatest wish fulfilled: the appearance of their son's first compositions in print. To Joachim, Brahms dedicated Sonata, Op. 1, and to Clara Schumann, Sonata, Op. 2. He found none of his works worthy of being dedicated to Robert Schumann himself, but his songs, Op. 3, he dedicated to Bettina von Arnim. Brahms had made the acquaintance of this remarkable woman at the Schumanns', having already come into contact with the Arnim family through their intimate friend Joachim. Above all, Bettina von Arnim seemed to the 'young Kreisler' the personification of the romantic muse. She had always stood in the center of the romantic movement, and her husband Achim, together with Clemens Brentano, had published a large compilation of German folk songs, Des Knaben Wunderhorn. The dedication of his songs to her was, therefore, a sign of his devotion to romantic art.

At last all his business in Leipzig was ended, and on 20 December Johannes went back to his parents. He spent some very happy days with them in their new and better apartment, Herr Brahms having meanwhile been promoted to the post of contrabass player at the town theatre. In Hamburg, too, Johannes's success had become known. From all sides relatives and friends came to hear him tell of his adventures, and his parents could not contain themselves for pride in this son who had in the last seven months 'advanced ten years.'

UNPUBLISHED LETTERS REFERRED TO:

1. Letter from Christiane Brahms, 11 June 1853.
2. Letter from Christiane Brahms, 23 July (1853).
3. Letter from Elise Brahms, 9 September 1853.
4. Letter from Christiane Brahms, 3 September 1853.
5. Letter from Christiane Brahms, 1 December 1853.
6. Various letters from Fritz Brahms, 1853-4.

IV

'STURM UND DRANG' *

(1854-1856)

THE first two months of 1854 passed in undisturbed contentment. In Hanover, Brahms worked at a new composition, the Trio in B major for pianoforte, violin, and violoncello, Op. 8; and his free time was spent with Joachim, at whose house he also met one of Jussuf's friends, Hans von Bülow, the highly gifted pianist and subsequent conductor. In spite of his close connection with the 'new German' musical movement, von Bülow was so impressed with Brahms's creations that he was the first pianist to perform a work of the composer's in public, the first movement of the *Sonata in C major*, at a concert in Hamburg on 1 March 1854.

At the end of January two beloved visitors appeared: the 'glorious' Schumanns spent a week in Hanover. These were, as Brahms wrote to Dietrich, 'high festival days, which make you really live.' Who could have foreseen that he who inspired all those about him with such intense intellectual life would only one month later no longer be numbered among the living intellects? On 27 February 1854 occurred the catastrophe in Robert Schumann's life. The nervous disorder which had already tormented him now became unbearable. He felt himself assailed by spirits; sometimes heavenly voices, sometimes demoniacal shrieks sounded in his ears. To escape this agony he sought death, and threw himself into the Rhine. His life was saved, but on his regaining consciousness the darkness of insanity enveloped him still more closely. On

* Storm and Stress.

4 March he had to be removed to an asylum at Endenich near Bonn. Clara was left with six children, and a seventh was expected in a few months' time. The financial burden imposed on this poor woman was dreadful enough, but how insignificant compared with the unspeakable sorrow of the separation from her adored husband.

This is not the place to speak of the Schumanns' married life, which in its peaceful harmony and mutual spiritual enrichment appears unique in the history of the personal relationships of artists. For fourteen years Robert had been to his wife a devoted husband and at the same time a wonderful artistic guide. How was Clara to find consolation now that the master could no longer help her, now that the man whom she so ardently worshiped was languishing in madness? How was this delicate woman to endure the various exhausting phases of her husband's illness, the changes from hope to despair, until at last it became a certainty that he was past recovery? In this terrible situation it was chiefly the sense of her duty to her children that supported Clara, and partly, too, the comfort derived from the knowledge that she had a companion in her grief, for at the news of Schumann's illness one man had instantly hastened to her side, willing to render aid with all the strength of his being.

When Brahms heard the terrible tidings, a sense of indebtedness to the man who had done so much for him prompted him to go immediately to Düsseldorf. His parents, too, agreed with him on this point. His mother even sent him money, and wrote: [1] 'We received a very sad, distracted letter from you today. That Schumann is so ill makes us unspeakably sorry. You were quite right to go there immediately.' Brahms, therefore, did his very best to help Schumann's wife to tide over this terrible time, and he achieved the miracle of saving Clara from complete despair. Various circumstances helped to make this possible. First, the young man's creative power, at this time breaking tumultuously forth, could not, even in her bitterest grief, fail to impress

the artist in Clara. Soon after the catastrophe, Brahms was
able to play his new Trio to her. She followed with deep
interest the shaping of a Sonata for two pianos, which, after
innumerable revisions, was ultimately to take the form of
the *Piano Concerto in D minor.* To give her pleasure he
composed, after the birth of her son Felix in June 1854, his
variations on a theme by 'him,' the beloved Robert, dedicated to 'her.' Clara felt that her profound sympathy inspired
the young composer, and this was a great consolation to her.
The artist who had rightly considered herself Robert Schumann's muse was comforted by the feeling that she was also
helping in the development of this young genius. And apart
from music, in her experience of life and in general culture,
she was greatly the superior of the young man who had
grown up secluded from the world and in restricted circumstances; so that she found satisfaction in assisting in the development of his personality in a cultural sense. Brahms expressed this perfectly when, on the occasion of a purchase,
he once wrote: * 'I am developing a sense of beauty, don't
you think? For when one associates with a beautiful woman
for a long time, and sees everything about one tasteful, and
at the same time genuine, one cannot help profiting by it.'
Lastly, the healing influence which the young man's fresh
susceptibility exercised on the tired woman must not be forgotten. The companionship of Johannes gave her a renewed
interest in life, and with him, as when they went on a walking tour along the Rhine in 1855, she enjoyed the beauties
of nature with a rejuvenated heart.

Brahms himself came more and more under the spell of
this remarkable woman, and if at first he had hurried to her
side from a sense of duty, it now seemed impossible for him
to stay away from her. When in August 1854 she went to

* This and the following quotations from the correspondence between Brahms and Clara Schumann are taken from *Schumann-Brahms
Correspondence,* by kind permission of the publishers, Messrs Mac-
millan & Co., London.

Ostend to recuperate, he set out on a tour through the Black Forest; half way, however, he turned back, because one should not travel if bound so fast to a place as I am now to Düsseldorf.' And when some months later she went to Holland on a concert tour, he followed her with his last money to Rotterdam, to be with her for a few days longer.

Bearing Clara Schumann's personality and appearance in mind, it seems only too natural that the reverent friendship which Brahms at first felt for her should gradually have changed to ardent love. In her the young man met a woman of classical and animated beauty, herself an eminent artist, intellectual and highly cultured. The fact that she was fourteen years his senior did not diminish his feelings for her; on the contrary, it added to Clara's charm for him that she had far more knowledge of life than he. Johannes, therefore, loved this exquisite woman with all that was best and noblest in his character, and this love was increased by his compassion for her in her great sorrow and his admiration for the way in which she bore it. In his letters to Clara, some of which have been preserved, he sometimes merely intimated his love, sometimes he spoke of it quite openly. From all the innumerable examples that might be cited, only the following need be singled out:

I should like to talk to you only of agreeable things. I regret every word I write to you which does not speak of love. You have taught me and are every day teaching me more and more to recognize and to marvel at the nature of love, affection, and self-denial. . . I wish I could always write to you from my heart, to tell how deeply I love you, and can only beg of you to believe it without further proof.

Clara, however, was the wife of his friend, who was wasting away under a terrible malady; she clung to her beloved husband with unchanging loyalty, and could only be a maternal friend to Brahms. She emphasized this by addressing him by the familiar *Du*, while he had strictly to keep to the more formal *Sie*. Brahms, therefore, liked to call her 'dear Mama.'

[44]

A few months later, however, the *Du* creeps more and more frequently into his letters, especially into their passionate conclusions. Nevertheless, he still tried to keep their relationship on a footing of friendship, and if he unguardedly wrote 'Beloved' he quickly added 'or beloved friend.' In these years Brahms's whole being was consumed by his love for Clara. He remained with her in Düsseldorf, although he had no opportunities for advancement there, and even when she was obliged, for her children's sake, to travel in pursuit of her artistic career, he wanted nothing better than to remain in Düsseldorf, in the atmosphere of her home, which he loved so dearly. So he kept his 'charming and comfortable room' in the Schumanns' house, even in her absence, looked after the children, and wrote endless letters to his 'fair and haughty lady.'

He sometimes found an opportunity of giving music lessons, but these brought in little money, and did nothing to improve his position. For the moment, however, he would not consider the question of giving regular concerts. His parents and Marxsen were in despair. Schumann had paved the way so magnificently for Johannes, and instead of making use of the interest awakened in him, and appearing publicly as pianist and composer, he buried himself in Düsseldorf. Joachim, too, realized this, and wrote of it to Gisela von Arnim: 'His unconcern for his livelihood is superb, splendid even. He is not willing to sacrifice a tithe of his spiritual inclinations. He does not want to play, partly out of disregard for the public, partly from laziness, although his playing is perfectly divine.' But this notion of Joachim's was perhaps somewhat superficial. It was not only laziness and disregard of the public that caused Brahms for the moment to adopt this imprudent attitude; it was before all his desire to devote his life entirely to Clara. This is plainly apparent, for example, in the answer he once returned to Joachim, who had proposed that he should give public performances in Hanover. After making all sorts of evasive objections, such as pointing to the advanced season of the year, and so on, he let out the secret: 'Frau Schumann leaves here on the 7th or 8th, so I don't want to leave two days earlier.' But he longed to see his parents after this separation of so many months. What luck that Clara had to play in Hamburg in November 1854! He could travel with her, and introduce her to them. Frau Brahms's delight was touching when she heard of this plan. She wrote·

Oh, how lovely, how wonderful that you are going to visit us and that the good Frau Schumann is also coming to Hamburg! How delighted we shall be to see her. You will know, as you know her best, if we can offer to put her up. It does look rather better here than it did last year, when the old kitchen range stood in the living room and Elise was ill. May the dear God spare us illness and then we shall all enjoy it the more. I am infinitely glad, for at Christmas I had no time to speak a word to you. Now we must make up for lost time. Come to us very soon, and stay a very long time. But please write when you are coming, so that we can make the thick oatmeal cakes that you like so much, cut in thick slices, the day before.[2]

This time Clara did not accept the invitation, but she often took her meals with these 'simple though respectable' people, with whom she 'felt so much at home,' and her leave-taking from 'the woman whose son had grown so near and dear to her heart' was quite sorrowful. Johannes spent the Christmas of 1854 with her in Düsseldorf. It was the first time he had spent this festival away from home, and the sensitive Clara felt compelled to make his parents a present in atonement. In a letter to his mother (reproduced here for the first time) she says:

MY DEAR FRAU BRAHMS,
   I have robbed you of your dear Johannes, just now at Christmas time: I cannot deny myself the pleasure of sending him to you in the portrait, which I hope will give you pleasure, and which may sometimes remind you of myself and my dearest husband, who will stand by Johannes all his life with true affection.

[46]

This assurance may be some little consolation to your mother's heart when he is far away from you. Greeting you all most cordially.

Yours very sincerely,

CLARA SCHUMANN [3]

This present gave the greatest pleasure in Hamburg, and when, in the following summer, Clara, who was on her way to the seaside resort of Düsterbrock, stayed the night for the first time in the Brahms's household, the relationship between the two women who were dearest to Johannes became much more intimate. While her Christmas letter had been rather reserved, Clara did not hesitate now to speak frankly of her friendship with Johannes. On 16 August 1855, she wrote:

From here, my dear friend, I can send you little or no good news. I am feeling the separation from Johannes too painfully, and I am leading the most solitary life. Düsterbrock is lovely, it is true, but just because it is so lovely, it is all the more painful that I must enjoy it alone, without my beloved husband and without the dearest friend I have in the world. And this Johannes is. If he were with me I could very well put up with it here. . . You made me so comfortable that day in Hamburg that I now feel doubly lonely. . .

The fact that Brahms, in obedience to Clara's urgent appeal, had at last resolved to play in public, had certainly helped to cement the friendly relations of the two women. A beginning was made by a joint concert given in Danzig by Clara, Joachim, and Brahms in the autumn of 1855. Performances of Beethoven's and Mozart's pianoforte concertos at Bremen, Leipzig, and Hamburg were soon to follow. In Hamburg Brahms received 'a quite enthusiastic reception—for Hamburg.' While in this way Brahms was gaining a standing as a pianist, his creative work was, of course, not unaffected by his emotional experiences. A battle was fought in his soul between his love for Clara and the wish to re-

[47]

main true to his friend and benefactor, whose recovery he desired with all his heart. These stormy moods are reflected in the somber and passionate ballads he began to write as early as the end of 1854; and above all in two other compositions, which were to receive their final form at a much later date, although they were conceived in this *Sturm und Drang* period: the first movement of the *Symphony in C minor*, and the *Piano Quartet in C minor*, Op. 60. Brahms himself explained to a friend the introductory movement of this tempestuous Quartet in the following words: 'Now imagine a man who is just going to shoot himself, because nothing else remains for him to do.'

These works, however, did not reach perfect completeness, and there came periods when all creative work ceased. These were times when the torturing mental conflicts had grown so overpowering that Brahms could not muster the objectivity indispensable to the production of artistic work. He tried to exorcize this unproductive spirit, which afflicted him chiefly in 1855, by making a fresh and intensive study of counterpoint. He agreed with his friend Joachim to exchange for criticism, once a week, the working out of difficult contrapuntal problems. While the overworked violinist preferred to pay the fine agreed upon—to be applied to the purchase of books *—to sending new material, Brahms was extremely conscientious in the fulfilment of his obligations. These studies certainly gave him greater facility in the handling of difficult forms; but they alone could not open up new creative sources. He had first of all to face the truth and work things out for himself: he had to clarify his relations with Clara, for this indecision was absolutely wearing him out. His mother, too, felt that her son was suffering, although she

---

* Among Brahms's books was a copy of the *Altdänischen Heldenlieder, Balladen und Märchen*, on whose flyleaf was the following inscription in the master's hand: 'Joh. Brahms, May 1856 (from J. Joachim as fine).'

JOSEPH JOACHIM, BY LAURENS

CLARA SCHUMAN, BY LAURENS (1853)

could not fathom the reason of his unhappiness, and she tried in her simple way to console him in a letter of congratulation on his twenty-third birthday:

I don't know what you are doing at this moment. I'm all alone and would like to talk to you a little. This morning I woke up at the exact hour when you saw the light of day for the first time twenty-three years ago. Half an hour later I held you in my arms, against my heart.—And now you are so far away; it is so hard that we cannot remain together.—Tonight we were all rather jolly, we drank the health of all of you, especially of the poor sick man. Johannes dear, if we only had the power to do something for the good Schumann! I beg you not to take it too much to heart; you cannot help him, and it only does you harm. . . Write quite soon how you have spent today. . .

Your tenderly loving
MOTHER [4]

Soon after this, fate took a hand in bringing about a decision. On 29 July 1856, Robert Schumann was delivered from his terrible sufferings by death. Even in the depth of her grief Clara, as Joachim wrote to Liszt, was 'still a noble example of God-given strength.' Profoundly moving and simple are the words in her diary with which she closes this period of her life: 'All happiness has gone with his passing. A new life now begins for me.'

What was this new life to be, and what place in it was Johannes Brahms to fill? They both felt that this question would have to be settled soon. But for the time being they were both so shattered by the dreadful experience that they longed only for relaxation and rest. With this in view Clara set out on a tour through Switzerland, accompanied by two of her sons, as well as by Johannes and his sister Elise. For some time past the brother had been suggesting that he must do something for the delicate girl; he now hoped that the mountain air would effect an improvement in her health. Clara, in her own charming fashion, helped Elise to make ready for the journey. As early as 6 August, a week after

Schumann's death, she had mastered herself sufficiently to write an exhaustive letter to Frau Brahms, in which she gave the inexperienced woman some practical advice. It is touching, however, to see how the pain of her irreparable loss found utterance even in this purely practical letter:

DEAR FRAU BRAHMS,

I am going to write to warn you of Johannes's arrival, because I should like to suggest a few more things for Elise. Johannes will probably arrive on Friday, and return here with Elise on Monday.—Well, I wanted to mention a few more things for Elise: Do not let her take too many things. If she needs two chemises a week, let her bring six chemises. If she is used to wearing only one, about four will be sufficient. Stockings, six pairs. She only needs two changes of dress; keep the nice blue one at home; it would be a pity if it were spoiled in the packing. If she has a black petticoat, this would be best for traveling, and then she will only want one white underskirt in case she sometimes wears a light dress; but if she takes only dark dresses she will not need the white petticoat. I am not taking one, too much luggage is so inconvenient on a journey, and laundry increases expense. She will need only one hat, in preference a dark straw. She probably has a warm shawl for the journey? Don't buy her any gloves, I can give her some, if she does not mind wearing washed ones. I think this is all. How glad I shall be if Elise benefits by this summer! You know how heavy my heart is. I don't want to talk of it; my heart bleeds at once. Johannes is my true friend and protector—what a blessing that I have him! I wish you and all your dear ones well.—With all my heart

CL. SCH.

So her brother fetched Elise—and his mother was worried by Johannes's appearance; he looked 'altogether too miserable' [5]—and now a new world was opened to the poor girl. Even in her old age Elise spoke with rapture of this one journey of her life, which took her to the Rhine, the Lake of Lucerne, the Lake of Constance, and Heidelberg. The constant association with the refined and lovable artist must have made a deep impression on Elise, and she always spoke of Clara in terms of the deepest admiration.

It is impossible to ascertain today whether the journey was equally happy for the two principal characters. For this decisive time we have to depend on pure surmise, and it is probable that full light will never be thrown on what took place between Clara and Johannes. From their correspondence, however, we can see that soon after Schumann's death the tone of Brahms's letters grew imperceptibly more reserved, and the ardent style of the sentimental youth gave way to that of a calm but deeply sympathetic friend. It is not easy to understand this change. Had not the adored master's death, even though it grieved Brahms profoundly, cleared the situation so far as mere externals went? Clara was now free, and the inner conflict from which the young man had suffered so unspeakably for the last two years no longer troubled him. At last he could think of declaring himself to his beloved and binding his fate to hers.

We can only guess at Clara's attitude. Although she was probably deeply attracted by Brahms, she must have felt the difference in age much more strongly than he did. There were also her seven children to consider. Could she and should she burden the young genius with such heavy responsibilities, and, if she did, would this be fair to her own family? Thus Clara, torn by conflicting emotions, must at least have raised strongest objections, even if she did not dismiss a union with Brahms as utterly impossible. Still, 'young Kreisler,' with the fire of his passion and devotion, might have made her give up the path of renunciation which the voice of reason recommended to her.

But did he really want to make Clara his wife? It was difficult for a Johannes Brahms to answer this question. How very much simpler such a decision had been for his father. He was almost the same age as Johannes now when he had contemplated marriage with a woman seventeen years his senior, and after realizing the advantages of the step he closed his eyes to the manifest difficulties, and married the old maid with cheerful unconcern. But Johannes, the genius, could not think in so straightforward a fashion as the simple musician Johann Jakob Brahms. For in all the great crises of his life, not only his personal well-being was at stake, but in an even greater degree his art. Certainly Clara embodied in every respect Johannes's ideal of womanhood, and he knew by experience how well suited they were to each other in all the lesser and greater affairs of life. As a man, then, he could not have wished for a happier fate than to be united to her, and the difference in their ages certainly did not dismay him. If, therefore, Brahms forcibly suppressed all the alluring dreams of union with Clara, and was content to remain her true friend for life, it must have been because the artist in him dimly felt that he must not definitely bind himself. An orderly life at the side of a beloved woman was not for him; he realized that he must sink deeply into the maelstrom of a life rich in joys and sorrows in order to create works which would truly express all the heights and depths of life. An unbridgeable chasm yawned between the longing of the man and the demands of his art, and with the unerring instinct of genius Brahms decided, as had other great artists before him, to tread the path of personal renunciation which was to bring his art to its fullest bloom. Unconsciously he subjected his life to the idea which three years earlier he had expressed in his letter to Joachim (see p. 32), that bitter experiences give the artist material for his work.

To this bitter experience, however, Brahms never really reconciled himself. Although he formed intimate friendships in later years, and although he loved several women, he was never again able to give himself so completely and unreservedly, never again was another permitted to gaze into the remotest corner of his heart. The days of his adolescence ended with his ardent love for Clara. He became more serious, quieter, and more reserved. The delicate tenderness, the romantic exuberance of his first creations gradually vanished from his compositions. In his life and in his work a new period had now begun.

UNPUBLISHED LETTERS REFERRED TO:

1. Letter from Christiane Brahms, 5 March 1854.
2. Letter from Christiane Brahms, 17 September 1854.
3. Letter from Clara Schumann to Christiane Brahms, 23 December 1854.
4. Letter from Christiane Brahms, 7 May 1856.
5. Letter from Christiane Brahms, 30 September 1856.

V

DETMOLD AND HAMBURG

(1857-1862)

THE days of dreaming were over. Now Brahms had to begin the battle of life, and shape his fate independently of his dearest friends. In 1857 he obtained his first official position, for after a very successful rehearsal he was engaged at the princely Court of Detmold from September to December. The little Residenz was as strict in matters of etiquette as any kingly Court, and in cultural matters, too, it tried to achieve the highest standards. Music was the dominating passion of the prince, who was not exactly overburdened with the business of government, and the Court circles naturally followed his example. Everybody in Detmold society who had the slightest inclination towards music learned to play the piano, or took part in the Court choral society, where they had the honor of singing with the members of the princely family.

At Detmold Brahms's duties were to give piano lessons to the music-loving Princess Friederike, to conduct the choral society, and to perform as pianist at the Court concerts. This position brought him many advantages. First, he could live modestly for the whole year on his three months' salary. But above all, it gave the young artist new possibilities of work, of which he availed himself with all the purposefulness of his nature. At Detmold he became a good choral conductor, and his work profited greatly by this practical experience. He had sufficient leisure for his own compositions, as in the mornings he was free from professional duties. A further amenity was the magnificent situation of the

Residenz in the Teutoburger Forest, whose beauties he came to know on his long, lonely walks. How unimportant seemed his individual fate in these dense, silent woods, where so many historical sites called to mind the mighty battles of the old Teutons with the Romans! Here one felt only an infinitesimal part of a mighty whole which one could but accept. The vivid impressions of Nature, together with introspection, gradually brought about a profound change in Brahms. More cheerful moods began to dominate him, and in a letter to Clara from Detmold he expressed views which a little while before he would certainly have rejected: 'Passions are not natural to mankind; they are always exceptions or excrescences. The ideal, genuine man is calm in joy and calm in pain and sorrow. Passions must quickly pass, or else they must be driven out.'

The compositions dating from these years at Detmold reflect, therefore, a certain quiet relief and a reconciliation with fate. Besides a number of choral compositions, there are the two charming Serenades, Op. 11 and Op. 16, and the fresh and colorful String Sextet Op. 18. The fact that Brahms continued to work on the daemonic *Piano Concerto in D minor* is no inconsistency. This was a previously conceived work that had not satisfied the composer in its earlier form as a symphony, and now underwent entire rearrangement. The sojourn at Detmold, therefore, was highly productive, and it is not surprising that Brahms, after the first trial year, was willing to make the same arrangement for the autumn of 1858. Nor did he waver from this decision when he received the following letter from Ferdinand Hiller in Cologne:

Next autumn the position which Franck has occupied for about eight years is falling vacant at our conservatoire. Would you like to take it over? You would have to teach two hours daily (piano, score reading, ensemble class, etc.). For four hours a week the salary is 100 thalers, therefore 300 thalers for certain, if you gave these 12 weekly lessons. You could easily earn another

100 thalers in our soirées of chamber music and at concerts. If you would agree to give some private lessons (for one thaler each) you would have a certain if modest income. Of all the other things you would find here, good and bad, I will say nothing. Only one thing I must say, that you would certainly find the very best reception, and that I, for one, would do all in my power to make your life here agreeable.[1]

The terms offered were not dazzling; Brahms received in Detmold, in addition to board and lodging, 566 thalers for the three months, or 25 per cent more than for the whole year in Cologne. Above all, however, Brahms was reluctant to bind himself for a whole year, and on that account he overlooked an advantage which Hiller emphasized in a subsequent letter,[2] namely that 'it would perhaps be better for so young a man to live in a large town.' Brahms was, it is true, very lonely at Detmold, his only friends being the first violinist Bargheer, a pupil of Joachim's, and the young son of the Court marshal von Meysenbug. Otherwise he remained a stranger to the stiff Court society, and often excited indignation by his unceremonious behavior. For example, he records in a letter to Hamburg: 'The other day I conducted my choral society, which is richly adorned with Serene Highnesses, without a necktie! Luckily I didn't have to feel embarrassed or vexed, as I only noticed it when I was going to bed!' One may imagine, however, that the 'Serene Highnesses' would not have overlooked their conductor's defective toilet!

Even in Hamburg, where Brahms remained with short interruptions up to the summer of 1858, he found few human interests, and when at last an opportunity of associating with his friends presented itself he enjoyed this long-missed pleasure with redoubled zest. He spent the summer in Göttingen, where Julius Otto Grimm (see p. 38) had recently been appointed to the post of musical director, and with his young wife Philippine, a daughter of the piano manufacturer Ritmüller, had got together a circle of young musical enthusiasts. And at Göttingen, where five years earlier Brahms had spent a delightful summer with Joachim, he was fated once more to receive decisive impressions.

In these gay and unconventional surroundings the young man made up for all that he had missed at the princely Court. Here he could be merry to his heart's content; he could wander about with congenial friends, and he could revel in music, unrestricted by etiquette. And when, in such a carefree frame of mind, one meets a lovely girl, a girl who sings one's own songs in a magical voice, whose tone Joachim compared with the strains of an Amati violin, it is only natural that this gay holiday mood should give way to a deeper feeling. The owner of this 'Amati-voice' was Agathe von Siebold, the daughter of a distinguished professor at the University of Göttingen; she was a very attractive girl, with dark, fiery eyes and lovely black tresses which provoked the gay young Joachim to exclaim: 'How delightful to run one's hands through such hair!' But if the great violinist neither could nor would resist her charm, it was not he but his friend Johannes who lost his heart to 'Gathe.' In her *Erinnerungen* Agathe sadly recollects 'the lovely summer-days transfigured by the glory of love'; and certainly these months were among the happiest in the lives of these two young people.

Nature had bestowed upon Agathe not only personal charm, but also temperament, a sense of humor, energy, and a mind highly responsive to all forms of beauty. This is very noticeable in her letters, which show more than an average literary talent, and which have been reproduced by Emil Michelmann in his interesting biography, *Brahms' Jugendliebe.* When we note how simple and profound were Agathe's impressions of Nature, how wholeheartedly she enjoyed her wanderings in the hills, we are ever and ever again reminded of Brahms, and we understand what a strong mutual bond this common interest must have formed. An even stronger bond was music. Terse but significant was Grimm's report to Joachim (23 September 1858): 'Johannes has written glorious songs which Gathe sings to us, and we are all agreed that this is a wonderful time.' As a matter of fact we owe the majority of the songs and duets in Brahms's Op. 14, 19, and 20 to his love for Agathe and her magnificent soprano voice. Yet apart from the delights of music, they found time for other things; for games such as hide-and-seek, blind-man's-buff, and the like, which only served to increase the young people's love.

Clara Schumann had contrived as usual to spend the summer with Johannes. But the serious woman was out of place in this high-spirited crowd, and Brahms was often overcome by something like a consciousness of guilt. At such times he left Agathe with the naive explanation that he must now be alone with Clara, to avoid making her jealous. But this was of no avail; Clara could not fail to notice Johannes's infatuation, and when during an excursion she saw him put his arm round Agathe's waist, she packed her things and left the same evening. Brahms, however, stayed on at Göttingen, and only when his departure for Detmold could no longer be postponed did he tear himself away.

This time Johannes could not adapt himself to the conditions at Court. Frau Brahms fathomed the reasons in her reply to his complaints: [3] 'You find it so narrow and boring there . . . that you would like to run away. Last year perhaps you found it easier. You have been spoiled at Göttingen.' To appease his longing, Brahms composed more songs, and wrote regularly to the Göttingen 'shamrock.' His correspondence with Agathe—for her a 'source of the deepest and purest joy'—has not been preserved, but even in his letters to Grimm and his wife the beloved maiden plays an important part. Brahms had no need to restrain himself in writing to this most happily married couple, as they were only anxious to favor the union of their two friends. This is shown in a hitherto unknown letter from Frau Philippine

[58]

Grimm. While Julius wrote chiefly of his music-making with Agathe, his wife took Johannes's affection for the young girl to be a matter of common knowledge, when she wrote to Brahms as follows:

Your dear letter has just arrived. Many thanks for it. I will at once send it to Agathe, she will be greatly pleased. . . But now I have a strange request to make. I should like to give Agathe a portrait of you for Christmas, but I have none. It would be very charming of you, my dear Johannes, if you would send me one. I should like to get it framed. But if you would like to give it to her yourself, I have nothing against that; I only want Agathe to get one, as I know how delighted she would be to possess one.[4]

Brahms's answer is characteristic of his tendency to leave the most important thing unsaid:

I am sorry, Frau Pine, that nothing can come of your kind intentions in respect of my head. There is only one very poor artist of the sort here, and I don't want to surrender myself to him, so we needn't consider further whether you or I . . . But . . .

'I,' one could perhaps complete the sentence, 'would have liked to know that Agathe had my portrait.'

When the term at Detmold had expired—that year it seemed unendurably long—on New Year's Day, 1859, Brahms rushed off to Göttingen, where he was able to spend a fortnight. With a full heart he enjoyed the delight of being near Agathe, and it never entered his head that in the little university town his friendship with the professor's daughter must long ago have given rise to general comment. In his happiness he lived only for the moment, and it was not until after he had left that his friend Grimm made it clear to him that after what had taken place Agathe's friends expected to hear of an engagement. Therefore, only two possibilities were open to him, either to declare himself, or never to see Agathe again. Again the artist had to put the same question to himself as in the tragic days after Schumann's death. And although Brahms had even consented, though secretly, to wear an engagement ring (as may be seen in a photograph taken at Göttingen), he was just as reluctant now as he had been three years earlier to tie himself down definitely. This appears quite clearly in a letter which he wrote to Agathe in response to Grimm's reminder, and which Agathe quoted from memory in her *Erinnerungen:* 'I love you! I must see you again! But I cannot wear fetters. Write to me, whether I am to come back, to take you in my arms, to kiss you and tell you that I love you.' Agathe was proud, and such words must have wounded her pride profoundly. How was she to understand that the love which had inspired Brahms to write his most beautiful songs was regarded by him as a burden? She, therefore, was the one to break the connection between herself and Brahms, by sending him a letter of refusal.

Both Agathe and Johannes were to suffer long from the wounds inflicted by this sudden parting. Even as late as 1864, Brahms enquired with suppressed emotion after the 'house and garden at the city gate,' where Agathe lived; and the second string sextet composed at that time was really dedicated to her. In the first movement (bars 162-8) the first and second violins three times invoke the name Agathe, playing the notes a-g-a-d-h *-e, and the composer has himself settled any doubts as to the meaning of the work by declaring to his friend Gänsbacher: 'Here I have freed myself from my last love.' It was natural that the great artist should mean very much more in Agathe's life. Not until ten years after her parting from Brahms could she make up her mind to marry, and only when she was an old woman was she able to forgive Brahms so far as to reply to a greeting sent through Joachim. In the end, however, she arrived at a complete understanding of his behavior, and we find towards the close of her *Erinnerungen,* which are written in the form of a novel, these forgiving words:

* German name for b natural.

But her memory of her great love for the young man, of the days of her youth, radiant with poetry and beauty, has never faded. . . Over and over again his immortal work has contributed to her happiness. He, however, strode by on his path to fame, and as he, like every genius, belonged to humanity, she gradually learned to appreciate his wisdom in severing the bonds which had threatened to shackle him. She saw clearly at last that she could never have filled his life with her great love.

In the critical days of January 1859, Brahms may not clearly have realized the depth of his pain, for at this time an event of great importance to the artist occurred. The *Pianoforte Concerto in D minor,* at which Brahms had worked so long, was first performed in public. The composer played it first in Hanover under Joachim's baton, and five days later in Leipzig, under Rietz. In Hanover, thanks to Joachim's influence, it was, in spite of a general lack of understanding, not unfavorably received. At Leipzig, however, the Concerto suffered a terrible defeat, such as Brahms had never known, and never again was to experience. In his account of the incident in a letter to Clara Schumann the composer professes to be quite indifferent:

My Concerto went very well. I had two rehearsals. You have probably already heard that it was a complete fiasco; at the rehearsal it met with total silence, and at the performance (where hardly three people raised their hands to clap) it was actually hissed. But all this made no impression on me. I quite enjoyed the rest of the music and did not think of my Concerto.

Despite his outward self-control, Brahms cannot have been in any doubt about the practical consequences of this defeat, and these may have contributed in the last resort to the break with Agathe. To be sure, the composer received some compensation in his native town, where two months later, under Joachim's friendly direction, he played this Concerto again. Here it achieved a modest success, and four days later his First Serenade was received with a cordiality unusual in the cold-blooded Hamburgers. The occasion of this little triumph was a musical evening organized by Brahms and Joachim in conjunction with a new friend, the gifted singer Julius Stockhausen, whom Brahms had met at the Rhine Music Festival at Düsseldorf in 1856. Before long, intimate friendship had sprung up between the composer and the singer, which led to their frequent co-operation at concerts in which Brahms figured as accompanist. If this connection was of definite practical value to young Brahms, the influence of the great artist on the work of his friend was even more important. Many of Brahms's loveliest songs were actually written for Stockhausen, and he was the first to introduce them to the concert hall. The fame of this magnificent singer remains indissolubly coupled with that of Brahms's songs.

Brahms now made a few friends among the resident Hamburg musicians. He saw a good deal of the music teacher Theodor Avé-Lallemant, who had great influence with the Hamburg Philharmonic Orchestra, the conductor Karl Grädener, and G. D. Otten, privileged to be the first to enable the adult Brahms to appear on the concert platform in his native city, 6 December 1859. Even more than intercourse with friends having the same interests, he enjoyed his work with a small ladies' choir, which met regularly under his leadership during the spring and summer of 1859, 1860, and 1861. Brahms was inspired by the clear, fresh voices of the singers to write new choral compositions. The companionship of these cheerful young women, the walks he took with them, to the accompaniment of continual singing—Brahms even conducted while sitting in the branches of a tree—meant personally a great deal to the young man, depressed by his recent experience with Agathe and his failure at Leipzig. In the choir there was a ladies' quartet, which he rehearsed separately, and so came into closer contact with its members. They were the sisters Betty and Marie Völckers, Laura Garbe, and Marie Reuter. Brahms rated their talent so high that he even allowed them to sing his works before such severe critics as Clara Schumann, Joachim, and Stockhausen. Later on, in Vienna, he begged for a photograph of these four ladies, who replied that he probably wanted their picture 'in order to enlarge his collection,' or to 'draw up the fire in a refractory stove,' [5] but actually they were only too pleased to accede to the request of their conductor, whose personality had greatly impressed them, as it had the other members of the choir.

It may perhaps be assumed that their acquaintance with Brahms had a decisive influence in the lives of several of these girls. At all events, of the quartet only Betty Völckers married early (and even her wedding was overshadowed by Brahms, for the ceremony concluded with the singing of three of Brahms's songs and cheers for the composer).[6] Marie Völckers did not marry until 1873, and the two other members of the quartet remained single. As late as 1875 Elise Brahms, in a letter to her brother, in which she told him that 'Donna Laura' had grown too fat, wrote maliciously of Laura Garbe: 'If she, therefore, is to become my sister-in-law, as you always used to call her, it had better be soon, or I won't accept her as such.' [7] Elise always kept in touch with the members of the ladies' choir, their adoration for their leader being transferred to his sister after his departure from Hamburg. And on the composer's birthday, or after any successful concert of his music, Elise, even in her old age, used to receive from them flowers, sweets, and even laurel wreaths for her brother's portrait.

Although Brahms himself cherished a warm affection for his 'dear girls,' only one, Bertha Porubszky, made a lasting impression on him, and she—to the annoyance of the Hamburg ladies—was a visitor from Vienna. It was through her that Brahms first came to know something of the Viennese character. This cheerful, simple, unaffected girl laid a spell upon him, and he was never weary of listening to the lovely Austrian folk songs if she would sing them to him. That his interest in Bertha was due less to a passing fancy than to an affection for the Austrian temperament which had its roots in the character of the Brahms family seems to be confirmed by the fact that Elise conceived a great liking for Bertha's brother Emil, who for some time rented a room in the Brahms's house. In the many letters which she later wrote to Johannes in Vienna she hardly ever forgot to ask after the jolly Emil Porubszky.[8] Her brother, however, expressed in his music, more warmly and gracefully than was possible in words, his impressions of the first Viennese girl he had ever met. His famous *Wiegenlied* (Lullaby) was written for Bertha after her marriage to Arthur Faber, and the rocking piano accompaniment of this song was taken from one of the slow waltzes (*Ländler*) which she had sung to him in the unforgotten summer of 1859.

When in the autumn of that year Brahms went back to Detmold it was with a heavy heart that he left Hamburg and parted from his ladies' choir, who presented him with a silver inkstand. Having learned that it was possible to form an intelligent musical community among his cool and reserved countrymen, he gradually conceived the hope that his beloved native city might possibly offer him sufficient scope for his artistic activity. Friedrich Wilhelm Grund, the aged conductor of the Hamburg Philharmonic Concerts, and of the *Singakademie*, would be resigning his position in the near future in favor of a younger man. Could he, Johannes Brahms, himself a Hamburger, and a man who had already done credit to the town of his birth, become Grund's successor? In the seclusion of Detmold this notion grew more and more alluring, so that before long he was unable to put it aside.

Every decision he had to take he now made on the assumption of a future position in Hamburg, and this was soon apparent in his whole attitude towards Detmold. His one idea was now to obtain practice in conducting an orchestra, and he therefore begged the prince to allow him to conduct the Court concerts, in which he had hitherto performed only as a soloist. In order to give a plausible reason for this request, he alluded to the constant friction between himself, as soloist, and the conductor August Kiel. The prince could not accede to this request, as he did not wish to hurt the feelings of the aged conductor, who had occupied this position for many years. As a compromise, therefore, he suggested that in the coming year Brahms should not play in the Court concerts, but should confine his activities to teaching the princess and conducting the choral society. Whenever he needed the orchestra in these choral performances he would, naturally, conduct it himself. Under these conditions, however, Brahms lost all interest in the Detmold post, and he surrendered its financial advantages in order to live permanently in Hamburg, and to gain a footing in the more influential circles of Hamburg society.

From the beginning of 1860, then, the artist lived for the most part in his native city. In his parents' house he could seldom find the quiet necessary for his work, so he rented from Frau Dr. Rösing 'a quite charming apartment with garden' in the suburb of Hamm. Frau Dr. Rösing was an aunt of the musical Völcker sisters, with whom he kept up his connections through the medium of the choir. Here in Hamm everything was suited to his taste: the quiet, airy rooms, the splendid garden, and the refined and friendly people, whom he was glad to meet for some pleasant hours of music-making, especially on the famous Friday evenings. In these surroundings, so congenial to a musician, many of his creations were developed and perfected. The series of pianoforte works was continued by the variations for four hands on a theme by Schumann, and the powerful Handel variations. At the same time, Brahms showed his mastery of the pianoforte quartet by his compositions in G minor

[65]

and A major. In the domain of vocal music the first of the exquisite *Magelone* romances came into being, and were dedicated to Brahms's incomparable interpreter and friend, Julius Stockhausen. One work alone of this inspired period did not at first bear the stamp of the fullest perfection. This is the String Quintet that Brahms afterwards rearranged as a Sonata for two pianos, and finally, in 1864, as the Piano Quintet, Op. 34. Brahms also began to come to the fore as a performer.

The Hamburg years, therefore, were filled with intense activity of various kinds, and everything was brightened by the hope of finding a profitable field of activity at home, where he was so deeply rooted. Occasional journeys, especially those to the yearly musical festivals, made agreeable interruptions. At the Cologne Festival, in 1862, Brahms came into contact with Vienna for the second time through a woman. The well-known singer, Luise Dustmann-Meyer, although hailing from Aix-la-Chapelle (Aachen), had for the last five years been working at the Court Opera House, in the Austrian capital, and had become completely Viennese. She could not speak highly enough of the beauty of the imperial city, and Brahms was even more fascinated by the singer's temperamental and unaffected manner, so different from that of the North German women. Memories of the charming Bertha Porubszky were reawakened in his mind, and the desire seized him to see the city that could produce such delightful people as Bertha and Luise. From the practical point of view, too, there was much to be said in favor of a visit to Vienna, which, moreover,.Clara and Joachim had often recommended. The city on the Danube led the world of music, and if Brahms could achieve success in the Austrian capital, he would certainly gain greater prestige with his own countrymen, and would have an even better chance of attaining the position he coveted. His mind was soon made up. On 8 September 1862, Brahms left his native town with the firm intention of settling there permanently after a short stay in Vienna.

UNPUBLISHED LETTERS REFERRED TO:

1. Letter from Ferdinand Hiller, 8 August 1858.
2. Letter from Ferdinand Hiller, undated (Autumn 1858).
3. Letter from Christiane Brahms, 12 November 1858.
4. Letter from Philippine Grimm, Thursday Evening (Autumn 1858).
5. Letter from Elise Brahms, 20 December 1862.
6. Letter from Elise Brahms, 31 October 1862.
7. Letter from Elise Brahms, 1875.
8. Letter from Elise Brahms, 12 February 1873.

VI

AT HOME AND ABROAD

IN 1887 Julius Grosser, a German author, addressed the following lines to Brahms, in recollection of his own stay in Vienna:

How lovely it was then; in spite of everything, the people there are much more easy-going and friendly than here; life is easier; Nature and the surroundings help us to overcome a lot of worries which are hard to shake off under these gray Northern skies. . . One thing is certain; whatever joy I possess in life, in its goodness and beauty, I acquired in Vienna, and I therefore cherish the most grateful feelings for this most charming of all cities.[1]

Brahms himself may have felt somewhat as this North German felt; for him, too, the principal attraction of the town on the Danube might have been summarized in the words: landscape and people; and, above all, the intellectual atmosphere. Many another artist who had come to Vienna had been irresistibly drawn under the spell of its unparalleled situation, which presents an ideal background for the growth and development of works of art. Nature here is not so magnificent and imposing that she overpowers man entirely, to the obliviousness of all else. The softly undulating hills, planted with vines, and sharply contrasting with the blue of the Southern sky; the woods of delightfully mingled trees, with here and there a pine, making the most glorious color-symphonies in spring and autumn; and the majestic Danube—all this beauty softly and gradually fills the heart with delight, and brings all hidden seeds to their fullest growth. That it is easy to live among the Viennese people Brahms was soon to learn with surprise and pleasure. The reserved Hamburger was delighted by the natural sociability of the Viennese families, the freedom and gaiety of life, and the charming thoughtfulness of the *Hausfrauen,* who were always proud to display their culinary arts to the newcomer. But above all he was attracted by the natural and innate musical talent of the majority of his acquaintances, who often gave excellent concerts in their own homes.

Friendly relations were quickly formed with many of his fellow musicians in Vienna. But it is interesting to note that Brahms liked best to associate with two musicians of the Liszt-Wagner circle: the composer Peter Cornelius and the pianist Karl Tausig. Brahms wrote in this connection to Joachim:

Wagner is here and I shall probably be called a Wagnerite, mainly of course out of the opposition to which any sensible per son is driven by the haughty way in which the musicians her talk of him. Besides I particularly like to be with Cornelius and Tausig who . . . incidentally, achieve more with their little finger than other musicians with the whole head and all their fingers.

Tausig, especially, fascinated Brahms by his brilliant virtuosity, and inspired him to write the Paganini Variations. Both musicians were not only fond of playing together, but also of philosophizing, and Tausig unsuccessfully endeavored to win Brahms over to the theories of Schopenhauer. That they were not, however, always engaged in such serious matters is clear from a remark of Tausig's in a later letter: 'Do you still remember Pressburg, where we three [probably Cornelius was the third] were perfectly drunk, and you kept on insisting that you must have your coffee? I hope we shall be as jolly together again. In the same spirit Grosser called the months which he spent with Brahms 'a mad time.' [2]

A connection was soon formed with a Viennese publisher whose acquaintance Brahms had previously made. This was J. P. Gotthard, manager of the publishing firm of Spina, who published two vocal compositions, the Psalm, Op. 27, and the Duets, Op. 28. Gotthard introduced Brahms to the musical historian Gustav Nottebohm, whose important researches into the works of Beethoven and Schubert were a source of inexhaustible interest to an artist of so strong a historical bias as Brahms (see p. 112). Next to an original MS. Nottebohm liked a good drink, of which Brahms, too, was rather fond. Further, Brahms found in Nottebohm, who was a confirmed bachelor, living a somewhat eccentric life, an excellent subject for his jokes. The following report, in a letter to Nottebohm from their common friend C. F. Pohl (the librarian of the *Gesellschaft der Musikfreunde*) is typical:

Since your departure our Kronprinz Restaurant flies a dark flag with an 'N' embroidered on it. Brahms assured Herr Weigl [the proprietor of the restaurant] that you had run away with two women. Weigl didn't believe it, explaining that 'Herr Nottebohm is a woman-hater,' whereupon Brahms murmured, 'Then you don't know much about him.' And then not satisfied with that, Brahms went to our café and told the amazed waiter a thrilling story about his friend Nottebohm's elopement with a woman. The waiter threw up his hands in astonishment, and cried: 'Oh dear, what is happening this year! I would never have believed such a thing of Herr Nottebohm.' [8]

We must not forget the beautiful women of Vienna who entangled the ardent young man in more or less serious flirtations. With Luise Dustmann he soon became very friendly, and she impressed him greatly as an artist, especially in the role of 'Fidelio.' The nature of their relationship is best revealed in the singer's letters, which were sometimes signed 'Fidelio,' and were preserved by Brahms; for example, the following:

I received your letter last night and hasten to answer it. My address is the one I gave you (in the suburb of Hietzing). I shall be giving audience there until the end of the month. . . My town address is surprisingly near you. But house painters and various other artists are in possession, which renders it impossible to receive you there as I should like. If, therefore, you don't

want to come all the way to Hietzing, on account of the badness
of the times [a joke, as the journey to Hietzing was neither long
nor expensive], my dressing room at the theatre remains the
only likely place for a rendezvous. There I can be seen tomorrow
from 5 to 6 p.m. as 'Heilige Elisabeth' [the leading role in
Tannhäuser]. Ever yours,

LUISE DUSTMANN [4]

On another occasion she wrote: 'I think I will summon
the gentleman from Hamburg, not for my piano, but for
myself. He is such an excellent tuner. Perhaps he will succeed in making my discordant strings resound again.' [5] Luise
Dustmann was probably the only person who thought of
addressing the reserved Johannes in her letters as 'Hansi,' a
Viennese pet name given only to children.

Brahms also kept up a friendship with Bertha Porubszky,
who had just become engaged to Arthur Faber. His relations
with the temperamental and highly talented singer Ottilie
Hauer were of quite another kind; Brahms used to go
through his songs with her, and she was presented with no
less than sixteen manuscripts by the master. She was a member of a small but select ladies' choir, which met regularly,
soon after Brahms's arrival in Vienna, at the von Astens',
who were friends of Clara Schumann's. This choir proved
to Brahms how musical the beautiful Viennese ladies were.
All, however, had to stand aside for Ottilie, and it happened
once again that a sweet voice sang its way into the artist's
heart. Later Brahms wrote to Clara 'of a very pretty girl with
whom he, God knows, would have made a fool of himself,
if, as luck would have it, someone had not snatched her up at
Christmas.' This can have applied only to Ottilie, who became engaged to Dr. Edward Ebner on Christmas Day, 1863.
In her recently published memoirs Ottilie's daughter mentions that her mother's family and all her friends had confidently expected the engagement of Brahms and Ottilie.
And many years later Brahms hinted in unmistakable terms
that Ottilie had inspired the writing of some of his songs.
When his friend Hermann Levi wrote of the excellence of

[71]

some woman singer, and added: 'With all respect to Frau Ebner, but this is quite different,' Brahms answered: 'Greetings to the artist who sings better. I'm sorry to say I have little understanding for this kind of talent. But this is probably natural; some can only repeat to us what others have made us create.' In this case also love changed into cordial friendship, which did not diminish in intensity as time went on.

Of even greater significance than the human relations he had formed was the reception he received from the leading musical circles of Vienna. The imperial city was at that time pre-eminent in all the branches of musical art. Young Otto Dessoff, an excellent artist, was director of the Court Opera House, and at the same time conductor of the Philharmonic Concerts, given by the operatic orchestra. The orchestral and choral concerts organized by the old and esteemed *Gesellschaft der Musikfreunde* were under the leadership of the fashionable and ambitious Johann von Herbeck. This organization paid most attention to oratorios and symphonies, whereas the *Singakademie*, founded in 1858, was interested mainly in *a cappella* singing. There were also numerous smaller choral organizations and chamber music ensembles, among which the Hellmesberger Quartet was the most prominent. And lastly, Vienna boasted a profusion of first-class soloists, both singers and instrumentalists. The famous Conservatory of the *Gesellschaft der Musikfreunde* attended to the training of the coming generation and the maintenance of the great musical traditions.

Into the company of these eminent Viennese artists came Johannes Brahms, whose works were as yet almost unknown to them. The composer of thirty was anything but a man of the world; he had not yet entirely overcome his shyness, and he was quite unable to push his own compositions. With such a temperament it may well have seemed difficult for him to gain prominence in this large and brilliant company; nevertheless, he attained it in a remarkably short time. First,

[72]

Julius Epstein, a very fine and able pianist, was completely carried away by Brahms's works, and introduced him to the Hellmesberger Quartet. They immediately decided to perform the Pianoforte Quartet, Op. 25, with Brahms at the piano, and thus he appeared before the Viennese public, as composer and as pianist, as early as 16 November 1862. His success was such that Epstein implored his new friend to arrange a concert of his own, and in order to forestall any possible opposition he engaged a hall in Brahms's name for 29 November. That evening the Pianoforte Quartet, Op. 26, and the Handel Variations were performed; and besides these Brahms played works by Bach and Schumann 'as unconcernedly as though he were playing at home to friends.' In a letter to his parents he explained this by the observation: 'This public, of course, stimulates one very differently from ours.' At a second recital he met with the same success, though it must be admitted that the pianist found far readier recognition than the composer. Nevertheless, the Viennese public was distinguished from that of other cities in that it listened to these unknown works with respect and sympathy, if not with understanding. Brahms's position in Vienna was further improved by the fact that the two conductors, Dessoff and Herbeck, were sufficiently interested in the foreigner to perform his two serenades; and lastly, a number of concert engagements won him still greater recognition. Thus a variety of circumstances co-operated to make his stay in Vienna agreeable.

It will be easily understood that his parents were delighted with the good news of their favorite son. Frau Brahms could not read the newspaper reports without tears, and when a batch of clippings arrived in time for Christmas, Fritz wrote in the name of the family: 'You could hardly have sent us a more welcome Christmas present. I needn't say . . . that I am as pleased as a king with your splendid reception. For us Hamburgers such a warm reception was astonishing.' [6]

On another occasion Frau Brahms wrote: 'You have so many friends already in Vienna! So you are probably not so home-sick any longer; otherwise I think you would be guilty of keeping me awake at night.' [7] And on 30 January 1863, she thanked him for a photograph sent from Vienna, in which her Johannes looked so gay and enterprising that she quite expected before long to receive the announcement of his en-gagement.

This time the sensitive woman was deceived by the ex-ternal facts. In reality Johannes was anything but happy in spite of his success, and all the artistic and human stimulus which the gay *Kaiserstadt* afforded him. For the second time in his life he had to overcome a disappointment which shook him to the very depths. Soon after his arrival in Vienna he received the news from Avé-Lallement, writing from Ham-burg, that his fervent hope of being elected as leader of the *Singakademie* and the Philharmonic Orchestra had not been realized. His friend, the singer Julius Stockhausen, was to be the successor to old Grund. The Hamburgers' motives were clear; they knew that Stockhausen enjoyed great popu-larity, and that he would be as great a 'draw' to the public as to the members of the choir. How little they had really considered their great son is shown by the fact that five years later, after Stockhausen had resigned this position, Brahms was again passed over, and Julius von Bernuth, of Leipzig, was elected. Some of his biographers state that the Hamburg patricians could not forget Johannes Brahms's origin in the *Gängeviertel*. This may in part have accounted for their behavior, but whatever their reasons, many years had to pass before Hamburg realized the greatness of its na-tive composer. The Handel scholar Chrysander, a friend of Brahms, who lived near Hamburg, wrote bitterly in 1869:

The other day your father mentioned that you would probably be coming here before long. May it be soon! Of course, I know only too well that no particular musical treat awaits you, but

[74]

rather the hidden enmity of small-minded men, who, alas, are influential enough to see that nothing of importance can happen in Hamburg.[8]

And as late as 1876 Marxsen complained, after a performance of the *German Requiem:* 'The artists of Hamburg, your so-called intimate friends, were one and all conspicuous by their absence!!!' [9]

So Brahms found himself disappointed in his fondest hopes, and the effect of this reverse of fate cannot be too strongly emphasized. It is best to let the artist himself describe it in a letter to Clara, in which, behind his carefully controlled words, we are conscious of the profoundest sorrow:

I feel that I must send you the enclosed letter [from Avé-Lallemant]. This is a much sadder business for me than you think, or can perhaps understand. As I am altogether rather an old-fashioned person, so I am in this, that I am not a cosmopolitan, but love my native town as a mother. . . And now this hostile friend comes and ousts me . . . perhaps for ever. How rare it is for one of us to find a permanent niche, and how glad I should have been to find mine in my native town! Happy as I am here, with so much that is beautiful to rejoice me, I nevertheless feel, and shall always feel, that I am a stranger and can have no peace. You have probably heard of the affair already, and perhaps you thought of me in connection with it. But I don't suppose it occurred to you that I had suffered so great a misfortune, yet it needs only a hint for you to see how much I am losing. If I am not to hope for anything here, then where? Where should I care to go, even if I had the chance? Apart from what you experienced with your husband, you know that, as a general rule, what our fellow citizens like best is to get rid of us altogether and to leave us to drift about in the void. And yet one wants to be bound, and to acquire the things that make life worth living, and one dreads solitude. Work in active association with others, with live social intercourse, and family happiness . . . who is so little human that he does not long for these things?

Clara, in her answer, did her best to take the matter less seriously: 'You are still so young, dear Johannes, you will find an abiding-place yet, and "the man who takes a loving wife finds heaven in every town." '

She was mistaken, however. With all the force and constancy of his nature Brahms held fast to the idea of a permanent position in Hamburg. And just because its realization was shattered by his countrymen's lack of understanding, this dream of settling down to a bourgeois life in his native place seemed doubly alluring. Sixteen years after Stockhausen's election the old resentment still burned in him with undiminished force. When, on the occasion of the Hamburg Orchestra's fiftieth anniversary, the greatest honors were bestowed upon him, he whispered excitedly to his friend, the poet Claus Groth: 'Twice they have filled the vacant position of director of the Philharmonic Society with a stranger, and twice they have passed me over. Had I been elected at the right time I might still have become a respectable citizen; I could have married and lived like other men. Now I am a vagabond.' Whether this was true—whether Brahms would really have led an orderly bourgeois life in Hamburg, who can decide today? The artist who avoided every possibility of marriage, who could never bear to continue long in one post, whether in Detmold or Vienna, could probably never have endured any such permanent ties, even at home. The professional duties of the choir and orchestra conductor would soon have become onerous, and he would then have risked everything to secure the freedom so indispensable to his art.

Brahms himself, however, was never able to consider the true state of affairs so dispassionately. All the discontent and restlessness in his nature (the causes of which will occupy us later) were focused on his humiliation in Hamburg. It is perhaps not too much to say that in the end it was this defeat, whose importance he absurdly overestimated, that gave rise to the great change in Brahms's demeanor. He hid his all too soft and vulnerable heart behind a mask of distrust, reserve, and sarcasm, and sometimes, as Hermann Levi said was even 'ridden by the demon of harshness and callousness.' This, however, does not mean that Brahms's character, so unusually kindly, had really undergone a change, for his life was full of supremely unselfish actions. He used, however, to utter a thousand little sarcasms, to give vent to the bitterness and disillusion gathering in his heart, which he never relieved by expressing it openly to his friends.

From the standpoint of the historian, however, Brahms's defeat appears in an entirely different light. Posterity is much more inclined to view this setback as providential and beneficial to his art. Feeling himself cast out of Hamburg, he was forced to find a new home, and with the sure instinct of the genius, he decided on the city which was most propitious to the development of his work. For the stolid North German especially, the atmosphere of Vienna, so foreign to his nature, resulted in an enrichment and expansion of his artistic personality, and many of his loveliest creations cannot be imagined as having flowered in another soil.

UNPUBLISHED LETTERS REFERRED TO:

1. Letter from Julius Grosser, 1 March 1887.
2. Letter from Karl Tausig, 10 April 1867.
3. Letter from Carl Ferdinand Pohl, 1 February 1876.
4. Letter from Luise Dustmann, 9 October (without year).
5. Letter from Luise Dustmann, undated.
6. Letter from Fritz Brahms, 28 December 1862.
7. Letter from Christiane Brahms, 6 December 1862.
8. Letter from Friedrich Chrysander, 16 December 1869.
9. Letter from Eduard Marxsen, 4 December 1876.

VII

FIRST APPOINTMENT IN VIENNA

(1863-1864)

LIKE every change in Brahms's life the transference of his abiding place from Germany to Austria was gradual. Ever and anon he drifted back from foreign parts to Hamburg, and to his parents' house. But as conditions there grew more and more unpleasant he resumed his wanderings after a short stay. Many years of an unsettled, wandering life were to pass before Vienna was to become his home.

In May 1863, Brahms, on leaving Vienna, went first to his friend Joachim. This time there were two reasons for his visit. Shortly before this, Joachim had become engaged to the lovely opera singer Amalie Weiss. In compliance with her fiancé's wish she gave up her theatrical career, and Brahms arrived just in time to be present at her farewell performance as 'Orpheus' in Gluck's opera. Her singing impressed the composer deeply, and many of his later compositions, in particular the *Rhapsodie*, Op. 53, were written for Amalie's magically soft contralto. Soon Johannes and Ursi (as Amalie liked to be called) were on the very best of terms, and many years later his loyal adherence to this friendship even resulted in a serious inner conflict (see p. 142). This visit, however, was also intended for Joachim the artist. The F minor String Quintet, the tonal quality of which had not satisfied the composer at a private performance in Vienna, was once more to be thoroughly rehearsed by Joachim. But even under his leadership no better result was achieved, and so Brahms gave up the idea of publishing this work as scored for strings.

From Hanover, Brahms went to Hamburg, where he arrived in time to celebrate his thirtieth birthday. The usual festive spirit, however, was this time not forthcoming. For this the bitter feelings which the artist now entertained for his native city were not wholly responsible; what was far worse was that gaiety and comfort had deserted his parents' house. Frau Brahms had aged suddenly. The consequences of her hard life now began to show themselves in this woman of seventy-four; she urgently desired to fold her hands in her lap and let others care for her. But this was impossible; although her daughter Elise loved her wholeheartedly, she was often unable, on account of her terrible headaches, to be of the slightest help. The atmosphere of suffering that surrounded the frail old woman and the ailing, melancholy girl was inevitably bound to be most distasteful to Jakob Brahms. With his fifty-seven years the jovial man was still very active and not in the least inclined to renounce the pleasures of life. Scenes and misunderstandings were unavoidable between the ill-matched pair, and Fritz and Elise did nothing to ease the tension. Doubtless the girl took her mother's part, while the son avoided his parents' home so far as possible. Johannes's intervention did something to improve matters, and thanks to his conciliatory speeches the quarrel was patched up. But his heart was heavy, as he was only too keenly conscious of the dangers that threatened a peace concluded with such difficulty.

Into this gloomy atmosphere a ray of light shone from Vienna. Before his departure some of his friends, notably the singer Joseph Gänsbacher, had inquired, in a noncommittal way, whether Brahms would be inclined to take over the leadership of the *Wiener Singakademie,* a well-known choral society. At the time Brahms had been undecided; now, however, the Viennese offer seemed very tempting. When, therefore, he received the official announcement of his election, he did not take long to consider the matter.

His friends had only to exercise a little persuasion, and he accepted his new position gladly.

The very first concert, on 15 November 1863, was a clear proclamation of his artistic faith. The ardent Bach devotee began his activities with the performance of the cantata *Ich hatte viel Bekümmernis*. This was followed by Beethoven's *Opferlied,* and several of Brahms's own adaptations of folk songs for four voices. It goes without saying that a work of his never-to-be-forgotten friend Robert Schumann was included in the program; the lovely *Requiem für Mignon* brought the concert to a close. Only six weeks were available for the preparation of this comprehensive program, and the success of the concert spoke well for the conductor, as well as the choir. Afterwards Cornelius wrote impulsively to Brahms. 'What a treat that was! You have unquestionably won the most perfect laurels. I really revelled—each piece was more beautiful than the last. I wish this concert had been the ultimate of the series, so that you could have closed your first season with this striking success.' [1] (With this last remark Cornelius unfortunately revealed prophetic gifts!) The Viennese critics also showed their utmost appreciation, and Brahms could be well contented with his first appearance as a conductor before so exacting an audience. Artistically, too, his new work was bound to please him, as it gave him an opportunity of acquiring a profounder knowledge of compositions which he particularly valued. How seriously the new conductor set about his task may be seen from the fact that he wrote a special organ part for the Bach cantata. This has been preserved in the archives of the *Wiener Singakademie,* and clearly shows the artist's conception of how the older music should be performed. The organ supports the choir and the orchestra, intensifies the important crescendos, and supplies the necessary fullness of tone and harmony. Apart from this, however, the conductor allows the organ a certain latitude when the leading melody is silent or needs relief. With the most refined taste, Brahms kept to the happy medium between too sparing and too lavish an accompaniment.

In every respect, therefore, his new work was pleasantly begun. Yet even in his first delight in his success he wrote Clara a letter whose content, although it is lost, may be deduced from her reply:

I should have liked, dear Johannes, to write you as soon as I received your letter, because I so much wanted to tell you with what deep pleasure I had heard of your splendid success. . . But in any case you damp my ardor almost immediately by saying that you don't after all think you will keep the post. . . I can't imagine why you think Dietrich's [a conductor in Oldenburg] and Stockhausen's positions enviable. In view of the small appreciation he gets in Hamburg, Stockhausen's position is on the whole certainly not enviable, for the public there is not nearly ripe yet for good orchestral performances. . . Once more, I can plainly see what a difficult position you would have had there as a native of Hamburg, and so young a man to boot. Your wings would soon have drooped with exasperation. How different things must be in Vienna.

The inner contradiction which Brahms's letter must have shown is obvious. Already the composer was tired of his work in Vienna, and the fault may have lain principally in the administrative work inseparable from public performances. It was essential to consider all the wishes and scruples of the different members of the board, to make arrangements with the soloists, occasionally to alter the appointed dates of performances, and so on. But in spite of his impatience with all these details, Brahms fervently desired to obtain similar work in Hamburg. This shows clearly how small a part logical considerations played in the decisive questions of his life.

Preparations for the second concert began, and this time Brahms went a step further in the choice of his program. He decided to perform, together with a Bach cantata, a large number of *a cappella* works of the seventeenth century. Difficult though it was for performers and audience to feel

[81]

themselves at home in this strange world, the conductor, inexperienced in the practical side of concert-giving, did not provide the necessary variety, but presented a succession of the gloomiest pieces. Such a preference elicited the jesting remark in Vienna: 'When Brahms is really in high spirits he gets them to sing "The Grave is my Joy." ' This serious concert was unsuitably placed at the beginning of the carnival season, and as the choir did not sufficiently master the *a cappella* pieces, the success of the performances was very doubtful. The next concert, with Bach's *Christmas Oratorio,* was given shortly after a wonderful rendering of the *St. John's Passion* by the much more highly trained *Singverein,* and so suffered in comparison. Even though the final concert on 17 April 1864, which was entirely devoted to Brahms's own compositions, found a much kinder reception, it will readily be understood what conclusions he drew from his first trial year. The *Singakademie* had the greatest faith in their conductor and elected him unanimously for the next three years, but Brahms declined. Although he complained that 'his purse had for some time been leading a remarkably limp and inactive existence,' he did not contemplate continuing his activities merely for the sake of financial security. As early as 17 January of this year he wrote to his friend, Adolf Schubring: 'While in any other city a regular position is desirable, in Vienna one lives better without it. The many interesting people, the libraries, the *Burgtheater,* and the picture galleries, all these give one enough to do and enjoy outside one's own room.'

Socially the winter of 1863-4 was very like the first Brahms had spent in Vienna. In particular his work as a teacher brought him into contact with a number of new acquaintances. One of his girl pupils, Elisabeth von Stockhausen, was so lovely and gifted that he was positively afraid of her; his experience with Agathe and Ottilie had put him on his guard, so he entrusted her instruction to Epstein, who, however, declared that he, too, found it impossible not to fall in love with the charming blonde. In later years Elisabeth, who married Heinrich von Herzogenberg, one of Dessoff's pupils, came to be one of Brahms's most sympathetic friends, playing no small part in his life. Another pupil was Amalie von Bruch-Vehoffer, to whose house Brahms also liked to go for an hour of comfortable gossip. Frau von Bruch died in 1871, leaving a chest full of music to her beloved master. Upon opening it, Brahms found in it, to his surprise, a purse containing a considerable amount of money and a note expressly bequeathing this sum to him. He was too proud, however, to accept such a gift; moreover, he was afraid that Herr von Bruch might misinterpret his wife's action. He therefore returned the money to the widower, explaining that it could only have been left in the chest through an oversight.

As for his male acquaintances, he was on terms of increasing friendship with the well-known critic Eduard Hanslick, who even sought the acquaintance of Brahms's family in Hamburg, sending his photo to the delighted Elise.[2] He continued to see much of Tausig and Cornelius and they in turn were anxious to arrange a meeting between Brahms and their friend Richard Wagner. The introduction was at last effected through the medium of a third common acquaintance, Dr. Standhartner, who took Brahms to see Wagner on 6 February 1864. The evening was a gratifying success: apart from classical music, Brahms played his Handel Variations, and Wagner could not but be impressed by this magnificent work. He expressed his admiration in the following words: 'One sees what can still be done with the old forms in the hands of one who knows how to deal with them.'

Never again were the two greatest German composers of their time to meet face to face. It would therefore seem appropriate to give some account of their relations here. In their art Brahms and Wagner had no points of contact whatever (as will be more fully explained in another chapter). Precisely because of their dissimilarity, one might have

[83]

thought that each could have respected the other's achievements. Actually, however, their relations—mainly owing to the intervention of third persons—became less and less friendly. The attack delivered upon the 'music of the future' by Brahms in 1860 can hardly be held responsible for this. In that year Brahms, together with Joachim, Grimm, and Scholz, drew up a manifesto in which they and a number of sympathizers sought to protest against the influence of the 'new German' school. Owing to an indiscretion, this manifesto, which was really aimed at Liszt rather than Wagner, was published with the names of the four principals only, and in this form excited mirth rather than anger in the camp of their opponents. In any case, this episode was not regarded as an obstacle to the meeting of Wagner and Brahms in the year 1864. The maturer Brahms was profoundly interested in Wagner's works. In the year 1870 he went to Munich for the performance of *Das Rheingold* and *Die Walküre;* he urgently invited his publisher, Simrock, to go with him to Bayreuth, and he studied with genuine interest the Wagner treasures in the possession of the Wesendoncks. Moreover, he expressly advised [3] the conductor Arthur Nikisch to perform one of the compositions of the Bayreuth master at his opening concert in Leipzig.

Brahms repeatedly expressed his appreciation of Wagner's music, while he seldom—even among his closest friends—said anything in criticism of his works. Wagner, however, as early as 1869, in his essay *Ueber das Dirigieren,* delivered a covert attack upon Brahms, referring in sarcastic terms to their meeting in Vienna. In later years his tone became positively vindictive, and the fact that his music was bitterly attacked by numerous critics of Brahms's circle increased his hostility. A rather unpleasant correspondence between the two composers, concerning the ownership of the autograph-score of the so-called 'Paris *Tannhäuser* scenes,' did not help to improve their relations. Brahms had received the manuscript as a gift from Karl Tausig, and was greatly surprised when their common friend, Cornelius, asked [4] him in 1865 to return the score to Wagner, as 'Tausig was undoubtedly in error when he declared that the score was his property.' Brahms was always reluctant to part with any of the treasures of his collection. He returned the manuscript, unwillingly enough, only when Wagner himself appealed to him, ten years later. Finally, the Bayreuth master felt deeply offended when the younger composer was awarded in 1879 the honorary degree of Doctor of Philosophy by the University of Breslau, while he himself could not boast of such an honor. At that time Wagner, in his *Bayreuther Blätter*, wrote a heated article against Brahms, in which he described him as a 'street singer,' a 'Jewish czardas player,' and so forth. Although this disparagement of Brahms was the fashion with Wagner's adherents, many of his more temperate followers were unable to agree with the master in this respect. Karl Tausig, for instance, in spite of the disagreeable incident of the *Tannhäuser* score, always remained a friend and admirer of Brahms; and it is interesting to read the following letter, which Tausig wrote from Berlin at a time when the idolized Wagner may have been working on the essay *Ueber das Dirigieren:*

I have received the [D minor] Concerto and the cadenzas; many thanks for them. I hope to see the father of these interesting children in the near future. Do come if possible; you will find it quite pleasant at my house. I take it for granted that I may put you up. Your room is ready and the large cigars languish while waiting for you to smoke them. You will find the Tiergarten more charming than ever, and you will be led so far into it that no sound of a street organ will reach your ears. . . Now you may realize my great regard for your music and what I think of you. I have said it at least a hundred times, and proved it to the best of my ability. [5]

Brahms, not forgetting this invitation, spent a night in Tausig's home when passing through Berlin in 1871; this was to be his last meeting with his friend, who was carried off by a cruel fate when barely thirty years of age.

More conspicuous still was Brahms's friendship with Mathilde Wesendonck. As is well known, the Wesendoncks offered Wagner a refuge (after his flight from Germany) in a cottage near their house 'on the green hill' and there the romance occurred between Mathilde and Wagner that he immortalized in his opera *Tristan and Isolde*. After Wagner's departure they corresponded for many years, friendship surviving even when the vicissitudes of life had loosened the tie between them. Considering how much Wagner's cottage must have meant to Mathilde, we are astonished to read the following lines in one of her letters [6] to Brahms: 'During the music festival the Stockhausens are going to be our guests; unfortunately I shall be absent. The little green nest near by with its hermit's gate will remain untouched; before I leave for St. Moritz I am going to see to it that at any time a light-hearted swallow can find a modest shelter there.' She, therefore, did not consider it irreverent to allow Johannes Brahms to occupy the rooms that once sheltered the ardently worshiped Wagner. As Brahms did not accept her invitation, she wrote even more pressingly in the following year: [7] 'Your rooms are always ready for you. For the New Year, let me now tell you all that you ought to have known long ago, and do know now, don't you? I should not like to have lived in this century without at least giving you a friendly and pressing invitation to join us at our fireside.'

Many more of Mathilde's letters, preserved by Brahms, as well as copies of her poems with personal dedications, bear witness to the sincerity with which she aspired to his friendship. In one letter she explained what it was—besides Brahms's art—that had made such a deep impression on her: 'You know . . . that it is my weakness to think of you as one of the best and most unprejudiced men of our time.' [8] In Wagner's case Brahms had the opportunity of proving this lack of prejudice, so rare among creative artists.

Let us return to 1864. Now that Brahms's work with the

Singakademie had come to an end there was nothing to keep him in Vienna, and he returned to Hamburg in June 1864. The situation at home was even more unpleasant than in the previous year. His mother had become feebler and more intolerant; while his father, who in his old age was overjoyed by the fact that Stockhausen had accepted him for the Philharmonic Orchestra, complained that he was not allowed to practice undisturbed. The son soon realized that separation was the only solution. He therefore took a room for his father in the *Grosse Bleiche;* his mother and sister remained for a time in their old home, only to move in November 1864 to a 'charming apartment with garden,' ⁹ where a room was always kept in readiness for Johannes. In many respects the dissension between his parents was a heavy blow to their son. He, who was so fond of both his father and his mother, was called upon by each in turn to deliver judgment on the other. Delighted by the realization of his father's musical ambitions, he could not but take his part, seeing that Jakob was hindered at home in his work. He knew, however, how deeply his mother was hurt by her favorite's attitude. The sensitiveness and kindness of the man is shown in his letters to his father—published in 1933 by Stephenson.* (Only those to the father have been preserved, the letters to his mother having been destroyed by Brahms himself.) How diplomatically he proceeded is seen in the following lines, written in October 1864, after his departure from Hamburg to Baden-Baden:

MY DEAREST FATHER,

I do indeed miss news of you, although I cannot hope to hear anything pleasant. That Mother and Elise have reserved a room for me would please me indeed if I could think that you would occupy it frequently! I hope that this will be the case. You can often take your afternoon nap in the company of my books. Don't stint Mother as regards my money; it is not important

* For this and other letters of Brahms's to his father and stepmother, see *J. Brahms' Heimatsbekenntnis,* by Kurt Stephenson, Hamburg, 1933.

that it should last until the New Year, and money can bring a smile to many a face which would otherwise frown. Do your best, even if things should be unpleasant at times. Help them with the moving, and don't let yourself be driven away; the time will come when she and all of us will thank you. . . Where do you have your meals? You do still go to Mother's? Could you settle a few small expenses for me with Mother? For example, the cost of sending some music to Vienna. Please make a note of this item; I will send the necessary amount at the first opportunity.

Yours most affectionately,

JOHANNES

It is touching to see how the son again and again did his best to find a pretext for bringing his parents together—whether he speaks of the unoccupied room in the new home, or the midday meal that Jakob was to take with his wife, or the sums that his father was to pay his mother.

Apart from his grief, the separation of his parents brought him material cares, as Brahms had undertaken to support his mother and sister. This was not easy for a musician who had no fixed income, and the burden was so heavy that Clara Schumann thought it necessary to intervene, asking Jakob Brahms to do more towards maintaining his wife, as Johannes was not quite so well off as his father supposed.[10] Her intervention had little success, for Jakob, who was now taking his meals at a restaurant, could not live as cheaply as he had lived at home. Johannes, therefore, had to provide for mother and sister. After Christiane's death he continued to support the delicate Elise, and in the course of the years the allowances to his father increased, as Jakob gradually retired from his profession. The manner in which Brahms met all these troubles shows the kindliness and nobility of his character. Even when in the greatest straits he never said a word about his sacrifices; as often as possible he tried to send more than he had promised, asking that the money should be spent on luxuries. The following lines to his father are characteristic: 'Whenever you need any money, whatever the sum, you write to me, won't you? Are you living comfortably? Do you buy as many geese as you can do with? If you don't I shall send again without being asked.'

Of this aspect of his family affairs Brahms rarely spoke, even to his best friends. When he did, however, no one could fail to notice the pleasure with which he referred to it. In his old age the musician Vincenz Lachner recalled such a scene in a letter to Brahms:

I remember when in my lodgings at Mannheim you strode up and down with a beaming face, waving a knitted purse in your hand, whose golden contents you complacently set out on my piano like a company of tin soldiers. This is for my dear father in Hamburg, you said. I could have flung my arms round you.[11]

Such golden gifts were sent to Hamburg again and again. One thing only he insisted upon: a prompt acknowledgment. Of Elise—apparently knowing that she was inclined to be extravagant—he demanded also an exact list of her expenditure, which she forwarded punctually every fortnight.

Having settled the dispute in his parents' house to the best of his ability, he went in the summer of 1864 to Lichtental near Baden-Baden, where Clara Schumann had bought a cottage. This famous spa is beautifully situated, and on the wooded hills Brahms was able to give full rein to his passion for the long, undisturbed morning rambles, during which the majority of his compositions were conceived. Baden-Baden, besides, was in many respects a stimulating place. Artists, diplomats, and royalty from every part of Europe assembled there; and gradually Brahms came into contact with a great variety of eminent men and women, such as the Landgravine of Hesse; the Russian novelist, Turgenieff; the famous singer, Pauline Viardot; the pianist, Anton Rubinstein; the Viennese 'waltz king,' Johann Strauss; the painter, Anselm Feuerbach, and many others.

With two of the men whom he met here, Brahms soon formed a close friendship: Hermann Levi and Julius Allgeyer. Levi was the conductor of the opera house in Karlsruhe; the young and gifted artist had long been a warm admirer of Brahms's works, and he was now fascinated by the composer's personality. On Brahms's departure in the autumn of 1864 Levi wrote to their mutual friend Clara Schumann: 'This close contact with Johannes has had, I believe, a deep and lasting influence on my whole character, such as I cannot remember having experienced at any other period of my musical life. In him I have seen the image of a pure artist and man; and that is saying much nowadays.' For Brahms, too, the connection with Levi was extremely valuable. 'This young man,' he wrote to Joachim, 'despite all his theatrical upbringing, is so lively and looks up with such bright eyes to the greatest heights, that everything done in his company becomes a pure joy.'

The young conductor studied his friend's compositions with all the exuberance of his nature. He loved to copy them out, in order to make them entirely his own, and he often received the original manuscript as a token of gratitude. In this way he witnessed the creation of many a work, and sometimes, like Joachim, he even influenced its final elaboration. For many years Levi considered it to be his chief duty to work for the recognition of his friend's compositions, and when in 1870 he received a call to Munich, Allgeyer wrote to Brahms: 'It goes without saying that Levi, as I do, feels that he owes it to you to accept this position. He considers it his duty to procure a fresh footing for you in this enlarged field of activity.' [12] Allgeyer, a gifted copperplate engraver and photographer, was a friend whose sterling nature must have delighted Brahms. The portrait Levi painted of this simple and modest man, in a letter to Clara Schumann, might have been the work of Johannes himself: 'He is a dear old fellow; true as gold. When I have spent an evening with him, I always feel as if I had taken a refreshing bath. Even his faults are lovable.' Allgeyer's heart was filled above all with love and admiration for Anselm Feuerbach,

[90]

of which his great biography of the painter is the best witness. However, he had also a deep admiration for Brahms's art and character, and he expressed this feeling very gracefully when writing to the composer himself:

To true greatness one may make such a confession without misgiving; in this strain, without feeling that I was doing anything undignified, I wrote to Feuerbach the other day: 'I wish I could sometimes be with you, even if I had to shine your boots.' You, my dear Johannes, are less concerned about the polish of your 'pedals' than our little darling of the Graces in Rome [Feuerbach], otherwise I should be ready for once to serve two masters.[13]

In a circle of friends so sympathetic and stimulating, still further enriched by Clara's presence, Brahms's art bore magnificent fruit. The F minor Piano Quintet received its final form, the Second String Sextet matured, and a series of songs was completed and sent to the publishers. Thus the summer of 1864 was a highly productive season; and during the composer's next sojourn in the same environment he was destined to reap an even richer harvest.

UNPUBLISHED LETTERS REFERRED TO:

1. Letter from Peter Cornelius, undated (November 1863)
2. Letter from Elise Brahms, undated (1864).
3. Letter from Arthur Nikisch, 5 September 1895.
4. Letter from Peter Cornelius, 18 August 1865.
5. Letter from Karl Tausig, 27 April 1868.
6. Letter from Mathilde Wesendonck, 12 June 1867.
7. Letter from Mathilde Wesendonck, 30 December 1868.
8. Letter from Mathilde Wesendonck, 24 November 1874.
9. Letter from Elise Brahms, 17 August 1864.
10. Letter from Jakob Brahms, 13 January 1865.
11. Letter from Vincenz Lachner, 24 January 1890.
12. Letter from Julius Allgeyer, 17 June 1870.
13. Letter from Julius Allgeyer, Christmas, 1872.

VIII

'A GERMAN REQUIEM'

IN the autumn of 1864, Brahms returned to Vienna, where he spent the whole of the following winter. This time Christmas was a sad festival, for the son's thoughts turned ever and again to Hamburg. Once more he made a hesitating attempt to reunite his parents. To his father he wrote: 'You must after all receive my greetings at this festival, although we lonely men don't see much of it. Aren't you going to spend one evening with Mother? Doesn't Fritz do his best to persuade you to go there? I myself shall be alone, and how lovingly I shall think of you!' Jakob, however, could not persuade himself to follow his son's advice; and before long fate intervened, making further efforts at reconciliation superfluous. On 2 February 1865, Johannes received a telegram from Fritz: 'If you want to see our mother once again, come immediately.' He hastened to Hamburg, but found his mother dead; a stroke had suddenly ended her life. Outwardly the son was amazingly composed, his common sense telling him that he owed a debt of gratitude to destiny for the long life that had been granted to his mother, and for her painless death. Nevertheless, he was deeply stricken, knowing well what a store of love, devotion, and tenderness he had lost in the passing of this old woman.

As a truly creative artist, Brahms could master his deep sorrow only by concentrated work, and a long-cherished plan was now slowly assuming a tangible form. His grief at Schumann's death, as Kalbeck states, may have inspired in Brahms the thought of composing a *German Requiem*. His mortification over the Hamburg defeat deepened his melancholy, and now the shock of his mother's death spurred him to work out this immortal composition. In the following years the *German Requiem* * grew slowly to completion, and by engrossing himself in the artistic shaping of it, Brahms succeeded in overcoming his melancholy mood. As Goethe had done by writing *Die Leiden des jungen Werther,* so Brahms freed himself from intolerable gloom by composing *Ein deutsches Requiem.* The composer, under the influence of the majesty of death, underwent a process of purification. In this mighty oratorio Brahms reconciled for the first time the conflicting energies of his creative genius. With the completion of this work, the composer reached his full creative power, and a new period in his work began: that of mature and consummate mastery. In himself, too, Brahms grew calmer, more lucid, more tranquil. He no longer rebelled against the inevitable, and the following words, which he wrote to Clara soon after his mother's death, might be taken as the motto of his newly found attitude to life: 'There is nothing to be altered, nothing to regret for a sensible man; it's simply a matter of carrying on and keeping one's head above water.' The events of the last few years, which culminated in his mother's death, had matured him as a man and an artist.

During this period of his inner transformation Brahms could never bear to stay long in one place. Although from time to time he made his home in Vienna, and often returned to his friends in Baden-Baden in the following years, he felt driven to lead the restless life of a concert performer; it was also necessary, in order that he might support his family in Hamburg. In the autumn of 1865 a series of recitals was begun in Mannheim, where the D minor Piano Concerto, under Levi's inspired conducting, received real appreciation for the first time. Touring the more important towns of Switzerland, he soon won a large following, which made this small country one of the most important and enthusias-

* This work is usually known as Brahms's *Requiem;* cf. p. 310.

tic centres of the Brahms cult. More concerts followed in Mannheim and Karlsruhe. At Christmas, Brahms went to Detmold, where the mature artist was received with open arms. The year 1866 opened with a real Brahms Festival in Oldenburg, where his friend Dietrich was working as musical director.

After this restless life the composer was in urgent need of undisturbed repose. This he found in Karlsruhe, in the quiet and cheerful atmosphere of Allgeyer's home, where the *Requiem* grew to completion. Then, however, the longing for vivid and unfamiliar impressions of Nature awoke in him. After a short stay in Winterthur with his publisher Rieter-Biedermann, in whose comfortable house Brahms felt very much at home, he spent the summer of 1866 on the Züricherberg. The view over the magnificent range of glaciers may have inspired the stupendous vision of the sixth movement, and the sunny blue lake the idyllic fourth. He soon found friends in the society of Zürich. Besides Schumann's pupil, Theodor Kirchner, he often met the conductor Friedrich Hegar, who all his life was one of Brahms's most enthusiastic adherents. He also appreciated the society of the eminent surgeon Theodor Billroth, who was an ardent musician in his leisure time, and was even permitted to play piano duets with Brahms, and to take a string part in the master's quartets. A lifelong friendship was formed between these two men. Further, from this time dated Brahms's relations with the hospitable Wesendonck family.

In the autumn of 1866 Brahms again made an extensive concert tour through Switzerland, this time in conjunction with Joachim, who had resigned his position after the King of Hanover's abdication. Brahms's piano playing developed a new beauty under the great violinist's influence; and they found the results of their partnership so gratifying that a year later they made a second tour, this time through Austria. The visit to Switzerland came to an end in December 1866, and after an absence of more than eighteen months

Brahms returned to Vienna. He spent Christmas in the Fabers' house, and was much more cheerful than he had been two years earlier, knowing that his *Requiem* was completed. Also he had no longer to think of his father as a lonely man, for at Christmas he had received the following gratifying news:

I am happy to sit down to write to you, but of course I never have anything to say. I have learned nothing, and lead as always a very retired life. But my home life is happy; I should like you to see it. It is as though God had sent an angel to make me forget everything. Heartiest thanks, my dear Johannes, for the ten napoleons with which you presented us at Christmas. I am only sorry not to be able to send you ten times as much.[1]

Who had brought about this change in Jakob's life? In order to understand this we must go back more than a year. As early as the summer of 1865, only a few months after Christiane's death, the tone of Jakob's letters had grown less discontented, and in one of them he told his son with satisfaction that he had at last found a good place for his midday meal.[2]

In October Brahms, to his surprise, received a long letter from his father, who was usually so averse to writing. This letter contained the following news:

Life, as I am now living, contains so little that is agreeable, it is so dull and empty, that I have decided to make a change; I believe and hope that this will be for my happiness. It is easily understood that I, who for thirty-four years had lived with my family, if not always very happily, must find it hard to accustom myself to the life I have led for the past two years. Therefore, if you think it over, you won't hold it against me if I tell you that I am thinking of marrying again, especially as my choice has fallen on a woman, who, though of course she won't make you forget your mother, has every right to your respect. She suits me, and I am sure I have not made an unbecoming choice. She is a widow, a homely body, forty-one years of age. It would make me particularly happy if this should be another reason for you to come here this winter. . . I hope, therefore, my dear Johannes, that we shall see each other soon, and I hope until then you think kindly of my intention, even if it rather surprises you. . .[8]

His choice had fallen on Karoline Schnack, at whose table Jakob Brahms had been taking his midday meal. The news could not at first be welcome to the son. Once more his father, now fifty-nine years old, was about to bind himself to a woman whose age seemed incompatible with his own, though this time he had gone to the other extreme; Jakob Brahms was as many years older than his betrothed as Christiane had been older than he. Would he not, in his later years, have to suffer as Johannes's poor old mother had done? However, in October 1865, when Johannes came to know Karoline, all his fears vanished, for she was a cheerful and capable woman, who loved Jakob faithfully and was able to organize his life just as he wished. In fact, Karoline made her husband's old age extremely happy, and Jakob did not exaggerate when he wrote [4] to his son that under her influence he had become quite a different man. At sixty he felt restored to youth; enthusiastically he made excursions from Hamburg, visited his native village of Heide, where he entered with all his heart into the gaiety of peasant weddings; and he even planned more extensive journeys. The son was delighted to witness his father's happiness, and he soon made up his mind that Jakob, who had never yet left the lowlands, must visit him in Austria and see the mountains. In the first months of 1867 Johannes realized sufficient money, thanks to successful concerts in Austria and Hungary, to invite his father to visit him; so, on returning from a visit to Heide, Jakob found the following letter:

MY DEAREST FATHER,

You are probably returning from Heide tomorrow, and I hope and wish that you are in such good spirits that you will immediately do what I ask you. Come to Vienna! Don't think it over too long; only consider that at your age traveling becomes more difficult and less enjoyable with every year; and don't forget that the summer is getting hotter and hotter in Vienna, and

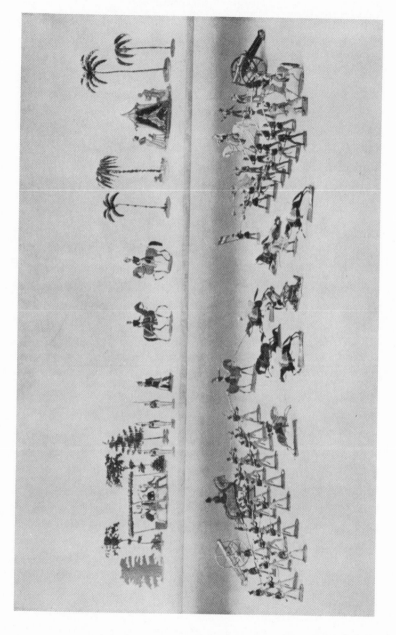

BRAHMS'S TIN SOLDIERS

BRAHMS AS A YOUNG MAN

less agreeable week by week. It goes without saying that this journey will cost you nothing, not even the loss of opportunities at Hamburg. Of course we will arrange everything so that this will not be too tiring for you. You must not and cannot gainsay me, and you are not to think over this offer too long. It would be best for you to start, if possible, this very night. . . I beg you, dearest Father, kiss Mother good-bye at once, and give her a kiss for me too. Off you go; you will enjoy yourself thoroughly, and you will give me the greatest pleasure. I am waiting impatiently for the announcement of your departure.

Yours,
JOHANNES

This letter contained also a number of practical details about train connections, and even the advice to drink a glass of grog every night during the journey, in order to sleep soundly. The son had forgotten nothing of the slightest consequence, and it will be readily understood that his father could not resist so pressing an appeal.

Jakob was enchanted with Vienna; he liked Johannes's friends enormously, and he quite understood that his son was happy there. In his later letters he always inquired after their mutual acquaintances and once he longingly remarked: 'After all, you live there hovering between heaven and earth.'[5] The Viennese, too, had taken a fancy to the cheery Hamburger: a lady of Johannes's circle, Frau von Bruch, even corresponded with Jakob until her death, and she regularly sent him newspaper clippings containing criticisms of his son's work.[6] The mountain tour in Styria and the Salzkammergut, which Jakob and Johannes made in the company of Gänsbacher, did not impress the old man so greatly as his son had anticipated, judging from his own impressions. At home, however Jakob was childishly happy in recounting his adventures to his astonished friends, and he openly confessed in a letter: 'You can imagine how many people envy me; of course, I exaggerate properly; I tell them I've climbed right to the top of the Schafberg (a mountain in the Salzkammergut, 5,400 feet in height), but I don't tell them that I rode on horseback three-quarters of the way.' [7]

This first journey was far from deterring Jakob from further adventures. On the contrary, in the following year Johannes took him to the Rhine and to Switzerland, a journey which the son would undoubtedly have refrained from making had his father really been lacking in appreciation, as some of Brahms's biographers have imagined. In 1870 Jakob even decided to travel alone with his wife to the Harz; long beforehand he was 'childishly,' and Karoline 'crazily,' looking forward to this journey,[8] and his detailed accounts,[9] written in the style of a diary to his son, show how many vivid impressions the man of sixty-four could still receive.

In 1867, at the end of the summer holiday with his father, Brahms returned to Vienna and wrote to Joachim:

Through the visit of my father and a little trip we made together, I felt the most delightful uplifting of spirit that has come my way for a long time. No small part of my joy was due to the pleasure my father derived from all the new sights . . . and it was anything but unimportant to him that here he came face to face with the Austrian Emperor and the Turkish Pasha, and in Salzburg with the Emperor in the company of Napoleon. Now I am sitting in Vienna again and here I shall quietly remain, but my soul is refreshed as is the body after a bath. My dear father has no idea how much good he did me; I almost went with him to Hamburg.

The next few months were devoted to the work of preparing for the performance of the *Requiem*. A beginning was made in Vienna, where on 1 December Herbeck conducted the first three movements in a concert of the *Gesellschaft der Musikfreunde*. Here the audience showed its distinct disapproval of the work, one of the reasons being the fact that the timpanist played the long-sustained D of the magnificent fugue in the third movement fortissimo, drowning all the other instruments. Brahms, however, would not be disheartened; he knew that the performance of his work had been entirely inadequate, and after making several changes in the ill-fated passage of the third movement, he confidently looked forward to the first complete performance of the *Requiem*. This was planned to take place under his own conductorship in the cathedral of Bremen on Good Friday of the following year. In January 1868 he left Vienna to reassure himself on the progress of the rehearsals, which were conducted by Karl Reinthaler. This artist had devotedly applied himself to the study of the magnificent work, and had transmitted his enthusiasm to the choir and orchestra, so that Brahms could rest assured that his work was in the best of hands. After he left Bremen to give concerts in several German cities and in Denmark, Brahms wrote to Reinthaler: 'I wish from all my heart that your people would maintain their zeal. I confess, I would have to admire you, if we could be quite happy in Holy week [when the *Requiem* was going to be performed]. My *Requiem,* after all, is rather difficult, and at Bremen they attack the high A more cautiously than in Vienna.'

But when at last 10 April arrived, Brahms had every reason to be 'quite happy.' All those who were present at this first performance of the *Requiem* felt that this was an important artistic event; this consciousness fired both singers and players to do their utmost, and inspired the audience to appreciation of all the beauties and subtleties of this wonderful work. When Brahms stepped up to the conductor's desk, a wave of emotion seemed to meet him. His dearest friends had come; his father, Clara Schumann with her eldest daughter Marie, Joachim and his wife, Stockhausen (an unparalleled soloist in the third movement), the Grimms and Dietrichs, the publisher Rieter-Biedermann, and many others. (The fact that Marxsen—on account of illness—was unable at the last moment to come to Bremen [10] was perhaps even more disappointing for the teacher than for the pupil.) In the choir, too, familiar faces greeted him; the former ladies' quartet of Hamburg had insisted on co-operating in this performance. Soon, however, all distinction between the composer's intimate friends and the innumerable strangers assembled there was to disappear, for one and all were spellbound by this new work. On that day Brahms, at the age of thirty-five, experienced fully, for the first time, complete success, and even though many such experiences were to be his he could rarely have enjoyed any of them as he enjoyed this first triumph.

And Jakob Brahms: how had this day of rejoicing affected him? An English eyewitness, John Farmer, subsequently teacher of music at Balliol College, Oxford, describes this in a letter that he wrote many years later to Brahms:

When I hear your works played, and there is seldom a concert in which Brahms does not appear, it brings back to me so clearly my first visit to Hamburg in 1861 or 1862, when I, through a letter of introduction from Rieter-Biedermann of Winterthur, saw you and heard you play for the first time. And afterwards, at Bremen at the first performance of your *Requiem,* when I had also the pleasure of meeting your father. I remember so well being near him, Frau Schumann, Joachim, and others on that grand occasion. He was the only one to remain calm—the rest were in tears even at the opening chorus 'Selig.' I remember so well when we were coming out of church after your great triumph I spoke to him and asked him if he was proud of his son's success, but all he said was: 'Es hat sich ganz gut gemacht' (It didn't sound bad)—and took a pinch of snuff. He was the only man who seemed calm, he took it for granted that his son would triumph. He remains for me the picture of a simple and strong man.[11]

This, at first, may seem astonishing. Had old Brahms really been so unresponsive to this great impression? Surely not; but he had the typical reserve and outward calm of the North German. The Holstein poet, Theodor Storm, complained that he used to send every new creation of his muse to his father without ever hearing a word of praise or blame from this otherwise most affectionate parent. The Holsteiner is silent when he is most profoundly moved. This fact should not be overlooked if we want to understand the character and the behavior of Jakob and also of Johannes Brahms.

The triumphal progress of the *Requiem* was irresistible. Before the month was out it had to be repeated in Bremen. After this Brahms added the wonderful fifth movement 'Ye now Are Sorrowful'; this part is the very heart of the whole work, which is dedicated to the memory of his mother, and the part that speaks most clearly of her character. In this final and complete form the work was performed in Germany no less than twenty times in the following year. London followed in 1871, Petersburg in 1872, and Paris in 1875. The fact that the *Requiem* was not only certain of success with the public, but was sung with special pleasure by the choir, is shown by an account from the pen of Hermann Levi, who rehearsed this work at Karlsruhe * in 1869. He wrote to Brahms:

Last night, after the rehearsal, when most of the people had left and I was sitting at the piano, lost in thought, I began unconsciously to play the first bars of your *Requiem*. Instantly those who were at the door turned back, their hoods flew off, and the girls crowded round the piano and began to sing, with radiant faces, until we at last got stuck in the third movement.

The success of the *Requiem* encouraged Brahms to further choral compositions. In Bonn, where he spent the summer of 1868, he not only completed the cantata *Rinaldo,* but also worked on the magnificent *Schicksalslied* (Song of Destiny), He then sought recreation in Switzerland in his father's company. Then followed concerts in Oldenburg, Hamburg, and Bremen; but more and more frequently his thoughts turned to Vienna. He had written from Bonn to Amalie von

* After the exceptionally successful performance at Karlsruhe, a special mark of courtesy was shown to the composer. As Brahms's liking for old music was generally known, he was presented with a beautifully written score of Georg Forster's *Ausbund schöner teutscher Liedlein,* a very rare choral work of the sixteenth century.

Bruch: 'You would not believe how often I think of Vienna! If only the journey there—and each journey back—were not so long!—One ought to just stay there.' [12] In December he was at last back in Vienna. At first he stayed at the hotel *Zum Kronprinz,* but presently the long-cherished plan was realized. He was tired of his restless, roaming life; even though he would have to give many more concerts, he wanted to have a home of his own, to which he could always return. He had come to love Vienna, and from year to year it became dearer still. On 30 April 1869, he therefore asked his father to cease reserving rooms for him in Hamburg; and the reason he gave shows that he had now resigned himself to the inevitable, in this as in other matters:

After all, I cannot wish to settle in Hamburg, and even if I visit you for shorter or longer periods, we can hardly for that reason keep two rooms empty all the year round. . . Besides, what should I do in Hamburg? Apart from you there is no one I want to see. You know well enough how little, in any respect, I get out of the place. In short I realize at last that I must have some sort of a home somewhere, so I think I shall try to make myself more comfortable in Vienna next autumn.

UNPUBLISHED LETTERS REFERRED TO:

1. Letter from Jakob Brahms, 19 December 1866.
2. Letter from Jakob Brahms, 9 July 1865.
3. Letter from Jakob Brahms, 14 October 1865.
4. Letter from Jakob Brahms, 19 December 1866.
5. Letter from Jakob Brahms, 8 December (without year).
6. Letter from Jakob Brahms, 15 January 1869.
7. Letter from Jakob Brahms, 3 September 1867.
8. Letter from Jakob Brahms, 7 June 1870.
9. Letter from Jakob Brahms, 26 June 1870.
10. Letter from Eduard Marxsen, 5 April 1868.
11. Letter from John Farmer, undated.
12. Letter from Brahms to Amalie von Bruch, 1 July 1868.

IX

ARTISTIC DIRECTOR OF THE 'GESELLSCHAFT DER MUSIKFREUNDE'

(1869-1875)

HARDLY had Brahms, in 1869, decided to make Vienna his home, when various opportunities arose of obtaining a position in Germany. Ferdinand Hiller again tried to draw him to Cologne. Comparing this urgent invitation [1] with the earlier one (see page 55) we can see how greatly Brahms's fame had increased in the ten intervening years.

You see that I am today writing on official stationery, although the contents of this letter are of a purely private nature. . . I take it, however, as an omen, I hope a good one. Rudorff is going . . . so his position falls vacant. It means giving ten to twelve piano lessons and a few lessons in harmony and counterpoint. As, however, the teaching alone could not interest you sufficiently, I should propose that they offer you the direction of the concert choir—not under me, but in co-operation with me. We would divide the work between us. . . Of course, I don't speak of the fact that it would give me personally the greatest pleasure to share my daily work with you, since that is no reason for taking such a decisive step. But you could count on my doing everything to make life agreeable for you, though naturally, after Vienna, Cologne is bound to seem a dreary place. . . Please do not let me wait long—give me at least your first impression, and tell me if I may hope. . .

Brahms first inquired of Rudorff what his experience had been in Cologne, but he added: 'The daily intercourse with Hiller and the work with the choir tempt me to go to

Cologne . . . the town itself and the giving of lessons frighten me.'

These misgivings were in the end decisive for Brahms, and he refused the post. The second temptation, which came to him in the same year, must have been far greater. The Royal Musical College (*Königliche Hochschule für Musik*) had been opened in Berlin under Joachim's leadership; and the new director naturally sought to secure the co-operation of the friend he so admired. Once again Brahms could not bring himself to accept the offer, but his reasons for refusing it are not really known. Possibly Joachim could not offer sufficiently good terms, or he approached Brahms at a time when the Berlin plans were still in the air. This, at any rate, is suggested by a letter from Marxsen: 'So it is really true that you have had propositions from Berlin! Up to now I rather doubted this, but felt sure that in case they did materialize you would refuse. The whole affair seems rather vague, and will probably always remain an ideal dream.' [2] However, the supposition that Brahms refused for personal reasons seems more likely. In spite of his love for his friend, he had always avoided living in daily contact with him and in the same town. This assertion may seem surprising, but it can be substantiated by a significant document, which we shall consider presently (see page 144). Finally, Brahms refused both offers all the more readily, inasmuch as he was already greatly attached to Vienna. Although he loved to grumble about 'the useless life' to which he was condemned there, at the bottom of his heart he clearly realized how important Vienna had become to his artistic development. He pretended to himself that he was diligently looking for a position in Germany, and in 1870 he even showed some interest in a directorship, recently resigned by Bruch, at the small Residenz of Sondershausen, a second Detmold. As soon, however, as a real possibility offered itself, he always found ample reasons for refusing it.

A delightful work of his dating from this year shows how

deep were the roots that already bound Brahms to Vienna. After he had rid himself of all grievous and oppressive thoughts by the composition of his magnificent funeral chant, the *Requiem*, his newly recovered joy in life found expression in the *Liebeslieder* (Songs of Love—piano duets with vocal quartet *ad lib.*). These delicately stylized Viennese waltzes are definitely Austrian in their charm and their lovable and frolicsome merriment. Brahms had a special place for them in his heart. When the score was printed, the composer, who never uttered a word of praise for his own works, unbent sufficiently to write to his publisher, Simrock: 'I must confess that it was the first time I smiled at the sight of a printed work—of mine! I will risk being called an ass if our *Liebeslieder* don't give pleasure to a few people.'

An artist of Brahms's complex character, however, could not long maintain such a cheerful acceptance of life. In 1869, the very year of the *Liebeslieder,* he was made particularly conscious of his loneliness by an event in the Schumann family. Julie, Clara's third daughter, had grown into an exceptionally lovely girl, to whom Brahms had become deeply attached during his stay in Lichtental in the summer of 1869. He was, however, anything but an outspoken lover, so it was quite possible that neither Julie nor her mother had an inkling of their friend's feelings. Just about the time when Elise Brahms, as she wrote to her brother,[3] was told in a Hamburg shop that a daughter of Clara Schumann's had become engaged to a certain Brahms from Vienna, Clara herself informed Johannes, in all innocence, of Julie's engagement to Count Radicati di Marmorito. Again this meant renunciation, and just because the decision—in contrast to his earlier love affairs, when Brahms had forced renunciation upon himself—came on this occasion from without, it hit him all the harder. Clara and her family noticed that Johannes suddenly seemed 'quite changed,' and he regained his self-control only when he had succeeded in giving expression to his grief in music. At the end of September,

Clara wrote in her diary: 'A few days ago Johannes showed me a wonderful work for contralto, male chorus, and orchestra. He called it *his* bridal song. It is long since I have received so profound an impression; it shook me by the deep-felt grief of its words and music.' The composition which moved Clara so intensely was the *Rhapsody*, Op. 53, on a text from Goethe, depicting, with a power that could only have come from personal experience, a solitary man, the prey of all the agonies of loneliness.

When Brahms returned from Lichtental to Vienna, the question of his accepting a position once more arose. Herbeck had been appointed to the Opera, and so his position as musical director of the *Gesellschaft der Musikfreunde* had to be filled. From the first Brahms's friends had been working for this appointment; but the reserved North German still had many enemies in influential circles, who had other candidates in view; so it was by no means certain how the fight was going to end. Brahms himself thought that 'the position was altogether too precarious' (as indeed every post was in his eyes). On the other hand, he felt strongly attracted by its artistic possibilities. How seriously he considered it—in contrast to all former proposals—is clear from the fact that in July 1870 he asked his friend Levi where he would be during the summer, as his advice might be badly needed in respect of the question of Herbeck's successor. Levi disapproved entirely of Brahms's plans, and in reply he wrote a letter in which he stressed his doubts.

I saw in Karlsruhe—and with unprejudiced eyes—that you have a gift for conducting such as no other man possesses. Nevertheless, you are not the man to contend successfully with the thousand-and-one petty vexations which are inevitably connected with any official position. I am afraid they would soon get the better of you. . . Just reflect: I strongly sympathize with your desire to find a settled home, to be absorbed in work that is independent of momentary moods and inspirations. . . But far more momentous than all this is your duty to persevere in the struggle, and to avoid setting the center of gravity of your life on soil which may be successfully cultivated by artistic journeymen, but never by the masters of art.

This admonition did not fail to impress Brahms, and he may have been glad that the decision did not for the moment rest with him, since the post was provisionally given to Joseph Hellmesberger, who was followed in 1871 by Anton Rubinstein. Brahms realized, however, that the question was by no means definitely settled. Meanwhile he quietly continued to live his usual life, spending most of the winter in Vienna, and the summer in Germany. In 1870 he attended the Munich performance of *Das Rheingold* and *Die Walküre,* and spent some time with Joachim in Salzburg. His intention of visiting Clara Schumann in Lichtental could not be fulfilled, owing to the outbreak of the Franco-Prussian war. He followed all the events of the war with the deepest interest, and the joy of the patriot in the German victories found direct expression in his magnificent *Triumphlied* (Song of Triumph). This composition was dedicated to the German Emperor, although Brahms had really written it for Prince Bismarck, for whom, after the events of 1870-71, he had a greater admiration, perhaps, than for any of his contemporaries. In his rooms there hung a picture of Bismarck wreathed in laurel, and later on he became honorary president of the Vienna branch of the club Z.A.D.P. (*Zum Ausspannen der Pferde*). This club (founded in 1894 by Sophie von Sell) was a society of Bismarck's admirers who had intended to honor the ex-Chancellor by unharnessing his horses and drawing his carriage themselves on his return to Berlin, after he had been dismissed by Wilhelm II. When this was forbidden by the police, the club sent the ex-Chancellor a laurel wreath and a poem, and subsequently missed no occasion of doing him honor. Brahms had some correspondence with Sophie von Sell,[4] as he liked to be informed of the club's activities.

Shortly after the *Triumphlied*, the *Schicksalslied*, started three years earlier, was completed. The first performance of this work took place on 18 October 1871, under Levi's inspired conductorship, at Karlsruhe; and thereby the composer paid a debt of gratitude to the friend whose influence had been so helpful, especially in respect of this particular work.

At Christmas 1871, an event of great importance occurred in Brahms's outer life. He moved into the apartment in Karlsgasse 4, which was so entirely to his taste that he retained it to the end of his life. The only improvement he made in this modest home—and not until he reached the height of his fame—was to add a third room to the original two, for the purpose of accommodating his extensive library, which had until then remained in Hamburg. At first he was satisfied with two very simply furnished rooms, regardless of the fact that every visitor had to enter by way of an unsightly corridor—passing the kitchen door, which was always open—and go through his bedroom in order to reach the sitting room. They offered him all that he demanded of a home. These rooms, built on the third floor, were very quiet, and afforded an exceptionally fine view of one of the columns of St. Charles's church—so beloved of Brahms—and the great square, with the Elisabeth Bridge and the little stream (Wienfluss), which had not then been built over. Moreover, they were in the center of the city, and were thus quite near the building in which he always found so much to do: the premises of the *Gesellschaft der Musikfreunde,* which, built in 1870, contained also the concert hall and the music library. Indeed, the convenient situation of Brahms's rooms gave rise to a jest: Carl Ferdinand Pohl, then the librarian of the *Gesellschaft der Musikfreunde,* who could not welcome Brahms too often to his Museum, wrote: 'Properly speaking, there ought to be a footbridge, leading from St. Charles's, across the Wienfluss, straight to our music building. It ought to be called the Brahms Bridge, and only the person of that name should have the key.' [5]

Soon after Brahms moved to his new home, there occurred

an event that bound him still more closely to Vienna. In January 1872 his stepmother wrote that his father had fallen seriously ill, and the son, deeply distressed, hastened to Hamburg. An advanced cancer of the liver had been diagnosed, and Jakob died eleven days after Johannes's arrival. The son's grief was profound. He knew how his father had enjoyed life during the last few years, and he cursed the fate that had robbed him of the joy of helping to make his father's life happy and free from care. A sense of loneliness overcame him, even deeper than before, for the bond with his native town was now entirely severed. Although both his brother and sister lived in Hamburg, they were almost strangers to him. He could not forgive Fritz for breaking off all connections with his family, and giving them no help, in spite of his good financial status (as a well-known music teacher he had a substantial income).

Although Fritz and Johannes were reconciled at their father's deathbed, the relations between them remained entirely superficial. As for Elise, she had married, shortly before this, a widower of sixty who had six children, and Johannes disapproved of her choice, fearing that her extensive duties might be too great a burden for her. Here, however, Brahms was mistaken. It was good for the lonely girl to have a home of her own, and in her many letters to her brother she always spoke of her husband's thoughtful and affectionate character; for instance, he surprised her on each anniversary of their wedding with a poem written by himself. So far as it was possible for Elise, to whom Nature had not been kind—even her only child died a few days after its birth—her marriage with the watchmaker Grund turned out very happily. Brahms soon realized this, and helped the Grunds continually in the most generous manner; he even paid for the education of the youngest of Elise's stepchildren, little Alfred. But nearer his heart than either his brother or his sister was Karoline, to whom he always remained grateful for making his father's last years so happy and contented. The very first letter to her after his return from Hamburg eloquently testifies to the warmth of his feeling for her.

[4 *March* 1872]

MY DEAR MOTHER,

Many a time I have put out the paper in order to write to you. I thought of you indeed, most affectionately; I thought further and further back into the past—but it couldn't be put into writing. Neither that, nor words of consolation. And even now I can't attempt to console you; I know too well what we have lost, and how lonely your life has become. I hope, however, that now you are doubly conscious of the love of others—and finally, my own love, which is entirely and wholly yours. Here I have received so many marks of sympathy that you would have been happy to see how Father was valued by all who knew him. . . I am sending you 1,000 thalers. Of that you can give Elise her share. May I ask you to write in good time when and how much money I shall send? Simply the sum you need. . . Now my most heartfelt greetings and as you assuredly know how I loved my father, so, too, be sure that I shall always, and for all time, in truest and most grateful love, be

Yours,

JOHANNES

It speaks of the profound loyalty of Brahms's character that he should have remained all his life so warmly attached to this simple woman. Over and over again he sent her substantial sums of money, and criticisms of his works, and although he disliked writing letters, he kept up a correspondence with her and her son by her previous marriage, Fritz Schnack. It is significant that almost the last lines which he wrote at the point of death were on a postcard to Karoline Brahms, in which he reassured her about his condition.

On his return to Vienna after his father's death, Brahms felt very strongly that this city was now his home. And as the possibility of securing a fixed position had now become more definite—Rubinstein had resigned, after a year, from the conductorship of the *Gesellschaft* concerts—he saw this problem in a different light. He was tempted to test his powers upon such splendid material, and he may also have felt pleased that he, who had been passed over in Hamburg, was now to receive a far more important appointment. The *Gesellschaft der Musikfreunde* agreed to all Brahms's conditions; they offered him a yearly income of 3,000 florins, and the final decision on all artistic questions, such as the choice of programs and soloists, was left to him.

Nevertheless, Brahms hesitated. The creative artist in him was afraid of unaccustomed restrictions, and the man whose character was so averse from the involved methods of diplomacy feared the intrigues and subterfuges to which the holder of a position of this kind was exposed. In the end, however, he decided to accept the appointment, and it may have been that such arguments as his friend Pohl put into the following humorous words induced him to take this step:

Although I truly believe I know and understand your feelings in the matter, I should like to convince you that after all, as in a dish of garnished beef [a favorite Viennese dish, consisting of boiled beef surrounded by various vegetables] the meat is the most important thing; with the rest you can do just what you like; and so here remember that you can do an infinite amount of good; and there are bitter pills to be swallowed everywhere.[6]

So Brahms agreed to become artistic director of the *Gesellschaft der Musikfreunde*, and he started his work in the autumn of 1872. He at once made a number of important reforms. First of all, he reorganized the orchestra, which consisted mainly of amateurs, replacing the weaker musicians by members of the excellent Court Opera orchestra. Moreover, he insisted on a second weekly rehearsal for the choir, and allowed the more difficult passages to be studied only by small groups at a time. The programs, too, made great demands on the intelligence of performers and audience alike. Although Brahms did not dare to proceed as drastically as in the case of the *Singakademie*, ten years earlier, the composition of the programs clearly proclaimed his artistic creed. Of the eighteen concerts given in the years 1872-5, two-thirds were devoted to the older music; nine works of Bach, five compositions of Handel, and four *a cappella* pieces of the seventeenth century were performed. Even when he came to the Viennese classics the new conductor was able to present absolutely unknown works, such as the *Davidde penitente* and *Venite populi,* of Mozart. Characteristically enough, Brahms himself was not very often represented in these concerts; but he organized the first Viennese performance of the *Triumphlied,* produced the *Rhapsody* and the *Schicksalslied,* and was induced by the general request to give a performance of the *Requiem* in his last year of office— an unforgettable artistic event in the annals of the *Gesellschaft der Musikfreunde.*

We have few accounts of Brahms's methods as a conductor. It is said that his movements were extremely energetic, and that the passion with which he felt every note was forcibly transferred to the performers; and such stern critics as Clara Schumann, Hermann Levi, and Hans von Bülow spoke highly of his achievements as a conductor. Though his gifts as a conductor were great, they were of less importance to his work as artistic director than his exceptional knowledge and understanding of old music. It was in this domain that Brahms exerted the greatest educational influence during his three years of office, and for this Vienna still owes him thanks. He combined the keenest artistic understanding with an exceptionally delicate sense of historical style, and performances of unique quality resulted from this blending of qualities. Even though Bach and Handel had been played in Vienna before his time, we may safely say that his renderings first helped the Viennese public to gain a deeper understanding of the magnificent works of the Baroque period. The Hamburg master, who had been so richly inspired by the Viennese atmosphere, paid his debt of gratitude in full by interpreting the old North German music for the Austrian people.

In the *Gesellschaft der Musikfreunde* a number of orchestral scores have been preserved, which were carefully arranged for performance by Brahms himself. Considered in its entirety, this hitherto unnoticed material gives a plastic image of the way in which Brahms thought works of the seventeenth and eighteenth centuries should be performed. (We find here scores of J. S. Bach: *Christ lag in Todesbanden, Nun ist das Heil, O ewiges Feuer, Liebster Gott;* of G. F. Handel: *Saul, Solomon, Alexander's Feast,* the *Dettingen Te Deum,* the *Organ Concerto in D minor,* and many others.) He refrained on principle from modernizing the instrumentation, a procedure not uncommon in the nineteenth century. His historical sense even caused him to retain antiquarian details, for example, the practice of having the solo voices accompanied by part only of the orchestra. He also used keyboard instruments for the continuo, as a matter of course, in producing works of the Baroque, and he meticulously avoided alterations such as those made by Robert Franz, who replaced the continuo by wind instrument parts inserted for the purpose. Brahms, however, did not invariably adhere to the orthodox archaic standpoint. Where small alterations would improve the color of a passage, he applied them without hesitation. He carefully avoided rigid interpretations; his graduations of tone were full of light and shade, affording not only supple and harsh contrasts, but also delicate tonal transitions; in particular, he was never tired of introducing numerous small crescendi and decrescendi.

His work as artistic director, therefore, must have given Brahms a certain satisfaction, and its success was all that could be desired. The original opposition among the members of the choir quickly gave way to frank admiration; the critics, his friends, and the public applauded enthusiastically, and the number of his persistent adversaries was insignificant. All this, however, could not prevent Brahms from resigning his position at the end of three years. The final reason was Herbeck's retirement from the management of the Court Opera. Brahms was sufficiently well acquainted with the ambitious character of this man to know that the former conductor of the *Gesellschaft der Musikfreunde* would adopt every device of intrigue to regain his previous position. The composer did not care to enter upon such a contest, but preferred to resign of his own free will. Herbeck's rivalry, however, was only the final cause of Brahms's action, and we should probably be justified in assuming that the master was well content with this turn of events. His interests as composer and as musical director had often clashed, as, for example, in the yearly difficulties in respect of the programs. For practical reasons the *Gesellschaft der Musikfreunde* liked the programs to be arranged early in the spring. Brahms, however, who spent this time of the year in creative work, usually disappeared without leaving his address, and could be found only with difficulty. The same sort of thing happened in other directions and Levi's prophecy came true. Brahms, who did all that he undertook with the greatest conscientiousness (it was said that he worked three months to prepare himself for a performance of the *St. Matthew Passion*), was bound to feel greatly hampered in his own creative activity by the many duties imposed on him.

This state of affairs could not be continued, and, even without Herbeck's rivalry, Brahms would, before long, have found some reason for resigning. That the artist was aware of this, and retired without the smallest ill-feeling, is evident from the fact that his relations with the *Gesellschaft der Musikfreunde* remained cordial and undisturbed. He was elected honorary member, and was to show his attachment in later years by appointing the *Gesellschaft der Musikfreunde* his sole heir, with the exception of a few personal legacies. On the other hand, the question arises: why did the society allow their eminent conductor to leave them? We must consider, in the first place, that Vienna was at the time undergoing a severe financial crisis, in which the musical world was deeply involved. It may, therefore, have seemed safer to the *Gesellschaft der Musikfreunde* to entrust their concerts to Herbeck, a man who for many years had stood in high favor with the Viennese public, and who, moreover, made it his business, more than Brahms ever did, to arrange attractive programs. Moreover, co-operation with the composer was probably not always quite easy, so that the management of the *Gesellschaft der Musikfreunde* may have found the change from the intractable Brahms to the versatile Herbeck not so inconvenient.

The master's creative activity, often hampered by the duties of his position, broke forth all the more impetuously during the summer months. The summer of 1873, which Brahms spent in Tutzing, near Munich, yielded a particularly rich harvest. In these months he mastered two new forms of music. He completed the two String Quartets, Op. 51 (dedicated to his friend Billroth), which, although not his first attempt at this type of work, were the first he thought worthy of publication. In the same summer Brahms wrote the brilliant Haydn Variations, Op. 56, in two versions: for orchestra, and for two pianos. He also composed the greater part of a volume of songs, Op. 59, at this time.

Brahms must have felt a sense of physical well-being in this charming village on the Starhembergersee, of which he wrote to Levi:

Tutzing is far more beautiful than we first imagined. We have just had a gorgeous thunderstorm; the lake was almost black, but magnificently green along the shores; usually it is blue, though of a more beautiful and deeper hue than the sky. In the background there is a range of snow-covered mountains— one can never see enough of it.

He lived a simple, rustic life, as he loved to do, and there was no lack of charming representatives of the opposite sex. Frau Dustmann permitted herself the pleasure of spending the summer with 'Friend Hansi,' and here too Brahms spent many agreeable hours in the company of a young musician from the Dutch East Indies, Lucie Coster, who, as she complained in a letter to him,[7] was a first-rate butt for his teasing and mischievous remarks. Above all, Brahms was not far from his good friends Levi, Allgeyer, and Franz Wüllner in Munich. Through the medium of these men he came into contact with the whole musical circle of Munich, and an outward sign of the appreciation of the Bavarian capital was his investiture with the Order of Maximilian, which occurred some months later.

The only discord in the harmony of this summer was a misunderstanding between himself and Joachim. A great Schumann Festival had been arranged for 17-19 September 1873, at Bonn, and the receipts were to go towards the erection of a monument over the deceased master's tomb. Joachim had been appointed leader of the Festival, and the committee tried to induce Brahms to write a special composition for the occasion. He refused, on the grounds that he could not find a suitable text, and justified his refusal with the generous words: 'I can't see why I ought to speak, when one is to be spokesman who knows my language better than I.' Joachim then suggested the performance of the *Requiem,* as the name of Brahms could not be absent from a Schumann Festival. Brahms had no objection; but his answers—probably as a result of his modesty—were couched in such a cool and constrained tone, that even his old friend could not understand him. Accordingly, when the committee decided against the *Requiem* on purely technical grounds, Joachim too dropped this proposal, believing that he was acting as Johannes would have wished. This, however, was not the case; Brahms had regarded the performance of the *Requiem* as a matter of course on such an occasion, and on learning of its withdrawal through the press, he was deeply hurt, and bore a grudge not only against Joachim, but also against Clara, who had influenced the arrangement of the program. Only Levi's intervention removed the misunderstanding. Brahms realized that he had expressed himself with too great reserve; he attended the Festival, and did his best to recover the old intimacy of friendship. Clara even wrote in her diary: 'I tried the new variations for two pianos with Johannes . . . they are quite wonderful. Johannes promised to come to Baden—we have spoken frankly to one another (as far as such a thing is possible with him).' These last words are significant and give a key to the whole episode. Brahms had reached such a degree of mental reserve and isolation that he could seldom make himself understood, even by people like Jussuf and Clara, whom he considered his very best friends. (That Clara must be counted among these, in spite of all his inner changes, is proved by innumerable letters, such as the following written in 1874: 'I love you more than myself and more than anybody and anything on earth.')

Brahms, however, avoided at this time any really personal friendship in the true sense of the word. He took all the more pleasure in cordial and unconstrained relations with people who understood the artist in him, who made kindly allowances for his decided tastes in matters of external conduct, and who never tried to look into his inmost heart. All this was true of the two new friends whom Brahms made at this time. The master gave several concerts in Leipzig in January of 1874 and there he met his beautiful ex-pupil, Elisabeth von Stockhausen, now Frau von Herzogenberg, who, like her husband (the esteemed composer and leader of the *Bachverein*), was a passionate admirer of Brahms's works. Elisabeth was lovelier than ever. Her exceptional musical talents had developed brilliantly; she was an excellent pianist, and had so remarkable a gift of perception and so retentive a memory that she was able to write down a new orchestral work of Brahms's after a single hearing. Now that Elisabeth was another man's wife, Brahms's former constraint disappeared, and it is not surprising that he felt extremely happy in her company. He had become 'so benevolent, mild, and amiable, that the old Brahms could hardly be recognized,' as Elisabeth wrote to Bertha Faber. After his departure from Leipzig a correspondence with his new friends gradually sprang up, and when he returned, three years later, it was almost a matter of course that he should stay with the Herzogenbergs. Now he learned that 'the slender woman in blue velvet, with the golden hair' was an admirable and considerate hostess, and on his return to his bachelor quarters the plaint escaped him: 'It was so beautiful with you; I still feel it today, as an agreeable warmth, and I should like to shut it up and lock it in, so as to keep it for a long time.' Brahms spent many such gay and pleasant hours with the Herzogenbergs, and few people contributed more to the happiness of the lonely and reserved master than the lovely and sympathetic 'Liesl.'

In the summer of the same year, 1874, which saw his growing intimacy with the Herzogenbergs, Brahms found yet another friend. After a Swiss music festival (at which his *Triumphlied* was performed) he spent his holidays in Rüschlikon near Zürich, and there made the acquaintance of the poet Joseph Victor Widmann of Berne, to whom he soon became greatly attached. He was fond of discussing general questions with him, and spent almost every day of the musical festival in his company. Later on the bond between the two artists became very close indeed, and Widmann's delightful memoirs, which are among the most informatory accounts of Brahms's character, show how thoroughly he understood the personality of his eminent friend. In Zürich Brahms often met the well-known pianoforte teacher, J. C. Eschmann. The enthusiastic terms in which Eschmann addressed Brahms may be taken as typical of the Swiss attitude to Brahms's work: 'My admiration for your compositions, and your lofty and noble ideals, is unbounded and entirely without reservations, and you could not easily find another man to whom your works have given such profound happiness, and who has received such spiritual satisfaction from their study.' [8]

In Rüschlikon, too, a number of compositions were completed. This time song writing occupied the foremost place, and the songs, Op. 63, the Vocal Quartets, Op. 64, and the second series of *Liebeslieder*, Op. 65, were written. The delightful summer on the Lake of Zürich finds a reflection in the cheerful mood that emanates from these songs. How Brahms enjoyed his life at Rüschlikon may be judged by a letter from Carl Ferdinand Pohl, written in answer to one of his own. The writer describes how, sitting alone in their favorite Restaurant Gause, he seems to hear the voice of his loyal table companion, and continues longingly:

The man who calls me sits far away beside the Lake of Zürich, admiring the view at Nydelbad; he drives to Küssnacht, eats freshwater fish and crayfish in the 'Sun,' drinks the excellent red wine at Erlenbach, or even better lakeside wine at Mariahalden . . . and saunters along to Horgen, which is one fragrant rose garden in June. . .[9]

In 1875 Brahms settled down for the summer at Ziegelhausen, near Heidelberg, where he was visited by many of his friends from the neighboring towns, and notably the painter Anselm Feuerbach. This summer, too, was marked by his first encounter with a conductor who was to be of great importance in the Brahms movement. As early as April the musicologist Hermann Kretzschmar,[10] who knew Brahms well, had asked him to accept the highly talented young Fritz Steinbach as a pupil. Now, at Ziegelhausen, the youth himself tried to persuade Brahms to accept him. Although he did not succeed in overcoming Brahms's inherent dislike of teaching, the master put his refusal so nicely that he quite won the young man's heart.

It goes without saying that Brahms's creative work did not suffer at Ziegelhausen. He completed the Duets, Op. 66, and the Piano Quartet, Op. 60, the first drafts of which had been written in his *Sturm und Drang* period; and in addition to these he wrote the gay and cheerful String Quartet, Op. 67, 'all of them,' as he wrote to Wüllner, 'useless trifles, to avoid facing the serious countenance of a symphony.' The master's mood in these months was full of happiness; he wrote to

Rheinthaler: 'My rooms and my daily life are most agreeable. Levi and Dessoff were here today, tonight Frank (a Viennese conductor working at Mannheim) is coming, tomorrow some charming lady singers from Mannheim—in short, life is only too gay.' We may not be far wrong if we assume that Brahms's gaiety was due not merely to the successful summer, but even more to his relief at having resigned his position in Vienna. A period of dissatisfaction and painful longing lay behind him. With his election by the *Gesellschaft der Musikfreunde* one of his most earnest wishes had been fulfilled, although not quite in the desired form of a post in his native city—and he was proud to know that he was capable of doing great things as a conductor. But three years' experience had shown him that in the end such a position had more disadvantages than advantages for him. With this realization he definitely made up his mind never again to accept a permanent post. Now he knew what life could offer him, and henceforth he abandoned all unrealizable dreams; he grew calmer, more balanced and content. New forces were set free in his soul and he turned to greater tasks.

In his outward appearance, too, a change took place. At forty he had often given the impression of a shy youth; now he began to grow a majestic beard, and even his outward appearance revealed the tranquillity of the mature man.

UNPUBLISHED LETTERS REFERRED TO:

1. Letter from Ferdinand Hiller, 2 February 1869.
2. Letter from Eduard Marxsen, 10 October 1869.
3. Letter from Elise Brahms, undated (September 1869).
4. Letter from Sophie von Sell, 5 February 1895.
5. Letter from Carl Ferdinand Pohl, 7 July 1872.
6. Letter from Carl Ferdinand Pohl, 11 June 1872.
7. Letter from Lucie Coster, 25 August 1873.
8. Letter from J. C. Eschmann, 16 October 1872.
9. Letter from Carl Ferdinand Pohl, 16 June 1874.
10. Letter from Hermann Kretzschmar, 3 April 1875.

X

ON THE SUMMIT

(1876-1879)

IN the second half of the 'seventies there began for Brahms a period of extensive concert tours. They contrasted with the former tours—for instance, those he had undertaken with Joachim or Stockhausen—mainly inasmuch as he now rarely interpreted the works of other composers. His steadily growing fame resulted in invitations from all sides to conduct or to play his own compositions. The artist's presence was desired by so many cities that he could have spent the whole year in answering such invitations. This, of course, was quite contrary to his plans, and he made it his general rule to devote about three months every winter to concerts. The autumn, and above all the spring, he liked to spend in Vienna, for—as he wrote once to Billroth—'it isn't really spring without a few evenings in the "Prater"' (Brahms's favorite park). In the early summer he went into the country so that, on his long undisturbed rambles, those works he had conceived during the past year might ripen and be given their final form.

To follow the artist in all his numerous tours would be too complicated a task, and of little interest today. In this book, therefore, only those concerts will be mentioned which made Brahms acquainted with the larger cities and significant personalities. First of all, the Dutch tour of 1876 must be mentioned in this connection. Next to Switzerland, it was Holland that showed early appreciation of Brahms's work, and the artist had promised some years earlier to go there. He stayed in Utrecht with Professor Engelmann, whose acquaintance he had made at Rüschlikon, and he spent a very agreeable time with him and his charming wife —the pianist Emma Brandes—whose inspired rendering of Brahms's works always gave great pleasure to the composer. The dedication of the String Quartet, Op. 67, to Professor Engelmann expressed Brahms's friendship for the brilliant scholar, and his cheerful letters to Utrecht make it clear how comfortable he had been in the Professor's hospitable home. His journeys to Holland gradually became a fixed institution during the following years, and everywhere he won loyal and enthusiastic friends. In Amsterdam, for instance, he stayed with J. A. Sillem, who describes his compatriots' delight in many cheery letters. In one of them he wrote:

The pleasure which your acceptance has given us is beyond description. We men, who are used to self-control, don't show it so stormily as some of our ladies; which is why I had to advise Herr Schiff to put his wife into a strait jacket at the time of your arrival. I had a passionate dispute with Frau Koopman as to where you were to stay. It was fortunately a bloodless battle, and was settled on the mutually touching condition that the one to whom you gave your preference should invite the other every day of your stay. In this way you cannot get rid of either of us.[1]

Apart from the profound impression that Brahms the artist naturally made, it may have given pleasure to the extremely house-proud Dutch hostesses to entertain anyone so grateful for every attention, for a well-arranged menu, a new dish, and so forth. Brahms, as a matter of fact, recalled with gusto, in his letters to the Engelmanns, the aspect of the table, freshly laid at all hours by the maid Antje, and he even had some schnapps sent to him from Amsterdam, which 'impressed him tremendously.'

Another country would, of course, have received him with the same enthusiasm, and it is to be regretted that Brahms never accepted any of the pressing and frequent invitations to visit England, where he had for many years aroused the greatest interest. It must always remain a proud record in the history of Cambridge that this University offered him the honorary degree of Doctor of Music at a time when it had not occurred to his own country to honor him thus. (Engelmann stoutly declared that the offer of this degree was 'a disgrace to the German Universities.') On 4 April 1876, Professor Macfarren wrote to Brahms:

MY DEAR SIR,

The Council of the University of Cambridge yesterday agreed to sanction a grace offering the honorary Degree of Doctor of Music to you and I must request the favor of your informing me within three weeks from this date if it will be agreeable to you to accept the same. This is the only country in which the Faculty of Music is represented in its Universities, and acknowledged by scholastic Degrees, and England has thus the opportunity of making the recognition of your high services to art, in which all earnest musicians will concur. For myself, I am happy on this occasion to address you, which enables me to thank you for the great pleasure I have experienced from your works.

I am, my dear Sir,

Yours with the highest esteem,
G. W. MACFARREN

P.S. The ceremony of conferring the Degree may take place on the 8th of May or on the first of June, the former being preferable. There will be a performance of your *Requiem* by the University Musical Society on the 23rd May, to which your presence would give great additional interest, and the members of the Society would be especially proud and pleased if you could be induced to conduct the work. It will be particularly fortunate if the ceremony and the performance could combine to bring you to Cambridge.[2]

This letter does not show clearly that Brahms's presence for the conferment of the degree was necessary. At first, therefore, the artist wrote to Joachim that he 'was extremely delighted with this great adventure'; but, when he received more detailed information from his friend, who was being similarly honored, he grew rather doubtful. A further letter [3] from Macfarren confirmed that Brahms was 'doctor *in posse*

not *in esse*' and that 'the Degree was not given until he had
been personally admitted to it.' They were ready to fix the
ceremony for any time convenient to Brahms; but the artist
could not make up his mind to undertake the journey to
England. He appealed to Gerard F. Cobb, of Trinity College, of which Brahms was to become a Fellow; Mr. Cobb
'fully sympathized with Brahms's feelings with regard to the
journey to England and the necessity of submitting to the
excitement of London,' and promised 'to do his very utmost
to try and induce the Vice-Chancellor to dispense, in
Brahms's case, with personal attendance on the occasion of
the conferring of the degree.' [4] In the end, however, Cobb
had to tell Brahms that no amount of good will could enable the University to confer the degree in his absence, as
according to the statutes it 'had no such powers.' [5] As Brahms,
nevertheless, would not contemplate a journey to England,
nothing came of the University's generous offer.

Brahms may have had a very prosaic reason for his refusal;
he seems to have been afraid of seasickness. It is well known
that he left a ship in Genoa, on which he and his companions had already taken passage, at the last moment, making
the hot railway journey through the whole of Italy to Naples
in order to avoid the sea. He may have heard gruesome accounts of storms in the Channel from Clara Schumann, so
that he, who laid so little stress on outward honors and material gain, could not understand why he should expose himself to such inconvenience. Apart from this fear, his inability
to learn foreign languages discouraged him from visiting
countries in which a strange tongue was spoken. Italy was
the only exception; her glorious works of art and the whole
Italian atmosphere had an irresistible attraction for him
(see page 135). He did not consider Holland a foreign country, as most of the people there understood German, and the
Dutch language itself strongly resembled his own dialect of
Low-German.

However, his English friends were not to be discouraged by the master's refusal, and continued their endeavors to win him over. In the year in which the honorary degree was offered to the composer, the well-known firm of Novello [6] offered him the munificent sum of 15,000 marks for an oratorio on the same scale as Mendelssohn's *Elijah*. In the following year the London Philharmonic Society awarded him their Gold Medal, which the Austrian Consul, Stockinger, presented to him.[7] His German friends, too, did not cease their endeavors to persuade Brahms to overcome his fear of going abroad. The famous Handel scholar, Friedrich Chrysander, made particularly strenuous efforts in this direction, and never tired of telling Brahms about the country to which he himself had become so deeply attached during his studies in London. He wrote: 'You need not be afraid of being pestered. You would be surprised how quiet and undisturbed a life you could lead in the middle of London.' [8] At another time he spoke of 'Brahms's English friends,' and added: 'you may well call them that, as they have twice listened to your violin concerto with the greatest intelligence; while the good Hamburgers the other day . . . still didn't know how they ought to take it. [9] The well-known German singer George Henschel, whom Brahms greatly admired, and whose great love for England had caused him to become naturalized, worked continuously towards the same end. In 1879 he declared: 'London does not take second place to any city in its admiration for you.' [10] Incidentally, it was Henschel who brought about a meeting between Brahms and a young English musician who was later to become an eminent composer. On 28 December 1877, he wrote the following lines to Brahms:

The bearer of this letter is an English girl, Miss Smyth, as talented as she is jolly and amusing. She wrote some quite charming little songs, even before she had had any lessons; she is burning to say just one word to you, or better still to hear you say it. Grant her that word, if it were only 'Get out!' Besides all this she can jump over chairs, back and all, she rides, hunts, fishes, swims, etc.[11]

Ethel Smyth, who wanted to show Brahms some old French songs, often had opportunities of exchanging more than a word with him, as she became a private pupil of Heinrich von Herzogenberg's, and therewith entered the master's circle of friends. In many of his letters to his Leipzig friends he sends his 'very best greetings' to 'the little one,' and it would seem that the strongly marked personal and artistic qualities of the girl of twenty did not fail to make the same impression on Brahms as on his friend Henschel. But in spite of his friendly feelings towards individual English people, his aversion to making a journey to England could not be overcome. Being rooted in his instinctive dislike of the sea and his inability to learn foreign languages, this fear could not be exorcized by rational arguments.

About the time when he allowed the Cambridge degree to escape him, Brahms also refused an offer from Germany. Wilhelm Rust (later Thomaskantor in Leipzig) wrote to him on 18 August 1876,[12] that he had happened to speak to President Bitter, who had told him of a plan to make a fresh appointment to the post of music director at Düsseldorf, which had been held since Schumann's illness by the mediocre Julius Tausch. In the first place they had considered Max Bruch, but had later dropped this idea because of the 'fear of being swamped with Bruch's compositions.' Rust now inquired whether Brahms would, on principle, be inclined to accept this post. Because of his reverence for Schumann, the artist felt at first compelled to give an affirmative reply.

Now began an endless correspondence in various quarters, and it seemed as though Brahms was once more on the point of losing his freedom. The terms were favorable; the city, the State, and the *Musikverein* collaborated in paying the music director a yearly salary of 6,000 marks. For this he would have, during the six winter months, to conduct all the Düsseldorf concerts, and also the annual Rhine Musical Festival. The possibility of Brahms's appointment roused the greatest interest in the musical circles of Germany. Clara Schumann changed her attitude several times, and kept on making fresh objections. Hiller eagerly entreated Brahms to accept, and offered to go to Düsseldorf for the purpose of gaining a clear insight into the situation.[13] Chrysander asked for details for a newspaper article on Brahms's new post; [14] Henschel was so excited that he enclosed a stamped post card in his letter,[15] requesting Brahms only to cross out the 'Yes' or 'No'; Marxsen [16] believed the affair to be settled; Pohl, however, wrote from Vienna: 'That was an ugly line in your card. Leave Vienna! Impossible! No, thrice no!' [17] At the bottom of his heart Brahms was of the same opinion; he did not want to leave Vienna for good, but he could not bring himself to refuse outright an appointment which the memory of Schumann endeared to him. Finally a possible retreat was opened to him; hearing that in Düsseldorf a strong party which favored Tausch was working against the appointment of a new director, he now had grounds for his refusal. In vain, beseeching letters and addresses were sent to him, bearing the signatures of eminent persons; [18] in vain he was told that at the election only 10 out of 39 votes had been cast for Tausch. Brahms declared that he would oust nobody from his post—and felt greatly relieved. This was the very last position which Brahms seriously considered. When, in the autumn of 1878, he was offered the post of Thomas-kantor in Leipzig he declined point-blank, although he was attracted by the thought that Elisabeth von Herzogenberg was living in Leipzig.

Even though Brahms had thus once again revealed his intention of permanently settling in Vienna, he liked to vary his choice of a place for his summer holiday. In 1876 his selection of a holiday resort was quite in opposition to his usual custom. This time he felt no longing for inland

mountains or sunny lakes; he went to the seaside, to Sassnitz on the Isle of Rügen in the Baltic Sea. It is noteworthy
that this sojourn in Northern Germany was unable fully to
satisfy one who was falling more and more under the spell
of Vienna. When Joachim visited Sassnitz in 1886, Brahms
wrote:

Rügen will greatly please you; it is quite magnificent and once I
endured it for a whole summer. I had to tell myself, however,
that in spite of all its beauty I wouldn't go there again. One
has to put up with too much discomfort and inconvenience, to
which I, who have made my home in the South, am not used
any more.

Nevertheless the artistic outcome of the summer at Sassnitz was most satisfactory, for it saw the completion of
Brahms's first Symphony, impatiently awaited by his friends.
The beginnings of this work go back to the *Sturm und Drang*
period (see page 48), and Clara Schumann had already heard
the first movement in 1862. At that time, however, Brahms
had not felt sufficiently mature to reconcile the opposing
forces of this tempestuous work, and fourteen years had to
pass before he considered himself equal to this great task.
The result fully justified him; for apart from the technical
mastery of the definitive version, Brahms could hardly have
risen to the hymnal exaltation of the Finale before going
through the spiritual changes of the past few years. As soon
as the work was completed, Brahms wanted to hear it and
wrote to Dessoff, who had recently been working in Karlsruhe: 'It was always my cherished and secret wish to hear
the thing first in a small town which possessed a good friend,
a good conductor, and a good orchestra.' Dessoff was of
course delighted, and the first performance took place on
4 November 1876, and met with great, but not overwhelming, success. After the concert, the orchestra, represented by
Carl Will, knowing Brahms's horror of speeches, thanked
the master in writing [19] for having proved that the last word
in the art of symphony-writing was not yet spoken. Perform-

ELISABETH VON HERZOGENBERG

AGATHE VON SIEBOLD

ances followed in Mannheim, Munich, Vienna, Leipzig, Breslau, Cambridge, London, and so on, with varying success—the least in Munich, the Wagnerian stronghold. Only with his next symphonic work was Brahms to achieve a decisive triumph as a composer in this domain.

The Second Symphony was written in the following summer in Austria, in the charming out-of-the-way village of Pörtschach on the Wörthersee, where Brahms thoroughly enjoyed himself. 'It is delightful here,' he wrote on 19 June 1877, to his publisher and friend Simrock. 'You surely cannot find the same comfort and friendliness on your own trip [on the Rhine]. I will never again spend the summer far away from the Prater' (see p. 121). The friendly Austrian atmosphere seems to radiate from the D major Symphony, and when Billroth played it for the first time he exclaimed: 'It is all rippling streams, blue sky, sunshine, and cool green shadows. How beautiful it must be at Pörtschach!' It will readily be understood that this work instantly found its way to the heart of the public, and the first performance at Vienna, on 30 December 1877, under Hans Richter's inspiring conductorship, was received so enthusiastically that the delicious third movement had to be repeated. Especially remarkable was the triumph Brahms won with this work at Hamburg. Here, in September 1878, was celebrated the fiftieth anniversary of the Philharmonic Society, to which the now famous Hamburg composer had received a pressing invitation. His old friend Avé expended all his eloquence, and the conductor of the concerts, J. von Bernuth, wrote to Brahms: 'You must know that there is no one in Hamburg who would not be delighted to see you at the conductor's desk.' [20] But Brahms declined; the wound inflicted on him by the Society sixteen years earlier had not yet healed. At the last moment, however, he could not bear to stay in Austria; he arrived in time for the festival, and had no cause to regret this sudden decision, for his native city received him with extraordinary enthusiasm. His best friends felt only too honored to play in the orchestra under his direction. None other than Joachim himself led the orchestra; among the violins were such eminent artists as Brahms's Detmold friend Bargheer, the well-known left-handed violinist Richard Barth (a pupil of Joachim, later Bernuth's successor in Hamburg), and J. Boie, the husband of Marie Völckers, whose acquaintance with Brahms dated from the jolly days of the ladies' choir. The performance of the Second Symphony was a great artistic event that could not fail to delight Brahms, even though his pleasure did not make him forget for an instant his grievance against his native city (see p. 76).

Next summer, Brahms remained faithful to the village that had inspired him to such splendid creative efforts. When passing the Wörthersee on his return from Italy (see p. 135) he could not refrain from visiting Pörtschach. 'I only wanted to stay there for a day,' he wrote to Billroth, 'and then, as this day was so beautiful, for yet another. But each day was as fine as the last, and so I stayed on. If on your journey you have interrupted your reading to gaze out of the window, you must have seen how all the mountains round the blue lake are white with snow, while the trees are covered with delicate green.'

In the summer of 1879 he again returned to Pörtschach, and only when the ever-growing popularity of the place threatened to disturb him did he decide to go elsewhere. These summers of 1877-9 in Carinthia were exceptionally fruitful; hardly at any later period did Brahms display the same powers of creation. The year in which the Second Symphony was written saw the birth of the First Motet, Op. 74, and the Ballads, Op. 75, and a wealth of the most lovely songs, Op. 69-72 (which, however, owed their existence to the springtime rambles in the Prater rather than to Pörtschach). In the two following summers Brahms composed several important piano works (Capricci and Intermezzi, Op. 76, Rhapsodies, Op. 79) and the First Violin Sonata.

The crowning masterpiece of the compositions of these

two years is, however, the Violin Concerto, which Brahms had written with Joachim in mind. It was Joachim who launched the Concerto in Leipzig on the New Year's Day of 1879. This original if somewhat difficult work was not at once fully appreciated. To England is due the honor of having first welcomed the Concerto with unqualified approval (see p. 125). Joachim played it as often as possible, and notwithstanding its great technical difficulties, other notable artists, such as Richard Barth, Hugo Heerman, and Adolf Brodsky, soon ventured to perform it. The next artist to attempt the Concerto was a girl of nineteen, Marie Soldat, whom Brahms had met in the summer of 1879. The great talent of this young violinist, then quite unknown, impressed him so favorably that he decided, contrary to his usual habit, to give a concert with her in Pörtschach. At his request his old friend, Luise Dustmann, who was spending the summer in the same resort, also took part in the performance. Brahms then aroused Joachim's interest in the young artist, and his friend admitted her to his master-class, where Marie Soldat's art developed to such a degree that she was allowed to attempt the difficult Brahms Concerto. Once, after 'the brave, little soldier' (as he liked to call her) had played his concerto 'incomparably well' in a Sunday noon concert, Brahms, as a treat, took her to his beloved Prater * where they sampled all the many merry-go-rounds and delighted in a Punch show. To round off the day suitably, these two insatiable souls went on to a performance of *Macbeth*.

Pörtschach was not only a pleasant place for Brahms to work in; the society, too, was quite to his liking. He associated with a number of people from Vienna—in the first place with the Kupelwieser family—and was visited by many friends from other parts: he loved, too, to talk to the Carinthian officials, doctors, and so forth, who met at the simple

* A beautiful reservation near the Danube, with a large amusement park.

table-d'hôte of Werzer's hotel. Often the 'pretty postmistress' —as he called her—Christine Werzer, came to help him with the packing of his manuscripts. When he praised one of her rolls of music to his publisher Simrock, she wrote on the accompanying card: 'It is a pleasure to do anything for such a charming gentleman.' Although many a woman was deeply impressed by Brahms's character, hardly another would have called the gruff, often sarcastic artist a 'charming gentleman.' Brahms, therefore, must have been exceptionally cheerful in pleasant Pörtschach.

Not always, however, was the master so agreeable and easy-going, as one of his best friends had painful cause to realize about this time. Hermann Levi had been working at the Munich Opera since 1872, and his views on Wagner, whom he had passionately opposed in earlier years, had undergone a complete change. This is quite comprehensible in an artist of Levi's fiery energy. He had recognized that his own talent lay principally in the domain of opera, and as a conductor of opera he felt it his duty to devote himself to the works of Richard Wagner, which had revolutionized the art of the music-drama. Levi, however, was unable to remain a neutral observer; he had always to take sides; he had either to love or to hate. On probing more deeply into Wagner's works, the technical difficulties at first arrested his attention; but he did not long resist these wonderful creations, and in the end he was constrained to give them his wholehearted approval. Brahms, however, could not understand this change in his friend, and never tried to do so, believing Levi's altered standpoint to be due to lack of principle. Long years of the Wagnerites' malicious attacks had made him distrustful; he could not, therefore, conceive that an enthusiastic adherent of Wagner's could, at the same time, champion his own work with the old fervor. Levi's protests were of no avail, and in 1875 a violent quarrel occurred, in which Brahms used 'very unkind words' that neither was to forget. Levi made a last attempt to explain his point of view in a letter, to which it would seem that Brahms never replied. Allgeyer, their mutual friend, intervened in a letter to Brahms: 'Do not rob me of the belief that you are too big and magnanimous to turn relentlessly from a man to whom, in spite of the change due to his excitable character and his exciting profession, you and your work were, are, and always will be, of the greatest moment.' [21] Brahms replied in an exhaustive letter of a purely personal nature, in which the name of their mutual friend was not even mentioned. His connection with Levi dragged on for some years, only to cease definitely in 1878. Though Brahms no doubt suffered from the loss of his sympathetic friend, he never really attempted to understand Levi's point of view and to bridge the chasm between them.

Characteristic of the composer was a certain fatalism in his dealings with others, however dear they might be to him. He admitted this openly to Clara Schumann with reference to the Herzogenbergs, when he wrote:

In this connection I cannot help thinking of my dear Leipzig hosts, whom I seem to have offended in some way. I should be particularly sorry to have done so, more especially in this case. But I leave the world to go the way it pleases. I am only too often reminded that I am a difficult person to get on with, I am growing accustomed to bearing the consequences of this.

This failing of his, that he never tried to clear up any misunderstanding, or to see other people's point of view, ended in his losing many of his best friends.

On the other hand, these years saw the growth of a significant friendship. Theodor Billroth had been summoned to Vienna in 1867, and this fact may have contributed to Brahms's decision to settle there. In Billroth he found an expert comprehension of his art, rare in its devotion and depth. The many letters which the eminent surgeon wrote to his friend in respect of each new work were so profound and brilliant that Brahms even sent some of them to Clara Schumann for her edification. Billroth, therefore, was often the first to see a new composition, and the composer waited with visible impatience for 'an unfriendly word on this quite worthless rubbish' (as he called, for instance, his famous Intermezzi, Op. 76, or the Motets, Op. 74). What Billroth's verdict really meant to him is clearly shown in the following letter, written by Brahms in answer to his friend's praise of the *Gesang der Parzen:*

You can't imagine how important and precious your approval is to me. One knows what one wanted, and how seriously one wanted it. Then one ought to know also what has really been achieved; only this one prefers to hear from another person, and is glad to believe the kind words. My heartiest thanks for praising my song and thus—giving it to me.

To Billroth, Brahms also owed a debt of gratitude for many pleasant and stimulating hours in the surgeon's beautiful Viennese home, where large receptions were held in the composer's honor, and where most of his chamber music was performed for the first time. But even this admirable friendship was not to remain quite untroubled in later years.

It is interesting to see how in Brahms's case a healthy egoism essential to the production of creative art was coupled with the rarest kindness and helpfulness. Today it is no longer possible to ascertain just how many people Brahms helped. Among the letters he kept are many from unknown persons, thanking him for gifts of money, loans, and recommendations. Even in towns which Brahms seldom visited he had his protégés. For instance, we find a letter [22] from Prague, from a certain Herr J. C. Hock, describing in detail the talents of a young musician in whom Brahms had taken such a 'generous interest.' The master may have read with greater sympathy another report from Prague, in which Franz Jauner,[23] director of the Court Opera in Vienna, wrote enthusiastically of a Bohemian musician, who had recently been discovered by Brahms. In this case the master's aid had notable results; for we are speaking of none other than Antonin Dvořák. As a member of a committee for the granting of scholarships, he had received a work from this wholly unknown composer. Brahms procured him the scholarship; persuaded Simrock to publish his works; influenced conductors and soloists to perform these compositions; found time to correct the proofs carefully before they went to press, as the composer himself was unable to do so; and repeatedly offered him material help, to lighten the burden of his poverty. At the beginning of their acquaintance Dvořák wrote the following letter of thanks to the master:

Your last most valued letter I read with the most joyful excitement; your warm encouragement, and the pleasure you seem to find in my work, have moved me deeply, and made me unspeakably happy. I can hardly tell you, esteemed Master, all that is in my heart. I can only say that I shall all my life owe you the deepest gratitude for your good and noble intentions towards me, which are worthy of a truly great artist and man.

Your ever grateful
ANTONIN DVOŘÁK [24]

This letter did not reach Brahms immediately. Ten days earlier the artist had realized a long-cherished desire, and had set out on his first journey to Italy. He traveled in the company of Billroth, who had an exhaustive acquaintance with the fine arts, and was, therefore, an excellent guide. Brahms traveled *via* Rome to Naples, visited Florence and Venice on his return journey, and, as he wrote to Simrock, lived through 'magical days.' The beauties of art and Nature gave him such delight that he paid eight further visits to that country, generally so arranging matters as to spend his birthday in Italy. Throughout the winter he looked forward to these journeys. He prepared for them with real North-German thoroughness, studied guide books and technical works, and felt so much at home in Italy that the return seemed quite 'wrong' to him. He loved to hunt through the old curiosity shops for engravings, and thought this a 'most fruitful and amusing occupation.' He who so disliked letter writing even sent long letters to Clara Schumann, urging her to undertake a trip to Italy. His old friend may well have been astonished to receive such enthusiastic lines as the following from the otherwise so reserved Johannes.

How often do I not think of you, and wish that your eyes and heart might know the delight which the eye and heart experiences here! If you stood for only one hour in front of the façade of the Cathedral of Siena, you would be overjoyed, and would agree that this alone made the journey worth while. And, on entering, you would find at your feet, and throughout the church, no single corner that did not give you the same delight. On the following day, in Orvieto, you would be forced to acknowledge that the cathedral there was even more beautiful; and after all this to plunge into Rome is a joy beyond all words. . . We have still the best time of the year before us. It is quite early yet, and everything is gradually coming out. You can have no conception of how beautiful it is, and you have only to take a little trouble to enjoy it in comfort. Next year you must see that you are free at the end of March, when I shall be able to be with you on the whole of the journey—by that time I shall have become a thorough Italian, and shall be able to be of use to you.

The music of this country appeared 'ghastly' to Brahms, which, however, did not detract from his pleasure, so much being offered to the eye that the ear for once could take a rest. We never, therefore, find any trace of the influence of Italian music in Brahms's work; nevertheless, his Italian travels were of the highest importance to him. The impression of the lucid beauty and gaiety of the South, together with the fine art of Italy, effected a reinforcement of those classical tendencies in the composer, which are more and more in evidence in the creations of his maturity. For Brahms, the man, the weeks in Italy may undoubtedly be counted amongst the happiest of his life. Rarely had it hitherto been his lot to yield himself to the joy of the moment so freely and unrestrainedly.

UNPUBLISHED LETTERS REFERRED TO:

1. Letter from J. A. Sillem, 26 December (without year).
2. Letter from G. A. Macfarren, 4 April 1876.
3. Letter from G. A. Macfarren, 27 May 1876.
4. Letter from Gerard F. Cobb, 27 November 1876.
5. Letter from Gerard F. Cobb, 12 December 1876.
6. Letter from Novello & Co., 28 July 1876.
7. Letter from Stockinger, 28 August 1877.
8. Letter from Friedrich Chrysander, 30 December 1878.
9. Letter from Friedrich Chrysander, 10 November 1879.
10. Letter from George Henschel, 2 December 1879.
11. Letter from George Henschel, 28 December 1877.
12. Letter from Wilhelm Rust, 18 August 1876.
13. Letter from Ferdinand Hiller, 24 December 1876.
14. Letter from Friedrich Chrysander, 13 November 1876.
15. Letter from George Henschel, 20 January 1877.
16. Letter from Eduard Marxsen, 29 October 1876.
17. Letter from C. F. Pohl, 14 October 1876.
18. Letter with numerous signatures, 8 January 1877.
19. Letter from Carl Will, 13 November 1876.
20. Letter from J. von Bernuth, 7 July 1878.
21. Letter from Julius Allgeyer, 11 March 1876.
22. Letter from J. C. Hock, 21 March 1880.
23. Letter from Franz Jauner, 25 March (without year).
24. Letter from Antonín Dvořák, 18 April 1878.

XI

OLD FRIENDS AND NEW

(1880-1885)

BRAHMS'S concert activities extended over an ever-widening sphere. In the autumn of 1879 Joachim and he toured through Hungary and Transylvania. Brahms had at first hesitated, because he felt that his taste and intentions differed too greatly from those of his friend. He liked, as he wrote to Simrock, 'to travel in leisure and comfortably, to see new countries and new people, and lightheartedly to earn just enough to cover the expenses. Joachim, on the other hand, wanted to give a concert every day, to see nothing, and only to earn money.' Nevertheless things appear to have worked out to his satisfaction, for he was easily persuaded to undertake a similar tour to Poland in February 1880, insisting only that he was to receive not more than a fourth or at the most a third of the receipts, as a bachelor did not need as much money as a married man with a family to support.

At the beginning of the same year Brahms once more gave a number of concerts on the Rhine, on this occasion visiting Krefeld for the first time. There he was received with a cordiality unusual even at that time, when he was at the summit of his fame. He was so enchanted by the artistic achievements of this little town that he gladly accepted later invitations to revisit it. He found another incentive in his friendship with Rudolf von der Leyen, a gifted musical amateur, in whose house Brahms stayed at Krefeld. Von der Leyen, and his relations, the von Beckeraths, whose individual members were living in various parts of the Rhineland, were now among Brahms's most intimate friends. Von der Leyen records these visits in his memoirs, and he gives also an amusing account of his meetings with the composer in Italy. Schwerin too, like Krefeld, became a center of the Brahms cult. At Schwerin the Director of Music was Alois Schmitt, whom the composer, after the first rehearsal with the orchestra, which had studied his work with devotion, addressed by the intimate pronoun *Du*. From Schwerin it is not far to Königsberg, so that Brahms was able to accept an invitation from the conductor Stägemann, which must certainly have amused him:

It is really an impertinence, but the wish is stronger than any other consideration. Could you bring yourself to conduct here? . . . For the last two years this request has stuck in my throat, and I utter it with the feeling that you will probably think me crazy. But we should so love to have you here for once. . . Perhaps a kind impulse may seize you, and our northern Königsberg, which is the ugliest town in the world, may excite your curiosity.[1]

So the months passed, in strenuous concert performances, and after Brahms had taken part, as conductor, in May 1880, in the solemn unveiling of Schumann's monument, it was time to look for an appropriate summer resort. He had had enough of Pörtschach; yet he would prefer to remain loyal to Austria, and so his choice fell on a watering place in the Salzkammergut, which was celebrated as being the summer residence of the Emperor Francis Joseph. This was Bad Ischl, which might be called the Austrian Baden-Baden, for there the best society used to meet. This Brahms did not resent in the least, and when Elisabeth von Herzogenberg asked: 'What brought to you to Ischl of all places? Is it comfortable and doesn't half of Vienna stay there?', he answered, somewhat belligerently: 'That half of Vienna comes to Ischl does not, at present, spoil it for me—even the whole of Vienna would fill me with anything but repugnance! Indeed, half of Berlin or of Leipzig would probably put me to flight, but half of Vienna is quite pretty and need not be ashamed of itself.

The composer was intimate with a number of Viennese artists and scholars. Among the musicians his favorite was the excellent pianist Ignaz Brüll, who had also won laurels with his opera *Das goldene Kreuz*. Brüll often had the honor of trying out Brahms's orchestral compositions on two pianos, with the master, before their first public performance. He had a good knowledge of French, which so impressed Brahms that he expressed the wish to converse in French with Brüll on their walks together. The initiated, however, asserted that on these walks they were generally silent—in French.

Another regular visitor to Ischl was Johann Strauss. Brahms greatly admired the graceful art of the Viennese 'Waltz King,' and had for many years tried to win his friendship. As for Strauss, perhaps he did not fully understand the Hamburger's art, which was so different from his own, but he recognized that here was a real genius. Strauss's many letters of invitation, generally signed: 'In sincere respect and admiration,' show a cordiality unusual even in this amiable Viennese. He also paid homage to the North German master by dedicating to him the waltz *Seid Umschlungen Millionen*. At Ischl Brahms was a regular guest in the beautiful villa of the Waltz King, who could not be dissuaded from inviting him to his large parties, although his sarcastic friend sometimes caused him painful embarrassment by ruthlessly showing his dislike for some fellow guest whom he found uncongenial. Johann Strauss's stepdaughter, Frau Alice von Meyszner-Strauss, still remembers her dismay at one such incident, when the unfortunate composer Moszkowski received a taste of Brahms's sarcasm. Towards his host and the family, however, Brahms always displayed the most perfect amiability. When Fräulein Alice Strauss asked him to sign her autograph-fan he wrote down the first bars of the famous *Blue Danube* waltz, adding: 'Leider nicht von Johannes Brahms!' ('Alas! not by Johannes Brahms!') At another time he even attempted to combine Strauss's art with his own by writing the opening bars of his Fourth Symphony, and, as a counterpoint to it, the beginning of the *Blue Danube* waltz, on the back of a photograph that he presented to Frau Adele Strauss. He was thus trying to find a pleasant way of expressing his sense of fellowship with the Viennese Waltz King.

Brahms soon became well acquainted with the various professional residents of Ischl; and although the weather, which is always very uncertain there, was at its worst in the summer of 1880, he was well contented. He wrote to Professor Engelmann: 'I can only say how wrong I think it that you should avoid our dear, lovely Austria. Why don't you all come here? There is a different air and a different life here—and how many other things are different!' His friend did not comply with his suggestion, but Brahms met him in September, as well as the Herzogenbergs, at Berchtesgaden, where he went with Clara Schumann in order to celebrate her birthday. To them he played what he had composed during the summer in Ischl, mainly two small orchestral works. The *Academic Festival Overture* was prompted by an external event. In March 1879 the University of Breslau, following the example of Cambridge, had conferred on him the honorary degree of Doctor of Philosophy. At first the composer was content with returning thanks —on a post card. When, however, his friend Bernhard Scholz, Director of Music in Breslau, drew his attention to the fact that the University expected him to express his gratitude in musical form, he wrote the *Academic Festival Overture*, which is built on a few popular student songs. In Ischl he also composed a pendant to this, making use of some old sketches, in the shape of the *Tragic Overture*. Clara pronounced both works to be 'magnificent,' and enjoyed them no less than Johannes's exceptional cheerfulness and good humor.

At Berchtesgaden Brahms had long talks with Joachim, with whom he had already arranged a meeting during the summer. Outwardly he was pursuing his intention of discussing with Joachim an arrangement for the violin of his new Hungarian Dances. In reality, however, he sought this meeting because he knew that his friend was going through a difficult time. For some years the Joachims' married life had been anything but happy, as the husband suffered from an almost morbid jealousy. which the life that Frau Joachim naturally had to lead as a concert singer only exasperated. The conflict had just reached a crisis, as Joachim suspected a mutual friend, Brahms's faithful publisher, Fritz Simrock.

At Ischl Brahms had received a letter from Jussuf which made him 'extremely sad.' The composer, who knew both husband and wife equally well, was convinced of the wife's innocence, and he did his utmost to cure his old friend of his tragic delusion. At first he seemed to succeed. When, however, Brahms came to Berlin the following December to hear a performance of his *Requiem* conducted by Joachim, he could not fail to observe that the affair had taken a turn for the worse, and all his arguments were of no avail. He sympathized deeply with the wrongly suspected wife, and after his return to Vienna, he felt compelled to write her, to 'free himself from a heavy burden.' This letter,[2] which is unique in the whole of Brahms's correspondence for its length and its warmth of tone, was to have far-reaching consequences. When it came to divorce proceedings between the couple, Frau Joachim produced this letter as a proof of their mutual friend's belief in her innocence. The result was extraordinary; the judge took the same view as Brahms, and acquitted Frau Joachim of any guilt. Joachim, however, was deeply wounded by his friend's action, which he regarded as disloyalty. He could not reconcile himself to the fact that Brahms had attacked him from the rear, at such a decisive moment of his life, after a friendship of almost thirty years; he therefore severed all connections between them.

When Brahms learned of the consequences of his letter, which he could no longer clearly remember, he asked Frau Joachim for a copy. This was sent to him by the singer's

brother, Franz Schneeweiss. I found it among the letters left
by Brahms, and part of it is given here:

DEAR FRAU JOACHIM,

If you had any notion how much I wanted to have a confi-
dential talk with you in Berlin just recently, and how I have
been longing to write to you since then, you would know what
a comfort your letter was to me, and what a relief it is to write
these lines to you.

I have known of your difficulties as long as they have existed;
therefore let me tell you, first of all, that I have never by thought
or word adopted your husband's view, for there was never any
reason to do so. I have always—and often—thought of you with
sympathy, but now, since I have been with you, how completely
I agree with you, how I wish I could do something!

Alas! I have no courage and no confidence left, and so I can
only feel the relief of sending you a word of sympathy . . . I believe that no one else can understand your case so clearly and
correctly as I. This may seem to you questionable, although you
know that my friendship is older than your marriage.

You may, however, have noticed that in spite of our friendship of thirty years' standing, in spite of all my love and admiration for Joachim, in spite of all the mutual artistic interests
which should bind me to him, I am always very careful in my
intercourse with him, so that I rarely associate with him for
long or at all intimately, and I have never even thought of
living in the same town and tying myself down to work with
him. Now I hardly need tell you that I knew, even before you
did, of the unhappy peculiarity with which Joachim torments
himself and others in such an inexcusable way. Friendship and
love I must be able to breathe as simply and freely as air. I take
alarm when I encounter these beautiful emotions in a complicated and artificial form, and the more so if it has to be maintained and enhanced by painfully morbid excitement.

Needless scenes, evoked by imaginary causes, horrify me. Even
in friendship a partial separation is sad, but it is possible. Thus
I have saved a small part of my friendship with Joachim by my
caution; without this I should have lost all long ago.

Dear friend, after this I need not write to you in detail . . . in
order to justify you. By Joachim's hopeless brooding the simplest
thing is so exaggerated and so complicated that one does not
know where to begin or where to end. . .

I therefore simply want to tell you, explicitly and plainly, as I have told Joachim innumerable times, that it is my opinion and belief that he has done you and Simrock a grievous wrong; and I can but hope that he will abandon his false and terrible delusions.

Your love, on the other hand, may be so great that you can forget all that has passed, his compliance and Simrock's good will so great that a tolerable relation between the two men may be possible. In this case, which is most devoutly to be wished, Joachim would have to admit his mistake, and he could not then require that you and Simrock should suffer for it. . .

You will see from this long letter how vainly I try to satisfy myself. If only you could feel a small part of the real affection with which I think of you and write to you (I am not ashamed of my emotion!) and if only I could hope that he would feel the same, and write to him in the same way! But it is hardly possible not to feel bitter towards him, or to hope that he would not receive well-meant advice in a bitter and wholly mistaken spirit.

Believe, then, that you have a really true friend in me. Dispose of me as and when you think I can be of use to you. Unfortunately, as you see, I have little hope of being able to help.

With all my heart,

Your devoted

J. Br.

Later, he wrote in reply to her request that she might in a given case make use of this letter: 'I have not told you any secrets. What I have said in this letter can be repeated by my letter or myself to anybody you wish' [8] (never dreaming that she would produce it in open court, any publicity being hateful to the artist).

Many aspects of this letter are illuminating. It clearly shows that it was Joachim's 'unhappy peculiarity' that made it impossible for Brahms to live in the same town as his friend, and to accept, for instance, a position in Berlin (see p. 104). Moreover, it throws light on Brahms's relations with certain other persons. There may often have been scenes which Brahms thought 'needless, evoked by imaginary causes,' while his friends—whether Levi, Joachim, Clara Schumann, or others—may have believed them to be essential for the purpose of clearing the air in respect of their relations with the rather difficult master. To Brahms such scenes were always 'horrifying,' and when they were unavoidable he preferred to break off all relations with a friend rather than expose himself to such 'painful and morbid excitement.'

Joachim and Levi, the two most understanding of his artist friends, were now lost to Brahms. Soon after this, another old friend to whom Brahms, in spite of his outwardly cool manner, had always been attached with undiminished loyalty was torn from him by fate. In the summer of 1882 the Beethoven scholar, Gustav Nottebohm, fell sick of a pulmonary complaint; after an unsuccessful cure at Gleichenberg he found himself unable to complete the journey to Vienna, and had to remain at Graz, where he lay seriously ill. In this terrible situation the lonely bachelor knew of only two men who were really attached to him: Carl Ferdinand Pohl and Brahms. Daily reports were exchanged between him and his two friends, and it seems as though Brahms had for once thoroughly overcome his dislike of writing; he sought to cheer Nottebohm by his reassuring letters, discussing the prospects of a trip to Italy. The news from Graz, however, grew more and more serious, and in the end Nottebohm sent the following message to Brahms through his nurse: 'I am getting worse and worse. I don't know what is going to become of me. Feeble, still feeble. I can't make up my mind. Probably I shall have to remain lying in Graz—and what then? Do I know? I need help and strength. I am too tired to write to Pohl as well.' [4] After receiving this letter Brahms hurried to the deathbed of his old friend; he was with him during the last days, until his death, and took upon himself the trouble and expense of his funeral.

While Brahms had at this time to lament the loss of many personal relationships, he had formed one new and very important friendship. Hans von Bülow, a pianist and conductor of genius, formerly an ardent apostle of Wagner's, had

turned away from the circle of the Bayreuth master's disciples, unable to get over the grievous disillusion when his
wife, Cosima, left him in order to marry his best friend,
Wagner. Now, as a pianist and conductor, he began to give
more and more attention to Brahms's works, which he had
formerly thought cold and dry, and followed the artist's development with growing sympathy and admiration. As early
as 1877 the two musicians had come into contact, when
Bülow gave the first performance of Brahms's First Symphony in Hanover, and then in Glasgow. Brahms, at this
time, regarded the conductor's co-operation as of great importance, as may be seen from one of his letters to Bülow,
which contains these, for Brahms, exceptionally cordial
words: 'I only hope that you will not lose on closer acquaintance (with the symphony) too much of that generous
sympathy which has given me such pleasure.'[5] Since 1880
Bülow had been Music Director of the small but highly
cultivated princely Court of Meiningen. He cherished the
principle that in art nothing is insignificant, that every least
detail is of importance. He therefore took unprecedented
pains in rehearsing single groups of the orchestra, the result
being model performances of singular beauty. A Berlin
critic, for example, wrote of his impression of a concert given
by the Meiningen orchestra: 'It seems as if the spiritual eye
were suddenly provided with a telescope, through which a
magnificent landscape, previously obscured by mist, becomes
fully recognizable to its smallest detail.' When, in the spring
of 1881, on the occasion of his Viennese concerts, Bülow told
Brahms of his innovations, the composer was deeply interested, and the impulsive conductor was accordingly impelled
to place his orchestra at Brahms's disposal for rehearsals of
his new compositions. It was not long before Brahms profited
by this offer. In the summer of 1881, which he spent in the
charming village of Pressbaum, not far from Vienna, he
completed an important new work, the Piano Concerto in B

flat major. First he played 'the long terror' (as he termed it) with Brüll on two pianos to 'the victims Billroth and Hanslick.' When this met with success, he announced his intention of bringing the concerto to Bülow in October. At first the conductor was not particularly pleased, since the orchestra was not at its best just then; however, he said nothing of this to Brahms, only asking him 'to pack all his store of good will and indulgence in his trunk.' All went well, however, and the public performance, on November 1881, to which Brahms invited the Herzogenbergs as 'they would not hear his music played so well in Leipzig,' was an outstanding success. Bülow was completely carried away by this new composition, and by Brahms's playing of it, and with passionate enthusiasm he placed himself at his new friend's disposal.

All the devotion he had previously given to Wagner was now lavished on Brahms. He arranged extensive concert tours with his splendid orchestra, the principal object of which was to make Brahms's compositions more widely known; and as pianist, too, he worked indefatigably for his friend. He who thirty years earlier had been the first to play a piano piece of Brahms's in public now organized whole 'Brahms evenings.' One of these was held in Vienna on 2 February 1882, and a rare visitor was in the audience: Franz Liszt. Through Bülow (Liszt's former son-in-law) the two artists, so different in temperament, got into touch again. Liszt had even courteously requested that the new Piano Concerto should be sent to him, and naturally Brahms had complied with this wish. Liszt's hitherto unpublished letter of thanks is so characteristic that it is worth reproducing here:

HONORED MASTER,
I beg you to forgive my delay in thanking you for so kindly sending me your Concerto. Frankly speaking, at the first reading this work seemed to me a little gray in tone; I have, however, gradually come to understand it. It possesses the pregnant

character of a distinguished work of art, in which thought and feeling move in noble harmony.

With sincerest esteem, most devotedly,

F. LISZT [6]

Brahms would not have been greatly troubled by this rather tepid judgment, as he was just then celebrating undreamed-of triumphs, thanks very largely to Bülow's glowing advocacy and support. Although he was sometimes unpleasantly impressed by his friend's tendency to abrupt changes of mood, Brahms could not but honestly admire Bülow's artistic genius and his upright and kindly character. The composer certainly disliked the notoriously aggressive speeches Bülow was in the habit of making before the concert began; but he was naturally delighted when a thoroughly successful performance of the 'Tenth' or 'Eleventh' followed (for so Bülow liked to describe Brahms's First and Second Symphonies, in order to express their kinship with Beethoven's nine symphonies).

The question whether the results of Bülow's enthusiastic propaganda were always profitable to Brahms cannot be answered by an unreserved affirmative. The quarrelsome conductor had many antagonists among his colleagues, and some of Brahms's earlier adherents were by no means pleased by this new alliance, as is shown by the somewhat malicious manner in which Ferdinand Hiller expressed his opinion:

No one was astonished that you rehearsed your Concerto at Meiningen—but the news that you were going to play in the *strolling* Bülow orchestra has filled many people with amazement. These concerts are nothing but an outlet for the Herr Baron's love of battle. He wants to show us all how one ought to conduct Beethoven, it is a pity, however, that he plays him in such a dull, dry, unfeeling, and unimaginative manner. . .[7]

Clara, too, at first thought Brahms's participation in these concert tours unworthy of his high position in music. When, however, she witnessed the triumphs that Johannes was now achieving, she was 'pleased and happy.' As for Bülow, his life acquired a new meaning from his work for Brahms, whom he believed to be, after Beethoven and Bach, the greatest and most sublime of composers. For Bülow life was worth living only if he could give himself heart and soul to a great purpose; he was not exaggerating, therefore, when he said that Brahms's music had 'restored him to health of body and mind.'

When Brahms one day, merely to divert him, sent him some spiteful criticisms of their performances, Bülow confessed that he was weak enough to be troubled by such things, and added:

Every blow aimed at you, even if it glances off, stabs me to the heart. Yes, indeed! . . . Even if Frau and Herr von Herzogenberg . . . may perhaps admire you with greater intelligence, they cannot give you deeper affection. . . Do you know—don't scold me for my presumption—to make patent the latent fire of your compositions is the most cherished task of . . . your most faithful baton.

Brahms answered:

So that my dispatch of today should not again arrive without a word [as often happened when Brahms sent music or criticism without bothering to write], I make the belated remark that it is intended only as a token of the pleasure your last kind and affectionate letter and your beautiful words have given me. They touched me so deeply that I cannot bring myself to send you any more Speidel [a Viennese critic who attacked both Brahms and Bülow]. In all affection,

Yours,
J. Br.[8]

A few lines from Daniela von Bülow, which were found among Brahms's papers, are likewise significant of Bülow's feelings for Brahms. Daniela, a daughter of Cosima Wagner's first marriage, lived with her mother in Wagner's house, and was among the most enthusiastic admirers of her stepfather. However, when Bülow was taken ill in 1882 with a nervous complaint, she brought herself to write to Brahms, who was anything but a favorite in Wahnfried, asking him to visit her father. In explanation of her motive she wrote: 'I know the esteem and affection he bears you, and I know that your presence now would be quite particularly beneficial to him.' [9]

Another result of this friendship was that Brahms entered into cordial relations with the ducal house of Meiningen. Duke Georg II and his wife, Helene von Heldburg, were distinguished connoisseurs of music, who fully appreciated the honor of receiving Brahms as their guest. They did all in their power to make the artist's stay in their Residenz agreeable. On the occasion of his first visit, the Commander's Cross of the Order of the House of Meiningen was conferred on him; the Grand Cross followed later, after an exceptionally splendid concert. At Meiningen, above all, Brahms was never oppressed by the requirements of etiquette, as he had been at Detmold. He was wholly at his ease with the ducal couple, and his stay at the castle differed from visits at the houses of other friends only in the fact that greater regard was paid to his comfort there than elsewhere. The luxury, the golden dishes, and the lackeys embarrassed the son of the little musician from the Hamburg slums not at all; though at times he thought sadly of his parents, with whom he would gladly have shared his happiness. Intellectually the days in Meiningen were highly stimulating. Brahms enjoyed the brilliant productions at the famous theatre, and repaid his hosts by his wonderful playing to a small circle of friends. The visits to the little Residenz came to be a fixed institution, to which Brahms remained true even when Bülow no longer worked there.

As token of his friendship for Duke Georg II, Brahms dedicated to him his latest composition, the *Parzenlied*. This work was written at Ischl in 1882, where Brahms had again spent the summer. The whole spirit of the composition may have been influenced by his Italian impressions—Brahms had paid an exceptionally pleasant visit to Italy in the spring of 1881—as was *Nänie*, which was finished at Pressbaum in the same year, and was composed in memory of the deceased painter Anselm Feuerbach. Both these choral compositions were first performed in Switzerland, where the choirs met with Brahms's particular appreciation. *Nänie* was heard in Zurich on 6 December 1881, and just a year later—on 10 December 1882—the *Parzenlied* was produced in Basle.

This summer at Ischl also saw the completion of two important pieces of chamber music, the Second Piano Trio in C major, Op. 87, and the radiantly joyous First String Quintet in F major, Op. 88. Kalbeck's conjecture that this work was written under the impression of Ignaz Brüll's engagement is refuted by the fact that this engagement took place—according to Brahms's letter to Billroth—on 29 August, whereas the Quintet was already finished by the end of June. Nevertheless, Brüll's gay music may have exercised a certain influence on the work, as Brahms himself announced this 'Spring-product' to Billroth with the humorous remark: 'By Brüll or myself—we are working together, and one could easily be taken for the other.'

In spite of Brahms's satisfaction with the result of his stay in Ischl, he again visited Germany in the summer of 1883. Great disappointment prevailed in Ischl on this account, as is shown by a letter from the proprietress of the Café Walter (where Brahms had been a constant customer):

In the name of the heart-broken Esplanade [Ischl's principal promenade], as well as of your humble servant, I take the liberty of asking you whether you are not going to honor us with your visit again this year. Although your faithful companion [Brüll] has entered into wedlock, I will do my best to give you good coffee and plenty of newspapers. The flower girls also would be delighted to get the sugar that is left over; in short, everything would be done to give you satisfaction. Herr Ignaz Brüll has even promised me that if you come, he and his brother-in-law will stay here and again become bachelors for an hour a day.[10]

His Viennese friends, too, joined Frau Walter in her request. Brahms, however, did not give way; he was faithless to the last six summers passed in Austria, and went to Wiesbaden, having several good reasons for this change. His friends Alwin and Laura von Beckerath, whose society he greatly enjoyed, lived at Wiesbaden, and he had always admired the surrounding country. But in the summer of 1883 a special magnet drew him to Wiesbaden, for there lived the young singer, Hermine Spies. Brahms had made her acquaintance at von der Leyen's home in Krefeld, in January 1883, after an exceptionally fine performance of the *Parzenlied*. At that time Hermine had as yet hardly outgrown her apprenticeship under Stockhausen, but the connoisseurs were confident that her talent, though as yet immature, was very great. In purely vocal qualities the young contralto could compete with the most famous representatives of her art; in her spirited rendering she surpassed most of them. Her emotional versatility was such that experienced managers advised her to go on the stage. Hermine, however, had no intention of doing so; it was enough for her to be known as the singer of the German *Lied*. To this end she devoted herself with all her youthful enthusiasm, and long before she had made Brahms's personal acquaintance his songs had found their way into her heart. No wonder that the man of fifty was deeply impressed by this highly talented and peculiarly attractive young woman, and the impression she had made upon him was confirmed by a summer at Wiesbaden. One critic summed up Hermine's charm in the concise words: 'An earnest voice and a jolly girl.' Hermine was a true child of nature, merry and good-humored. If, like most girls of her age, she felt in awe of the great master, she was able to conceal this under her unembarrassed friendliness. Better, perhaps, than any other woman heretofore, she understood Brahms's teasing and malicious remarks, to which she never failed to respond in kind. Brahms, therefore, was completely fascinated by the 'gay and pretty Rhineland girl.'

During the next few years he followed her brilliant career with the greatest sympathy, and did his utmost to help her. She became his favorite interpreter of the *Alto Rhapsody;* he gave her a brilliant introduction to the musical circles of Vienna, and sent her some of his songs in manuscript. Many of the songs of this period, especially those contained in Op. 96 and 97, reveal such warmth of feeling that Billroth, an excellent judge of human nature and of music, wrote to Brahms: 'If these songs are really new, you must be in the grip of such a strong and wholesome midsummer passion as is in keeping with your healthy and indefatigable nature. I believe there is something behind this. So much the better; one doesn't choose such words and write such songs out of the mere habit of composing.' That Brahms had really thought of marrying Hermine will seem very unlikely to those who understand his character—though according to Elise Brahms [11] his engagement was regarded as an accomplished fact in Hamburg. One thing is certain, however, that for some years he sought every possible occasion of meeting his 'Hermione-ohne-o' (Shakespeare's Hermione without the *o*). He was always exceptionally cheerful and carefree in her presence, and it was surely not the singer alone that he loved. He recognized, however, that the mode of life which he had chosen was the only one that suited him, and he may have resigned himself in this case without any great inner conflict. Hermine, for her part, who was well aware of Brahms's feeling for her, repeatedly declared in her letters that she had never considered a closer relation. Yet she openly admitted her 'Johannes-passion,' and even in July 1887, after the climax of their friendship was over, she still wrote with enthusiasm of the man of 54 in her letters to their mutual friend, Claus Groth (in whose recently republished memoirs are several letters of Hermine's in which she speaks of Brahms). '*What* a splendid fellow is Brahms! Once more I was absolutely overwhelmed, enraptured, enchanted, carried away. And what a dear he was! In a really happy, youthful, summery mood! He is eternally young.'

Not only in beautiful songs—as in Op. 96, 97—did Brahms's love for Hermine find expression. She inspired and stimulated the creative artist in various fields, and it may be more than pure chance that many of the composer's finest works date from the next few years.

The summer of 1883 was a period of the greatest importance, for in the wonderfully situated studio, high above the town, which Brahms occupied that year at Wiesbaden, the Third Symphony saw the light. This composition gave Brahms the long-desired opportunity of renewing his relations with Joachim. Having unburdened himself to his old friend at the Musical Festival that year in Koblenz, Brahms now asked Joachim whether he would be interested in the first performance of the symphony in Berlin. Naturally Joachim, whose admiration for the composer was unaffected by their personal differences, took the 'proffered hand,' thereby giving Brahms the 'greatest and most solemn joy.' Before it was performed in Berlin, however, the symphony was first produced in Vienna, by the Philharmonic Orchestra under Hans Richter, on 2 December 1883—not a completely successful performance. In the Austrian capital the adherents of Wagner and Bruckner had prepared themselves for a vigorous assault on Brahms, whom they could not forgive for his ever-growing fame, and whom they held—without justification—responsible for the sharp attacks upon their party delivered by Brahms's friend, the greatly dreaded critic, Eduard Hanslick. Brahms's fieriest antagonist was young Hugo Wolf, at that time still quite unknown as a composer. His criticisms in the insignificant Viennese *Salonblatt* were so recklessly exaggerated that they merely tickled Brahms's sense of humor. Once, for instance, he called Brahms's symphonies 'disgustingly stale and prosy, and fundamentally false and perverse,' adding that 'a single cymbal-stroke of a work by Liszt expressed more intellect and emotion than all three symphonies of Brahms and his serenades taken to gether.'

In spite of all their efforts the Wagnerites did not succeed in bringing about the failure of the Third Symphony. In Vienna the majority of the public was on Brahms's side, and the performances that followed in other cities—Berlin alone heard the Symphony three times in close succession— were sufficient proof to the composer of the great response everywhere evoked by his magnificent work. The performance at Meiningen, where Bülow produced the work twice in the same concert, was particularly fine. The fame of the Symphony spread even to France, which had hitherto shown but little interest in Brahms. Benjamin Godard invited [12] the composer—although in vain—to conduct his work for the *Société des Concerts Modernes*.

Soon after the first performances of the Third Symphony, Brahms received yet another invitation to Cologne. In the spring of 1884 the aged Ferdinand Hiller wrote to him:

DEAR FRIEND,
You will be able to guess the contents of this letter. When I left Düsseldorf thirty-four years ago, I wrote to Schumann—to-day I beg you to become my successor. My desire is not really egotistical, for I shall not derive any glory from it. But I love my Cologne Institute, and I should like to secure for it an increase of efficiency, and, let us say, of glory. I hope to be able to over-come some of your objections. Cologne is not a beautiful place, but it is neither too large nor too small. . . On the whole, the people are decent folk, and to you they will behave particularly well, for they will be proud to have such a conductor. They will let you have as many holidays as you want. . . Don't, at least, refuse beforehand. . . I feel sure they will accede to all your requests, as far as ever they can. And so I venture to hope that after having done so much to improve the conditions here, I am doing the best thing of all by encouraging you to become the leader of the municipal orchestra.[13]

Brahms received also an official communication, in which he was offered a yearly income of 12,000 marks, or twice as much as Düsseldorf had offered him eight years previously. As might have been expected, he declined the appointment; and in his official reply he could not refrain from writing:

How I used formerly to long for such employment, which is not only desirable and even essential for the creative artist, but is necessary to enable him to lead a decent and fitting existence. I am thinking now of Hamburg, my native city, where, since the time when I consider I began to count for something, my name has repeatedly been—absolutely ignored.

His motives were well understood in Cologne, and when he proposed that the position should be filled by Franz Wüllner, a conductor whom he always highly esteemed and who was then working in Dresden, his candidate was accepted.

After a series of successful concerts he was able to think of his holidays. To begin with, he spent some enjoyable days on Lake Como at the enchantingly beautiful Villa Carlotta, which belonged to the Duke of Meiningen. Then his choice fell on the little town of Mürzzuschlag in Styria, which he had visited seventeen years earlier on the memorable walking tour undertaken with his beloved father.

Again the summer visitors to Ischl were disappointed, and Ignaz Brüll wrote reproachfully:

Well, what a fellow he is! He means to take rooms in Ischl for the summer, and then one morning he wakes up in Mürzzuschlag! I had been looking forward to our walks, on which I would not have disturbed the heavenly peace by a single sound, whether German or French . . . to our pleasant coffee parties, and much besides—and most of all to the playing of new duets— and now all my hopes are turned to water (hence all this rain!).[14]

Brahms, however, who may have chosen this new resort in the desire for new impressions and possibly because he dreaded the rainy weather so frequent at Ischl, may not so greatly have felt the loss of his friend, as he found many agreeable acquaintances in Mürzzuschlag, such as the Fellinger family. Richard Fellinger, manager of the important industrial firm of Siemens and Halske, and his gifted wife (whom we have to thank for some excellent photographs, portraits, and busts of Brahms) were among the master's most intimate Viennese friends. The sensitive and tactful manner of the Fellingers, who tried to divine the artist's every wish but never forced themselves upon him, was particularly soothing to the aging and lonely bachelor. He often invited himself to the Fellingers' house on Sunday, knowing that he could count on his favorite dishes; and in other respects he was not unwilling to be spoiled by his friends' affectionate forethought. Frau Fellinger knitted his stockings, as his mother had done, and made the sort of neckties that he liked to wear, and one day Herr Fellinger delighted Brahms by installing electric light in his rooms.

Clara Schumann, too, came to Mürzzuschlag, and many another Viennese friend decided on an excursion to the pretty little town, which was not very far from the capital. Billroth came to see him, with Hanslick, Epstein, Kalbeck (subsequently his biographer) and—at Simrock's request—a painter arrived from Berlin to paint the master's portrait. Brahms, however, as usual, flatly refused to sit for the artist, who had to go away with the portrait unpainted.

In spite of so many social engagements a great new work, the mighty Fourth Symphony, made such good progress that Brahms was well satisfied with Mürzzuschlag, and went there again in 1885 for the purpose of completing this composition. When the Symphony was finished, the composer was obliged to admit to himself that he had produced a very unusual work, and the first impressions of his friends—even of the sympathetic Elisabeth von Herzogenberg—told him that he was not fully understood. He therefore felt that it was all the more important to rehearse the Symphony 'nicely and comfortably' at Meiningen. Bülow, of course, agreed, and Brahms arrived at Meiningen in time to hear the first performance of the F minor Symphony by the young Richard Strauss, in whose work he had taken an interest since Strauss, at Bülow's request, had sent [15] him his Suite, Op. 4.

As usual, in the case of young musicians, Brahms's verdict was extremely laconic—but by no means unfavorable. Richard Strauss, for his part, received an unforgettable impression of the new Brahms Symphony, the Andante of which 'reminded him of a funeral procession moving in silence across moonlit heights.' Bülow, too, was enchanted by the Symphony's 'unparalleled energy,' and he rehearsed it with such devotion that, at the first performance at Meiningen, on 17 October 1885, Brahms was able to inspire the perfectly prepared orchestra to achieve a magnificent performance. The success of the Symphony was so great that during the ensuing concert tour with the Meiningen ensemble this composition was the main feature of the program. Brahms accompanied the orchestra, but was far more than an 'extra conductor,' as he had first termed it. He conducted the Symphony in nine cities, so that the energetic Bülow had hardly enough to do; especially as Brahms was unwilling to allow any other striking composition to precede the Fourth Symphony.

This gradually aroused a degree of ill-feeling that needed only a little provocation to find an outlet. The occasion came only too soon. Brahms, while absent from the orchestra for a few days, had been persuaded to perform the Fourth Symphony in November 1885 with the Frankfort orchestra, just before the already-planned performance in that city by the Meiningen orchestra. Bülow, who had particularly wished to conduct the new Symphony himself at Frankfort, where many of Brahms's friends were living, above all, Clara Schumann, felt that this behavior was a proof of a grievous lack of confidence. He was not only personally hurt, but he felt that his professional honor, as head of the Meiningen orchestra, had been so deeply wounded that he resigned his position. Brahms was greatly perturbed by this unexpected result of his thoughtless but in no way ill-meant action, and he declared that this misunderstanding pained him far more than Bülow realized. He could not, however, regard concerts as 'serious affairs' and he would have to wait until Bülow could take the same point of view. In his heart he knew that Bülow was too closely linked to him to intend an absolute rupture of their relations. When, after more than a year's separation, Bülow came to Vienna, a calling card of Brahms's, on which a few notes of music were written, was enough to restore peace between them. The notes were from *The Magic Flute*, and in the opera they accompany the following text: *Soll ich Dich, Teurer, nicht mehr sehen?* (Shall I, Beloved, see thee no more?) Bülow, deeply moved, made haste to call on Brahms that very day, 'chatting with him for a bewitching hour.' Soon he could announce triumphantly that he and Brahms were *d'accordissimo* in their way of thinking, and that 'the satisfaction which he felt, mentally and emotionally lent him the strength of a giant.'

The Fourth Symphony played an important part in yet another friendship. Joachim was so delighted by this work, which was his favorite among the four Symphonies, and conducted it with such understanding, that the reticent Brahms, carried away for once, wrote to his friend: 'Praise and sympathy such as yours are not only highly gratifying, but necessary. It is as though one had to wait for them for permission to enjoy one's own work!' Now, once more, after an interval of many years, he asked for Joachim's advice in respect of technical details; and before long a new composition was to give Brahms an opportunity of renewing his relations with the friend of his youth, relations which became as cordial as could be expected after the stormy disputes that had preceded them.

UNPUBLISHED LETTERS REFERRED TO:

1. Letter from Max Stägemann, 15 January 1879.
2. Letter from Brahms to Amalie Joachim, December 1880.
3. Letter from Brahms to Amalie Joachim, December 1880.
4. Letter from Gustav Nottebohm to Brahms, 26 October 1882.

5. Letter from Brahms to Hans v. Bülow, October 1877.
6. Letter from Franz Liszt to Brahms, 15 April 1882.
7. Letter from Ferdinand Hiller to Brahms, 5 November 1881.
8. Letter from Brahms to Hans v. Bülow, undated.
9. Letter from Daniela v. Bülow to Brahms, 7 November 1882.
10. Letter from Amalie Walter to Brahms, 27 May (1883).
11. Letter from Elise Brahms, 26 April 1883.
12. Letter from Benjamin Godard to Brahms, 7 December 1884.
13. Letter from Ferdinand Hiller to Brahms, 17 April 1884.
14. Letter from Ignaz Brüll to Brahms, undated (Summer, 1884).
15. Letter from Richard Strauss to Brahms, 19 November 1884.

XII

A FRUITFUL AUTUMN

(1886-1890)

Brahms spent the summer of 1886 in Switzerland. For Widmann's sake his choice fell on Hofstetten, near Thun, on the Lake of Thun, not far from Bern, where his friend lived. Here there was much to recall the happy summers spent in Pörtschach. Once more Brahms enjoyed so greatly his stay beside a lake that he visited the same place for three summers in succession; once more, surrounded by a landscape that delighted him, he did an astonishing amount of creative work, following, to some extent, the lines laid down at Pörtschach. Two Sonatas joined the First Violin Sonata; the Violin Concerto was continued by the Concerto for Violin and 'Cello—in writing which he had again his friend Joachim in mind. In these summers in Thun the master wrote also the Second 'Cello Sonata, Op. 99, the C minor Trio, Op. 101, the passionate *Zigeunerlieder* (Gipsy Songs), and a number of his most famous songs (Op. 105-7). Many of these Swiss works are more vigorous and powerful in character than the older compositions, just as the Swiss landscape is more magnificent than the delightful country round Pörtschach. From the windows of his rooms, which were situated on the Aar, Brahms enjoyed an indescribably beautiful view of the glaciers of the Bernese Oberland, and we can understand why many of the compositions written here have something of an Alpine majesty.

Brahms invited his friends to join him at Thun. Many of them did so, and the master spent pleasant hours with Stockhausen and Kalbeck, the Dutch composer, Röntgen, and the philologist, Gustav Wendt, for whom he had a great esteem. The Dutch organist, S. de Lange, was also a welcome guest, and he wrote to Brahms after his departure: 'I must tell you what a joy it was to us to meet you, and how your cordiality made our rainy days in Thun the brightest of our trip to Switzerland. We should be delighted to receive a line from you. But if you have music to write, do that instead; it will give me even greater pleasure, and will delight thousands of others.' [1] Most of all, the composer may have enjoyed the visit of the poet Klaus Groth, for they were now linked by yet another bond. The composer of fifty-three and the poet fourteen years his senior both loved Hermine Spies, and when they were together they never tired of bantering one another. Twice during these three summers Hermine herself came to Thun, and then there was glorious music at Widmanns', where Brahms, inspired by '*his* singer,' played for hours on end to his enchanted friends. But even without this special attraction, Brahms arrived at the Widmanns' punctually every Saturday, spending the day with them, or even several days; carrying off, for his own perusal, the latest books which the editor had received for review, indulging in endless debates with his host, delighting in pointing out little inaccuracies in Widmann's editorials, eating large slices of his favorite plum cake, and taking a friendly interest in all that concerned each member of the household, including the dog. When he returned to Vienna, Brahms wrote: 'After all, people are what matters most; when I remember magnificent Thun, it is the memory of you that gives me by far the dearest, the most valuable, and the most heart-warming thrill.'

This intimate friendship with a writer who had had some success as a librettist gave rise to rumors that Brahms was composing an opera to a text of Widmann's. This was not the case, but the rumor was not wholly unfounded, as in previous years Brahms had seriously discussed the question of operatic libretti with Widmann. But the poet's attempts were just as fruitless as the indefatigable efforts of Allgeyer and Levi had been. Brahms found insuperable defects in every libretto submitted to him, and at the time of his visits to Thun he had definitely abandoned the idea of composing an opera. This decision was deeply founded in Brahms's artistic personality. The composer was so firmly rooted in the world of absolute music, regarding the compact musical form as irrefutable law, that—as he clearly expressed himself —he could contemplate only an opera consisting of compact single numbers, loosely bound by spoken dialogue. On the other hand, Richard Wagner's musical drama had impressed him so strongly that he could not ignore the great importance of that type of opera, in which the whole text is set to music. He refused, of course, to imitate the Bayreuth master; yet he did not feel that he was the proper person to effect such an original renewal of the classical opera as he had in mind. (His prototypes were *Don Giovanni* and *Fidelio*.) He found no proper solution of this inner conflict, and as he possessed no real dramatic sense, his plans for writing an opera, much as he liked to dwell upon them, did not proceed beyond the stage of theoretical speculation.

Although it was a painful disappointment to Widmann to find that artistic co-operation with the composer whom he so admired was impossible, this disappointment struck no discordant note in their friendly relations. Brahms conceived an increasing respect for Widmann's intellectual gifts, and felt he would be the ideal companion on his visits to Italy. In the spring of 1888 his wish was at last granted— in 1887 his companions were Simrock and Kirchner— and Brahms so greatly appreciated the poet's company that he entreated Widmann, year after year, to repeat the visit to Italy. On two further occasions he enjoyed this experience, and the poet has given a delightful description of these visits in his memoirs.

In the second summer at Thun, Brahms entered into an extensive correspondence with Frau Fellinger in respect of a matter that had become very important to his comfort. Ludovika Vogl, who had for many years sublet to Brahms the furnished apartment in the Karlsgasse, had died, and he could now have rented the unfurnished flat directly from the landlord. But who should keep house for him? This question greatly embarrassed Brahms, and the position was made no easier by the fact that a large number of ladies wrote to him stating that they would only be too happy to become his housekeeper. He therefore confided his trouble to Frau Fellinger, complaining that widows and spinsters had applied to him from the four corners of Europe, including Constantinople, but he always mislaid their addresses, treating 'the whole affair as carelessly as he did his composing, and the matter was really more important.' His relief was great when Frau Fellinger took the affair in hand, attending, in the first place, to the provisional furnishing of his rooms. All that he asked was that everything should be as simple as possible; he really needed nothing but a washstand and a bed. Only after prolonged discussion did he make a trifling concession, writing to his friend: 'I am a perfect angel, and I consent to curtains, but only in the music room.' In the end Frau Fellinger hit upon an excellent solution. She arranged an interview with Frau Dr. Celestine Truxa, the widow of a writer, who was willing to take the unoccupied rooms of the flat for herself, and also to look after Brahms. She provided the composer's three rooms with furniture of her own, and arranged everything to Brahms's taste. Her reserved manner and her inconspicuous way of performing little services were exactly what the master wanted, and he was well content with his new landlady. A great lover of children, he was delighted with Frau Truxa's two 'darling boys,' and one of his principal pleasures was the giving of Christmas presents to these boys, whose Christmas tree was always set up in his library.

Once his household problems were solved, Brahms divided his day in a more and more definite manner, which he observed to the end of his life; this regularity to some extent replaced for the aging bachelor the comforts of domestic life. Brahms was a very early riser, and liked to prepare his own breakfast and make his beloved coffee, which an admirer of his, Frau Fritsch-Estrangin, sent him in large consignments from Marseilles. The morning was devoted to work. His lunch, and as a rule his evening meal, he took in his favorite restaurant *Zum roten Igel* (The Red Hedgehog), which, thanks to Brahms, had become the rendezvous of the musical circles of the capital. He characteristically avoided the elegant dining-room, which was frequented by officers and high officials, feeling at ease only in the more modest 'general dining-room,' where he ordered the simplest fare. However, they knew how to prepare his favorite dishes and kept in the cellar a small barrel of the finest Hungarian Tokay for his private consumption. So the composer remained faithful to his 'prickly pet,' and even on his summer holidays breathed 'a sigh of tender longing' for it. Brahms liked to joke about the affinity between himself and the name of his favorite inn and he once wrote to Marie Brüll: 'On Saturday Herr Röntgen arrives with his sister and they both look forward to the lunch, the hedgehog, and to myself. Couldn't you also join the two pricklies?' ² The composer's preference for this restaurant was soon so well known that even princes—as, for example, the Landgrave of Hesse—liked to patronize it, in order to lunch or dine with Brahms. After his lunch Brahms used to take a stroll in the lovely *Stadtpark,* where he drank a cup of black coffee. The afternoon was devoted to further work, or to social engagements; in the evenings he often returned to the *Igel,* drinking his last cup of Mocha, very late at night, in a café near his flat.

About this time the composition of his circle of Viennese friends began to undergo certain changes. Brahms was deeply grieved by the death of the 'good, touchingly good,' Carl Ferdinand Pohl, whom he had to thank for many a happy

and stimulating hour. When we read the many letters addressed to Brahms by the famous biographer of Haydn (who
had to give the composer the 'historically noteworthy pen'
with which he had written the last chapter of Volume II of
his book), we are enchanted by the gay and unconstrained
manner of Pohl's approach to his eminent friend. Brahms's
work is never once mentioned; Pohl was far too modest, and
too sensitive, to speak of it, knowing that Brahms allowed
only a few of his very intimate friends to discuss his creations
with him. Pohl took, however, all the more interest in the
affairs of the master's everyday life. When Brahms was absent from Vienna, it delighted Pohl to do him little services,
and he executed all the composer's commissions with the
greatest care, describing his incidental adventures with delightful humor. After Pohl's death, Sir George Grove, who
was a friend of his wrote a spontaneous letter of condolence
to Brahms. No less than the understanding words which
Grove dedicated to Pohl's memory, Brahms may have welcomed the sincere admiration expressed by the famous historian for his own compositions.

Before I end, let me express to you some small part of my
feelings for the three great works of yours which have come to
London this last week. . . Even such slight acquaintance serves
to increase, if possible, the debt of gratitude and admiration
which I abundantly feel towards you. I only speak the senti-
ments of a great many Englishmen when I thus thank you most
warmly for the invaluable benefits that we derive from you, and
for which we are so deeply indebted to you.[3]

Simultaneously with the tidings of Pohl's death, which
reached Brahms only in May 1887, at Thun, after his return from Italy, he received a second and almost more distressing message. Theodor Billroth had fallen dangerously
ill with pneumonia. Brahms immediately sent urgent en-
quiries to Vienna; at length a moving letter in his friend's
own hand convinced him that all danger had passed. Billroth recovered his health, although to Brahms he no longer

seemed quite the man he had been. As late as 1889 the composer wrote to Clara that it made him uncomfortable to
look at his friend; his cheerfulness seemed to be forced and
unnatural. Like many healthy people, Brahms confronted
illness and physical pain without understanding, even with
a certain dread, and it may have been that he betrayed his
feelings too openly to his friend. In any case their intercourse, in spite of all mutual esteem, lacked its former intimacy, and before long this fruitful alliance began to decline. Other reasons may have been partly responsible. Billroth, who had lost his old vitality, was more easily offended
by those aspects of Brahms's character which had always been
alien to him: the master's love of sarcasm and his bad manners. Brahms, on the other hand, became estranged from his
old friend by a series of misunderstandings. Dr. Gottlieb-
Billroth, in his highly interesting preface to the correspondence between Brahms and Billroth, points to two incidents
of this kind. On the wall of Billroth's new study hung a portrait of Brahms, with a manuscript line from Brahms's own
pen underneath it. This line the surgeon had simply cut out
from the original score of the A minor Quartet, which had
been presented to him by Brahms. The composer, who had
always been a passionate collector of musical manuscripts,
could not but be horrified by such a mutilation of his manuscript. Billroth, however, who set no great value on autographs, had placed the line under Brahms's portrait simply
that he might have always before him something from the
pen of the beloved master.

Even worse was another misunderstanding. The musical
critic, Eduard Hanslick, showed Brahms some beautiful letters that Billroth had written when still under the impression of Brahms's music, quite forgetting that one of them contained a remark not destined for the composer's eyes. In this
Billroth declared that Brahms the man would never quite
rid himself of the consequences of a neglected education.
The master naturally was deeply hurt (all the more, perhaps,

as there was a grain of truth in Billroth's statement) and, as at Hanslick's request he never spoke of the matter to Billroth, his wrath exploded on an absolutely irrelevant occasion. Billroth had invited some of his most intimate friends to dinner, and when Brahms was asked to play some of his new works he replied in such a sarcastic and even hostile tone that the surgeon had not the courage ever to invite him again. None the less, the intellectual bond between the two men was too strong to permit of a permanent estrangement. Though the old cordiality was not regained, they still continued to exchange ideas until Billroth's death.

Though Brahms was certainly not blameless in respect of the decline of his friendship with Billroth, the aging musician did endeavor in other respects to preserve old friendships. In 1887 he wrote to Billroth: 'What you say of your increasing loneliness sounds a little melancholy. I have a sympathetic understanding for such feelings, and I only wish you would take timely precautions. I myself do so—who have always been and still am a shocking "outsider." ' It was due to Brahms's initiative that his friendship with Bülow was renewed, while his Double Concerto was inspired mainly by thoughts of Joachim. In 1887, at Baden-Baden, the composer rehearsed it, with the violinist and the excellent 'cellist Hausmann, in Clara Schumann's presence. Thus, after a lapse of many years, the two artists once more cooperated, to their mutual delight.

Moreover, a new form of social life was offered to Brahms by the *Wiener Tonkünstlerverein*, founded in 1885. He was elected honorary president of this society in December 1886, and took a keen interest in its development, believing that the performances of the *Tonkünstlerverein* were an important influence in the training of the younger generation of musicians. The social side of the activities, however, pleased him even more than the artistic. He never failed to attend the pleasant sociable meetings of the *Verein,* and there were many of its members whom he was glad to see on

Sundays, and accompany on excursions into the Wiener-
wald. Only those, however, who could keep up with his rapid
gait were welcome; as, for example, his old friends Julius
Epstein, Ignaz Brüll, and Carl Goldmark, with the sensitive
composer, Robert Fuchs, and the distinguished pianoforte
teacher, Anton Door; and of the younger generation the
composers Richard Heuberger and Ludwig Rottenberg, with
Richard v. Perger, subsequently the conductor of the *Gesellschaft* Concerts; and above all the master's particular
famulus, Eusebius Mandyczewski. Largely owing to the introduction of Brahms, who as long ago as 1879 had warmly
recommended the young musician, Mandyczewski succeeded
Pohl as librarian of the Museum of the *Gesellschaft der
Musikfreunde*.

Thenceforth it seemed as though Brahms had transferred
to Mandyczewski the affection he had formerly bestowed
upon his predecessor. The master had a great esteem for
Mandyczewski as an artist of versatile culture, both musical
and literary. It pleased him, too, that the young librarian
raised no objection to performing insignificant services for
him—as, for example, the packing of postal parcels, which,
to Brahms, was the most distasteful chore on earth—yet did
not hesitate, when needful, to criticize the revered master's
compositions. The historian made himself indispensable to
Brahms by bearing in mind the master's unfailing delight
in the gems of an earlier age; and in this way he filled the
gap caused by the deaths of Nottebohm and Pohl. Lastly,
'Mandy' won Brahms's heart by sharing his peculiar sense
of humor. The master, for instance, delighted in rallying
the young man on his conquests in the excellent women's
choir which he conducted, offering him three Overtures by
Dvořák for the archives of the *Gesellschaft der Musikfreunde*
with the words: 'Would you like to have Smetana's *Kiss*, too?
Or does the ladies' choir furnish a better article?' With
Mandyczewski, too, Brahms could indulge in his love of
endorsing his letters with musical allusions only the initi-

ated could understand. Thus, he once wrote a letter from Ischl, in which he asked 'Mandy' to do various errands for him, and with a feeling of guilt he jotted down on the envelope, under the address, the opening of his own eleventh waltz from *Liebeslieder*. The words to the music, omitted on the envelope, were: 'Alas, there is no getting on with the people' (*Ach, es ist nicht auszukommen mit den Leuten*); words that Mandyczewski would immediately supply. Brahms sought the company of his faithful amanuensis as often as possible, and even wrote from Ischl to arrange a meeting in Vienna:

> On Tuesday, in the good old way, I shall go to the 'Igel' for lunch, and afterwards into the Stadtpark. It would be too delightful were you to greet, on this occasion,
>
> Yours sincerely,
>
> BRAHMS

For his own part, Mandyczewski saw in Brahms not only the surpassing genius, but also the man of rare kindliness, who took an ever-ready interest in all his personal concerns —from his professional difficulties to his domestic relations— and never hesitated to help his young friend by word or deed. When Mandyczewski had finished his great task, the complete edition of Schubert, Brahms sent a thousand marks to the always impecunious musician, with the characteristic words:

> I suppose one might regard this as a sort of 'grateful endowment'? Isn't it permissible in one to whom, as you know, you have given such peculiar pleasure by your last admirable work, and who is, moreover, as you also know, sincerely attached to you?

The three years 1886-8, whose summer months Brahms spent in Thun, show a pronounced decline of his concert activities. He was now concerned only to perform his new compositions. On 24 November 1886, he played his 'Cello Sonata with Hausmann in Vienna; on 2 December of the same year his A major Violin Sonata with Hellmesberger, and the C minor Trio in the same month with Hubay and Popper in Budapest. The Double Concerto was first performed in Cologne on 18 October 1887, and his last Violin Sonata in Vienna on 22 December 1888, with Hubay.

Brahms gladly went also to Meiningen, where the orchestra, under young Fritz Steinbach—who had soon replaced Bülow's successor, Richard Strauss—was doing excellent work. Not only did Brahms enjoy the splendid performances of his own works there; he also permitted himself the pleasure of hearing unknown works of Bach and Mozart performed for his special benefit. On the whole, however, he avoided traveling as much as possible, feeling happiest when in Austria. It was, as he wrote, quite a peculiar pleasure for him to see the first Austrian train guards and waiters, when returning from a trip abroad. When the spring of 1889 arrived, he decided to spend the summer within easy reach of Vienna. He returned to Ischl, and was so well satisfied that he remained faithful to it to the end of his life. He never wearied of telling his friends of the advantages of this summer resort; besides the beauty of the surrounding country, the gay and friendly nature of the inhabitants pleased and refreshed him, who was 'serious enough at home.'

From Ischl Brahms often visited the adjacent town of Gmunden, where he found the hospitable family of Miller von Aicholz, in whose beautiful house he always felt at home. Viktor von Miller and his wife Olga were among the most faithful of Brahms's friends, and their home was a regular meeting place for the Brahms circle. Shortly after the master's death, Herr von Miller expressed his admiration for his friend by establishing a remarkable memorial, in the form of the Brahms Museum at Gmunden which contains all the furniture of the composer's rooms in Ischl—down to the very window frames—as well as numerous pictures, letters, and manuscripts. It is to Viktor von Miller's son, however, to Herr Eugen von Miller, that we owe a number of delightful snapshots, taken in Brahms's later years, which show us the master in his more social moods, and even reveal the hard-boiled bachelor as a worshiper of the fair sex. Most of these snapshots have been assembled in the *Brahms Bilderbuch,* which is one of the most attractive examples of Brahmsiana.

At Ischl, in the summer of 1889, Brahms received news of two distinctions that had been conferred upon him. The Order of Leopold had been bestowed by the Austrian Emperor, and on 23 May the following telegram arrived from Hamburg:

I am happy to be able to inform you that the Honorary Freedom of Hamburg has been conferred upon you. Further details to follow,
BURGOMASTER PETERSEN

This was a great distinction. So far only twelve persons had received the honorary freedom of the city of Hamburg, and among them were men whom Brahms regarded with sincere admiration; for example, Blücher, Moltke, and Bismarck. How had this astonishing change in the opinion of his native city come about? One word will suffice to explain it: Bülow. Since 1886 the conductor had been working in Hamburg, and a close friendship had sprung up between him and the aged Burgomaster Petersen. Bülow, aware of Brahms's feeling for Hamburg, was anxious to obtain some reparation for the old but never-forgotten wrong done to the composer. He therefore suggested to the Burgomaster that Brahms should be thus honored, and he was able to inspire him with such enthusiasm that Herr Petersen succeeded in overcoming all opposition in the Senate.

Brahms was greatly pleased with this distinction, even though every honor awarded by his native city evoked a certain bitterness, and the feeling that it was all 'too late.' He returned thanks to Hamburg by attending the festival of the Industrial and Commercial Exhibition held in September 1889; and by offering a new choral work, his *Fest- und Ge- denksprüche,* Op. 109, to the Cecilia Society for its first per- formance. The formal ceremony of presenting Brahms with the diploma of citizenship took place on 14 September, and the accompanying festivities at the Burgomaster's country house resulted in the formation of a pleasant friendship be- tween Brahms and the Petersen family. When the *Fest- und Gedenksprüche* were published, the composer thought it only appropriate to dedicate them to the Burgomaster, and he received the following letter of thanks:

To me, as a layman, a great honor has been paid. Fortunately, one need not be an expert in order to derive joy from music, and just as I enjoyed this beautiful work at the Exhibition, so I hope often to feel happiness and peace of mind on hearing it in future. Your work and your name will long outlive mine; so it is pleasant to think that through the medium of your dedica- tion my name will be handed down to posterity.[4]

Although Brahms, characteristically enough, did not thank Bülow, to whom he owed this honor, in so many words, their relations became more cordial than ever, and when, some months later, on 8 January 1890, Bülow celebrated his sixtieth birthday, the master sent him the autograph copy of his Third Symphony, for which the conductor had a special affection. In Hamburg Bülow's birthday was celebrated with great festivities, and a few lovers of music took this oppor- tunity of contributing the sum of 10,000 marks, with the stipulation that the recipient was to use the money for an artistic purpose which he deemed worthy of support. When Brahms heard of this, he wrote the following characteristic letter to the conductor:

MOST HONORED FRIEND!
You are always giving me so much reason to write to you, and, what is more, to write exhaustively and gratefully in the best and most varied sense of the word, that it is only too easy to postpone

my letter—or never to write it at all. Sittard's book [*Johannes Brahms als Symphoniker und Eduard Marxsen*] is . . . bad. . . I have never before seen anybody write such sinuous lines. [This sentence Brahms wrote in the shape of a snake.]

As far as I know, he was warmly on my side from the outset; he also occasionally sent me his reviews. Perhaps I was ashamed to answer merely by a post card—the most I can do in such cases —but card or no card: he does not know that I am a poor recluse, who really feels much more comfortable when the world takes no notice of him. . . What will you do with the 10,000 marks? I hope, no stipends for pianoforte-houris? I often think it would be seemly to make a presentation to Chrysander on the completion of his edition of Händel. However, I am not the right person to stage such a matter, as I dread publicity even in such a case.

Most affectionately yours,

J. B.[5]

Although Bülow did not see eye to eye with Chrysander, whether in musical or in personal matters, he gladly followed Brahms's suggestion; he was, however, somewhat disappointed when Chrysander replied with a long letter describing his researches, but never once mentioning the munificent gift. Brahms did not approve of the ungracious manners of his compatriot, but he thoroughly understood him; so that the following letter to Bülow is of interest as affording a clue to the master's own character:

MY DEAR FRIEND,

When one has performed, or has intended to perform, a just and kindly action, one can quietly abide the consequences. You are in this position and you should forbid your thoughts to indulge in idle imaginings (his 'not finding it worth while,' etc.). Chrysander is a queer customer, but you can't know or even guess what is going on in his mind. He may or may not want to accept your gift—he cannot but have the very highest opinion of you and your offer. I can see myself in the shoes of either of you, and you could each of you teach me something. In Chrysander's place I should need to be taught the lesson that in such a case one should immediately give at least a provisional

·answer; but in your place my imagination, too, would be only too apt to go astray in the gloomiest minor key! Finally, I can't help saying that it delights me to think of Chrysander's declining (with the sincerest and most joyful thanks) because he absolutely didn't need more money. . . Dear Friend, I am shocked at my garrulousness. But I think that the first sentence of this letter really says all that is needful. If you think otherwise—and still haven't heard from Chrysander—let me know, and I will write to him. I may do this the more easily, as I can, as I have said, see myself behaving in just the same way.

Most affectionately yours,

J. B.[6]

Further steps on Brahms's part were, however, unnecessary, as Bülow presently wrote that the whole affair had been cleared up, and that Chrysander had accepted and been profoundly moved by the gift.

The year 1890 was barren of outward events. In March Brahms enjoyed a magnificent performance of the *Fest- und Gedenksprüche* and the new *a cappella* Motets, Op. 110, at Cologne, conducted by Wüllner. He was 'as merry as a grig' at having with him on this occasion his old friends, the Grimms (see p. 56). Then Brahms went to Italy with Widmann, where, though he visited only well-known places, he constantly found new and unexpected beauties. A delightful work, the String Quintet, Op. 111, was completed during the summer at Ischl. Its fluent energy in no way betrays the master's increasing years. Brahms, however, had the feeling that with this work he had exhausted his powers. Holding that one should never compose a line without inner inspiration, he decided to anticipate a possible decline of his creative powers, and to write no more after this perfectly finished Quintet. A lifework of great wealth and variety lay behind him. He was fifty-seven years of age, and thought that he had earned the right to peace and leisure. Now he could look back over what he had done, destroy what he deemed to be worthless, finish what had been successfully begun, and make certain dispositions concerning his material possessions. In the autumn of 1790 he began to consider the provisions of his last will and testament.

UNPUBLISHED LETTERS REFERRED TO:

1. Letter from S. de Lange, 10 August 1886.
2. Post card from Brahms to Marie Brüll, 26 February 1896.
3. Letter from Sir George Grove, 2 May 1887.
4. Letter from Carl Petersen, 19 March 1890.
5. Letter from Brahms to Hans von Bülow, January 1890.
6. Letter from Brahms to Hans von Bülow, January 1891.

XIII

NEARING THE END

(1891-1897)

A T Ischl, on his fifty-eighth birthday, Brahms drew up his will in a letter to his publisher and friend Fritz Simrock. In it he provided, in the first place, for his sister Elise—his brother Fritz had already died, in 1886—and for his stepmother; secondly, for his faithful landlady, Celestiné Truxa, and his landlord in Ischl, which had become his second home. Further, he made donations to various musical associations of a charitable nature in Vienna and Hamburg, as well as to the *Gesellschaft der Musikfreunde,* to which he bequeathed, apart from his books and music, his valuable collection of original manuscripts.* While he was thus settling matters that had long been occupying his mind, the master had, in fact, already outgrown this melancholy mood of farewell. It is true that for the time being he undertook only tasks that did not require much creative effort; he revised for publication a collection of canons, most of which he had written in the days of the Hamburg ladies' choir; and he completed the Vocal Quartets, Op. 112, which he had begun in 1888.

Soon, however, he felt a surge of fresh creative power.

* The most outstanding pieces are the full scores of Mozart's Symphony in G minor, and of Haydn's six 'Sun' Quartets, two sheets of music, showing on the front page Beethoven's, on the back page Schubert's handwriting, various songs and dances by Schubert, numerous sketches by Beethoven, the first version of Schumann's Symphony in D minor, and the close of the concert version of Wagner's Prelude to *Tristan and Isolde.*

His good resolutions on the subject of opportune retirement availed him nothing; the powers of inspiration proved irresistible. Two months after he had made his will he sent from Ischl the score of his Clarinet Trio to his faithful 'Mandy,' and in response to the latter's enthusiastic praise he confessed that this work was only 'the twin to a far greater folly,' which he was now trying to 'feed up.' He was alluding to the wonderful Clarinet Quintet, a pearl among Brahms's chamber music. In both these compositions the preference for the clarinet is striking, as it was an instrument Brahms had hitherto never used for chamber music. The credit for having, unknowingly, inspired the master in this respect was due to the eminent clarinettist of the Meiningen Orchestra, Richard Mühlfeld. When visiting the ducal Court in March 1891, Brahms had been deeply impressed by the wonderful playing of the artist; thenceforth he bestowed his love upon this melancholy singer of the orchestra, whose tone was particularly appropriate for the serious mood of his later compositions. It goes without saying that *Fräulein Klarinette,* or 'his dear nightingale' as Brahms was wont to call Mühlfeld, on account of the exceptional sweetness of his tone, took part in the first performance of both works. This was given in Berlin, on 12 December 1891, in a concert of the Joachim Quartet, and the enthusiasm was so great that the Adagio of the Quintet had to be repeated. The famous historical painter, Adolf Menzel, was in the audience, and he was so impressed by the performance that he made a sketch of Mühlfeld as a sort of Greek god; and a few months later he sent the drawing to Brahms with the following words: 'We often think of you here, and often enough, comparing notes, we confess our suspicions that on a certain night the Muse itself appeared in person (disguised in the evening dress of the Meiningen Court) for the purpose of executing a certain woodwind part. On this page I have tried to capture the sublime vision.' [1]

During the musician's stay in Berlin a close friendship had

sprung up between Brahms and Menzel, who regarded each other as colleagues, each having received the Prussian Order *Pour le mérite*. They understood each other excellently in their general views of life and the world, and they also shared a peculiar appreciation of the more prosaic joys of life. The painter prepared mighty banquets in honor of his new friend, at which they ate, drank, and debated indefatigably; and even after spending as much as seven hours in this fashion, neither the seventy-six-year-old Menzel nor the all but sexagenarian Brahms felt in any degree tired, but positively refreshed. In April 1892 a nephew of Menzel's, Otto Krigar-Menzel, wrote to Brahms: 'I can truthfully assure you that we have never yet had such fine and enjoyable carousals as those of the December days when you were with us.' [2] We may gather from the same letter that Brahms had sought to obtain Menzel's assistance in procuring the *Pour le mérite* Order for Billroth—a proof of the affection which he still felt for his friend; the more so as it was never easy for him to make any request of the kind. It was, however, impossible for Menzel to fulfil Brahms's wish, as he had always insisted on the drawing of a strict line between the artistic and the scientific branch of the Academy. Brahms, of course, respected this attitude, and his friendship with Menzel remained undiminished, a constant joy and stimulus to both.

During these festive days in Berlin in 1891, Brahms—as he wrote himself—had Clara constantly in mind. Between these two friends of almost forty years' standing something had occurred which neither had thought possible: a difference of opinion that became so pronounced as to lead to a temporary rupture of their friendship. The cause was comparatively insignificant. Schumann's Symphony in D minor existed in two separate versions, which differed widely. Brahms, who possessed the first of these drafts, did his best, as early as 1888, to get it published, thinking it of far greater artistic value than the version already printed. For instance he wrote to Wüllner: 'I think it quite charming to

see how the beautiful work was given right away the loveliest
and most appropriate clothing. That later on Schumann
draped it so heavily may have been due to the bad Düsseldorf orchestra; thus all beautiful, free, and graceful motion
became impossible.' Wüllner quite agreed with his friend
and it was he who, on Brahms's instigation, edited the original score for Breitkopf & Härtel. Brahms repeatedly inquired whether Clara would agree to such a procedure. She
never gave her consent, but as she also never refused outright, he believed himself justified in taking her agreement
as a matter of course. In 1891, however, when the work appeared in print, Clara, who was always afraid of injuring
her husband's reputation by the production of works unpublished at the time of his death, was greatly surprised and
highly indignant. She replied to Brahms's attempts at an
explanation with a letter so worded that it was, as Brahms
said, quite apart from their friendship, 'too harsh even for a
merely honorable person,' and made further discussion impossible.

Brahms's impulsive reaction is quite comprehensible; ob-
jectively considered, Clara was in the wrong, as he had actually written to her on the subject of the Symphony. This
quarrel, however, was only a final pretext. For many years
past, a certain bitterness had been growing in Clara's heart,
as she increasingly missed in Brahms the confidence and
warmth and sincerity in which she herself was so rich. She
could not reconcile herself with Brahms's cool irony, and
she treated all his witticisms—which were sometimes clumsy
enough—in deadly earnest, often remembering for days, as
a bitter offense, some hasty word of his, which he himself
had at once forgotten. She also felt herself to be neglected
for new friends, and she was jealous of Elisabeth von Herzogenberg and Billroth, who were better able than she to
give utterance to their artistic impressions, so that they were
often the first to hear new works of the composer's. Now, in
her old age—Clara was already seventy-two—she was growing

increasingly sensitive. Every little difference with her beloved friend moved her deeply, and it is easily understood
that with a nature as open as Clara's their continuous small
misunderstandings had inevitably to bring about a crisis.
Much as Brahms was inclined to remain passive in such
cases, and to let things take their course, on this occasion he
felt uneasy. Was not his friendship at stake with one who,
despite the rich experiences that life had brought him, was
nearest to his heart? Now, when he searched his conscience,
he began to understand that he had deserved, by his conduct,
the 'great pain of her estrangement.' He realized that Clara
might have been outwardly in the wrong, but that essentially
she was in the right; and so for once it was he who took
the first step towards a reconciliation.

At Christmas 1891, he humbly approached her with an
affectionate letter of congratulation. Clara, too, could cherish her grievance no longer. Tentatively and hesitatingly
they regained the old cordial tone. The last decisive step was
taken by Brahms on Clara's next birthday. In order finally to
clear up their misunderstandings, he forced himself to confess the grievance he had been cherishing for years, and
which may have influenced his whole manner towards his
friend. In the complete edition of her husband's works, Clara
had failed to include several of Schumann's compositions for
the pianoforte first published by Brahms, and the composer,
with his inveterate distrust, had concluded that she had not
cared to see his name published in connection with that of
her beloved Robert. It was incomprehensible to Clara that
after so many years of artistic co-operation he could have
thought her capable of so base a motive, and she declared
that the omission could only have been due to sheer thought-
lessness on her part. Now Clara finally removed this grievance by asking Brahms to undertake the editing of a supplementary volume of the complete edition of Schumann's
works, in which not only the piano pieces in question, but

also other posthumous works, selected by Brahms, were to be included.

In this way the clouds on the horizon of their old friendship were dispelled. From now onwards Brahms's attitude to Clara was transformed; he was warm and cordial in his language, and indefatigable in such whimsical conceits and little attentions as might cheer and console the ailing old woman. The man's fundamental kindness of heart, too often concealed by a harsh exterior, was now clearly revealed. In the letters he wrote to Clara in these years is the mood of a quiet evening landscape bathed in the last rays of sunset.

A gentle tranquillity, combined with a certain unworldliness, increasingly took possession of the aging man; even when the circle around him grew smaller, as death robbed him of some of his dearest friends, this mood was essentially unshaken. In January 1892, Frau von Herzogenberg was carried off by a disease of the heart. It is true that Brahms's relations with 'wonderful Frau Liesel' had diminished in cordiality for some time past. The cause of this change is unknown, but it may have been due simply to the composer's deep-rooted horror of invalids—for first Heinrich von Herzogenberg and then his wife had been seriously ill for years. Now, however, when he had lost his friend forever, her graceful image recovered its former brilliance, and her memory was so sacred to him that he even refused to give some of her letters to her husband, for a projected publication of her correspondence, as they were for him 'one of the dearest memories of his life.'

His sister Elise died in the same year. There had never been any real spiritual bond between them, but if only for the sake of his beloved mother, who had always been on the best possible terms with Elise, Brahms would have thought of her with tenderness. He had, moreover, always made the most affectionate provision for her, and since nothing gave him such joy as to be able to help others, he must have felt her death as a grievous loss.

[182]

Through Elise's death, the necessity arose of altering his will. He asked Simrock to return his letter, and on the back of it made notes for a new draft, which show that, apart from a few legacies, he intended to leave the whole of his property to the *Gesellschaft der Musikfreunde*. Brahms omitted, however, to put this new will into legal form, so that after his death it was contested by various distant relatives, and an arrangement was reached only after prolonged discussion. Under the terms agreed upon, the *Gesellschaft der Musikfreunde* received all the books and music in the master's possession, as well as all letters, unless they had been claimed by their writers.

In 1893, hardly a year after her marriage, gay Hermine Spies died at the age of thirty-six. When Brahms received the news, he sat for a long time with the telegram before him, 'first without being able to think at all, then with his thoughts in a whirl.' He was bound to be deeply stricken by so cruel a fate, even though Hermine Spies the artist had been, for him, overshadowed by another star. Since the beginning of 1890, the master had taken the warmest interest in the contralto Alice Barbi, a singer of positively classical beauty, and quite unusual artistic accomplishment. Kalbeck's assumption that Brahms did not really discover Alice Barbi's artistic perfections until the year 1892 is disproved by a letter of the master's to Clara, dated February 1890, in which he declared that many things could not be sung more beautifully than by Barbi. In the autumn of the same year he arranged for her to visit Clara, wishing to give his friend an exceptional pleasure. His admiration for the singer constantly increased; he spoke to his friends of her achievements with unprecedented enthusiasm, and he, who now appeared publicly as a pianist only under the most exceptional circumstances, undertook to accompany the whole program of the farewell concert that Alice Barbi gave before her marriage to Count Stomersee; and even some years later than this he wrote to Clara that he had postponed his departure to Ischl because the singer had kept him in Vienna.

Without the Barbi episode we should not have a complete portrait of the elderly Brahms. He was imbued with a certain serene resignation; he was less sarcastic and bitter than in former years, and more considerate of others. The increasing wisdom of age, however, was often scattered to the winds by some poignant experience; for then the heart of the stout little man with the white beard beat as stormily as a youth's.

The sixtieth birthday of a musician who now enjoyed universal esteem was the occasion of many festivities. It will readily be understood that the artist, who had always been averse from such things, made a timely escape from Vienna. Fortunately his friend Widmann was free to join him on a visit to Italy. How much Brahms had longed for that is shown in a letter he wrote to Bülow a year previously:

So I arrive just in time while you gaily pack your trunks, to wish you from my heart everything fine and pleasant for your trip. By the way, the fact of your going to Italy, to breathe that glorious air and to bask in beauty . . . is a proof to me of the excellence of your health. Why don't I go myself to a country where every visit has disclosed more beauties and been more beneficial? Well, why should my usual and dear companion, I mean Widmann of Berne, have to stay at home? For such an adventure we need not only the same outlook but also the same robustness of limb.[3]

Unfortunately it was Widmann's leg, so highly praised by Brahms, that suffered on this Italian trip, which took the two friends, together with the conductor Friedrich Hegar and the pianist Robert Freund, to Sicily. On the return crossing to the mainland Widmann slipped so unluckily that his left ankle was broken, and Brahms spent his sixtieth birthday in a somewhat original manner, at his friend's bedside.

Many congratulations reached Brahms even in Italy. Thus Adolf Menzel wrote: 'Heartiest good wishes on your sixtieth birthday!!! Were I with you, I would draw a picture of you

—on your knees praying to St. Rosalie of Palermo!' [4] This, of course, was a jest, for Brahms was a strict Protestant. A telegram from the teaching staff of the Vienna Conservatoire, which erroneously congratulated the composer on his 'seventieth birthday,' was returned by him with the words: 'Not accepted: I protest!' [5]

After Brahms's return he had, as he wrote, 'to cut his way without too much shedding of blood and ink through more than fifty telegrams and countless letters.' As a special honor the *Gesellschaft der Musikfreunde* had commissioned the sculptor Scharff to design a Brahms medal, of which the master received a gold impression for himself and a number of bronze copies for distribution among his friends. He corresponded with Mandyczewski from Ischl in regard to the choice of recipients, and was glad to accept the latter's carefully drafted list of some fifty names, including the most faithful members of his circle—and, of course, not excepting Alice Barbi, and of English recipients, Sir George Grove. Brahms himself had more important business at Ischl. He continued, in Op. 118 and 119, the series of pianoforte pieces begun in the previous year with Op. 116 and 117. Among these there were several pieces of an earlier period, which were now marked by the style developed in the last few years.

Apart from these, he began a task that had long been tempting him, though the pressure of creative work had hitherto made its accomplishment impossible. Since his youth, he had always been greatly attracted by the German folk songs, and had collected them with untiring zest; and he now began to revise his favorites for a practical edition. He added a piano accompaniment, which revealed, notwithstanding its great simplicity, all the characteristics of his art; he compared the variations in the text with the earnestness of a philologist, and maintained, in connection with his work, an extensive correspondence with 'Mandy.' He derived the greatest enjoyment from this work; he told all his friends about it, speaking with an enthusiasm he never betrayed when his own creations were in question. To the publisher Simrock he wrote: 'I believe they will dazzle the Berlin Philistines like a ray of sunlight.'

When, however, the great series of seven-times-seven songs was completed, a melancholy event clouded his joy. During this work, his thoughts had often rested on the one friend who would especially appreciate them. This was the eminent historian, Philipp Spitta, who had for many years been among Brahms's most intimate friends, and to whom the Motets, Op. 74, had been dedicated. Brahms admired in Spitta the Bach biographer of genius and a pioneer of musicology, and he knew that the scholar was entirely at one with him in respect of the new publication. In the spring of 1894 he sent him songs for inspection, and was stricken with grief on receiving, instead of a reply, the news of Spitta's sudden death.

Altogether the year of 1894 was a painful one for Brahms. On 6 February Billroth died, and in him Brahms lost the friend whom he possibly had to thank—apart from the professional musicians of his innermost circle of friends—for the greatest intellectual stimulus. When Widmann sent his condolence, Brahms answered:

You express sympathy at the loss of my friend. I have felt this loss for years and shall feel it again and more and more strongly in the years to come. But just now I have had, as have probably many of his friends, a feeling of relief. . . His nature was extremely active right up to the last day of his life, but to me this activity was unpleasant and embarrassing as a mere shadow of his former energy and joy of life. . . Billroth had all the qualities, great and small, to ensure popularity. But I wished you could witness as I do, what it means to be loved in Vienna. This we [the Viennese] understand, while you [the Swiss] do not. Others don't wear their hearts so openly, they don't show their love so warmly and beautifully, as it is done here, mainly by the best of them; I mean: the real people, those occupying the cheapest seats in the theatre.

[186]

Only six days after Billroth's passing Brahms suffered another irreparable loss: his 'faithful baton,' Hans von Bülow, was released from his sufferings by death. Brahms was so profoundly shaken that he could not bring himself to write a personal letter of condolence to von Bülow's widow.* He asked Toni Petersen, the daughter of the burgomaster of Hamburg, to buy a wreath for him; at the same time, however, he honored Bülow's memory by giving a thousand marks each to two institutions that provided pensions for German musicians. Great was his wrath when, through Símrock's indiscretion, these gifts were made known to the public; and he complained to his friends: 'Now I look like any vulgar benefactor.'

A letter which he received from Hamburg in April 1894 may well have caused him grief of yet another kind. Now, at the age of sixty-one, the position was offered him that he had desired so fervently as a younger man. New members had been elected to the governing body of the Hamburg Philharmonic Orchestra—men who sincerely desired to make amends for the grievous wrong done to Brahms by their predecessors. Accordingly, after von Bernuth's retirement, they offered him the conductorship of the concerts, explaining beforehand that they would agree to his remaining at the head of the society for a year or two only if his creative work made a longer engagement impossible. As was only to be expected, Brahms refused, but he could not refrain from uttering the following words:

There are not many things that I have desired so long and so ardently at the time—that is at the right time. Many years had to pass before I could reconcile myself to the thought of being forced to tread other paths. Had things gone according to my wish, I might today be celebrating my jubilee with you, while you would be, as you are today, looking for a capable younger

* A beautiful performance of his own *Requiem* under Wilhelm Gericke, which Brahms attended at that time in Vienna, must have been of a particularly deep significance for the composer.

man. May you find him soon, and may he work in your interests
with the same good will, the same modest degree of ability, and
the same wholehearted zeal, as would have done yours very sincerely,

J. BRAHMS

Thus we see that this, the deepest wound in the master's
heart, was not yet healed, notwithstanding all the appreciation he had found, and in spite of the resignation of age.
To the uninitiated, however, Brahms must have seemed a
happy man, for it was his lot—a lot which has fallen to few
of the great masters—to receive universal admiration and understanding in his old age. If 1894 was the year of his deep
grief, 1895 was the year of the great Brahms festivals. The
festivities at Leipzig in January had a certain symbolic value,
showing, with particular clearness, the revolution in public
opinion. No less than three Brahms concerts were given in
a single week. In two concerts of chamber music the two
wonderful Clarinet Sonatas composed in the previous summer were performed, besides earlier works.* These were succeeded by an orchestral concert in which, in addition to the
Academic Festival Overture, both the Pianoforte Concertos
were played. This was a daring venture, and all the more
daring in Leipzig, where the D minor Concerto had suffered
so overwhelming a defeat thirty-six years earlier. Their success, however, was above all expectation. The composer himself conducted, and at the piano sat Eugen d'Albert, whose
art Brahms most highly esteemed. For a long while this excellent pianist had been among Brahms's greatest admirers,
and the idea of playing both Concertos on one evening was
due to his enthusiasm. It was no wonder that, thanks to the
co-operation of two such magnificent artists, these compositions made an unforgettable impression on the audience.

How warm d'Albert's feelings were for Brahms may be

* According to Lienau's *Memoirs,* Brahms was in his best form at
the piano, although he had partaken of an enormous lunch which
lasted until 3.30 P.M.

[188]

seen from the pianist's letter of thanks for the gift of a bust
of Brahms (by Tilgner):

Sincerest thanks for your kind words and good wishes, which
gave me great pleasure. This was indeed a happy time for me—
the arrival of the charming little bust made the day a festival.
For this, with all my heart, I give you my best thanks. The bust
stands always before me when I write, and reminds me of the
wonderful and unforgettable hours it was granted me to spend
with you. In the most sincere and ardent devotion,

Yours,

EUGEN D'ALBERT [6]

In September 1895 a music festival, lasting three days,
was held in Meiningen under Fritz Steinbach's leadership.
There Bülow's dogma of the 'three great B's' was realized
in the most impressive manner. Apart from the works of
Brahms, only compositions by Beethoven and Bach were performed, the audience feeling that the place of honor next
to these giants of tonal art was the rightful due of the living
master. Enthusiastic homage was also paid to Brahms at the
Zürich Music Festival in October 1895, where the *Triumphlied* was played before Beethoven's Ninth Symphony. Here,
too, Brahms was gratified by an honor of an exceptional
kind. In the painting on the ceiling of the newly erected
Tonhalle he saw his own portrait, together with those of
Beethoven, Mozart, and other immortal masters.

But above all triumphs and honors, among which the
conferring of the *Ehrenzeichen für Kunst und Wissenschaft*
by the Austrian Emperor must be mentioned, Brahms was
deeply moved by the act of an unknown English admirer.
The wealthy music-lover Adolph Behrens had always been
an ardent champion of Brahms's music. Years ago the first
English performance of the *Requiem* had been financed by
him, and he had also borne the expense of engaging the
clarinet player Mühlfeld, in order to provide the finest possible rendering of Brahms's last chamber-music works for

his compatriots. After Behrens's death his brother wrote to Brahms:

DEAR HERR BRAHMS,—I have to inform you on behalf of my brother, Mr. Frank Behrens, and myself that we hold at your disposal the sum of £1,000, which we know it was the desire of our late brother, Mr. Adolph Behrens, that you should regard as a slight token of gratitude and admiration for your art. May I ask you to be good enough to write and inform me to what banker you would wish the money to be remitted for your account. . .[7]

Brahms, who was besieged with letters, petitions, and inquiries from all corners of the earth, and who even had cards of refusal printed for troublesome writers, appreciated the rare delicacy and tact of the man who had apparently never thought of seeking personal contact with the master, in spite of his great admiration for him. Brahms was 'very deeply and sincerely moved,' and thought that one could not experience 'a finer or more beneficent action.' He used the magnanimous gift in the way most agreeable to him; that is, for donations of all kinds. The *Gesellschaft der Musikfreunde,* among others, received 6,000 florins, under the condition that the donor's name should not be mentioned, and that 1,000 florins should go to the Museum.

Just at this time such tactful homage was peculiarly grateful to Brahms. The master was in a softened mood. Clara's condition had for some time past been alarming, and on 26 March 1896 she had suffered an apoplectic stroke. Brahms could not close his eyes to the danger of her condition, and he had to familiarize himself with the inevitable. His mind dwelt upon his beloved friend, and he saw the shadow of death was drawing closer and closer. Just as thirty years earlier, so now the artist could find escape from the thought of death only in creation. After his mother's death he had completed the *Requiem;* now his fears for Clara and his prescience of her approaching end, and his own, found expression in the *Vier ernste Gesänge* (Four Serious Songs).

This work, which Brahms was never willing to hear performed at a concert, fearing that it would move him too deeply, was written in the first week of May 1896 and was finished on his birthday. On this day Clara sent him a few lines, whose meaning was not very clear; three days later a second stroke followed, and on 20 May 1896, the great artist and admirable wife and mother breathed her last. Brahms had lost the friend who, in his own words, was 'the most beautiful experience of his life, its greatest wealth and its noblest content.'

The news of Clara's death reached Brahms in Ischl, after some delay, his landlady having forwarded the telegram in a letter from Vienna. He started at once for Frankfort. In his mental preoccupation, however, he took the wrong train, and had to go back for some distance, arriving at Frankfort too late to attend the funeral service. Clara was buried at Bonn; he therefore continued his journey, and, after traveling for forty hours without a break, he arrived in time to throw a handful of earth into his beloved friend's grave. The great exertion, and even more the emotional strain, left their mark on the constitution of the man of sixty. After spending a few days with his Rhenish friends (Rudolf von der Leyen and his circle), days which were dedicated to the memory of Clara by the performance of noble and beautiful music, he regained some measure of outward calm. But when he returned to Ischl, and attempted to resume his accustomed mode of life, his changed appearance and sallow complexion attracted general attention. The young composer Richard Heuberger finally plucked up courage and urged Brahms to see a doctor. The master admitted that he did not feel well, and allowed himself to be examined by Dr. Hertzka, the Ischl physician. Hertzka diagnosed jaundice, and advised a cure of Karlsbad salts; for the sake of precaution, however, he called in the famous Viennese physician, Professor Schrötter, for the purpose of a consultation. Schrötter reassured Brahms, but told the worried Heuberger, in confidence, that he considered the master a lost man, his liver being greatly enlarged, and the gall ducts obstructed. Before long, cancer of the liver was plainly apparent, the same dread disease to which Brahms's father had succumbed.

After the failure of the cure of Karlsbad salts in Ischl, Brahms was sent to Karlsbad itself. He was accompanied by the faithful Dr. Fellinger, who had spent the last few days with Brahms at Ischl. The composer wrote a grateful letter to Frau Fellinger: 'I have reason to praise your husband to the skies, and to be grateful to him for his most touching kindness. . . It meant much to me at that time, and I can hardly tell you how pleasant it was. I do not like to be reminded of my body, and probably I should have stayed in Ischl in sheer sulkiness.' In Karlsbad, too, he was encompassed by his friends' care. Theodor Leschetitzky, the famous pianist, carefully warned the physician, Dr. Grünberger, and Frau Anna Seling, the proprietress of the hotel where Brahms was going to take his meals, of the composer's idiosyncrasies. Hanslick, moreover, saw to it that two musicians who were working in Karlsbad—Emil Seling and the choirmaster Alois Janetschek—were helpful to Brahms in every way. Several of his friends came to see the master: Faber, Brüll, Kössler (a composer and teacher of composition from Budapest, for whom Brahms had a great liking), and Amalie Nikisch, the wife of the conductor. Finally, Professor Engelmann of Utrecht came to Austria, ostensibly for professional purposes, and went to Karlsbad as a matter of course. When he had examined his friend the gravity of Brahms's condition was obvious to him. He could not, however, believe that the case was utterly hopeless, and accordingly, a few months later, he sent his son-in-law, an eminent surgeon, from Holland to Vienna for the purpose of a fresh examination.

It may be doubted whether Brahms realized his own condition. He who had always looked on illness as a blemish would be the last to admit that he himself was seriously ill.

BRAHMS AT THE AGE OF TWENTY, BY LAURENS

Accordingly, he kept up his spirits, and jested over the 'petty-bourgeois jaundice,' which was changing his 'Norman into a Gothic style.' He replied with equanimity to an anxious telegram from Frau Adele Strauss, the wife of the Waltz King: 'Your telegram was a very friendly greeting and I thank you sincerely for it. I have every reason to be well satisfied with my stay here—I hope I shall continue to be so, and am looking forward to an early and happy meeting.' [8]

Inwardly, however, he may have foreseen his approaching end. The only work written in the summer of 1896 (published after Brahms's death) was the *Eleven Choral Preludes* for the organ. They are, as it were, beyond the reach of earthly cares. It is doubtless of symbolic significance that the last piece of this series, containing, indeed, the last notes that Brahms ever wrote, is a fantasia on the chorale *O Welt ich muss dich lassen* (O World, I Must Depart from Thee).

On 2 October Brahms started from Karlsbad, and Janetschek arranged with the State railway that the carriage in which the composer was traveling should be heated, although according to the railway regulations the heating of carriages would be begun only a fortnight later. In Vienna it was soon manifest that Brahms had derived no advantage from the cure. His strength began to fail with alarming rapidity. Only a few months previously he had given all who encountered him the impression of a man in the full possession of his physical and artistic powers. Significant, for example, is the fact that the composer Edvard Grieg, who had spent some wonderful days with Brahms in Vienna in March 1896, asked the man of sixty-three to undertake the journey to Norway, and—what is more—expected great new works of him. He wrote at the time:

If you would only come to Norway. I could not indeed show you a 'frantic night' [referring to Mozart's *Figaro* with the subtitle 'A Frantic Day'], but something far better, 'a luminous night.' And quite certainly . . . something more: the secret place where the treasure—your Fifth Symphony—lies hidden!

Therefore, please, please come! The Norwegian landscape is great and solemn, as great and as solemn as your most beautiful inspirations. It is *bound* to be to your liking.[9]

Now, however, in the autumn of the same year, everyone who saw Brahms knew that a sick and aged man was before him. His appearance was so greatly changed that casual acquaintances did not recognize him. At parties he often fell asleep from sheer exhaustion; he became so thin that his clothes hung loosely upon him (although faithful Frau Truxa secretly took them in again and again, in the hope of making him believe that he had put on a little weight), and he also had an apoplectic stroke, the results of which the doctors explained to him as 'facial rheumatism.'

With all his gigantic energy he fought against the rapid increase of his illness. He still courageously took walking exercise as long as he could do so; after a time, however, this was no longer possible, and he therefore suffered his friends, mainly the faithful Millers and Fabers, to persuade him to go driving with them 'to keep them company.' He still was to be seen in the circle of his friends, and even at concerts, although seriously ill. The Christmas Eve of 1896 he spent, as he loved to spend it, with the Fellingers. On 2 January he attended a magnificent performance by the Joachim *ensemble* of his G major String Quintet, which moved him deeply—perhaps by the knowledge that he was soon to bid farewell to that great artist and friend. Joachim succeeded in drawing the reluctant composer on to the platform, and this elicited tumultuous applause. Even more impressive was the homage rendered by the Viennese on 7 March 1897, when Hans Richter conducted the Fourth Symphony at a Philharmonic Concert. Brahms sat in his usual place, the directors' box of the *Gesellschaft der Musikfreunde*. All who saw the beloved and familiar figure, now so terribly changed, were full of anxious compassion. Once again one and all wanted to show their love and respect for the beloved master, and the applause that broke forth after each movement was indescribable. The audience and the performers alike waved, shouted, and wept, with that genuine emotion which Brahms had himself so often praised in the Viennese. This was the last public performance of a work of his own that Brahms was to hear. On 13 March he made an effort for the sake of his dear Johann Strauss, and attended the first performance of the friend's new operetta, *Die Göttin der Vernunft*. After this, however, he was content to visit only his most intimate friends. Soon even this was too much for him. On 24 March he wrote to Joachim: 'I am going downhill; every word spoken or written is a strain.' Next day he took his last lunch outside his home. He visited the Millers, who were especially devoted to him; the other guests were his faithful 'Mandy' and 'Fräulein Klarinette.' On 26 March, however, he could no longer leave his bed.

Outside Vienna little was known of the change for the worse in Brahms's condition. In February Harold H. Widdop of Bradford had asked Brahms's permission to name the orchestral society of his native city, which played a Brahms work at every performance, the 'Brahms Society,' adding, in explanation, 'We all feel that we should like to establish a living statue of your great great genius in our town.' [10] At the same time the composer Frederick Cowen [11] asked Brahms to write a new work for the Cardiff Festival of the following year. Brahms's old acquaintance, Frau von Holstein, who had, when a young girl, written so charming a description of the young 'Messiah' promised by Schumann (see p. 38), unsuspectingly advised him to have his portrait painted by Vilma von Parlaghy, who had painted Kaiser Wilhelm and Bismarck as well as herself. Jokingly she remarked: 'It was hard to convince me that a pretty picture could be painted of an ugly woman; to my greatest amazement, however, I see that Parlaghy sees through to the ideal being and puts it on canvas without departing from the likeness.' [12]

Already Brahms was far beyond such things. Yet it may perhaps have pleased him that a friend should send [13] the

first violets from Rolandseck, as a greeting from the Rhine,
the sight of which had filled the youth with such joy forty-
four years previously. And the Rhine wine from the cellar
of his old friend Deichmann, with whom he had kept in
touch since the glorious year of 1853, may have afforded him
a last pleasure. But he soon sank deeper and deeper into
unconsciousness. When any help was given him, the master
who had, throughout his lifetime, been so appreciative of the
least friendly service, recovered sufficiently to show his gratitude; for the rest he was in a state of coma, and on 3 April
1897, at half-past eight in the morning, he breathed his last,
fortunately without great suffering.

The obsequies were eloquent proof that a prince in the
realm of music was being borne to the grave. The City of
Vienna and the *Gesellschaft der Musikfreunde* (the organ-
izers of the funeral) did their very utmost to honor the departed master. Other important musical centers sent representatives, and these came not only from Germany, but from
foreign countries also; from London, the faithful Cambridge
(which again in 1892 had offered Brahms the honorary degree of Doctor), Amsterdam, Paris, and many other cities.
In Brahms's native city, moreover, the flags were flown at
half-mast on all the ships in the harbor.

No near relatives walked behind the master's coffin, no
wife, no children; of the women who had made his life
beautiful only Alice Barbi did him the last honor.

Nevertheless, Brahms was escorted by true lovers to his
final resting place. Loyal and affectionate friends such as
Fuchs, Mandyczewski, Perger, Brüll, Door, Heuberger,
Henschel, Kalbeck, Fellinger, Miller, and Simrock shared
the honor of carrying the funeral torches. These names, however, are but a few taken at random. The funeral procession
that passed through the streets of Vienna extended further
than the eye could reach, and immense numbers of people
lined the road on either side. And these, too, were only a
small part of the vast community of all nationalities which

mourned this day for one of the greatest in the realm of tonal art.

The words of Agathe von Siebold, the great love of the artist's youth, had come to pass. Brahms could not belong to one alone. Unwedded and childless he had to tread life's paths, that he might bestow on all the riches of his soul, his mind, and his art.

UNPUBLISHED LETTERS REFERRED TO:

1. Letter from Adolf Menzel, 30 April 1892.
2. Letter from Otto Krigar-Menzel, 26 April 1892.
3. Letter from Brahms to Bülow, undated (April 1892).
4. Letter from Adolf Menzel, 7 May 1893.
5. Telegram in the possession of Alice von Meyszner-Strauss.
6. Letter from Eugen d'Albert, 7 April 1893.
7. Letter from E. Behrens, May 1896.
8. Letter from Brahms to Adele Strauss, 9 September 1896 (in the possession of Alice von Meyszner-Strauss).
9. Letter from Edvard Grieg, 1 April 1896.
10. Letter from Harold H. Widdop, 18 February 1897.
11. Letter from Frederick Cowen, March 1897.
12. Letter from Hedwig von Holstein, 16 March 1897.
13. Letter from Julie Schnitzler, 29 March 1897.

PART TWO

HIS WORK

XIV

BRAHMS'S LIFE WORK

Brahms's artistic development proceeded slowly and steadily. Nevertheless, research reveals several landmarks in the master's creative activities, which can be co-ordinated with special events in his life. Thus it is possible to distinguish four periods in Brahms's artistic development, each of which has a character of its own.

The *first period* of Brahms's development included the earliest existing works up to 1855. This was the time of his growing friendship with Joachim, his affectionate relations with Robert Schumann, and his passionate love for Clara Schumann. Under the influence of a highly romantic nature, Brahms then considered the purport of his work to be more important than its form. The classical symmetry of his later compositions was sometimes lacking in these works of the *Sturm und Drang* period, but the emotional expression was often of elemental strength. The young Brahms was hard, almost to harshness; he loved blunt expression and sudden contràsts, and avoided concessions to mere comprehensibility; nevertheless, his works were imbued with simplicity and a profound tenderness. Already in his creative work the folk song played an important role. In the use of instruments Brahms showed a certain monotony, for—as with the young Schumann—the piano was his principal means of expression.

Brahms never disowned these first works of his youth; but in a certain sense he very soon detached himself from them. With his friend Joachim he began fresh studies of counterpoint, and when, after an apparent pause, he came forward with new compositions in the year 1855, his style had changed considerably. The romantic, highflown youth had developed, both in his life and in his work, for both his intellectual outlook and his mode of self-expression had acquired lucidity and tranquillity. In the works of the *second period* he sometimes directly followed classic models. The violent eruptions of his earlier works were abandoned, and his compositions became mellower, softer, more intimate and meditative. His 'twilight' style, with its peculiar blending of moods, was already in evidence. As yet Brahms had not found his wonderful counterpoise of romantic longing and classical repose, and it is characteristic of this second period that he often completely recast a finished work. An example of this is the F minor Piano Quintet, which was originally a string quintet, then a sonata for two pianos, before it acquired its final form. At this time Brahms had not a permanent home, nor had his style as yet achieved a definite form. He was clearly passing through a period of transition, in which youthful vigor was coupled with the symptoms of approaching maturity. It is therefore comprehensible that he should have turned his attention mainly to chamber music. The piano, which had attracted him so strongly in the first period, no longer seemed adequate; yet the way to the great choral and orchestral works could be covered only step by step.

The *third period* opened with the elaboration of the *German Requiem,* the first great choral composition written by Brahms, which was also the first to make his name generally known. Although its conception belongs in part to the previous ten years, the final form was given to it in the middle 'sixties. At about the same time Brahms introduced a certain degree of definite order into his life by establishing himself in Vienna. In this period the master's art attained its climax; the peculiar 'Brahmsian' combination of the spirits of the sixteenth, seventeenth, eighteenth, and nineteenth centuries reached its highest development. Now the formal perfection of his works fully equaled their content; the composer reached the highest peak of his development in the use of tonal resources, and all his big orchestral and choral works were created during this period. Intellectual and spiritual concentration became the guiding principle of his work; he expressed himself in as concise and pregnant a manner as possible, and his compositions gained thereby in power, and even in tragic violence. Gradually the emotional content of his work became more serious, and we find more of those singularly lusterless pieces, full of indefinite melancholy, which form an essential constituent of the whole body of his work. It is characteristic of this period that the joyous and effervescent Scherzo of his youthful works gave way to quieter and serener forms.

In the year 1890, after the completion of his G major String Quintet, Brahms felt that his creative powers were exhausted. He regarded his life work as finished, and a little later, in the spring of 1891, he made his will. Henceforth he purposed only to set his older unpublished works in order, to destroy what seemed worthless, and to revise other compositions for publication. But Brahms had resigned himself prematurely. Before long his creative impulse revived and he began to produce works that were in many respects unlike his former compositions. In the *fourth period* his style was still more serious, more reticent, and at the same time more natural. There are no great orchestral or choral compositions in this period, for Brahms had reverted to the chamber music, the pianoforte music, and the songs of his youth. His technical refinement increased and his intellectual concentration became more intense as he diminished the external scope of his work. His inspiration occasionally lost something of its freshness; but up to the very last there was no decline, rather an increase of spiritual potency and formal constructive power.

In the following chapters we shall group Brahms's works

[203]

under the instruments for which they were written, and arrange them chronologically within each group. The changes in style distinguishing one period from the other will become especially clear if we consider together those works that employ the same means of expression.

XV

COMPOSITIONS FOR THE PIANOFORTE

THE earliest of Brahms's compositions for the pianoforte is the *Scherzo in E flat minor*, Op. 4, which was composed in 1851. In more than one sense the boy of eighteen follows closely on the heels of his predecessors. The unconscious resemblance in this work to the opening of Chopin's B flat minor Scherzo (Brahms, b. 10 *et seq.*; Chopin, b. 1 *et seq.*) is of no great importance; of greater significance, however, is the derivation of one of the main themes (b. 45 *et seq.*) from the Overture to Marschner's *Hans Heiling*, and finally, the inclusion of two Trios—so unusual in Brahms —points to the influence of Schumann or his disciples. Nevertheless, this first work reveals individual features both in its vigorous, virile, astringently cheerful spirit, and in the art with which the different motives of the piece are organically connected. Note, for example, how the second subject in the Scherzo is linked to the first by the same percussive motive, and how in the second trio (b. 80 *et seq.*) a theme from the first trio (b. 38 *et seq.*) recurs. And last but not least, the peculiar style of the composition, which is set as though for strings and wind instruments, gives one the impression that Brahms was really writing the piano score of an orchestral composition. Numerous sequences of octaves and sundry passages demanding great width of span contribute to this character. Apart from the absence of sequences in thirds and sixths, and the rhythmic changes between the hands that Brahms favored so greatly in the ensuing pianoforte pieces, the essential characteristics of his technique in the first two creative periods may already be detected in the Scherzo.

Brahms followed up the E flat minor Scherzo with the

powerful triad of Pianoforte Sonatas, of which the earliest is the *Sonata in F sharp minor,* Op. 2, written in November 1852. In this work, the fair, youthful head of the inspired disciple of Jean Paul Richter seems to be gazing out at us. Here we have the utterance of youthful exuberance, passion, and stubborn rebellion, together with passages that have the tenderness and intimacy of folk songs and vague, dreamy, tone pictures. In this Sonata, Brahms does not conceal his intimate relation to the Romantic movement, although he still endeavors to achieve the ideal outward forms of Haydn, Mozart, and Beethoven. For instance the titanic opening of the first movement (b. 1-15) gives one the impression of a rhapsodic introduction rather than the main theme so necessary for the construction of a Sonata movement. The *sostenuto* at the beginning and end of the Finale, in which we find runs of the hand that the composer was elsewhere so careful to avoid, only shows the artist's desire to break away from the conventional laws of form, which are still felt as fetters, by the insertion of vague, impressionistic passages. But Brahms would not have been himself if he had not, on the other hand, tried to counterbalance any tendency towards a romantic loosening of form. This he did partly by the characteristic contrapuntal blending of the different themes (cf., for example, first movement, b. 162 *et seq.*) afterwards applied by Wagner in the Prelude to *Die Meistersinger.* He also utilized the old principle of thematically relating the different movements, which he found employed in the nineteenth century by Liszt. The Andante, probably the most valuable movement in the Sonata, introduces three free variations on a simple and tender theme inspired by the *Winter Song* of a German Minnesinger (Kraft von Toggenburg). The theme of the Scherzo is really a fresh variant of the same idea. In the same way the beginning of the introduction to the Finale has a certain resemblance to the principal theme of the first movement. Everywhere we find a romantic overflow of imagination in conflict with a sense of form influenced by classic models. And it is just because these contrasting qualities are not always perfectly balanced that this youthful Sonata is particularly lovable.

In January 1853, shortly before Brahms left Hamburg, the first, second, and fourth movements of the *Sonata in C major* for the pianoforte were created. The Andante was written the year before. In this composition Brahms at last felt that he had written something worth offering to the world as his Op. 1, and rightly so; for it is greatly superior, in its unity and concentration, though not in its musical value, to the earlier Sonata. This is especially true of the first movement, which is full of vigor and vitality—and a proof of Brahms's devotion to Beethoven. It is probably only by chance that the first theme is reminiscent of the beginning of the *Hammerklavier Sonata*, but it has a symbolical significance. The repetition of the joyous first theme a tone lower than in the beginning (compare the *Waldstein Sonata*), the gain of the transitional passage from the contrapuntal elaboration of this subject, the effective preparation for the tender secondary subject, the tense development, and the powerful Coda attached to the recapitulation—all this is conceived in the spirit of Beethoven. The wonderful, lyrical second movement, which shows the closest relation to the Andante of the F sharp minor Sonata, includes free figural variations on an old German *Minnelied* (*Verstohlen geht der Mond auf*), to which the master returned on several occasions in later years. Here the simple melody, which has the quality of a folk song, assumes a form greatly beloved by Brahms, that of a dialogue between soloist and chorus, above which Brahms even copied the text. This quiet, simple movement is followed by a loud and almost brutally gay Scherzo. One can understand why the ailing Schumann was shocked by this movement, although he must have been profoundly moved by the wonderful, romantic, soaring Trio (*Più mosso*). In the Finale—a Rondo with Coda—the main theme of the first movement is repeated with rhythmical changes. Even in this movement, so full of wild vitality, a simple theme, like a folk-song melody (A minor, 6/8 time) provides a temporary rest. Brahms himself stated that one of Burns's songs (*My Heart's in the Highlands,* which was also set to music by Schumann) had inspired him in this movement.

The third *Sonata, in F minor,* Op. 5, is the last and greatest of Brahms's Sonatas for the pianoforte. Its first, third, and fifth movements were written in October 1853 and the second and fourth at an earlier date. In its formal construction this Sonata is a significant experiment. Instead of the usual four, there are five movements, as was customary in the old *divertimenti.* The sequence of tempi is now quick-slow-quick-slow-quick, securing all the more symmetry inasmuch as the two slow movements are closely related in thematic material. It seems a pity that Brahms failed to employ this form in his later Sonatas. The introductory movement of the Sonata is developed with indomitable energy. The opening bars seem to be beaten out of steel by cyclopean hands, and the leading motive (b. 1, 2nd and 3rd quarter notes), with appropriate modifications, prevails during the whole movement. Having recognized the themes introduced in bars 7 and 23 as variants of this motive, one can but admire the intense concentration of this movement, a concentration which Brahms achieved again only in his ripest works. And what tremendous progress he made in a single year, from the fantastic, almost formless, introductory movement of the Sonata in F sharp minor to the compression of this dramatic composition! The second movement, in its general mood, is closely related to the slow movements of the first two Sonatas. A line from a love song by Sternau, printed at the beginning of this section, indicates the emotional content of this tender and dreamy Nocturne. It is not surprising that the impressive Coda of the Andante flashed through Wagner's mind (he had heard the Sonata in 1863), when he wrote the lovely passage in *Die Meistersinger:* 'A right good bill has the bird that sang today!' The Scherzo, with its wist-

ful Trio, is followed by the fourth movement, an Intermezzo, *Rückblick* (Reminiscence) which repeats in a modified form the main theme of the second movement. In this
movement the almost orchestral inventive quality, so characteristic of Brahms's early works, is very pronounced. Ever
and again one seems to hear kettledrums, contrabasses, wood
wind, strings, and sometimes a full orchestra. The Finale,
written in free Rondo form, brings the composition, in the
manner of Beethoven, to a victorious conclusion. Through
various contrasting moods it fights its way with irresistible
power to a mighty and triumphant end.

With this imposing third Sonata Brahms took a final leave
of the Pianoforte Sonata. He had found a satisfactory solution of its problems, which he approached in many different
ways. Now a fresh task attracted him of hardly less importance for his creative work: the composition of variations.
And a decade later, when he seemed to have mastered this
form also, and had arrived at full artistic maturity, he lost
interest in compositions for the pianoforte as such, and reserved the Sonata with several movements for chamber music
and the orchestra, henceforth writing only small pieces, in
a single movement, for the piano.

In the spring of 1853, the *Variations on a Hungarian Song*
were composed during the concert tour with Reményi. They
were published as Op. 21/2. These were not only the first set
of Variations to be published by Brahms as an independent
work; they were also his first composition that dealt with
the Hungarian folk song, which was to play such an important part in his future work. The racy theme of this work
(changing in alternate bars from 3/4 to 4/4 time) is the
basis of a number of characteristically vigorous variations;
Brahms's art of allowing the individual variations to proceed
logically one from another, and welding the short pieces
into organically self-contained groups, is already fully developed in this first work. This is particularly clear in the
last five variations, where the tempo constantly accelerates,

until at last, in the *doppio movimento,* the vigorous Coda commences. In a purely technical sense Brahms keeps scrupulously to the melody of the theme in these variations. Now it is transposed into the bass, now into the minor key; now some of its intervals are modified, or intervening notes are inserted here and there; but the structure of the melody is always preserved and is clearly discernible.

In the summer of 1853 Brahms made the acquaintance of the Schumanns. Before long an intimate friendship developed, and the feelings that the young master entertained for the two artists found expression in the *Variations on a Theme by Robert Schumann,* Op. 9, of which Nos. 1-9 and 12-16 were written in June and Nos. 10 and 11 on 12 August 1854 (Clara Schumann's *Saint's Day*). The manuscript of this composition is in the possession of the *Gesellschaft der Musikfreunde,* and bears the title *Little Variations on a Theme of His, dedicated to Her.* The whole work is an act of homage to the beloved pair. The young man's devotion is expressed not only in the choice of the theme, which is taken from Schumann's first *Albumblatt,* Op. 99, or in the fact that his ninth variation is a paraphrase of Schumann's second *Albumblatt,* while the thirtieth bar of the tenth variation begins with the 'theme of Clara Wieck' from Schumann's *Impromptus,* Op. 5 (No. 1, b. 17 *et seq.*). It is even more significant that this wonderfully vivacious and emotional work follows, in the whole of its formal arrangement, in the steps of Schumann's art, as revealed, more particularly, in his *Etudes Symphoniques.* They are fanciful variations, which do not adhere strictly either to the formal structure or to the harmonization of the theme, but are freely superimposed upon its melody. Not only the treble of the theme, but the bass also is modified in three variations (Nos. 2, 10, 16), in which the bass melody sometimes becomes the treble. Following the example of Bach's *Goldberg Variations,* Brahms displays all the resources of contrapuntal art. No. 8 introduces a canon in the octave, No. 14 one in seconds, and No. 15 one in sixths. In No. 10 the melody (originally the bass of the theme) is even employed as a canon of the inversion: every interval that carries the treble downwards is answered in the bass by a rise of the same interval, and vice versa. At the same time the middle voices repeat the subject in diminution. It should be noted that this *non plus ultra* of contrapuntal art, which was written, together with the eleventh variation, in a day, bears in the manuscript the superscription, 'Roses and Heliotrope have bloomed.' It is characteristic of Brahms that a purely romantic idea could inspire him to a creation of the strictest structural perfection.

To give Schumann pleasure (he was then at Endenich), Brahms sent him the Variations. While under the first impression of the work, the invalid wrote on a slip of paper, on which various notes and drafts of letters were jotted down, an impulsive letter of thanks. As this—hitherto unknown—document deals principally with the Variations, it may be reproduced in this connection:

MY DEAREST FRIEND,
What very great pleasure you have given me with your Variations! My Clara has already written to tell me how delighted she was with them. That you have studied counterpoint deeply is apparent in all the Variations. How tender. how original in its masterly expression, how ingenious every one of them! How I should like to hear you or Clara play them! And then, the wonderful variety! The third, the fourth, the fifth, the sixth with its retrogression in the second part. The following Andante, how tender; the eighth with its beautiful second part. Then the ninth, how beautiful in form; the tenth, how full of art, how tender; how individual and delicate the eleventh, and how ingeniously the twelfth joins it! Then the thirteenth, with its sweet metaphysical tones, and next the Andante, with its witty and artistic canon in seconds, and the fifteenth in G flat major, the sixteenth beautifully and blessedly ending in F sharp major. How sincerely my Clara and I have to thank you for your dedication!

I thank you also most heartily for giving so much of your precious time to my Clara. Write to me; I should be delighted.

Your admiring friend,

ROBERT

Schumann never dispatched these lines. The letter of thanks actually written to Brahms on 27 November 1854 shows a more carefully revised style, but does not deal with all details of the composition and does not so clearly express the first enthusiasm of the writer.

That same summer of 1854 witnessed the birth of *Four Ballads*, Op. 10. The first, a setting of a Scottish ballad, *Edward*, is frequently heard, and rightly, for the tragic power of this tremendous piece could hardly be surpassed The entirely successful experiment of describing the catastrophe in a major key in the middle section, or the Epilogue (Tempo I), expressing quivering unrest by triplets following the beat, would alone suffice to betray the hand of a master. The maturer and more tranquil Brahms was much less capable of dealing with this strange and daemonic subject, which he set to music for a second time twenty-three years later (Op. 75/1). In the other Ballads also passages of the greatest merit occur. For example, the Intermezzo (No. 3) is closely related in mood to the E flat minor Scherzo—but how much more concise and effective Brahms's expression has become in the short span of three years! No. 2 rivets the attention as much by the tender melody of its main section as by the interesting coloration of the middle portion (B major). In its mood No. 4 is akin to Schumann, whose influence may be discerned also in the simplification of the pianoforte technique.

The *Ballads* are the last composition for the pianoforte of Brahms's first creative period. He began a new series of studies in composition for the purpose of learning the secret of the effortless style of classical polyphony, which, despite all that he had already achieved in this respect, still seemed to him the ideal towards which he must strive. Only a few of these studies have been preserved; among them are the two *Gigues* and two *Sarabands* written in 1855. They show how completely Brahms had familiarized himself with the style of J. S. Bach. Although one should not judge these pieces as independent compositions, it may be noted that Brahms took from the first Saraband some essential themes for the slow movement of his String Quintet, Op. 88, composed almost thirty years later.

In his new studies of composition, Brahms included the Variation form. According to a letter to Joachim, written in June 1856, he was striving towards a severer, purer form of variation, the result of which is shown in his *Variations on an Original Theme,* Op. 21/1, written about this time. Adherence to the melody of the theme (or even to its bass), which was characteristic of the variations of his first period, is now completely neglected, whereas in this astringently flavored work he adheres strictly, in all the variations, to the periodic structure and harmonies of the theme. In the fifth variation, with a canon of the inversion, he penetrates again into the region of counterpoint. In this composition Brahms's requirement, expressed in his letters and his teaching of G. Jenner, that the bass carrying the harmony, or, to put it more simply, the harmony of the theme, should be easily discernible in each variation, is realized for the first time.

In the *Variations and Fugue on a Theme by Handel,* Op. 24, written in 1861, Brahms reached his completest mastery of the Variation form. In this work all the principles of variation followed in the older works are united for the first time. In the great majority of the twenty-five variations the harmonic and periodic structure of the theme is scrupulously preserved, while due regard is paid to the melody. Precisely because of the strict limitations the master imposed upon himself, the wealth of imagination and technical skill he displays in this work give it a very special position among his compositions for the pianoforte. It is not easy to say which deserves greater admiration—the logical concatenation of the individual variations, their firm organic cohesion, the profound spiritual vitality of the work, or its purely technical effectiveness as pianoforte music. Passing from the quietly gay first variation, still in the spirit of Handel, through the two softly veiled pieces in the minor key (Nos. 5 and 6), the trumpet variations (Nos. 7 and 8), the delicate canon (No. 16), the Siciliana (No. 19), the 'Musical Box' (No. 22), and the great final climax (Nos. 23-5) to the powerful crowning Fugue—the whole is a masterpiece, in which the strictest adherence to the rules and the greatest freedom are miraculously balanced.

In November 1861, Brahms wrote his first piano duet, *Variations on a Theme by Robert Schumann*, Op. 23. This theme is Schumann's *Letzter Gedanke* (Last Inspiration), which the artist, already mentally unsound, wrote shortly before his attempted suicide, on 27 February 1854, as a basis for variations, in the belief that the spirits of Mendelssohn and Schubert had given him this inspiration.* Brahms's composition is in every respect conceived as an act of homage to the memory of his deceased friend. The principle of the Handel Variations is followed here also, but in a modified degree; there is greater freedom in the outline of the variations—a legacy from Schumann, with the result that there is a resemblance to Brahms's earlier Schumann Variations. The melancholy mood of the theme is preserved throughout the work, and when the last variation closes with a triumphant funeral march, it seems as though Brahms were speaking to the spirit of his friend in the words of St. Paul, which he set to music in his *Requiem:* 'Death is swallowed up in victory.'

* Actually, the tender tune was inspired by the main theme of the slow movement of Schumann's own Violin Concerto, composed a few months earlier, a fact that escaped the notice of the composer as well as of his friend. See the publication of Schumann's own set of variations by the author of this book (London, 1939).

The last set of variations of his second period is the *Variations on a Theme by Paganini*, Op. 35, headed 'Studies for the Pianoforte,' consisting of two volumes, each containing fourteen variations. They were written in the years 1862-3, as the result of the technical exercises at which Brahms worked together with the pianist Karl Tausig at the time of his first stay in Vienna. In these variations on a theme, which offers hardly more than a harmonic skeleton, the classical variation technique of Op. 24 comes into its own again. From an artistic point of view, however, these two volumes cannot be compared with the earlier work. All Brahms's skill in writing pianistically difficult passages—runs in thirds, sixths, and octaves, passages with both hands in rhythmically contrary motion, glissandi, and tremendous stretches—is here brought into play, in order to exhibit the pianist's virtuosity. Even the quieter episodes—e.g. No. 11 of the first or No. 4 of the second series—do not affect the main characteristics of the work. It is a brilliant and effective composition for the concert hall, and, by way of exception, one in which the technical interest predominates, rather than the spiritual.

In connection with the Paganini Variations the Pianoforte Studies should be mentioned, in which Brahms merely arranges the works of other composers, or devises ingenious finger exercises. Such pieces were written by the composer throughout his life. They serve to perfect the playing of sixths (*Etude, after Chopin*), the development of equal strength in both hands (*Presto, after Bach*), or the technique of the left hand (*Rondo, after Weber; Impromptu, after Schubert*), and the use of the left hand alone (*Chaconne, by Bach*). The *Fifty-one Studies for the Pianoforte* contain the essential qualities of the whole of Brahms's pianoforte style and are most valuable for the practice of both hands, and especially for the absolute independence of either hand. As a matter of fact, Brahms wrote a great many more exercises for his own use, or for teaching purposes, than he ever published. In a manuscript owned by the Viennese pianist Paul Wittgenstein we find, for instance, the following exercises for the development of the technique of the thumbs and the width of span:

EXAMPLE 1

(Mit dem Daumen) With the Thumb

(Mit dem Daumen) With the Thumb

Brahms's humor is apparent in the title, for the admirer of the romantic poet E. T. A. Hoffmann calls these dry exercises *Fantasiestücke in Callots kühnster Manier* (Imaginative Pieces in Callot's Boldest Manner). In this connection may be mentioned the cadenzas to the Concertos of Bach (D minor), Mozart (G major and D minor), and Beethoven (G major and C minor). Although the author adapts himself in every respect to the spirit of the original work, his personality and the individuality of his technique are very apparent. For the sake of completeness we may mention the adaptation for the piano of a Gavotte from Gluck's *Paris and Helen,* made for Clara Schumann, in which piece Brahms creates a real orchestral atmosphere.

In the winter of 1863-4 Brahms worked on the arrangement for two pianos (published as *Sonata* Op. 34b) of his String Quintet in F minor, composed in 1862. Later we shall return to its third and final setting as a pianoforte quintet, but here we need consider only its specific qualities as a composition for the pianoforte. This version, as well as the original string quintet which Brahms himself abandoned, does not always sound quite satisfactory. Two pianos, of course, cannot produce contrasting effects of timbre, and the rich invention of this comprehensive work in four movements is sometimes masked by its too dense and monochromatic content. The full effect of the magnificent composition is realized only in its final setting for two contrasting types of instrument (piano and strings).

With the Paganini Variations, Brahms took leave of the titanic technique of his youth. What he in later years thought of his earlier works is shown by a volume of his early pianoforte pieces in the possession of the *Gesellschaft der Musikfreunde*, Vienna, containing a number of comments by the composer himself. In one place, in the Scherzo of the Sonata in F sharp minor, which requires an exceptionally wide span, he gave an alternative easier rendering. headed by the words *più facile*. The passage in the introduction to the Finale of the same Sonata is marked with an impatient 'N.B.' (Nota bene). And the overelaborate tenth variation of the *Variations on a Theme by Robert Schumann* is marked not only with 'N.B.,' but with a query as well. Only the Ballads and the Handel Variations seemed to give him full satisfaction.

The first of his pianoforte compositions of the third period, a work neither difficult to play nor to understand, is a simple and charming cycle of sixteen *Waltzes* in duet form, which Brahms wrote in January 1865 and published as Op. 39. With this delightful work Brahms enters into the artistic spirit of the city of Schubert and Johann Strauss. The Viennese *Ländler* and waltzes predominate, but there is also a Hungarian note. It would be difficult to conceive that this joyous, carefree music was the work of the North German master, were it not for the last item, a more thoughtful and contemplative waltz in double counterpoint.

Even more. than the waltzes, the *Hungarian Dances* for two pianos, of which the first two volumes were published

in 1869, are proof of the master's versatility as a creative
artist. In this work Brahms arranged Gipsy tunes which he
had collected at various times after his concert tour with
Reményi. It is not surprising that these Dances achieved an
unparalleled success, for in them Brahms contrived, while
preserving the characteristic melody, harmony, and rhythm
of Gipsy music, to give it an artistic form which raised it to
a higher level. None of his many predecessors or followers
has approached his success in this direction. Only a musician
with Brahms's knowledge of folk song would have been
capable of this twofold achievement. In 1880 two more volumes of Hungarian Dances were published, comprising also
three original compositions (Nos. 11, 14, 16). This second
series is more artistically written and more profound, and
therefore a little more Brahmsian than Hungarian. Is it astonishing that this series achieved less popularity than the
first?

The *Variations on a Theme by Joseph Haydn,* Op. 56,
completed in the summer of 1873, will occupy our attention
later in their more significant form as an orchestral composition (see p. 251). Here we will mention only the edition in
which they appear as a pianoforte duet, which, according to
Orel, was the first version to be written, although from the
outset Brahms had intended to write an orchestral work.
Very elaborate preliminary sketches of this work were preserved, an unusual course for Brahms, and these are now in
the possession of the *Gesellschaft der Musikfreunde.* These
sketches comprise no less than twelve closely written pages,
and are apparently the first draft of this work. Although
Brahms revised and altered them to some extent, it may be
noted that in this first sketch all the characteristics of the
complete work are already evident. This is the case even in
the masterly *basso ostinato* of the Finale, which is already
full of significant details. Brahms had apparently developed
this powerful composition to a great extent before writing
it down. If what has been said of the eleventh variation of

Op. 9 is recalled, it will be clear that the master's imagination rose to the greatest heights when under the constraint of the strictest laws. The pianoforte setting contrasts favorably in clarity and lucidity with the earlier *Sonata for Two Pianos*. With its sparse application of color effects this lovely work makes a profound impression even in its initial stages.

The Haydn Variations were the composer's last extensive work for the pianoforte. They are followed by the *Klavierstücke*, Op. 76, written between 1871 and 1878. Four quietly reflective Intermezzi and four Capriccii, with considerably more movement, though they have no real relation to one another, make a loosely bound sheaf of characteristic pieces. The diminished formal scale of the work corresponds to a technical limitation. As in the duets of his mature period, so here the pianoforte setting is much simpler than in the compositions of his youth. Brahms had relinquished his orchestral method of writing, and had approached more nearly to the style of Schumann and Chopin, which is particularly suited to the nature of the instrument. In general it is characteristic of Brahms's mature compositions that their performance is conceivable only upon the instrument for which they were written. In their mood the pieces of Op. 76 are introspective rather than outwardly brilliant. So the agitated first, the delicate second, the third, with its characteristic color effects, the tender seventh, and the swiftly gliding eighth, are all more suitable for playing in private than in public.

The *Two Rhapsodies*, Op. 79, written in the summer of 1879, are the most temperamental of the pianoforte compositions of the third period. From the dramatic, ballad-like character of the magnificent pieces it might almost be imagined that they were works of Brahms's youth. On closer inspection, however, a fundamental difference becomes apparent. Although Brahms has chosen a larger form for the weightier contents of the Rhapsodies, especially for the more important second Rhapsody, a severity and clarity is here attempted which he never attained before his maturity. We may compare the final Rondo of the Sonata, Op. 1, with the Rondo of the first Rhapsody; or the Sonata form of the first movement of Op. 2 with that of the second Rhapsody: the advance effected in the intervening twenty years towards the goal of simplicity and concentration will be clearly apparent.

Four collections, published in 1892 and 1893, and belonging to the master's fourth period of creation, conclude Brahms's compositions for the pianoforte. We shall consider them together, because of their spiritual affinity. They are the *Fantasien*, Op. 116, comprising three Capriccii and four Intermezzi, the three *Intermezzi*, Op. 117, the *Klavierstücke*, Op. 118, including four Intermezzi, one Ballad, and one Romance, and the *Klavierstücke*, Op. 119, including three Intermezzi and one Rhapsody. Some of these compositions may have been written at an earlier period; particularly the Capriccio, Op. 116/1, which recalls the mood of the *Edward* Ballad, and the melancholy and magnificent Rhapsody, Op. 119/4. Also the folksong-like Intermezzo, Op. 117/1, prefaced by the first lines of an old Scottish cradle song, reminds us of the slow movements in the Sonatas of his youth, although the older Brahms, too, was much occupied with folk song. However this may be, all these works received their final form in the master's fourth creative period. This fact is already indicated by the simple three-part song form in all the twenty numbers of these four works. Moreover, the striving for simplicity and concentration is very pronounced in these later compositions. The modulations are more limited, the harmony less complicated, the rhythm more uniform, and the art of musical economy is almost unsurpassed. On closely examining the Intermezzo, Op. 119/2, the surprising discovery will be made that the soft, sweet Viennese middle section in E major and the austere and sharply contrasting preceding and following sections in E minor are built upon the same theme, which comprises only a few notes. The characteristic leaning of the composer, in later years, to pre-classical art is expressed in these pieces; for instance, in the middle section of Op. 118/5 the same bass subject returns again and again, in the manner of an *ostinato*. In this series, however, the mood of the tenderly veiled idyll predominates, and it is typical of the resigned attitude of these pieces that Op. 119/4, the last number, though it begins in the major key, closes in the minor. Bach and Beethoven liked to follow the opposite direction. The fact that Brahms occasionally allotted the melody to the middle voice (e.g. Op. 117/1, 118/5, 119/3) enhances the impression of mystery, and at the same time adds to their colorful charm. The musical invention is absolutely suited to the instrument, as is the case with all the compositions of his last two periods; a fact strikingly confirmed if we remember that Brahms's attempt to arrange the quickly popularized Intermezzo, Op. 117/1, for the orchestra was a failure, owing to the purely pianistic design of the middle section. It is impossible to characterize the individual pieces of these four masterly series; one can at most call special attention to such works as the intensely emotional Op. 116/4; the Op. 117/1, which Brahms himself called 'the lullaby of my griefs'; the dramatic Ballad, Op. 118/3, with its sweet middle section; the nebulous Op. 118/6, with its wonderfully enhanced middle section; and the magnificent Rhapsody, Op. 119/4; although in so doing we hardly do justice to their almost equally important neighbors.

With these pieces Brahms has reached the close of his development as a composer for the pianoforte. It has carried him through many stages, from the broad sweep of a fresco to the delicacy of a miniature painting.

XVI

COMPOSITIONS FOR THE ORGAN

A T Düsseldorf in 1856 Brahms turned his attention to
playing the organ, with the result that his studies in
counterpoint, in which Joachim was his collaborator,
were often written for that instrument. Of the studies composed during this year, and the beginning of 1857, only
four are known. Brahms himself subsequently published two
of them (the Fugue in A flat minor, the Choral Prelude and
Fugue on *O Traurigkeit*), while two others (Prelude and
Fugue in A minor, Prelude and Fugue in G minor) appeared only recently. In these works Brahms has evidently
followed the great masters of the Baroque period. The quasi-
extempore parts of the G minor Prelude resemble analogous
parts in the compositions of the great Thomas Cantor, and
in the forceful ending of the Fugue in A minor, referring
back to the Prelude, one perceives the 'Ur-Bach-Handel' effect so justly praised by Joachim. The Fugue in A flat minor
is the culmination of these early works, in which composition the youthful and enthusiastic composer does not hesitate to employ an unusual key in order to express himself
more fully. Brahms's skill in counterpoint is no less remarkable here than in the other two pieces; but here one feels
that it is employed only as a means of inspiring the melancholy mood of the piece with pulsating life.

Both compositions on *O Traurigkeit* are noteworthy, because Brahms re-adopted their technique in the summer of
1896 for his *Eleven Choral Preludes*. The later compositions
are reminiscent partly of the earlier choral prelude and partly
of the earlier choral fugue; now the more or less transformed
melody of the hymn, transferred to the soprano, is merely

provided with fresh counterpoints, now the parts of the choral melody employed as *cantus firmus* are introduced or interrupted by fugal preludes or interludes. On the whole, however, there is a characteristic difference between these works, separated as they are by forty years. In the composition of 1896 there is an incomparably closer relation between the set chorale and the added melodies than in the earlier compositions. One may observe, for example, how in No. 5 the counterpoint in sixteenth notes is derived from the choral melody itself, and how in No. 1 the fugati preceding each line of verse are sometimes thematically derived from the following choral melody. All these are unmistakable signs of the art of the mature Brahms. These choral preludes are in no way inferior in their emotional content to a romantic song or pianoforte piece, despite their consummate contrapuntal skill. The prevalent mood of this late work is explained by the fact that Brahms wrote it, when seriously ill, in memory of Clara Schumann's death. Although a feeling of peaceful serenity No. 8), and even of restrained joy (No. 4), is not totally lacking, yet the whole atmosphere of this collection is that of the profoundest grief. The composer is prepared for death, and even longs for it. It was not by chance that the master wrote two renderings of the chorale *Herzlich tut mich verlangen nach einem sel'gen End* (to the melody of O Sacred Head now Wounded), and two of *O Welt ich muss Dich lassen*. The hymn *O Welt,* in its second version, is the concluding item of this collection, and also the last piece of music Brahms ever wrote. With this soul-stirring composition, in which each line of the chorale fades like an echo, Brahms takes leave of his life and of his work.

XVII

CHAMBER MUSIC

At the head of Brahms's chamber music, as of his compositions for the pianoforte, stands a single *Scherzo*. Brahms composed it in October 1853, as a contribution to a Sonata for Violin and Piano, whose other movements were written by Schumann and A. Dietrich. The work was inscribed 'F.A.E.,' an abbreviation of *Frei Aber Einsam* (free but lonely), a motto of Joachim's, to whom the Sonata was presented by his three friends when he visited them in Düsseldorf. In 1906 Joachim had the Scherzo alone of this work printed, while he kept back the other three movements. In this Scherzo different rhythms are employed simultaneously, and all the spirits of romanticism are at play, but the form is nevertheless extremely concise and clear. This is not surprising; Brahms understood how to construct a Scherzo, even before he had mastered the sonata form. If it were not that the naively boastful C major Coda bears the instruction *sempre ff e grandioso,* the critic might be tempted to place the Scherzo among the works of a later period.*

In the summer of 1938 Breitkopf & Härtel in Leipzig published a Piano Trio in A major which the editors, Ernst Bücken and Karl Hasse, called a posthumous work of Brahms. The basis of their publication was a manuscript written by an unknown copyist, which Ernst Bücken found among the music left by Dr. Erich Prieger of Bonn. The title page of this manuscript was cut out and nothing is known of the identity of the copyist who wrote it. Nevertheless Bücken contends that the work was composed by Brahms

---

* The complete *F.A.E. Sonata* was first edited in 1935 by Erich Valentin and Otto Kobin.

OTTILIE HAUER

AUTOGRAPH-FAN OF JOHANN STRAUSS'S STEP-DAUGHTER (WITH DEDICATIONS BY GOLDMARK, BRAHMS, LEONCAVALLO, NIKISCH, AND OTHERS)

in Bonn or Mehlem during the summer of 1853. A critical analysis of the Trio in four movements reveals a definite dependence on the models of Beethoven, Schubert, and Schumann. A certain resemblance to the style of Brahms's Trio, Op. 8, is also obvious, and Friedrich Brand justly points out that Brahms always liked to write two works of the same type in quick succession (compare his two sextets, the two piano quartets in C minor and A major, the two string quartets, Op. 51, two overtures, two clarinet sonatas, etc.). It is therefore not impossible that a Trio in A major preceded the Trio, Op. 8, in B major. Even if this should prove to be the case—and the proof does not seem conclusive to the author of this book—it can hardly be claimed that the newly discovered work equals Brahms's Op. 8 in value. In particular the first movement of the A major Trio lacks the impetus and monumental character of the corresponding movement in Op. 8. For a work that takes more than three-quarters of an hour in performance, the newly discovered composition is not attractive enough, and if Brahms really was its author, we can readily understand why he never published it.

In January 1854 Brahms completed the *Piano Trio in B major*, Op. 8. This earliest example of his chamber music to be published by the composer himself impresses one by its youthful freshness and tenderness of conception, its soft and sensual tonality, and its rich variety of moods. Even in his later days, Brahms hardly composed anything more beautiful than the broad, swinging introductory theme of the first movement, the elves' dance of the Scherzo, the opening of the Adagio with its inspired religious pathos, and the Schubertian cantilena in F sharp major of the Finale. Only in one characteristic point was the youth of twenty-one lacking: he could not contain himself. To begin with, the enormous first movement, with its five clearly separated themes, which comprises almost five hundred bars, has interpolated, in the recapitulation, a sort of secondary development in the form of a Fugato. In the Adagio Brahms is not satisfied with one contrasting theme, but inserts an Allegro, considerably endangering the unitary character of the movement. Similarly, in the final Rondo the romantic disintegration of form due to excess of invention is unmistakable.

Owing to the necessity of publishing a new edition, the composer was obliged to examine and revise this work in the beginning of 1890. As he himself explained in a letter to Grimm, he 'did not provide it with a wig, but just combed and arranged its hair a little.' This seems, however, a typical Brahmsian understatement. The copy used by the master for this purpose has been preserved by the *Gesellschaft der Musikfreunde,* and in its innumerable pencil marks it affords evident proof of the complete transformation which the work has undergone. The revision culminates in the effort to simplify the work and restrain its youthful exuberance. From this point of view no detail is too insignificant for the master. In the tempo-indication of the Finale, *Allegro molto agitato,* he strikes out the *molto agitato.* At the beginning of the first movement he omits a disturbing violin motive; and to obtain greater homogeneity of tone at the opening of the Scherzo (b. 5-9), he gives the imitation played by the 'cello to the bass part of the piano. Yet these, and dozens of similar revisions, do not satisfy him, and he finally rewrites whole sections. In the first movement he replaces several individual themes by a new, sharply outlined subsidiary theme. This change makes it necessary to work out afresh the development and the recapitulation, now left without a Fugato. The Adagio and Finale. share the same fate. Only the Scherzo receives mercy from the mature Brahms, the Coda alone being modified. Altogether the work lost more than a third of its length through the 'new setting,' but gained enormously in its vigorous concentration.

At Detmold, through the practical work of conducting, Brahms became familiar with the compositions of the classical masters. The earliest chamber-music work of his second creative period, the *String Sextet in B flat major*, Op. 18, composed in 1859/60, shows clear signs of this influence. Depth of feeling, richness of melody, and beauty of sound, all characteristic of the creations of his younger days, are here combined with traits from the works of the Viennese school. Now the spirit of Schubert is invoked (cf. first movement, second and third themes), then that of Beethoven (Scherzo) or Haydn (chief subject of the Finale). Far more important than these derivative features is the fact that Brahms acquired from the works of his Viennese models a sense of clarity and harmonious proportion. Further, we may observe a striving towards greater comprehensibility rarely to be noted in the bulk of his work. This is already apparent from his simple method of variation in the slow movement, and the insistence with which the principal themes are introduced in the first and last movements, first by the 'cello and then again by the violin. In this Sextet Brahms writes for the first time with the lightness of hand which he was later to reveal in his Waltzes, Op. 39, and his Hungarian Dances.

In the years 1857-8 he began the *Piano Quartet in G minor*, Op. 25, which, according to the manuscript (formerly in the possession of Wilhelm Kux), was completed only in September 1861. The fact that this work was composed within a very short time after the Trio in B major is unmistakable. Again both the first and the last movements contain an abundance of vigorous themes. In the first movement a second development is inserted, after the apparent recapitulation in b. 161, and the wonderful march of the third movement has a strong orchestral flavor (b. 75 *et seq.*). All these signs indicate an early creative period. However, although Brahms had failed in the B major Trio, the final version of the Quartet shows that he succeeded in thoroughly mastering the manifold difficulties of the form. Consider how he connects the second group of themes of the first movement with the first group, by accompanying both with the same passionate motive in sixteenth notes (cf. b. 27 *et seq*. with b. 79 *et seq*.), or how in the whole of the powerful development of this movement, he elaborates only the first group. The interlude (Intermezzo) of the second movement has nothing in common with the Scherzi of Brahms's first works. It is written in a subdued, mysterious mood frequently to be found in his later creations. The wonderfully romantic third movement was originally twenty bars longer. Later, however, in order to make this movement more concise, Brahms omitted part of the recapitulation between b. 206 and b. 208 of the final form (corresponding with b. 40-52 of the first section). The *Rondo alla Zingarese* in the fourth movement betrays for the first time in a chamber-music work the master's partiality for Hungarian tunes. With its breathless rhythm it is the most suitable Finale for this fresh and youthful composition.

We may assume that the *Piano Quartet in A major*, Op. 26, originated about the same time as the G minor Quartet. The A major, far more than its twin, shows a certain transitional character. Although in the first movement an interesting experiment is made—the inclusion of three variations of the principal theme in the development (b. 140 *et seq*.)—the formal structure is firmly built. Also the 'wonderful Poco Adagio with its ambiguous passion' (Joachim) shows a complete equilibrium in its various parts. In the deliberate third movement, however, a certain breadth of treatment is unmistakable, resulting mainly from the fact that even here Brahms was striving after the complicated sonata form. Moreover, the following Allegro, with its 519 bars in which the Hungarian fire of the Finale of Op. 25 is quenched by a touch of the Viennese spirit, impresses the hearer as being almost too long. The whole work shows—like the B flat major Sextet—a certain leaning towards the works of the classical Viennese period. The idyllic first movement leads one into a Schubertian atmosphere, and the trio of the

Scherzo reminds one, in its canon-like progress, of the Minuet in Haydn's Quartet, Op. 76/2.

The most significant chamber-music work of the second period is perhaps the *Pianoforte Quintet in F minor,* Op. 34, completed in the autumn of 1864. In the lively first movement a number of themes, often contrasting sharply in mood, are concisely elaborated. Despite its five expressive themes, this piece, whose components are welded into a homogeneous form, contains barely three hundred bars. The tender and impressive second movement is followed by a Scherzo, which, with its changes from major to minor, from 6/8 to 2/4 time, from a shadowy gliding motion to a powerful and joyous theme, recovers the emotional wealth of the first movement. And the powerful sigh of liberation at the opening of the trio is genuinely Brahmsian. The broadly traced fourth movement—as is often the case with the composer's Finali—cannot readily be classed with any of the recognized typical forms. A romantic introduction, serving as the germ of the whole movement, is followed by the real exposition (b. 41-183). The most important ideas of this section return again in a second part (b. 184-342), which might equally well be described as the recapitulation or the development. Finally, in the Coda (b. 343-492), the whole material appears again in a somewhat varied form. Brahms never adheres strictly to the schematic form, but creates, as he proceeds, the form best adapted to his thoughts and feelings.

In 1862 Brahms composed the first two movements of his *'Cello Sonata in E minor,* Op. 38, together with an Adagio, subsequently canceled. The Finale was written in June 1865. In accordance with the whole of his artistic development, Brahms mastered the form of the Duos for piano and a stringed instrument through writing first for the larger ensembles of trios, quartets, and sextets. In the first two movements of this Sonata the 'cello is treated with assurance, bringing its sonorous tone into relief, and showing what experience Brahms had already gained by the composition of chamber music. The subsequently added Finale, composed in the style of a fugue, is not quite so felicitous. In this piece the solo instrument does not always find it easy to hold its own with the brilliantly treated pianoforte part. Notwithstanding the lyrical tenderness predominant in the first two movements, the whole work is in a certain sense an act of homage to the venerated J. S. Bach, for the main theme of the first movement is closely related to the 'Contrapunctus 3' from Bach's *Art of Fugue*, while the fugato theme in the Finale of Brahms is astonishingly like the Contrapunctus 13' from the same work. It is characteristic, too, that Brahms gives the *Valse triste*, which constitutes the second movement, a stricter form by prefacing it with a four-note motive, which plays an important role throughout the movement, especially in the trio. This Sonata is a genuinely Brahmsian composition, in which romantic feeling and severe construction are perfectly balanced.

The *String Sextet in G major,* Op. 36, begun in September 1864, and completed the following May, impresses one as quieter and more restrained in mood, and more artistic in form than the first Sextet. It betrays far more of the essential nature of its creator than the earlier work, and this perhaps is the very reason why it was not so quickly appreciated. The iridescent flickering of the main theme between G major and E flat major, and the persistence of the rocking accompaniment in eighth notes, give the first movement a peculiar mystical charm. The following Intermezzo, entitled *Scherzo,* has a sort of weary grace, rising to real gaiety only in the spirited, effervescent *Presto giocoso* of the middle section. The third movement, an Adagio with five variations and Coda, has a curiously vague theme, but its poetic intention cannot be misunderstood: to progress, in the course of the variations, from an oppressed and lacerated mood to a blessed peace. The Finale exhibits an interesting mixed type; the original sonata form approximates to the

Rondo by repeating, in the manner of a ritornell, the same idea (b. 1-6) throughout all parts of the movement. Here we find already the idea of a 'motto,' which plays an important part in the work of the mature Brahms (cf. First Symphony).

In 1865 Brahms wrote the *Trio in E flat major,* Op. 40, a most peculiar setting for piano, violin, and French horn. The master's characteristic aversion for outward effects is betrayed here by his express choice of the old-fashioned French horn and rejection of the valve-horn, which was already in general use. Thereby he deprives himself of many technical possibilities, but recovers the original noble tone of the French horn. The spirit of the horn imbues the whole work with a delicate melancholy and an intense feeling for Nature. The veils are lifted only in the cheerful hunting scene of the Finale, while a faint trace of melancholy clings even to the humor of the Scherzo. The first movement is particularly original, a thrice repeated Andante, with two more agitated episodic parts. To accentuate the natural and simple character of this work, Brahms even resigns the sonata form (the only instance of the kind among his instrumental pieces in several movements). The third movement, with its wonderful depth of feeling, is admirably linked up with the Finale. Like an exquisite promise in the quiet solemnity of the *Adagio mesto,* the idea introduced in bar 58 soon reveals itself (b. 63) as an allusion to the main theme of the Finale. Brahms might have done this in an effort to create a more organic union between the somber first, second, and third movements and the Finale, which is full of the joy of life.

After the Horn Trio, an interval of eight years elapsed before Brahms wrote any more chamber music. And when at last, in the summer of 1873, he completed the *String Quartets in C minor and A minor,* Op. 51, he had not only conquered a new form of ensemble, but at the same time his style developed to its full maturity. He had now achieved an economy which refused to tolerate a single superfluous note, but at the same time he had perfected a method of integration that would give an entire work the appearance of having been cast from one mold.

In the C minor Quartet we can see that the first eight notes of the violin part in the first movement are employed also as the main theme of the Finale, and in part as the main theme of the *Romance*. The union is even more intimate between the several sections of each movement. Consider how, in the first movement, the leaping motive in eighth notes, accompanying the main theme from b. 24, continues even when a new idea is introduced in b. 35. By this expedient, already employed by Brahms in earlier works (cf. the G minor Quartet), the first and second subjects are quite naturally united. Towards the end of the exposition, the dotted rhythm of the main theme recurs, dominating almost the whole development, and thus contributing to the unity of the movement. In the A minor Quartet the thematic relation of the different movements is not so easily recognizable. The main motive in the Finale is contained in b. 4 and 5 of the first movement. The three eighth notes of this b. 4 appear in the Minuet as triplets (b. 2). Moreover, they are, in modified form (cf. b. 161 of the first movement), the nucleus of the beginning of the second movement. The union of all sections in the first movement, however, is still closer than in the C minor Quartet, because the whole movement, with all its different episodes, arises from the first nine bars of the main theme.

The same striving for unity may be seen in the mood of these works. The first, like the fourth, movement of the C minor Quartet is dominated by a somber passion and sullen determination. The *Romance* begins rather idyllically, even solemnly, but soon passes into a restrained and melancholy theme (b. 27 *et seq.*). Similarly, the F minor Intermezzo of the third movement, with its artistic double melody, played by violin and viola, becomes carefree and cheerful only in the trio. While in the C minor Quartet the same fundamental mood is maintained throughout the work, the A minor Quartet shows a perfectly natural progression of feeling. In the first movement a tender melancholy prevails; but the solemn character of the second movement is effectively interrupted by the powerful imitative duet of the first violin and 'cello. The amiable mood of the Minuet is still further brightened by the Finale, which has a certain Hungarian flavor. Thus, from the earnestness of the beginning, Brahms progresses to vigorous gaiety at the end. The composition recalls Beethoven in its spiritual atmosphere, in the strict discipline of its musical thought, and in the wonderful transparency of the setting for stringed instruments, born of a perfect understanding of the nature of chamber music. Brahms declared that he had written many quartets before publishing Op. 51, and it is obvious, if we examine the first works of this kind to be published, that he had acquired mastery in this type of composition.

Brahms's *Piano Quartet in C minor*, Op. 60, originated from two different creative periods. The first movement, originally in C sharp minor, was composed in 1855, as also the Andante in E major. Since the work did not altogether satisfy the composer, he put it away, and did not take it up again until the winter of 1873-4. At that time the already existing original Finale was replaced by a new one, and a Scherzo was added. Although Brahms certainly subjected both the old movements to a revision, they still show clear traces of their earlier origin. In the first movement the tragic despair of Brahms's *Sturm und Drang* period prevails, a fact explained by the composer himself in a reference to Goethe's *Werther* on the verge of suicide. Further, an experiment in form reminds us of an early work, the introductory movement of the A major Pianoforte Quartet, for here too Brahms employs variations in the sonata form. His second theme (b. 70 *et seq.*) is an eight-bar idea, which is at once elaborated in four variations. On the other hand, the last two movements are typical products of the master's maturity. The somber Scherzo is so concise that it can hardly contain a regular trio, replacing it by a brief episode in the major key. And in the Finale, Brahms, in his striving after compression, for once overshot the mark. As is shown by the manuscript (in the possession of the *Gesellschaft der Musikfreunde*), Brahms subsequently inserted b. 155-88 in order to mitigate the excessive conciseness of this movement. Moreover, he gave it, later on, a slower tempo. The manuscript was marked by him subsequently with *Presto, Tempo giusto,* and *Un poco presto,* which directions were changed to *Allegro commodo* only in the published form.

The *String Quartet in B flat major,* Op. 67, composed in 1875, forms a joyful, bucolic counterpart to the two earlier works of this category. It has a light impetuous rhythm, is pastoral in mood, and is conceived with a sense of humor. This perhaps explains why one has to look for the nucleus of the whole work in the Finale. This movement introduces eight variations on a simple folksong-like theme. After the first six variations have followed the usual course, the seventh introduces a joyful bugle call, which the master had already employed as the main theme of the first movement. Moreover in the eighth variation we find an idea that plays an important part in the first movement (b. 50 *et seq.*) as a transition to its third theme. The Coda combines the melody of the seventh variation with the original theme, and leads the joyous movement to its climax. In other respects, however, in this cheerful offspring of his Muse, Brahms avoids any marked adherence to strict form. The first movement, with its teasing change from 2/4 to 6/8 time, is loosely formed; and also the tender Andante contains a more freely conceived, almost improvisatory part (b. 45 *et seq.*). Originally, as shown by the autograph manuscript formerly owned by Wilhelm Kux, it read as on page 235 (Example 2).

Subsequently Brahms pasted over more than a page of the manuscript with the definitive version. It is not difficult to see the reason for this correction. The cadenza-like sec-

EXAMPLE 2

there follow b. 12–18 and then b. 73 *et seq.* of the printed version.

tion had to be extended in order still further to enhance the unrestrained character of the whole work.

In the summers of the years 1878-9, Brahms wrote at Pörtschach his first *Violin Sonata in G major*, Op. 78. In this work the master found a characteristic solution of the problem of the Duo for pianoforte and a stringed instrument. In Haydn's Violin Sonatas the pianoforte part was so predominant that the violin part was marked *Ad libitum* and could even be omitted altogether. Since the days of Mozart and Beethoven, a good balance between violin and piano has usually been maintained. Brahms's first 'Cello Sonata also clearly strives after this ideal, as in the Finale one fugue part is given to the 'cello, but the others to the piano. But precisely in this movement Brahms may have realized that with an even treatment of the two performers the stringed instrument is at a disadvantage when opposed by a full piano part. The lesson learned from this is apparent in the G major Violin Sonata. Here the pianoforte part is thin and transparent, and as the violin part generally has the leading melody, the balance is displaced to the advantage of the stringed instrument. Again the nucleus of the three-movement work is really contained in the Finale. Brahms proceeds, in Schubert's manner, from two closely related songs of his own, the *Regenlied* (Rain Song) and *Nachklang* (Memories) from Op. 59. The dotted rhythm of the beginning, the famous 'three D's,' are to be found also at the opening of the first movement and in the *Più Andante* of the second movement. Further, in the Finale (b. 83 *et seq.*) the opening of the second movement recurs. The whole work reflects the atmosphere of the beautiful Carinthian holiday resort where it was created. It is a composition full of restrained sweetness and that yearning tenderness which —as so often in Brahms—seems to smile through tears.

The first movement of the *Piano Trio in C major*, Op. 87, was composed in March 1880; the other three movements in June 1882. The characteristic features of the mature period are to be found in the introductory movement. It contains not a note too much or too little, and the whole piece develops in such a natural manner that one could almost believe that Brahms had nothing more to do, after working out the first few bars, than to complete the movement in accordance with the inner laws of its themes. The treatment of the chief subject (b. 1-4) shows the master at the summit of his art. Since the theme is eminently suited for strings, it is always played, apart from the final reinforcement just before the end, only by the violin and 'cello. Further, Brahms was able, in the development, completely to transform the character of this theme. No greater contrast could be imagined than that between the energetic beginning and the mystical, longing *animato* part (b. 165 *et seq.*). In the *Andante con moto*, five variations are written on a passionate-pathetic theme of a slightly Hungarian coloring. While the first, third, and fifth variations are supported chiefly by the theme-melody, played by the strings, the second and fourth depend more on the accompaniment of the theme in the piano part, so that the whole movement assumes a rather rondo-like character. A mysterious Scherzo, with its solemn trio, is followed by a lively Finale, which is no less concise, yet more loosely built and more artless than the first movement. It culminates in the Coda (b. 170 *et seq.*) which occupies nearly a quarter of the whole movement. It is characteristic of Brahms that even in a lighter movement the energy does not diminish, but rather is intensified towards the end.

In the spring of the year 1882 Brahms wrote his *String Quintet in F major*, Op. 88, and the whole joyous composition is full of the spirit of the spring. Since the completion of the first String Quintet (see p. 216), which the master himself had destroyed, as it refused to 'sound right,' twenty years had elapsed, and the composer seems to have learned an adequate lesson from the defects of this earlier work; for if ever a piece of chamber music 'sounded right,' the F major Quintet does so. Comparison with the unpreserved older composition is of course impossible. We can only say that Brahms did not use two 'cellos in his Op. 88, but instead of so doing, doubled the part for the viola, his favorite instrument, thus giving the alto pitch the preponderance over the baritone. The carefree, amiable first movement shows the same formal excellence as the introductory movement of the C major Trio. A remarkable feature is the mighty organ point, which with minor interruptions forms the foundation of the whole of the second part of the development and prepares the way most effectively for the re-entry of the recapitulation. The second movement assumes a rondo-like form, and combines the characters of the Adagio and the Scherzo. A *Grave ed appassionato* serves as a ritornelle, whose chief theme Brahms took from an earlier work (see p. 213). The passionate gloom of this composition of the *Sturm und Drang* period is gradually transformed, in its twice-repeated recurrence, into a mood of reconciliation in correspondence with the general character of the Quintet. A tenderly mocking *Allegretto vivace* and its variation in *Presto* are inserted as episodes. For the Finale Brahms chose the combination of fugue and sonata form favored by the classical composers, the Finale of Beethoven's String Quartet, Op. 59/3, providing the immediate model. As the different themes of this movement are nothing more than variations of the fugue-like main theme or in counterpoint to it, the inner unity of this Finale is perfectly preserved in spite of all its variety.

Only after an interval of four years was the F major Quintet followed by new chamber-music works. Then, however, they came in a torrent. During the summer of 1886 Brahms composed at Thun a 'Cello Sonata and a Violin Sonata, as well as a Pianoforte Trio. The first movement of the *'Cello Sonata in F major,* Op. 99, differs in some respects from other compositions of the mature period. Its ardent pathos would be less surprising in Brahms's youthful compositions, and the clear transparency of the piano part in the Violin Sonatas is lacking here and there. Although the 'cello part has in general a much higher pitch than in the first Sonata, great strength of tone is required if the player is to assert himself against the tremoli of the piano, here employed to an extent which will hardly be found in any other work of the composer. It may be that Brahms did not 'go for so many walks' with this work as was otherwise his wont. In any case

EXAMPLE 3

the original manuscript, now in the possession of the *Gesellschaft der Musikfreunde,* was subsequently corrected by the composer in pencil, or by pasting over several bars. For instance in the third movement, a somber, shadowy *Allegro passionato,* b. 71-80, read originally as in Example 3. Subsequently Brahms replaced the syncopated motive by a descending passage, whereby the movement gains greatly in variety. In a similar manner the alterations in other parts of the manuscript serve to enrich the composition or to give it a more artistic form. Lastly, it may be mentioned that the Finale—a rather hastily elaborated Rondo—seems to have been written with quite peculiar speed, as though the master could hardly write fast enough to put the rush of ideas on paper.

The *Violin Sonata in A major,* Op. 100, displays a strong contrast to the 'Cello Sonata, written at the same time. While in Op. 99 masculine defiance predominates, the main characteristics of the Violin Sonata are its feminine sweetness and tenderness. In the first movement the master cites one of his own songs (cf. the second theme with Op. 105/1), and this is not the only trait wherein Brahms's work recalls the composer of the *Trout Quintet* and the *Wanderer* fantasy. The lyrical basis of this tenderly spiritual work and its simple, concise, construction, remind us of Schubert's marvelous Op. 137, the Sonatinas for Violin and Piano. It has been pointed out, only too often, that in the opening theme of the first movement the first three notes correspond with the opening of Wagner's *Preislied* from *Die Meistersinger.* However, it would be an insult to Brahms to waste a single word in his defense. The second movement, as in the F major Quintet, combines the slow movement and the Scherzo. Between a beautiful and expressive melody on the violin and its two repetitions is inserted a gay *Vivace* with its variation. The whole of this delicate piece, together with the Coda, comprises barely 170 bars. In the following Rondo, also, which in its dreamy tenderness breaks away from the typical joyous and carefree Finale, Brahms reveals himself as an idyllic composer. He saves his epic weight and power for the third work of this summer's trilogy.

The titanic first movement of the *C minor Trio,* Op. 101, is one of the most powerful and at the same time most concise of the master's creations. One single motive, consisting of the second, third, fourth, and fifth notes of the left hand at the beginning of the pianoforte part, dominates the whole movement, and the terseness of the form is so extreme that Brahms—as the manuscript shows—subsequently even crossed out the originally intended repetition of the exposition. The succeeding movements bring a certain relaxation. The lightly gliding *Presto non assai,* with its strange arpeggio-like *pizzicati* of the strings in the trio, is followed by a charmingly tender *Andante grazioso*. Brahms originally wrote this movement in manuscript in 7/4 time, and only later decided to alternate one 3/4 with two 2/4 bars. In spite of its complicated rhythm, this melody is wonderfully simple and natural, almost reminding us of Mozart. It is one of the secrets of the mature Brahms that his mode of writing, if we look at the notes, seems to become more and more complicated, whereas the internal structure of his works becomes even simpler and more natural. The Finale, handled rather rhapsodically, in its broadly treated Coda transforms the grim humor of the beginning into radiant mirtn. In this triumphant ending the weariness and resignation often attributed to Brahms's works of this period are by no means apparent.

The *Violin Sonata in D minor*, Op. 108, the principal outlines of which were also composed in the summer of 1886, although the work was completed only in 1888, is more broadly planned, more brilliant, and also more vehement than the two preceding violin sonatas. No delicate dreamer, but rather an untamed and fiery spirit speaks to us here. The whole introductory movement is dominated by the first theme, in which not only the treble but also the bass is employed to elaborate it. The strict development may be considered as an enhancement of the technique of Op. 88, for it is built up entirely over an organ-point. It is interesting to note that the rocking violin figure at the beginning of this part (b. 84-5), which at first hearing seems to have only a coloristic value, reveals itself on closer inspection as a combination of the beginning of the main theme and its bass. It is just in Brahms's mature period that his logical mode of thinking is most sharply manifested when it is least expected. A profoundly felt Adagio with a broadly rhythmical violin cantilena leads up to a mysterious movement in the manner of the Scherzo of the C minor Trio. The impetuous Finale, with its fiery brilliance, borne onwards by intense emotion, is so richly endued with structural and intellectual values that it is able to hold its own with the first movement, and indeed almost to surpass it. Perfect as each movement of the three Violin Sonatas is, they seem, in this last movement, to have reached their culminating point.

The *String Quintet in G major,* Op. 111, written in the summer of 1890, is related to the mood of the first String Quintet. Here masculine strength is coupled with cheerful gaiety. The energetic first movement, with its Viennese second theme, the tender G major Trio in the *Valse triste* of the third movement, and the Finale, ending in a dashing Czárdás, are full of a pleasant, genuinely Austrian liveliness. And as the idyllic mood forbids a too strong accentuation of the purely intellectual, the variations of the Adagio are treated with a fantastic freedom not very frequent in Brahms's work. It is common knowledge that in the beginning of the first movement the 'cellist finds it especially difficult to make the main theme audible amid the fluctuations of the four accompanying parts. Brahms was implored to rectify this, and he jotted down on a sheet of paper, which is today in the possession of the *Gesellschaft der Musikfreunde,* the following less massive accompaniment for the violins and violas:

EXAMPLE 4

In spite of the evident advantages of this arrangement, Brahms could not make up his mind to disturb the uniform line of the accompaniment, and he retained the old version in print.

With the G major Quintet, Brahms thought to terminate his creative work. Nevertheless, in the following year he resumed his creative activity, but the character of his work had undergone a fundamental change. In all four chamber-music compositions of this last period, the clarinet, the rather faintly sweet, melancholy songster of the wood-wind instruments, has the leading part, and this fact alone indicates the character of these pieces. Their mood is more somber and serious than that of the works of Brahms's maturity; the invention, perhaps, is not always so fresh and abundant, though the technical mastery is no less remarkable. Further, these compositions show a very definite inclination towards the means of expression employed by the older masters.

The first of these works, the *Trio in A minor for Clarinet, 'Cello, and Pianoforte,* Op. 114, composed in the summer of 1891, is typical of this period. The inventive conception of the themes, born of the spirit of the wind instrument, and, more especially, the harmonious blending of the tones of the clarinet and the 'cello, are magnificent (Mandyczewski wrote to Brahms: 'It is as though the instruments were in love with each other'). Yet this noble work is not wholly free from a certain weariness; the themes are not quite so inspired, nor is their elaboration quite so captivating as usual. It is interesting to note that in the first movement (b. 51 *et seq.*), as in the last (b. 48 *et seq.*), the second theme is introduced as a canon of the inversion. With the pre-classical Viennese composers, as with the early Haydn, it was usual to arrange the second subject as a canon. Was this perhaps known to Brahms, who, as he grew older, felt himself more drawn to the music of the past? Had he consciously revived the old technique? I shall not attempt to decide this question; but the peculiar analogy is deserving of mention.

In the same summer Brahms composed one of his most beautiful pieces of chamber music, the *Quintet in B minor for Clarinet and String Quartet (Clarinet Quintet)*, Op. 115. It is a work of retrospection, a farewell. Pictures of the past, pleasures and sorrows, longing and hope, pass before the elderly master, who expresses them once again in delicately restrained and melancholy tones. A cornerstone of Brahms's creative work, the art of variation, forms the basis of this Quintet also. The nucleus of the whole composition lies once more in the Finale; in the Clarinet Quintet, even more than in the String Quartet, Op. 67. This last movement forms a series of variations of a rondo-like character, since the third and fifth variations express the theme much more distinctly than the others (cf. Piano Trio, Op. 87). In the fifth variation there appears as counterpoint to the theme a figure in sixteenth notes, which Brahms has used, in a slightly modified form, at the beginning of the first movement. But to make the composer's intention perfectly clear, the Coda of the Finale leads directly to the beginning of the first movement. Moreover, one realizes, on closer inspection, that a motive which plays a very important part in the opening movement (b. 3) is actually derived from the beginning of the Finale (b. 1-3). But even this is not enough for Brahms. The second movement is built up on a single motive (Clarinet, b. 1), not only in its first and third sections, but also in its fantastic middle section, which reminds one of the Hungarian Gipsy music; this motive, however, seems to be like an extract from the chief theme of the first movement. Again, at the opening of the third movement, we find an idea which is varied in its middle section. But this idea begins like the main theme of the Finale.

In its choice of instruments, and the narrow range of the principal keys used in the different movements (B minor, B major, D major), the Clarinet Quintet is akin to the old forms of Suite and Divertimento; even to a definite type: the Variation-Suite, in which one movement represents the theme and the others its variations. Doubtless Brahms was acquainted with this form, so often used in the seventeenth and eighteenth centuries, as Haydn's *Feldpartita,* containing the *Chorale St. Antonii* from which Brahms took his theme for the Haydn Variations, is just such a Variation-Suite. In this connection it may be mentioned that the method of the Clarinet Quintet, which brings out the actual theme only in the fourth movement, had already been employed in the Variation-Suite. There it was always the rule never to begin with the theme, but to let it appear only in the second, third, or fourth movement, so as to give more variety to the work.

The two *Clarinet Sonatas in F minor and E flat major,* Op. 120, written in the summer of the year 1894, are the last chamber-music works of Brahms. Their manner is familiar: a wonderful exploitation of the possibilities of the clarinet, particularly in the effective change from the higher to the lower registers, coupled with a certain austerity of tone; a tender melancholy, which seldom breaks out into more energetic or joyous accents; and a splendid perfection of form in all the movements. And yet, amid these typical features, what a profusion of individual attributes! In the F minor Sonata, for instance, it is remarkable how in each of the three sections of the beautifully proportioned introductory movement the lyrical opening rises gradually to epic strength, leading to final victory in the softer mood of the Coda. The combination of the movements in the second Sonata is also highly individual. The work begins with an *Allegro amabile;* there follows an impetuous, agitated, scherzo-like movement; lastly an *Andante con moto* with variations, of which only the last but one is an Allegro in the usual finale tempo. Thus Brahms, with a predominantly slow movement, bids farewell to chamber music, which throughout his career was his special predilection, and it seems only natural that he should have written this piece in the variation form, to which he was more strongly inclined than other composers. There exist in the archives of the *Gesellschaft der Musikfreunde* sketches of the Clarinet Sonatas, which afford us an interesting insight into the master's workmanship. On inspecting the drafts of the first movement of the F minor Sonata, it is apparent that the composer first jotted down only the melody and the bass; the middle voices were lacking as yet. Brahms could not consider details in his first hasty notes; yet it should be noted that the skeleton of the work corresponded almost completely with the final version. Again and again it is evident that Brahms— like Mozart—perfected his compositions before writing them down.

XVIII

COMPOSITIONS FOR ORCHESTRA

THE compositions for orchestra belong mainly to the mature period of Brahms's art. In his first creative period only a single orchestral work was attempted, and this was not finished until some years later. The second period produced the Serenades, orchestral compositions bearing a certain resemblance to chamber music. Not until his art was fully mature did Brahms become a master of purely orchestral composition, which he approached by way of his great works for choir and orchestra. Then, however, a time of intense productivity followed, and within a period of fourteen years (1873-87) no less than ten works were completed. Again, there is a complete lack of orchestral compositions in Brahms's last creative period, when he confined himself to the smaller forms of chamber music and pieces for the pianoforte. Lastly, it should be noted that Brahms's First Symphony occupies only the fifth place in the order of creation of his orchestral works. Although he had always given the greatest attention to the problems of the Symphony, he schooled himself, before attempting this form, by composing a Concerto, two Serenades, and Variations for Orchestra.

Brahms's earliest orchestral composition, which he wrote during the years 1854-9, has a curious history. Having in his mind the scheme of a symphony, he drafted his work first for two pianos, just as he did later on in the case of the Haydn Variations. The orchestration of the work, however, did not proceed happily under his untrained hand. He could not rid himself of the sound of the piano, and yet the use of the orchestra seemed indispensable for the realization of his ideas. He therefore devised the expedient of molding his ideas into the form of a Concerto for Piano and Orchestra. In so doing he discarded the Saraband-like funeral march of the original version, only to employ it later, in a changed form, as the second movement of the *Requiem*. Further, he composed a lively Rondo as a Finale to the new work, which was published as the *Pianoforte Concerto in D minor*, Op. 15. It goes without saying that a work created in such an unusual way does not conform to the ordinary conception of a solo concerto. In this passionate outpouring of the master's *Sturm und Drang* period, technical brilliance as an aim in itself will be sought in vain. The piano and the orchestra are treated as equally important, and though the solo part is anything but easy, the listener never feels that it is a piece of ostentatious virtuosity. It is an interesting fact that Brahms repeatedly entrusted to the piano in the first movement ideas that are only remotely, if at all, connected with the thematic material of the orchestral part. This is somewhat reminiscent of the 'Vivaldi Concerto-form,' often employed by J. S. Bach, wherein the solo instrument and the orchestra elaborate different subjects. This may be more than a coincidence, as Brahms at that time was devoting himself to the study of Bach's works. As in Schumann's orchestral compositions, there is in this Concerto a certain plastic fullness and massiveness of orchestral color that harmonizes most happily with the passionate and melancholy content of the work.

Owing to certain remarks which Joachim had made to Kalbeck, the Concerto was subjected to rather fantastic attempts at interpretation. Thus, the gloomy first movement was supposed to represent the terrible impression of Schumann's attempt at suicide. Gustav Ernest has demonstrated the improbability of this theory. The manuscript of the second movement bore the inscription: *Benedictus qui venit in nomine Domini*. These words, well suited to the tender, solemn mood of the piece, were subsequently omitted. Knowing that Brahms was in the habit of addressing Robert Schumann as 'Domine,' Kalbeck has also made the amazing suggestion that the composer intended to announce himself as the trustee of the Schumann inheritance, and to paint a sort of self-portrait in this Adagio. Apart from the fact that the peaceful and serenely solemn mood of this movement had nothing in common with the temperament of the young composer, it would be a gross misconception of the artist's character to assume that he had conferred on himself the role of a species of Messiah. On the contrary, it is far more likely that the 'blessed person' who came 'in the name of the Lord' was Clara Schumann, who, after her husband's death, worked untiringly for the recognition of his genius. This interpretation is confirmed by a remark in a letter Brahms wrote to Clara on 30 December 1856, in connection with the Concerto: 'I am also painting a lovely portrait of you; it is to be the Adagio.' The final movement alone has been spared attempts at programmatic explanation. In this movement Brahms set himself the task of writing a composition which, despite its fundamentally defiant character, is not without a certain mirthful liveliness. Such a mood was foreign to his nature during his *Sturm und Drang* period, and it is therefore not surprising that on Joachim's advice this movement was subjected to repeated alterations and corrections.

Brahms's second orchestral work, the *Serenade in D major*, Op. 11, dates from the years 1857-8. It bears witness to the young artist's industrious study of classical scores at the Detmold Court. Some of the subjects might well have been written by Haydn or by the young Beethoven. The orchestral score does not—with the exception of the four horns—exceed the classic limits, and the composition is full of joyous humor, even audacious mirth (cf. the first Minuet, with its imitation of fife and bagpipes). The Serenade, originally meant for eight solo instruments, was finally arranged for a complete orchestra. The new form—according to the title of the manuscript preserved by Breitkopf & Härtel, Leipzig—

was to be a 'symphony-serenade,' but luckily Brahms did not carry out this plan. Even in its final version this work has no relation to a symphony; the instrumentation is still quite pellucid, and the frequent use of the wind instruments for solo phrases, forbidding a heavy string ensemble, emphasizes the serenade-like character of this work. A greater contrast than that existing between this composition and the Piano Concerto is hardly conceivable, the one being tragic and passionate, the other graceful and charming. In the Concerto the method of scoring is massive; in the Serenade it is intermingled with solo parts. In the older work a wealth of emotional power is forced into three movements, while the six movements of the newer work show (especially in the outer parts) a certain careless diffuseness. In the few years that had passed between the beginning of these two compositions a new spirit had entered into Brahms's creative work.

Brahms wrote his Second *Serenade in A major,* Op. 16, during 1857-60. Almost more than the first work of this genre, it is a true *divertimento.* It consists of short movements; two horns are used instead of four, and not only trumpets and drums, but also the violins are omitted—as in Méhul's *Uthal*—which gives the composition a peculiar sonorous charm. The violas are the highest strings used; the bassoons and the lower register of the clarinets are especially favored; hence a deep, warm ground tone prevails, which in the long run is a trifle monotonous. The whole mood of this work is soft, tender, and rather pensive. It is not as lively as the First Serenade, but has far greater depth. The Adagio, with its *ostinato*-like bass, even tends towards a more strictly contrapuntal conception. Brahms was particularly attached to this composition, and when he was arranging the piano-duet score he wrote to Joachim: 'I was in a perfectly blissful mood. I have seldom written music with such delight.' And as late as 1875 he undertook the task of carefully revising a new edition of the score first published in 1860. The copy used by the master for revision has been preserved by the *Gesellschaft der Musikfreunde*. It is sprinkled with expression signs, and with phrasing marks which are also included in the new edition in general use today. Even in the orchestral score slight alterations can be found. For example, it is only in the second edition that Brahms has included the horn part in b. 173-4 and 177-8 of the first movement, or the oboe part in b. 263-4 of the fifth movement. The main features of the orchestration, however, were not in any way modified. It is incorrect to say—as some authors have done—that Brahms gave the work its final form as late as 1875, by omitting the violins, trumpets, drums, and two of the horns.

In November 1870 Joseph Haydn's *Feldpartita*, in B flat major, was shown to Brahms by his friend C. F. Pohl, the well-known biographer of Haydn. This interesting work, which Haydn wrote towards the close of the eighteenth century for the band of Prince Esterházy's troops, may well have fascinated Brahms, not only by its inventive charm, but also by its unusual setting for two oboes, two horns, three bassoons, and a 'serpent' (a kind of bass horn, obsolete in the nineteenth century).* At all events, he wrote down in his notebook, in which he had previously entered a number of musical phrases by the older composers, the second movement of the *Partita*, which was probably based on an old Burgenland pilgrims' chant, and was entitled *Chorale St. Antonii*. Brahms could not resist this original little melody, and used it as the theme for the *Variations on a Theme by Joseph Haydn*, Op. 56, which he wrote during the summer of 1873, in two different settings. We have already discussed the pianoforte version (see p. 218); we may now consider the orchestral. According to the manuscript in the possession of the Vienna National Library, Brahms's first idea was to arrange the theme, originally written for wind instru-

* As Haydn's composition had been hitherto unknown, it was published by me for the first time in 1932.

ments, for strings. Happily, however, he dropped this plan, and allowed the *Chorale St. Antonii* to retain its peculiar character Haydn had given it by the predominant use of the oboes and bassoons. The variations themselves present, in the technique of their orchestration, a very different picture from that of the Second Serenade of fourteen years previously. Brahms had acquired the technique of his maturer years, which was fundamentally an intensification of the 'broken work' (*durchbrochene Arbeit*) of the Viennese classical school. The motives and themes rove continually from one instrument to another; long-drawn-out melodies are divided among the various instruments, so that the lead is permanently changing from one section of the orchestra to another. Although Brahms hardly ever seeks inspiration from the tonal color of the individual instruments—as Liszt and Berlioz did—his orchestral tone is always richly varied, vivacious, and free from overloading. Again and again we are fascinated (cf., for example, third, fifth, and seventh variations and the Finale) by amazingly refined and ingenious combinations and antitheses of sound. In the technique of his variations Brahms here follows the same lines as in the Handel Variations. The eight variations strictly observe the rhythmic structure, the harmony, and, to a certain extent, even the melody of the theme. With ever-increasing significance, the work builds itself up to a magnificent climax, until the culminating point is reached in the grand Finale. This Finale, again, in the manner of a passacaglia, presents variations on a five-bar *basso-ostinato* idea, derived from the theme. Again we find that Brahms's imagination was gloriously kindled by the strictness of the various limitations imposed by his task. This work is so rich in variety that we feel tempted to give a special place to the Haydn Variations, not only among Brahms's variations, but among the whole of the master's orchestral compositions.

Brahms had worked for a very long time on the *C minor Symphony*, Op. 68. His earliest ideas for the first movement were already conceived in his *Sturm und Drang* period, but the movement was only partly completed as late as 1862. In the years 1874-6 he took it up again, added the slow introduction, and composed the three other movements. In September 1876 the Symphony was completed, as can be seen by the date on the manuscript. Brahms's close affinity with Beethoven, especially with his two symphonies in minor keys, can hardly be overlooked in this work. This affinity is not limited to the slight resemblance, often overemphasized, of the theme of Brahms's Finale to the *Ode to Joy* in the Ninth Symphony; nor does it consist in the intensity and subtlety of the musical elaboration alone, but rather in the similarity of the poetic content. The fundamental theme of human strife and creative impulse, the eternal motto *per ardua ad astra* has inspired alike Brahms's First and Beethoven's Fifth and Ninth Symphonies. The mood of the gloomy, painfully struggling first movement recalls the years, so full of conflict, before Schumann's death, while the dark, lowering, sometimes almost over-abundant instrumentation reminds us of the D minor Concerto. The rare art of the thematic treatment, however, clearly points to the maturer years of the master, during which the work received its final form. This movement is dominated by a sort of musical motto, which plays an important part in the Introduction, supplies the counterpoint to the main subject, and is the leading feature in the second subject and the development. This motive appears again and again in different places and in different forms, and helps to give the whole movement its perfect homogeneity. The two middle movements, however, are lighter and shorter; indeed, Hermann Levi thought them more suitable for a serenade than for 'a symphony so largely planned.' This opinion would seem to be justified by the delicate instrumentation of the second movement, with its oboe and violin solo, and by the graceful Allegretto, which seems to smile through its tears. On the other hand, it must not be overlooked that these two movements provide the indispensable moments of relief in the dramatic action of the whole composition. For not only the first movement, but the beginning of the Finale, conjures up a vision of a gloomy Inferno. Everything in this last movement seems to be hastening towards a catastrophe, until suddenly a horn solo sounds a message of salvation. Then the broadly flowing, hymn-like Allegro proclaims its triumph over all fear and pain.

Between Brahms's First Symphony and the *Second Symphony in D major*, Op. 73, completed in 1877, there is a contrast similar to that between Beethoven's Fifth and Sixth Symphonies. After several years' work upon his mighty C minor Symphony, the older master apparently felt the desire to create a light, carefree piece of the same category, and within a few months he wrote his Pastoral Symphony, which contrasts the heroic pathos of the Fifth with a serene idyllic atmosphere. Similarly, the Second Brahms, which is likewise inspired with a profound feeling for nature, was written much more rapidly than the C minor Symphony. The whole atmosphere of this work is reflected in its instrumentation, which is more delicate, more translucent, and definitely brighter than that of the First Symphony, the pastoral flutes, oboes, and clarinets receiving particularly prominent parts. Nevertheless, Brahms does not renounce the heavy artillery of the trombones and tubas, which provide, in the outer movements, dim and spectral effects (first movement, b. 33 *et seq.*), or impressions of power and strength (Finale). Also in the D major Symphony, a motto-like idea appears in the first bar of the introductory movement, which is marked by an almost Southern romanticism. Although this idea reappears in various parts of the movement, it has not—by reason of the mood of the piece—the same inevitable persistence as the corresponding motto of the C minor Symphony. The following Adagio, serious and pondering, serves as a retarding element before the gay and bucolic playfulness of the third movement. This graceful Allegretto—one of the most easily accessible movements in all the symphonies of

Brahms—assumes the form of a rondo, consisting of three ritornelli and two episodes. The first episode is built on a variation of the ritornello, while the second episode, reminiscent of a Hungarian folk song, is again a sort of inversion of the first. Confident happiness speaks to us from the broadly flowing Finale. Here violent contrasts are avoided. The concise middle section even lacks any real development, consisting mainly of a lyrical episode (b. 221-34) based on a modification of the first bar. The shortened recapitulation leads to a powerful Coda, which ends in a burst of Dionysiac jubilation.

The *Violin Concerto in D major*, Op. 77, which was completed in 1878, is governed by the same principles as Brahms's first Pianoforte Concerto. Although this work demands exceptional technique on the part of the soloist, virtuosity for its own sake is entirely excluded. For Brahms, the artistic idea was always of supreme importance; and just as in his orchestral compositions the sound of the instruments inspired him only in a minor degree, so, in the Concertos, he was not particularly interested in writing gratifying parts for the soloists and impressing the audience. Notwithstanding his small acquaintance with violin technique, tacitly admitted both by Brahms and by his friend Joachim, this work confronts the soloist with a whole series of new and difficult, though by no means insoluble, problems. These, with few exceptions, tax the left hand of the violinist; the greatest demands are made in respect of double-stopping, the ability to span large intervals, and certainty of attack in playing high notes after low. It is characteristic of Brahms that he conscientiously asked his friend's advice on all technical questions—and then hardly ever followed it. The German State Library in Berlin owned the manuscript of the violin part, with Joachim's suggested emendations; also the letters exchanged between the two friends show how much attention Joachim had given to this work. But the result of all the great violinist's suggestions, which were almost entirely directed to excluding excessive difficulties from the solo part, is comparatively small; for example, the addition of *ma non troppo* to the tempo-direction *vivace* of the Finale was made at Joachim's request. In the first movement, before the violinist's intervention, Brahms had written (b. 535 *et seq.*): This may be of

EXAMPLE 5

greater musical consequence, but it is less gratifying for the violinist than the version suggested by Joachim, which was finally printed.

In its mood the Violin Concerto is closely related to the D major Symphony. The first movement, inspired by a dreamy romanticism rising to joyous energy, is in its whole aspect reminiscent of the first movement of Beethoven's Violin Concerto. A delicate Adagio, with beautiful arabesques in the violin part, leads up to the fiery Rondo-finale with its suggestion of Hungarian melodies. Although this whole movement is inspired with a cheerful vitality, Brahms modifies his fervor in the last bars. When with an upward rushing D major run (b. 337-9) the triumphant climax seems to have been attained, the master adds a few meditative, restraining. bars before the final chords. In this slight gesture, if nowhere else, we must recognize Brahms.

In 1880, as a mark of gratitude for his nomination to the honorary doctorate of the university of Breslau, Brahms wrote the *Academic Festival Overture,* Op. 80. The description, 'a cheerful potpourri of student songs *à la* Suppé,' given by Brahms himself, is certainly not appropriate. Nor is the profound symbolism which many authors like to attribute to this work. The *Academic Festival Overture* is the lively, 'occasional' composition of a genius. To take it too seriously would not be fair to Brahms. Thematic development, which was always his strong point, does not find any great oppor-

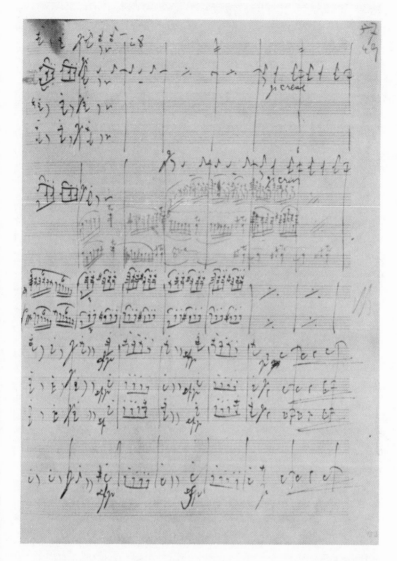

A PAGE OF BRAHMS'S DOUBLE CONCERTO (MS.) WITH PENCIL
CORRECTIONS (IN THE 7TH AND 8TH STAVES), BY JOACHIM

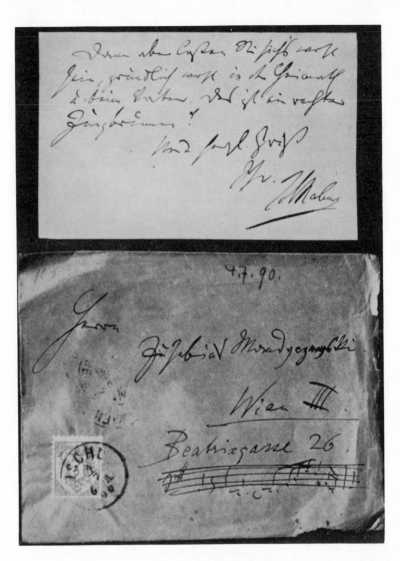

END OF A LETTER BY BRAHMS TO MANDYCZEWSKI, WITH ENVELOPE ON
WHICH BRAHMS NOTED THE BEGINNING OF HIS STRING QUARTET, OP. III

tunities in this work. The underlying ideas, in which four student songs are conspicuous (*Wir hatten gebauet, Der Landesvater, Was kommt dort von der Höh'*, and *Gaudeamus igitur*), follow too quickly on each other's heels for extended elaboration. The hand of the master is revealed, however, in the way the Overture grows from the mysteriously soft, almost somber opening in C minor, to the pealing jubilation of the concluding *Gaudeamus igitur,* played by the full orchestra. The composer succeeded in investing each of the songs with a specially effective instrumental garb; the comic scoring of *Was kommt dort von der Höh'* for bassoons and oboes is particularly noteworthy. If one were to cast about for humor in Brahms's work this passage would at once come to mind.

The *Academic Festival Overture* nas a companion piece in the *Tragic Overture,* Op. 81, which was completed in the years 1880-81. Brahms probably planned this as a prelude to a new production of Goethe's *Faust* in the Viennese Burgtheater. But it has not hitherto been realized that the first drafts of this composition must be more than ten years older. The *Gesellschaft der Musikfreunde* has a small sketchbook of Brahms's, containing sketches for the *Liebeslieder,* Op. 52, and the *Alto Rhapsody,* Op. 53, and in the midst of these, on two pages, the backs of which are covered with drafts of the Rhapsody, there is a fairly long sketch of the *Tragic Overture.* These sketches, apparently, as well as all the rest of the little volume, date back to the end of the 'sixties. The draft is set down—as is usual in Brahms's sketches—in two staves, which contain little more than the melody and the bass, the middle voices or the chords being entered only by exception. The sketch begins with b. 120 of the final version, and extends to b. 184 inclusive, i.e. to the end of the exposition; at which point Brahms put a repeat sign. As overtures, even when in sonata form, do not generally include a repetition of the first part, it seems doubtful whether the master had originally conceived this work as an overture; and it is, indeed, more likely that he reverted at a later date to the old draft, in his desire to create a companion piece for Op. 80. From b. 120 to 170, inclusive, the sketch is almost identical with its final form; the whole part, however, is written a fourth higher. After b. 171, Brahms noted two concluding passages for the exposition, which terminated—as in the published edition—in F major; one was of fourteen bars, and the other a longer one of thirty bars. The shorter passage was rejected, whereas of the longer one the last fourteen bars were used for the Overture. These fourteen bars, which correspond with b. 171-84 in the Overture, were already drafted in the key of the printed version. As in the final elaboration Brahms transposed the first fifty bars a fourth lower—i.e. from B flat major to F major—part of the modulating transition in the sketch could be canceled. In short, we may assume that a considerable part of the exposition—incidentally, one of the most effective passages in the whole work—was conceived as early as the end of the 'sixties. Its slow growth and possibly altered design did not improve the Overture. In spite of the unquestionable nobility and grandeur of its melodies, in spite of its beauty of form, this composition seems to lack inspiration. Its general effect is serious, sad, and colorless, but it is incomparably less tragic than the beginning of the D minor Concerto or the C minor Symphony. It is hardly possible that anyone, in listening to the *Tragic Overture,* would be conscious of that *katharsis,* that relief which the drama should bring to the soul of the hearer—according to Aristotle's definition—by exciting terror and compassion.

On his return from his first Italian journey, in the spring of 1878, Brahms made sketches for his *Pianoforte Concerto in B flat major,* Op. 83, which was finished three years later, in the summer of 1881. This work is extremely hard to master technically, because of its massive chords, its wide spans, its passages in octaves, thirds, and sixths, and its complicated rhythm. Greater still are the demands it makes on the intellect and understanding of the player. The soloist must not only succeed in asserting himself; he must also share, as an equal partner, with the other instruments of the orchestra in the development of the work, or he must content himself with the role of accompanist. The piano part is hardly more gratifying than that of a chamber-music work, although it demands the technique of a virtuoso. The character of the composition shows a certain freedom, of a kind unusual in Brahms's work. The violent and tragic mood of the First Concerto has vanished. The composition is full of a wonderfully balanced, one might almost say a Hellenic, serenity. To the usual three movements Brahms added a fourth, the Scherzo, wherein this work also resembles the Symphonies and the chamber music. The single movements are not as concise as is usually the case in the works of Brahms's mature years, and in their structure they frequently depart from the classic rules. In the first movement the exposition is preceded by a prelude-like dialogue between solo and orchestra; the Scherzo, instead of the traditional *da capo* after the trio, has a sort of free recapitulation. Similar innovations will be found in the last two movements. Finally, Brahms wanted to ensure that the work should be performed in a thoroughly rhapsodic style. The manuscript in possession of the Hamburg State and University Library shows a number of directions for small changes of tempo. For example, in the first movement: b. 118, *animato:* b. 128, *poco sostenuto:* b. 286, *sostenuto,* and so forth. Later, however, Brahms crossed out these directions, since he found that a too literal observance of them might spoil the continuity of the individual movements.

In the *Third Symphony in F major,* Op. 90, completed in 1883, the climax—as in so many works of the composer's maturity—is not at the beginning, but at the end of the work. The first movement has a comparatively short development, after a comprehensive exposition; the catastrophe, however, with its ultimate solution, is deferred to the Finale. This procedure is a complete renunciation of the principle, so often applied in the eighteenth century, and sometimes by Brahms himself, of regarding the last movement merely as a light and cheerful 'happy ending.' The mature master husbanded his resources, in order to reserve some of the most significant ideas until the end. Like the first two Symphonies, the Third is introduced by a 'motto' (b. 1-3); this at once provides the bass for the grandiose principal subject of the first movement (b. 3-5), and dominates not only this movement, but the whole Symphony. It assumes a particularly important role in the first movement, before the beginning of the recapitulation. After the passionate development the waves of excitement calm down, and the horn announces the motto, in a mystic E flat major, as a herald of heavenly peace (b. 101-8). Passionless, clear, almost objective serenity speaks to us from the second movement. No Andante of such emotional tranquillity is to be found in the works of the youthful Brahms. Particularly attractive is the first theme of the following *Poco Allegretto,* which (in spite of its great simplicity) is stamped with a highly individual character by its constant alternation of iambic and trochaic rhythms. Further, Brahms contrived to make the concise threefold form of the movement more effective by orchestrating the *da capo* of the first part in quite a different manner. Such a mixture of simplicity and refinement is characteristic of Brahms in his later years. The Finale is a tremendous conflict of elemental forces; it is only in the Coda that calm returns. Like a rainbow after a thunderstorm, the motto (b. 299-302), played by the flute, with its message of hope and freedom, spans the turmoil of the other voices. The orchestration of this work has a peculiar deep-toned luminosity.

How carefully Brahms worked at the scoring of this Symphony may be seen from the manuscript in the library of the collector Jerome Stonborough. It shows a large number of small penciled revisions in the orchestration, which the master probably made during the rehearsals. Thus, for instance, the change of the clarinets in the first movement (b. 36), from B flat to A, was not originally planned; and for the second movement Brahms wanted to make use of trumpets and drums, but subsequently dispensed with these, as not conforming with the mood of the Andante. On the other hand, the bassoons in b. 93-5 and the trumpets and drums in b. 91 and 233 of the Finale were later additions. Such meticulous consideration of the slightest subtleties of orchestral coloring belies the thoughtlessly repeated catchword that Brahms was not greatly interested in the problems of instrumentation.

The first two movements of the *Fourth Symphony in E minor*, Op. 98, were written in the summer of 1884, the third and fourth in the summer of 1885. This last symphonic work of the master is more stringent and more compact than the previous three. More than ever before was Brahms's mind directed towards the past. He found a wealth of inspiration in pre-classical music, which revealed peculiar possibilities of enriching his musical language. The principal theme of the first movement is largely characteristic of the whole work. Distinctive of the 'later Brahms' is the art with which an ample and far-flung theme is developed from a motive of only two notes; and no less so is the assurance with which the imitation of the theme in the wood wind is employed as an accompaniment to the theme itself. Again, the clear and passionless tranquillity of this idea, equally remote from pain and joy, is characteristic of this period of his work. The movement has no motto, like those of the first three Symphonies. On the one hand, the logical progression of ideas in this piece is so compelling that there is no need of a closer linking of the different sections by a special expedient; on the other hand, the Symphony possesses, in the Finale, a movement of such iron resolution and concentration that a similar formation in the first movement had to be avoided. The *Andante moderato* with its four monumental introductory bars, allotted to the horns and wood wind, leads off in the medieval Phrygian mode. Slowly the warm and fragrant E major makes itself heard. Notwithstanding its wonderfully tender song theme (b. 41 *et seq.*) introduced by the 'cellos, this whole movement seems to lie, as it were, under the shadow of an inevitable fate. A sturdy, high-spirited *Allegro giocoso* follows. If the first two movements and the Finale seem inspired by Sophocles' tragedies, which Brahms had read about this time in his friend Professor Wendt's translation, this movement might be sponsored by Breughel. A sturdy gaiety reigns supreme, and the orchestration is broader and more plastic, more calculated to secure massive effects. The master supplemented the scoring of both the preceding movements by the addition of piccolo flute, contrabassoon, and a third kettledrum. The Finale is the crowning glory of the whole work. Just as Brahms took leave of his chamber music, so, too, he bade farewell to his symphonic creations with a movement in variations, somewhat reminiscent of the old form of the Chaconne. A simple theme of eight bars (b. 1-8), is repeated thirty-one times, in the lower, middle, and upper voices, without a single modulation or transitional passage, providing the framework of this movement. How wonderfully the master's genius unfolded itself within this restricted form! With what skill he avoided spoiling the unity of the work is shown by the close interlacing of the successive variations, and by the addition of a second series of variations after the return of the theme in the fifteenth variation (b. 129-36). This second series is, as it were, a free repetition of the first. However, the technical mastery is as nothing compared with the power and magnificence, the defiance and lucidity of thought. This movement leads, as Kretzschmar says in his fine analysis of the Symphony, into the domain 'where the human bends its knee to the eternal.'

According to the manuscript, which is in the possession of the *Gesellschaft der Musikfreunde,* Brahms's last orchestral composition, the *Double Concerto for Violin and Vio-*

loncello in A minor, Op. 102, was written in the summer of 1887 at Thun. Although the master probably derived the inspiration for this work from the old *Concerti grossi* for two violins and one 'cello, and from Beethoven's Triple Concerto, his choice of the violin and violoncello for the solo instruments was quite original. The music, too, is modern, even though Brahms smuggled into the first movement (b. 90 *et seq.*) a reminiscence of Viotti's Violin Concerto in A minor, which he and Joachim loved so dearly. The soloists, from the technical point of view, have not here such a difficult task as in the Violin Concerto, and at the first rehearsals with Joachim and Hausmann their parts were actually made more difficult, instead of easier, as was the case with the earlier work. Joachim urged his friend to arrange several passages for the solo violin more effectively. This is clear from the original manuscript, which contains a number of subsequent corrections, and also passages that do not coincide with the printed edition, and were probably altered during the correction of the proofs. Thus the passage shown in Example 6 appears in the original manuscript, after b. 328 of the final movement. Joachim did not agree with this, and inserted in Brahms's manuscript a suggested alteration in pencil .(Example 7). Brahms admitted that Joachim's criticism was justified, but did not approve of his friend's suggestion, and wrote above it a third version for b. 330 *et seq.* of the Violin (Example 8).

For publication, however, he finally decided on a fourth version. So, too, with the b. 408-9 of the first movement. Here, again, Brahms's and Joachim's versions are written one above the other, and a third is substituted in the published edition. Further examples of Brahms's efforts to increase subsequently the brilliance of the Concerto might easily be given, since the master, whose sense of responsibility grew with increasing age, was anxious to create a true Concerto, and not another Symphony in disguise. This may also be the reason why, in this work, he dispensed with the

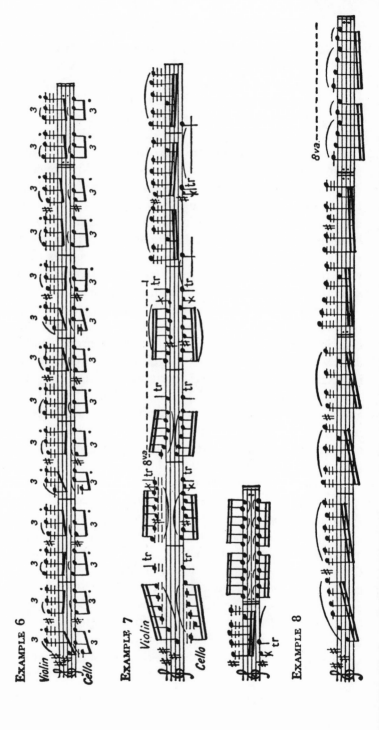

four movements included in his second Piano Concerto, and returned to the usual three—i.e. a powerful Allegro, an expressive Andante, and a cheerful Finale, in the manner of a Rondo. On the other hand, in accordance with his artistic principles it was utterly impossible for Brahms, especially in his later days, to write a really brilliant solo concerto. Thus he was faced with an inner conflict, which may be one of the reasons why this work lacks the magnificent power and inner necessity so strongly expressed in the last two Symphonies. The master could not fail to be aware of this, and since in his last creative period he generally aimed at a simplification of his means of expression, he henceforth lost all interest in orchestral composition, and gave his undivided attention—in the domain of instrumental music—to works for the pianoforte and chamber music.

XIX

SONGS FOR ONE, TWO, AND FOUR VOICES
WITH PIANOFORTE ACCOMPANIMENT

ALTOGETHER about 380 songs for one, two, and four voices were published from Brahms's pen.* Among them—including the folk songs—are about three hundred songs for solo voice and piano, twenty duets, and sixty quartets. It is impossible to discuss them one by one, as we have done in the case of the major instrumental works. On the one hand, this would exceed the limits set for the present volume, and on the other hand, it would entail an excessive amount of repetition in the study of the manifold stylistic interrelationships between the songs. For this reason it seems more expedient here to state the fundamental principles of Brahms's song writing, and then to discuss the most important features of each separate period.

In Brahms's songs the importance of the voice part is paramount. The composer values before all else a fluent, rhythmical, and expressive melodic line, carefully adapted to the text. He is even ready to sacrifice correct declamation, which in general he respects with the greatest conscientiousness, where the uniform flow of the melody is endangered. Second in importance comes the bass of the songs. With the mastery of the musician trained in contrapuntal thinking, he writes

---

* A new edition of Brahms's solo songs with excellent English translations of the texts and historical notes by Henry S. Drinker was published in 1945. In this and the following chapters the English names of the songs and choral works are quoted from this edition, as well as from the same author's *Texts of the Vocal Works of Johannes Brahms in English Translation.*

bass parts which not only constitute the foundation of the melody, but even emulate the voice part in intrinsic vitality, power of expression, and abundance of motives. As for the rest of the voices in the piano accompaniment, while it is true that Brahms's never-failing invention offers new modes of expression, which reveal the momentary mood of the song, these chords and figurations are of slight importance in comparison with the two main voices that are the basis of the composition. It seems almost as though the technique of the Baroque period, in which only the melody, together with the bass voice, was of importance, while the middle voices were not even noted, was trying to return to life in Brahms's music. Confirmation of this statement is afforded by his rough sketches, where sometimes only a figured bass appears instead of the middle voices (see p. 280). In this mode of construction Brahms contrasts very sharply with his contemporary Hugo Wolf, who in his songs gives the absolute lead to the pianoforte and emphasizes not so much the melodic line as the most careful declamation in the voice part.

A further feature of Brahms's songs is their splendid organic unity and completeness. He links the different parts of a composition, as well as the voice part and the piano accompaniment, by the use of similar motives. And further, a clearly articulated form will almost always be found as the basis of Brahms's songs. Next to the purely strophic songs, he particularly favors a form in which the individual strophes are more or less varied. But, even in the songs that depart entirely from the stanza form, the composer is careful to ensure the recurrence of the same, or at least related passages. If we examine a Brahms song merely from an architectural standpoint, we shall almost always find a symmetrical, beautifully complete, and even form.

After these few fundamental remarks, let us turn to the songs of the first creative period. They are: eighteen songs for solo voice with pianoforte, which date from the years 1851-3, and which appeared as Op. 3, 6, and 7, and also

Mondnacht (Moonlight), published in 1854 without opus number. In these earliest songs preserved, the young Brahms stands clearly before us. Op. 7/6, *Heimkehr* (Returning Home), the oldest song he thought worth preserving,* is like a scene from an opera. One would be inclined to place this *Allegro agitato,* with its vigorous triplets, its passionately rushing bass, and its sudden vociferous *fortissimi,* as a *recitativo accompagnato,* followed by a concluding *arioso,* in a serious Italian opera. Again, the somewhat superficial imitative description of the nightingale's song in the pianoforte accompaniment of Op. 6/6, *Nachtigallen schwingen* (The Nightingales), points to the composer's youth. There are even a few clumsy passages, as for instance in Op. 6/1, *Spanisches Lied* (Spanish Song), where the voice, together with the bass, passes from E to C sharp in the 20th, 22nd, 40th, and 42nd bars, and thus forms the prohibited octave-parallel with the bass. Finally, it is interesting to note that Brahms, in the first edition of his Op. 3, fairly sprinkled the voice part with expression marks. When, however, in later years, the songs appeared in a new edition, the maturer master canceled nearly all these marks—in order to give more freedom to the singer.

Although there is no lack of symptoms of the composer's youth, there are among these early opus numbers songs that give definite promise of future maturity. How characteristic is Op. 7/5, *Die Trauernde* (The Griever), where Brahms's preference for the sparse harmonies of the Renaissance and early Baroque periods is manifested! How impressive is its sudden change from major to minor, and its unusual rhythm! The text of Op. 6/1, *Spanisches Lied,* was set to music also by Hugo Wolf nearly forty years later; and although the poem inspired the younger master to write one of his most wonderful compositions, Brahms's gay and amiable song,

* Henry S. Drinker has an interesting theory that the first version of Op. 43, No. 3, probably antedates *Heimkehr* by four years (see *Solo Songs of Johannes Brahms,* vol. II, pp. ix, x).

with its original declamation and colorful accompaniment, can well hold its own in any comparison. Of the early songs Op. 3/1, *Liebestreu* (True Love), is the finest. Just as Schubert published the *Erlkönig* as the first of his songs, so Brahms sets in the forefront of his songs one of his most perfect creations. The deep tenderness of emotion and the marvelous economy of expression were scarcely ever surpassed in his later works. Consider the effect produced by the artist in making the voice part sometimes imitate and sometimes sing in unison with the bass accompaniment. What a brilliant result is obtained by the temporary modulation into E flat major from the gloom of the predominant E flat minor! One might quote Wagner's remark on Brahms's Handel Variations in connection with this song of only slightly varied strophes: 'What things can still be said in the old forms when someone comes along who knows how to handle them!'

To Brahms's second creative period belong the Eight Songs and Romances, Op. 14 (composed in 1858); Five Songs, Op. 19 (comp. 1858-9); Nine Songs, Op. 32 (comp. 1864); *Regenlied* (Rain Song) (comp. 1862, or perhaps 1866, published in 1907); and further, Three Duets, Op. 20 (comp. 1858-60); Four Duets, Op. 28 (comp. 1860-2); and Three Quartets, Op. 31 (comp. 1859 and 1863). To these must be added fourteen *Volkskinderlieder* (Children's Folk Songs), set in 1857-8, which Brahms himself published anonymously, and twenty-eight *Folk Songs,* which belong to the year 1858, but were published posthumously in 1926.

Brahms's deeply rooted love of folk song is particularly emphasized at this period. It is true that he gave much attention to it during his first creative period, but it was only at Detmold, when he began to study the music of the past with particular interest, that he became intensely preoccupied with folk song. He took the melodies and texts from the collection of Kretzschmer and Zuccalmaglio, which he particularly valued (see p. 288). He himself, however, composed the accompaniments, which first revealed the hitherto un-suspected beauties of these songs. Take, for example, the impression of wonderful quiet in No. 10 of the *Volkskinder-lieder,* the *Wiegenlied* (Cradle Song), evoked by the per-sistence throughout the song of the pedal-point on C, and the delicate trickling of the sand in the *una corda* quaver accompaniment in *Sandmännchen* (The Little Sandman). The twenty-eight *Folk Songs* are not quite so perfect, and these Brahms wrote rather as studies for his own use than for publication. It was not until his later years that he pub-lished many of them with altered accompaniments—some arranged for four-voice choir. It is most instructive to com-pare the first manuscript with Brahms's own 1894 edition of the forty-nine *German Folk Songs.* Contrast the two settings of *Feinsliebchen, du sollst mir nicht barfuss gehen* (You Must not Go Round without Shoes), and you will be aston-ished to see how greatly the accompaniment has gained in spirit and character in the later setting. How clear is the dis-tinction between the knight's and the maiden's speech in the pianoforte part, and how wonderfully the climax is reached by the simplest means in the last two verses! By comparison the setting of 1858 produces an almost meager impression. In contrasting other examples, however, the older collection does not come off so badly. Thus the older, power-ful setting of *Wach auf, mein Hort* (Now Hark and Heed) compares by no means unfavorably with the later and far richer version. His preoccupation at this time with folk song had also a profound influence upon Brahms's own work. The Eight Songs of Op. 14 were written to folk-song texts, and several of them, such as Nos. 1, 6, and 8, were likewise composed in the melodic manner of folk song. Brahms's en-deavor to deliver the short solo song from its isolation and to make it part of a cycle is already manifest in this opus. Some sort of a connection is also to be found between the nine songs of Op. 32. In spite of all his efforts to free himself from his beloved, in the end the man unconditionally admits

her sovereignty. Brahms's gift for making a logical connection between different song texts was—as we shall see—to
bear even finer fruit in his maturity. Also in a purely musical
fashion the composer often tries to link his songs together. In
Op. 19, *Scheiden und Meiden* (We Must not Part) and *In
der Ferne* (Far Away) begin in the same way. Thus the connection between the songs, which arises from the text, is
strongly emphasized.

Such imperfections as sometimes occur in the songs of the
first period are hardly to be found in these. On the other
hand they comprise a comparatively large number of masterpieces, which may be counted among Brahms's most priceless
songs. We need mention only Op. 19/4, *Der Schmied* (The
Smith), to the folksong-like melody of which Brahms has written an accompaniment that, without too obvious a realism,
suggests the sound of the light and the heavy hammer of the
blacksmith and his apprentice. More effective still, as far as
color is concerned, is the next song, *An eine Aeolsharfe* (To
an Aeolian Harp), in which the composer gives a masterly
portrayal of the ethereal tone of that strange instrument.
The Duets, Op. 28, in point of time, and also in their power
of expression, approach the verge of Brahms's maturer period.
The simple duet, *Die Nonne und der Ritter* (The Nun and
the Knight), is profoundly moving; whereas the next song,
Vor der Tür (Before the Door), with its conflict between the
increasingly urgent man and the obstinately unapproachable
girl, is full of mischievous gaiety. The pleasant *Wechsellied
zum Tanz* (Dialogue at the Dance), from the Quartets, Op.
31, betrays the composer's assiduous study of the older music
at Detmold. Schubert, and even more certainly Mozart, are
the godfathers of this lovely little minuet-like song. The
opening number of Op. 32, *Wie rafft ich mich auf* (In the
Night), is a powerful composition. With its dramatic entry,
its tremendous climax, and the wonderful interlocking of the
voice and the almost symphonic accompaniment, it rivals
the greatest songs of the later Schubert, by whom Brahms is

here perceptibly influenced. Even though there are many retrospective features in Brahms's work at this time—especially obvious in the archaic harmony of *Vom verwundeten Knaben* (Of the Wounded Lad), Op. 14/2—yet at times it points far into the future. Consider the stammering, hesitating declamation in Op. 32/2, *Nicht mehr zu dir zu gehen* (No More to See You), whose realism far outstrips the current conceptions of beauty in music, the heavy bass of the pianoforte, which, without breaking into an ordinary accompaniment, adds to the effect of the recitative, the passionate explosion in the middle section, the hopeless relapse into the mood of the beginning; this complete admixture of expressionism and naturalism would in no way surprise us in a work of the twentieth century. The most popular of all the songs of this period is perhaps the last, *Wie bist du meine Königin* (Fair, ah, how Fair). It is written in the varied strophe form especially favored by the composer. The first, second, and fourth stanzas recur almost unchanged; the third, however, is in strong contrast to them. In such narrowly restricted forms Brahms is—as we have seen—particularly successful. This song, with the ecstatic fervor of the voice part and the profoundly moving accompaniment, so simple, so entirely natural, and yet so affecting, is a work such as only a master could write, combining as it does the utmost skill with the simplicity of the folk song.

Brahms's third creative period covers about a quarter of a century. In this period such an enormous number of songs was written that it will be expedient to subdivide them. First we shall deal with the songs composed up to the spring of 1875, and then with the compositions of the following years.

In the period between the completion of the *Requiem* (1866) * and Brahms's resignation from his last permanent

---

* In this connection no regard is paid to the fifth movement, as the remaining six movements were already completely finished in 1866.

post as conductor of the *Gesellschaft der Musikfreunde* in Vienna (spring of 1875), he composed or completed the following songs: Fifteen Romances, Op. 33 (comp. 1861-9); Four Songs, Op. 43 (comp. 1857-68); Four Songs, Op. 46 (comp. 1864-8); Five Songs, Op. 47 (comp. 1858-68); Seven Songs, Op. 48 (comp. 1855-68); Five Songs, Op. 49 (comp. 1864-8); Eight Songs, Op. 57 (comp. 1871); Eight Songs, Op. 58 (comp. 1871); Eight Songs, Op. 59 (comp. 1870-73); Nine Songs, Op. 63 (comp. 1873-4); Four Duets, Op. 61 (comp. 1874); Three Quartets, Op. 64 (comp. 1862-74); Eighteen *Liebeslieder* (Love Songs) for vocal quartet and four-handed pianoforte accompaniment, Op. 52 (comp. 1868-9); and Fifteen *Neue Liebeslieder* (New Love Songs), Op. 65 (comp. 1874). We must add Five *Songs of Ophelia* from Shakespeare's *Hamlet,* written by Brahms in 1873 for Olga Precheisen, later the wife of the actor J. Lewinsky. These hitherto unknown songs were in 1933 published by me for the first time.

The most striking feature of this collection is the fact that the origin of many of these song cycles must be referred to the second or even the first creative period. We noted the same thing when considering the instrumental works. Brahms at the height of his powers was constantly returning to his earlier ideas. This had a decisive influence on his style. His music reached its highest perfection without developing any fundamentally new features.

We see that Brahms has still a special affection for the folk song. Pieces like Op. 47/3, *Sonntag* (Sunday), or the beginning of Op. 58/4, *O Komme* (Summer Night), have the natural unconstraint and slightly stereotyped quality of the folk song in spite of their artistic accompaniments. Also Op. 59/5, *Agnes,* with its fascinating change from 3/4 to 2/4 time, belongs to this group. But by far the most famous of all these songs is the *Wiegenlied* (Lullaby), Op. 49/4. The sweet and simple, yet highly original melody is constructed in strophic form above an organ-point and the soothing syncopation of the piano. Only a Brahms could have made technical perfection seem so like natural utterances.

Although Brahms was instinctively drawn to the North German folk music, there are plenty of allusions in his songs to the national art of his adopted land, Austria. Interwoven in the accompaniment of the *Wiegenlied* we find a genuine Upper-Austrian waltz song whose words are in dialect: 'Du moanst wohl, du glabst wohl, die Liab lasst si zwinga.' Moreover, in his thirty-three *Liebeslieder* and *Neue Liebeslieder,* Brahms paid the highest homage to the art of the Austrian capital. They are real Viennese waltzes and *Ländler,* in which Brahms, despite all his stylistic refinements, succeeded in recapturing with amazing fidelity the tone of the Austrian folk music. Together with the four-handed waltzes, Op. 39, they hold in numerical quantity alone a respectable position in the collected works of Brahms, so that we can judge how he loved this whole category of music. In the duet, Op. 61/1, *Die Schwestern* (The Sisters), Hungarian, and in Op. 48/1, *Der Gang zum Liebchen* (Going to the Loved One), Czech influences are apparent. One of his best songs, Op. 43/1, *Von ewiger Liebe* (Eternal Love), written to an originally Wendish text, shows unmistakable signs of Slav influence. Brahms, however, is not content with this. In the Serenade, Op. 58/8, the guitar-like tones seem to lead us to Spain. In the seventh of the Romances from *Magelone,* Op. 33, *War es Dir* (Was It for You), the peculiar rhythms and the stereotyped and persistent accompanying figures are suggestive of Oriental music.

To this group also belong the folksong-like *Songs of Ophelia* from Shakespeare's *Hamlet.* In spite of their conciseness, due to their employment in the drama, and the simple accompaniment, consisting principally of chords, they evoke the sinister atmosphere of the tragedy. In the whole melancholy cycle only the third number, the song of *St. Valentine's Day,* which assumes the role of a soothing

[274]

trio, strikes a somewhat brighter note. In this piece, with its dance-like, rocking accompaniment, and the tender, simple melody, the composer's individual note is most clearly audible.

Apart from folk music, Brahms's interest in the musical art of the past was uninterrupted. Pieces like Op. 43/3, *Ich schell mein Horn* (I Blow my Horn), with its peculiarly rigid harmonies, or *Vergangen ist mir Glück und Heil* (Dame Fortune Smiles no more on me), Op. 48/6, composed in the Doric mode, show his extraordinary insight into the art of the sixteenth century.

In his maturer years Brahms characteristically preferred to set poems which in mood and meter attempted to resuscitate the Greco-Roman lyrics of antiquity. To these belong *Der Abend* (Evening), Op. 64/2, a quartet which breathes a spirit of classic peace, and above all, Op. 43/2, *Die Mainacht* (May Night), one of his most beautiful songs. Hölty, the author of *Die Mainacht*, and of *Der Kuss* (The Kiss), Op. 19/1 (set by Brahms in his second period), wrote both songs in the meter of the Asclepiadic ode. It is instructive to observe the sovereign mastery with which Brahms at the height of his powers treats this complicated form, having almost failed, only a few years previously, to arrive at a full understanding of it.

If we are surprised at Brahms's perfect grasp of the most varied modes of expression, the multiplicity of the emotions conveyed by his songs is no less remarkable. Brahms had dedicated the Romances from *Magelone*, Op. 33, to his friend Julius Stockhausen. However, the majority of the songs of this period are fundamentally masculine in conception, not merely because Brahms was involuntarily thinking of the familiar voice of the great singer, but rather because it was his nature to express, even in his lyrics, robust and virile emotions. Brahms would never have attempted a work like Schumann's *Frauenliebe und Leben*, which is entirely rooted in the sphere of feminine emotion. Apart, however, from this unifying factor, the wealth of moods and characterizations in Brahms's lyric works is quite astonishing. If we compare *Botschaft* (Message), Op. 47/1, or the quartet *Fragen* (Questions), Op. 64/3, with *Schwermut* (Melancholy), Op. 58/5, or the cycle *Heimweh* (Homesickness), Op. 63/7-9, we shall find that hardly any shade of emotion is lacking, from joyous humor to intolerable grief. He has mastered even the gamut of hot sensuality (cf. the Eight Songs of Op. 57) and tempestuous passion (in Op. 47/2 *Liebesglut,* The Ardor of Love, and Op. 63/5 *Meine Liebe ist grün,* My Love is Green). He by no means disdains the hallucinating methods of tone-painting. In Op. 46/1 *Die Kränze* (The Garlands) he describes the dropping of tears quite in the manner of Bach. The first Romance from *Magelone* seeks to evoke the impression of a galloping horse, while Op. 59/3, *Regenlied* (Rain Song), and Op. 59/4, *Nachklang* (Reminiscence), describe the monotonous downpour of rain. But never does Brahms lose himself in detail. If, as in the last examples, he represents the sound of the rain, or, as in Op. 59/2, *Auf dem See* (On the Lake), the quiet rise and fall of the waves, he does so in order to relate these portrayals of Nature to the emotions which fill the human heart. The magical peace of the sunlit lake is reflected in the soul of the happy man, and the indefinable sadness occasioned by the equable rustle of the rain matches the melancholy thoughts of bygone childhood. To be sure, this method of animating Nature with the emotions of the human heart is by no means peculiar to Brahms. It is inseparably bound up with the character of romanticism, and in the songs of Schubert, which Brahms loved above all other songs, Brahms found this method raised to its highest perfection. This only proves once more how deeply Brahms, in spite of all preference for the classical, was rooted in romanticism.

Brahms's endeavor to deliver the single song from its isolation and to combine two or more songs in a larger unity was already perceptible in the second period, and became more pronounced in his maturity. In Op. 63 are two songs of related content under the common title of *Junge Lieder* (Songs of Youth), and three others are combined under the common title of *Heimweh*. In Op. 59 the two related songs, *Regenlied* and *Nachklang,* are musically connected by their rain motive. This endeavor reached its climax in the 'sixties, when Brahms was selecting short passages from the Bible for the text of his mighty *Requiem.* The composition of the fifteen Romances from Tieck's *Magelone* falls within this period. Only those who are familiar with Tieck's work can appreciate its close relationship of textual content. (The lack of such familiarity has prevented, and is still preventing, these beautiful works from becoming well known.) * Yet no one can fail to note their internal musical relationship. This is emphasized by the fact that at the end of the fifteenth song Brahms refers back to the first. Moreover, in all these fifteen pieces we find an unwonted breadth and boldness of structure. Brahms avoids the simple form of the folk song even as he avoids the simple strophic song; he is even less bound by the details of the text than in the other songs. Each Romance develops into a spacious scene, in which the piano is granted ample room for its independent prologue, interlude, and epilogue. It is hardly surprising that the Romances sometimes become more than a little operatic (cf. No. 3) and even Wagnerian (b. 82-5).

A light-hearted pendant to the Romances is found in the *Liebeslieder* (Op. 52) for piano duet and voice *ad lib.* This direction *'ad lib.,'* inserted by the publishers for the purpose of obtaining a larger sale, is completely misleading; for although nearly all the actual notes of the voice part are contained in the piano part, these pieces lose their special charm

---

* Guided by this consideration, Henry S. Drinker (*Solo Songs of Johannes Brahms,* I, pp. xix-xx) has told Tieck's whole story, showing in which place each Romance comes in. In a performance, Mr. Drinker's outline should be recited between the songs or incorporated in the program notes.

without the magical sound effect of the voices singing in waltz time and the beauty of the uttered words. The *Liebeslieder* are really vocal quartets, with four-handed pianoforte accompaniment. By deleting the misleading *ad lib.* from the second series of *Neue Liebeslieder,* and thus declaring the singing voice to be indispensable, Brahms did only what was musically an obvious necessity. It is certainly more than pure coincidence that the *Liebeslieder* stand in close proximity to the two string quartets of Op. 51. The doctrine held since the eighteenth century, that the combination of four voices is particularly well balanced and expressive, is not unjustified, and it is therefore hardly surprising that Brahms, as he matured, felt strongly drawn towards the quartet, both in instrumental and vocal composition. But we shall look in vain in the *Liebeslieder* for the organic completeness of the two string quartets. They constitute a loosely bound wreath of songs; the separate items were only gradually given their final form and their place in the sequence. Both the sketches for the *Liebeslieder* and the original manuscripts contain a number of deviations from the printed version. No. 13 had originally an eight-bar instrumental prelude, which Brahms later canceled; a piece whose concluding passage appears in the manuscript, was likewise excluded, only to be later reinserted in a new form, as No. 14 of the *Neue Liebeslieder.* Similarly, among the sketches for Op. 52 there are two waltzes, which Brahms included only in the second series, as Nos. 5 and 17. We see that he elaborated this cheerful offspring of his muse not only in his mind, but to some extent on paper; a sure sign that he was not dealing with a strictly constructed form, but a more loosely planned composition.

Shortly after the completion of the *Liebeslieder* Brahms was asked by his friend, Ernst Rudorff, to orchestrate the part of the piano duet for a Berlin performance. The composer liked the idea and wrote, in the winter of 1869-70, a little suite of nine waltzes for voices and small orchestra.

Eight of them were taken from Op. 52, a ninth one was a new composition that Brahms later incorporated in a slightly altered and improved form as No. 9 into his *Neue Liebeslieder,* Op. 65. The orchestrated *Liebeslieder* Suite, which was first performed on 19 March 1870 in Berlin, consists therefore of the following waltzes: Op. 52 Nos. 1, 2, 4, 6, 5; Op. 65 No. 9; Op. 52 Nos. 11, 8, 9. According to Brahms's wish, the solo voices were retained in this version, as a chorus would have unduly obscured the light and transparent orchestration. Throughout the whole suite, only two flutes, two oboes, two clarinets, two bassoons, two horns, and strings are used; and in Nos. 3, 5, and 6 the small group of wind instruments is even further reduced. The result is a series of little waltzes in true Viennese style, displaying the greatest economy in the use of orchestral instruments. The composition was first published in 1938 from Brahms's own manuscript. The editor, Wilhelm Weismann, emphasizes that even a performance of the instrumental parts alone, without the voices, is effective; there cannot be any doubt, however, that it would not have met with Brahms's full approval.

The *Neue Liebeslieder* compare with Op. 52 much as the second series of *Hungarian Dances* compares with the first. The happy freshness of inspiration which distinguished the earlier work is often replaced by especially careful workmanship. It is significant that the most exquisite piece of the second series, *Zum Schluss* (Ending), occupies a special position, as regards both its text and its music. A sole exception among all the *Liebeslieder,* the words are taken not from Daumer but from Goethe, and the music composed for them differs in character and rhythm from the waltz. This number is a Chaconne with a canon-like middle movement; and it is just here, where he is turning from a light to a more serious mode of writing, that Brahms gives of his best.—A further cycle of Daumer songs probably owed its origin to the work done on the *Liebeslieder.* These are the Eight

Songs, Op. 57, which are linked together by a glowing and yet dematerialized passionateness of expression. At that time such an emotional basis for song was rare. For this reason even some of Brahms's friends did not appreciate the cycle.

There are sketches not only for the *Liebeslieder* but also for the solo songs. Particular interest attaches to the preliminaries of the song Op. 58/7, *Vorüber* (Gone), in the possession of the *Gesellschaft der Musikfreunde*. In general, only the voice part and text are written down, except where the voice is silent, and then the treble part of the accompaniment is noted, and in a few places a figured bass. The bass, however, is by no means always present. The song was at first in E flat major, a whole tone lower than in the printed edition. Approximately the sketch follows the lines of the final version, until bar twenty-two, when it continues otherwise. Brahms was obviously dissatisfied with it, for after twelve bars he suddenly broke off and began the song again, this time in the right key of F major. At the critical point, 'Denn nun ich erwache' (And now I awake), at the beginning of the second part of the song, he stops short again, and here the sketch comes to an end. This little piece proves clearly enough the statement made at the beginning of this chapter, that Brahms considered the singing voice paramount. The second place he gave to the bass and its harmonies, which last he wrote as figures, in the old-fashioned way, over the bass. It was only when these foundations were laid that he turned to the details of the accompaniment. The groping after the final form of the composition shown in this sketch was certainly not confined to this song alone. Brahms, who frequently did not publish his songs until years after composing them, liked to get his *Lieder* down on paper as soon as the inspiration came to him, giving them to the public only after they had been carefully chiseled and polished.

Finally, before turning to the next group, let us consider a few exceptional songs which have not yet been mentioned.

In Op. 43/4, *Das Lied vom Herrn von Falkenstein* (The Song of the Lord of Falkenstein), he has given us a convincing work whose tone is that of the ballad. It is characteristic of Brahms that in the printed edition he added the defiant and challenging ninth verse, which is not in the manuscript. The tender, poetic accompaniment in Op. 47/1, *Botschaft* (Message), with its jerky combination of couplets and triplets at *Eile nicht* (Hasten not), is deserving of special mention. The restrained power of expression in Op. 49/1, *Am Sonntag Morgen* (On Sunday Morning), is extremely moving. Here the drama unfolds itself without departing from the narrow confines of the pure lyric, and is doubly impressive owing to these limitations. Both the beautiful quartet, *An die Heimat* (To the Homeland), Op. 64/1, and the three songs *Heimweh* (Longing for Home), from Op. 63, belong to the works in which the composer set to music his unquenchable longing for the home in which he could make no abiding stay. There is, however, no lack of artistic contradictions. We made their acquaintance in the Waltzes and *Liebeslieder,* and we find an amusing little trait, which confirms them, in the fact that Brahms wanted to begin his song Op. 57/1 with the-words 'Von Dornbachs schöner Höhe' (From Dornbach's lovely highland). Later he restored the words 'Von waldbekränzter Höhe' (From lofty wood-crowned highland), from the original text, renouncing, out of respect for the poet, the little compliment to Dornbach, that beautiful Vienna suburb.

In the second half of Brahms's third creative period the following songs were written: Nine Songs, Op. 69 (comp. 1877); Four Songs, Op. 70 (comp. 1875-7); Five Songs, Op. 71 (finished 1877); Five Songs, Op. 72 (comp. 1876-7); Six Songs, Op. 85 (comp. 1877-82); Six Songs, Op. 86 (comp. 1877-8); Five Songs, Op. 94 (comp. 1884); Seven Songs, Op. 95 (comp. 1884); Four Songs, Op. 96 (comp. 1884); Six Songs, Op. 97 (comp. 1884); Five Songs, Op. 105 (comp. 1886); Five Songs, Op. 106 (comp. 1886); Five Songs, Op.

107 (comp. 1886); Two Songs for Contralto and Viola, Op. 91 (comp. 1863-84); Five Romances and Songs for one or two voices, Op. 84 (comp. 1881?); Five Duets, Op. 66 (comp. summer 1875); Four Ballads and Romances for two voices, Op. 75 (comp. 1877-8); Four Quartets, Op. 92 (comp. 1877-84); and eleven *Zigeunerlieder* (Gipsy Songs), Op. 103 (comp. 1887).

In these songs—numbering over a hundred—we shall find again, as a rule, all those features we have already noted in the songs of the first half of Brahms's mature period. However, many minor details have been modified; features which were formerly in the foreground have receded, while others are now more conspicuous. Thus the general picture shows in some respects an altered aspect.

Brahms is no longer so naively wedded to the folk song in this period of his greatest artistic refinement. However, we still notice many little traits in the more elaborate songs which show how completely the master had adopted the language of the folk song. Thus, in Op. 105/5, *Verrat* (Betrayal), there is often a repetition of the last words at the end of each line. This is a little trick of expression native to the folk song, which contributes not a little to its emotional power. The change from 2/4 to 3/4 time in Op. 97/4, *Dort in den Weiden* (In the Shade of the Willows), has a similar significance, for the expansion and contraction of the rhythm are two of the small liberties characteristic of the folk song. Nevertheless, simple and downright directness of effect peculiar to the folk song is rarely found among the songs of this period. In this connection it is interesting to examine the songs *Spannung* (Strained Relations), Op. 84/5, *Dort in den Weiden*, Op. 97/4, and *Trennung* (Finis), Op. 97/6, which Brahms later included, with their original melodies, in his forty-nine *Volkslieder*. The difference between the genuine folk song and Brahms's rendering is considerable. It is also characteristic of Brahms that in Op. 86/1, *Therese*, he subsequently wanted to replace the simple original melody by something much more complicated, and was persuaded to retain the first version only by the energetic representations of his faithful friend, Frau von Herzogenberg.

Much the same thing may be observed in respect of the non-German folk music. In Op. 85/3, *Mädchenlied* (Maiden's Song), Op. 95/1 *Das Mädchen* (The Maiden), and Op. 95/5, *Vorschneller Schwur* (The Rash Oath), the spirit of Serbian song is expressed with surprising fidelity. The last two songs, however, belie in their later stages the specifically Serbian opening. Directly the text expresses a more cheerful mood, Brahms frees himself from the shackles of Slavic melody. The song gains in impetus, at the same time losing its expressly national stamp, as though the composer wished to show that hilarity and gaiety should have a more general character. The same thing may be said of the *Zigeunerlieder*, Op. 103. Brahms took translations of the Hungarian folk song for his texts. The airs are all in the favorite rhythm of Hungarian national music: 2/4 time; and sometimes the composer has permitted himself to be inspired by the original melodies; but the Hungarian character is not nearly so prominent in these songs as in the Hungarian Dances. He wished to produce artistic music in the spirit of the Hungarian airs, but by no means a mere copy of national folk music. The cheap effect of the imitation of the Gipsy cymbalom or dulcimer is rarely adopted by Brahms (compare No. 10); and it is significant that in No. 7, one of the most delightful pieces of the whole cycle—as in the second series of the *Liebeslieder*—the national character has almost entirely disappeared. Even in this period the master gladly derived inspiration from the national music of foreign countries, but when he had something decisive to say he involuntarily lapsed into his own mode of expression. It should be mentioned in this connection that in this period there are fewer compositions in the manner of the sixteenth century, and he wrote fewer settings of poems of classical form and content. The wonderfully impressive *Sapphische Ode* (Sapphic Ode), Op. 94/4, is almost an isolated example among the songs of this time.

Although Brahms to a certain extent restricted the scope of his song writing, he made up for this restriction by the undiminished and even increased variety of his own style. He is equally successful in men's, girls', or women's songs. From the archness of Op. 69/8, *Salome,* and Op. 107/3, *Das Mädchen spricht* (The Maiden Speaks), the comfortable humor of Op. 107/2, *Salamander,* the soulful tenderness of Op. 95/2, *Bei Dir sind meine Gedanken* (My Thoughts Are There), to the ethereal delicacy of Op. 70/2, *Lerchengesang* (Lark's Singing), and the somber passion of Op. 75/1, *Edward,* not a shade is missing from his palette. From the pure lyric, Brahms passes with his songs of a ballad-like character (cf. Op. 97/3, *Entführung* (Abduction), and the Ballads in Op. 75) to the realm of the epic; many of his songs have even the character of the dramatic scena. To this group belongs Op. 105/4, *Auf dem Kirchhofe* (In the Churchyard), in which Brahms ingeniously introduces the grand old Protestant Chorale, *O Haupt voll Blut und Wunden* (O Sacred Head Now Wounded), and above all Op. 94/5, *Kein Haus, keine Heimat* (The Tramp), which, in its compact structure and the short, sharp notes in the accompaniment, might have been included in any realistic opera of the time. Indefatigably he strives to increase the possibilities of expression. In the second half of the accompaniment of Op. 95/3, *Beim Abschied* (When the One Goes), the time was originally in 3/8, as in the voice part. In his printed copy, however, Brahms altered this for later editions to 2/4, without changing the time in the voice part. An element of painful unrest is introduced by these rhythmic discords, which is admirably suited to the character of the song. In Op. 72/5, *Unüberwindlich* (Irresistible), Brahms introduces a quotation from a Scarlatti Sonata, which in its dry, prosaic tone greatly enhances the comic effect of this humorous piece. And how completely Brahms has succeeded, with the help of a sudden, unexpected general pause, in depicting the treacherous effect of an overdose of wine! In Op. 91—perhaps inspired by Bach—Brahms adds the viola, his favorite string instrument, to the pianoforte and contralto voice parts. In *Geistliches Wiegenlied* (Cradle Song of the Virgin), the second of these two songs, the wonderful old German cradle song, *Joseph, lieber Joseph mein* (Blessed Joseph, Joseph Dear), is given to the viola, while the voice contributes gentle, floating melodies. This song is especially significant not only for its peculiar color effects, but even more for its profound emotional content and the imaginative use of the *canto firmo* technique. The first song, *Gestillte Sehnsucht* (When I Yearn no More), once more expresses Brahms's deep love of Nature. How delicately is the soughing of the wind portrayed by the broken chords gliding across the strings of the viola! In fact, Brahms's love of Nature is an inexhaustible theme. This is shown not only by such a masterpiece as *Feldeinsamkeit* (In Lonely Meadow), Op. 86/2, where the gentle moving quaver passages, deep pedal-points and a far-flung melodic line give a picture of a dreamy summer day with its slowly moving clouds, which has few counterparts in the whole of musical literature, but also by the weary dripping of the mist in the quartet *Spätherbst* (Late Autumn), Op. 92/2, the gentle and incessant ripple of the waves in Op. 96/4, *Meerfahrt* (At Sea), the wonderful, equable stillness of the night only just becoming audible in Op. 96/1, *Der Tod, das ist die kühle Nacht* (To Die Is Like the Cool of Night); all this shows that Brahms perceived the happenings of the outer world not only with quickened senses, but also with an open heart, and reproduced them in his work.

Lastly, let us enumerate a few of the best-known songs of this period which have not already been mentioned. Reminiscences of a Styrian *Ländler* seem unconsciously to have crept into the deeply moving *Minnelied* (Love Song), Op. 71/5. The composer's relations to Austrian dance music were so intimate that it entered into his mind on the very slightest pretext. In *Alte Liebe* (Old Love), Op. 72/1, the dreamy mood of a spring day, akin to both joy and sorrow, is wonderfully reproduced. In *Vergebliches Ständchen* (Fruitless Serenade), Op. 84/4, Brahms treats the same subject as in *Vor der Tür* (Before the Door), Op. 28/2; here, too, a presumptuous suitor is energetically repulsed by his lady-love. Whereas he intended an actual duet in the earlier work, the master's direction 'for one or two voices,' in *Vergebliches Ständchen* and all the other songs of Op. 84, is perhaps hardly to be taken seriously. The contrast between the two persons in the dialogue should be pointed—so far as this is not done by the accompaniment—by the dramatic skill of a single singer. Such an outward simplification, which ultimately increases the difficulties of the performer, is not seldom to be found in the works of this period. The inspired *Immer leiser wird mein Schlummer* (Fretful Slumber Veiled in Sorrow), Op. 105/2, is all mood and emotion. The famous *Ständchen* (Serenade), Op. 106/1, is hardly less steeped in emotion; a pastel, full of subtle passages, which, despite its tenderness, safely escapes the rocks of sentimentality. The last song of Brahms's mature period is *Mädchenlied* (Maiden's Song), Op. 107/5. The accompaniment is very simple, derived as it is from the regular rhythm of the spinning wheel. The voice part is arranged in strophes, and is given a certain freedom only in the second half of the song. But how powerful is the effect that Brahms obtains in spite of, or rather by means of, this extreme economy! In the third strophe the melody, by the simple means of two interpolated quaver rests, is obstructed in its free rhythm, conveying the impression of hopelessness. How poignantly despairing is the outburst: *Wofür soll ich spinnen?* (What use is my spinning?) where the basic melody recurs at a higher pitch! The refinement of simplicity, so characteristic of the older Brahms, is especially well exemplified in this song. The beautiful quartets Op. 92, like the four-part songs Op. 64 of the preceding group, deserve to be better known. They are lovely pieces of ensemble music which can stand comparison even with the instrumental quartets of the period.

Here we must also mention Brahms's arrangements of vocal works by other composers. For thirteen Chamber Duets and two Terzetti of Handel's (published 1880) the master composed a thorough bass. It is imaginatively planned, and reveals a vigorous life of its own, without, however, forcing its way into the foreground or taking precedence of the solo voices. In a quiet, simple, but always spirited manner the middle voices follow the prescribed upper and lower vocal parts. Seven of the thirteen duets were first published in 1870, and ten years later a new and greatly expanded edition was issued, in which Brahms had made a number of slight modifications. They give us an opportunity of studying the development achieved by Brahms even in the elaboration of a Continuo part. With only small alterations and revisions he succeeds, in this second version, in giving the accompaniment a more natural flow, and also a greater vitality.

To Brahms's last creative period belong only three works: the forty-nine *Deutsche Volkslieder* (German Folk Songs), without opus number, begun in his first period but not finished until 1894; the *Vier ernste Gesänge* (Four Serious Songs), Op. 121, completed on Brahms's sixty-third birthday, 7 May 1896; and the Six Quartets, Op. 112, composed 1888-91.

A wide gulf separates the *Vier ernste Gesänge* from the other solo songs of Brahms. The choice of the texts is unusual enough; their settings are still more so. His remarkable knowledge of the Bible enabled Brahms to select texts from both the Old and New Testaments and to combine them in an overwhelming Hymn to Death. A rugged pessimism dominates the first two songs, in which the vanity of all things earthly is proclaimed with hopeless austerity. There is no lightening of this dark mood until the third song, which at its close sings of the blessedness of death for all the weary and heavy-laden. The climax comes in the fourth and concluding song, which glorifies the power of love in the words of the incomparable Epistle to the Corinthians. Thereby the musician, who was nearing his end, made a last confession: that even the terrors of death are vanquished by all-conquering love. For such an unusual content he had perforce to choose an unusual mode of treatment. The *Vier ernste Gesänge* are a tremendous solo cantata, or even—if the expression is permissible—a sort of solo oratorio. There is preserved in the *Gesellschaft der Musikfreunde* a sketch of this work, with a draft of the orchestration. Even if the idea of an orchestral version of the work had never occurred to Brahms, the choice of Biblical texts, the declamatory style of the vocal part, inclining now to the recitative and now to the aria, the partially archaic style of the composition and the orchestra-like treatment of the piano part, all make one think of an oratorio. This last vocal work is the most characteristic example of the last Brahms. It compresses the greatest content into the smallest space; it is in some ways a continuation of the Protestant Church Cantata of the Baroque period, and yet, in the fundamentally unecclesiastical content of the first two songs, it was conceivable only in an age of skepticism. The musical language tells the same story: it is definitely Baroque and archaic, and at the same time, in countless details of its harmony, rooted in romanticism.

A curious problem is presented by Brahms's attitude to German folk music, and here we are referring not to the folk-song traits in his own songs, but to his treatment of original folk texts and melodies. Friedländer, who has gone deeply into this question, comes to the conclusion that Brahms had no unerring sense of the genuineness or spuriousness of old folk songs, because side by side with the gems of the older German folk music he did not scruple to publish imitations by Reichardt, Nicolai, Zuccalmaglio, and others. However far this reproach may be justified, it hardly

BRAHMS WITH HIS FRIEND, I. BRULL, 1894

BRAHMS WITH HIS FRIENDS, SHORTLY BEFORE HIS DEATH. *Standing, from left to right:* EPSTEIN, MANDYCZEWSKI, HAUSMANN. *Seated:* HANSLICK, BRAHMS, JOACHIM

BRAHMS AND FRAU NIKISCH

OLD BRAHMS SITTING IN THE GARDEN OF MILLER V. AICHHOLZ AT GMUNDEN

approaches the problem from the right side. In spite of his historical sense, which was unusually developed for a composer, Brahms was first of all an artist. He selected the texts and melodies according to their value and expressiveness, and not from the scientific point of view. At the same time, he was anxious that his choice should be justified in the eyes of an expert. He therefore studied, for purposes of comparison, all the compilations of folk songs made by Kretzschmer-Zuccalmaglio, Nicolai, Arnold, Simrock, and Erk-Böhme within his reach, and did his utmost, while respecting historical truth, to obtain the most beautiful and most accurate reading of text and melody. He was never weary of corresponding with the ever-helpful Mandyczewski, sometimes discussing a single word, or even a letter; but who would reproach him for attaching more importance, in the last resort, to artistic rather than to historical truth? He retained the songs from Zuccalmaglio's collection, which he had cherished in the past, even when some doubt of their genuine character had arisen; on the other hand, the inartistic, though historically correct mass of songs of greatly differing value in Erk-Böhme's collection was abhorrent to him.

It is obvious from a letter to Spitta (6 April 1894), that Brahms was fully aware that the air to No. 13 of his Folk Songs, *Wach auf, mein Hort,* was of much later origin than the text. Nevertheless, he included it in his collection, and to this conscious failure of historical criticism we owe one of the most characteristic and loveliest of the master's *Volkslieder.* A pamphlet of quite respectable size would result from the enumeration of all the small refinements Brahms introduced into the accompaniment of these songs. He adhered faithfully to the texts and melodies of the originals (except that he often omitted the less important stanzas). In Nos. 43-9 of the *Volkslieder* he even adopted the division into solo singer and chorus prescribed by Zuccalmaglio in many of the songs of his collection. But the accompaniment changes in accordance with the psychological situation

[289]

of the song. One of Brahms's most precious gifts, economy in expression, is here seen to the greatest advantage. With the most modest means, and without ever betraying the character of the simple folk song, he aims at the maximum impression. This he achieves, for instance, by a simple syncopation, or a few dispersed chromatic intervals. Only once did Brahms take a portion of a melody from the original and compose the rest of it himself: in the case of the wonderful No. 42, *In stiller Nacht* (In Dead of Night), the second half of which he supplied. But how magnificently the melody is continued in the very spirit of the song! Who could detect the work of the restorer, and who could fail to recognize that this stylistically faithful continuation of an older melody was possible only after a complete absorption of the spirit of folk song?

Of the Quartets, Op. 112, the first two pieces, *Sehnsucht* (Longing) and *Nächtens* (In the Night), are among the most melancholy of all Brahms's songs. Although these quartets were written as early as 1888, they are inspired by all the pessimism which predominates in the first two of the *Vier ernste Gesänge*. To be sure, they have not the monumental greatness of the later work. Although in *Nächtens* the somber bass cantilena which recurs several times in the pianoforte part seems to symbolize the rule of an inexorable destiny, yet the piece, with its restless bass tremoli, is completely possessed by subjective and emotional romanticism. The collocation of these two mournful quartets with four further *Zigeunerlieder* is due only to external causes. These *Zigeunerlieder* do not entirely escape the curse which has sometimes fallen upon the second series. They are not quite equal to the first series in freshness originality, or wealth of invention.

Thus, by the elaboration of folk songs, the Brahms of the last phase brings to its conclusion a task begun in his early youth. Infallible taste, a sense of style and economy—those attributes with which the aging master achieved such great things—these still persisted, while fewer demands were made on his creative powers, now beginning slowly to decline. But the eternal theme of death and love inspires the artist, himself approaching death, to his last creative effort. Reverting to the first great work of his mature period, the *Requiem*, in his own inimitable manner he created the mightiest synthesis of the old spirit and the new.

XX

SMALLER CHORAL WORKS

IN his first period Brahms wrote nothing for chorus. He had neither the occasion to do so nor the necessary technical mastery of choral writing. It was in his second period that, thanks mainly to his posts as conductor in Detmold and Hamburg, he became familiar with the choral form in actual practice, and also in theory, as the result of exhaustive study. The number of works of this period which he himself thought worthy of publication is considerable. They are: *Geistliches Lied* (Sacred Song), Op. 30, for four-part mixed choir, with organ or pianoforte accompaniment (composed in the Spring of 1856); the *Marienlieder* (Songs of the Virgin), Op. 22, for mixed choir *a cappella* (Summer, 1859); *Der 13. Psalm* (Psalm 13), Op. 27, for female choir with organ or pianoforte accompaniment, strings *ad libitum* (Summer, 1859); Two Motets, Op. 29, for five-part mixed choir *a cappella* (Summer, 1860); Three Songs, Op. 42, for six-part mixed choir with pianoforte accompaniment *ad libitum* (1859-61); Five Songs, Op. 41, for male choir *a cappella* (1861-2?); three *Geistliche Chöre* (Sacred Choruses), Op. 37, for female choir *a cappella* (1859-63); Twelve Songs and Romances, Op. 44, for female choir with pianoforte accompaniment *ad libitum* (1859-63); *Dem Dunklen Schoss* (In Earth's Dark Womb) for four-part mixed choir *a cappella*. Further, the great majority of the canons written by Brahms belong to this period. At all events, this is true of at least half of the twenty canons he is known to have written: the canon *Spruch*

(Maxim) (written 1856-8); six of the thirteen canons for fe-male voices, which were not published until 1891 (Nos. 1, 2, 8, 10, 11, 12, all written before 1862); *Grausam erweiset sich Amor* (Cruel Hath Love Been to Me) (version for four voices, written before 1862); *Zu Rauch muss werden* (In Dust Will Vanish) (before 1864); and *O wie sanft* (Ah How Slow) (be-fore 1864). Besides, Brahms arranged twenty-four German folk songs for four-part mixed choir *a cappella* (completed before 1864), fourteen of which were published by the com-poser himself in 1864, and four in 1926 by Max Friedländer; while the remaining six, in possession of the *Singakademie* in Vienna, were published by E. Mandyczewski in 1927.

An interesting supplement to this material has been pro-vided through the researches of Sophie H. and Henry S. Drinker. In 1935 they acquired a number of *Stimmenhefte* (part books) and scores which belonged originally to mem-bers of Brahms's women's chorus in Hamburg and were cop-ied directly by the singers from the composer's own manu-scripts. They contain a number of works Brahms subse-quently published as women's choruses (Op. 17, 27, 37, 44, etc.); moreover they comprise about fifty folk-song arrange-ments and a number of original works for women's chorus which the composer later adapted for mixed chorus or a solo voice, while the first version remained unknown. From this valuable source the following works for four-part wo-men's chorus have been published by Henry S. Drinker since 1938: *Vineta* (1860), subsequently published as a six-part mixed chorus, Op. 42/2; *Es geht ein Wehen* (A Sigh Goes Floating), subsequently published as a five-part mixed chorus Op. 62/6; *In stiller Nacht*, although partly an origi-nal composition by Brahms, subsequently published among his Folk Songs for solo voice; *Dein Herzlein mild* (Thou Gentle Heart), a completely new setting of the same text for five-part mixed chorus, subsequently published as Op. 62/4; *Marias Kirchgang* (Mary and the Boatman), subsequently published as a four-part mixed chorus, Op. 22/2; *Töne lin-*

dernder Klang (Music However Soft), a canon subsequently published for mixed chorus; *Seven Folk Songs* for three- and four-part women's chorus, partly arranged later on for mixed chorus or solo voice. A comparison of the women's choruses here listed with the versions for mixed chorus shows as a rule no fundamental difference. Apart from minor changes in melody and harmony, the subsequent arrangements exhibit various transpositions and a fuller setting, but no really new ideas.

The basis of Brahms's choral works of the second period is once more folk song and the music of the past. Indeed they sometimes show so pronounced a historical bias that the personal note of the composer recedes into the background. In the choruses for female voices, Op. 37, for example, the art of the sixteenth century seems to return to earth. In *O bone Jesus* there is a canon in contrary motion, sung by the first soprano and the second contralto. The same device is repeated in the two solo parts of *Regina coeli*. *Adoramus* even contains a four-part canon, in which the second voice enters a fourth below, the third voice a fifth below, and the fourth an octave below the first. Also the long, equable values of the notes and the severely simple harmonies have an archaic effect. It is therefore not surprising that the strict Cecilians were delighted with this Neo-Palestrinian writing, and hailed the appearance of the choruses with enthusiasm (cf. *Chorwächter* of 1 December 1878). In the five-part Motets, Op. 29, Brahms stands on the solid footing of Bach's art. In the first Motet, *Es ist das Heil uns kommen her* (The Grace of God Has Come to Man), the harmonized chorale is placed at the beginning. The melody of each individual verse is then treated as fugue, the theme being sung by the first bass, in the manner of a *canto firmo*, in notes of long duration. The second Motet, however, *Schaffe in mir* (Create in Me), contains two fugues, each preceded by a canon. Other instances of Brahms's astounding mastery of contrapuntal writing may be found among these

[294]

choral compositions. The *Geistliches Lied*, Op. 30, contains a double canon in ninths, the tenor imitating the soprano and the bass the contralto; similarly the *Märznacht* (March Night), Op. 44/12, has a double canon in sixths. And needless to say, there are many delightful little works of art among the smaller German canons. Op. 113/6 (like the canon without opus number, *O wie sanft*) is written *in motu contrario;* Op. 113/9 is in the form of a double canon; *Zu Rauch* is even a double canon *in motu contrario,* the soprano part being reversed in the contralto, and the bass in the tenor. Especially interesting is Op. 113/13, where Brahms has revived one of the oldest forms of polyphonic music. The two contralto voices imitate each other, forming the basis of the composition; at the same time an independent four-part canon is sung by the sopranos. This is precisely the form of the famous canon *Sumer is icumen in,* written many hundred years earlier. That Brahms used a Schubert melody—*Der Leiermann*—for a work cast in so antique a mold lends it a certain piquant charm.

Notwithstanding the very great technical achievement of these works, it would hardly be fair to regard them—as is sometimes done—as mere academic exercises. The supremacy of Brahms's art is shown by the fact that he never paraded his skill. In the case of the *Geistliche Chöre*, Op. 37, it was Brahms's original intention—as the manuscript formerly in the possession of Jerome Stonborough shows—to explain the canonical imitation in each piece by means of comments in Latin. Subsequently he deleted these additions, as such a display of erudition was repugnant to him. And the fact that these pieces became a standby in the repertoire of the Hamburg women's choir was certainly due not to their technical merits, but to their artistic value. Again, it is probable that no one would suspect a contrapuntal *tour de force* in the introductory movement of the Motet, Op. 29/2. The music flows on in soft tranquil chords, whereby the highly wrought canon *per augmentationem* is concealed rather than revealed.

So, too, the chorus for female voices, *Märznacht* (March Night), Op. 44/12, so imbued with the feeling for Nature, is as far removed as may be from a dry contrapuntal exercise. The contrapuntal and chromatic writing serves only to depict the peculiar fluctuation between winter and spring, dismay and delight. This is true also of the smaller compositions in canon form. Brahms himself described the pieces grouped together under Op. 113 as 'love poems, such as a pretty girl would find easy, and like to sing.' He took three typical nursery rhymes (Nos. 3, 4, 5), the melodies of which he had previously employed in his children's folk songs of 1858; and the artistic form of the canon did no violence to the naive and innocent character of these little tunes. No. 11 and the passionately somber No. 12 likewise depict moods of a genuinely romantic character; as does the canon *Mir lächelt kein Frühling* (The Spring Smiles no Longer), which sinks deeper and deeper into the abyss of hopelessness, and the gentle and resigned *Töne lindernder Klang* (Music However Soft). Although in these works Brahms was building on the foundation laid down by the older masters, it would be incorrect to say that he merely made their language and idiom his own. For Brahms, indeed, no less than for them, the most complicated forms of counterpoint were a natural means of expressing his emotions. As Palestrina or Bach succeeded in giving spiritual significance to their technique, so Brahms could turn a canon *in motu contrario* or a canon *per augmentationem* into a pure piece of lyrical poetry.

No less expressive than his polyphonic works are Brahms's homophonic choruses, in which once more he revived the art of bygone centuries. Especially moving is the chorus for male voices, Op. 41/1, *Ich schwing mein Horn ins Jammertal* (I Blow my Horn to Sorrow's Vale), which the composer afterwards arranged as a song for solo voice and pianoforte (Op. 43/3). The harmonization of this piece—in which only triads occur and even chords without thirds are employed—the narrow compass of the melody, and the full accent at the beginning when none is expected are features reminiscent of the art at the close of the Middle Ages. In *Darthulas Grabesgesang* (Darthula's Dirge), Op. 42/3, a setting of a translation of a poem by Ossian, Brahms has allotted the six voices to a higher and a lower chorus, singing in antiphonal responses, after the manner of the sixteenth century. In the first and third parts of the composition the harmony too is wholly archaic. But shortly before the beginning of the middle part (*poco animato*) the mention of the Sun initiates a passage of modern chromatic writing, which introduces the urgently tender Trio in G major. By discarding the fetters of the archaic style in this transitional passage and in the trio itself, Brahms achieves a contrast of overwhelming effectiveness.

The second element in the choral works of this period is the folk song. It is characteristic of the deep affection that Brahms cherished for folk music that he would frequently arrange the same air for women's chorus and also for mixed chorus or solo voice, and would even set a folk song twice for the same ensemble. Examples of this have already been given in the case of the solo songs. A mixed chorus also, *Wach auf* (Wake Up), was written in two versions: the one (arranged before 1864) is preserved in the archives of the *Singakademie* in Vienna; and the other (arranged about 1873), a product of the master's maturity, by the *Gesellschaft der Musikfreunde*. The older version is simply harmonized; the later is more elaborate, with short excursions into polyphony. It is interesting to see how over and over again Brahms matches his simply harmonized folk songs with polyphonal choruses in the manner of the old madrigal writers. In such pieces nature and art are fused in a bewitchingly unconstrained manner. No inferior work is to be found among Brahms's folk-song arrangements; but especially noteworthy are *Von edler Art* (Noble Thou Art), *Vom heiligen Märtyrer Emmerano* (The Holy Martyr Emmerano),

[297]

In stiller Nacht, Morgengesang (Morning Song), *Schnitter Tod* (Death the Reaper), *Wach auf,* in both versions, and *Dort in den Weiden* (A Cottage Stands) (belonging to the third creative period).

The influence of folk song may be detected as readily in the choruses composed by Brahms as in his songs. Examples may be found in the 'Songs and Romances,' Op. 44, among which pieces of definite folk-song character predominate. From the *Minnelied,* with its delightful dance-like character, and *Der Bräutigam* (The Bridegroom), with its gay horn call, and the sweetly tender *Barcarole,* to the strange melancholy of *Die Braut* (The Bride), an unaffected simplicity is preserved, so that it follows as a matter of course that almost all the songs of this series also are composed in strophic form.

The archaic tendencies and the leaning towards the form of folk song are not always clearly dissociated in the choruses; on the contrary, some especially attractive effects are obtained by their combination. This is seen clearly in the *Marienlieder,* Op. 22. The first and third parts of *Marias Kirchgang* (Mary and the Boatman) are strongly reminiscent of the medieval custom of giving the melody to a middle voice; here the contralto has the principal melody, while the soprano merely provides a colorful accompaniment. On the other hand, the imitation of bells in the middle section of the same song strikes an irresistible note of naivete. The chorus *Magdalena* sounds like an ancient pilgrims' chant, and the last piece of the series, which begins in 4/4 time, and then changes into 3/4, reproduces in its rhythmic alternation a very old trait of folk-dance music. Brahms's description of his *Marienlieder* as pieces 'in the manner of old German church music and folk song' is justified in every number of this series.

Only in a few of his choral works does Brahms seek affinity with the music of the nineteenth century. One such is *Vineta,* in Op. 42. This charming piece with its gently rocking rhythm reveals the composer's knowledge of Mendelssohn's choral works, while his strongly masculine genius avoids the imminent danger of lapsing into the sentimental. *Vineta* is a favorite bravura piece for choirs, and for all its winning charm is 'genuine Brahms.' Nos. 2-5 of Op. 41 have much in common with contemporary compositions for male voice choirs; they are soldiers' songs, grave or gay, and express the composer's ardent patriotism. Perhaps the most expressive is the humorous *Marschieren* (Marching), and the foreboding, prophetic *Gebet acht!* (On Guard!) It is a pity that these, the only male choruses which the master wrote, are not more widely known.

Before turning to the compositions of the next period a word must be said in regard to the accompaniment to the choruses. Brahms added a piano score to the Motets, Op. 29, 'only as a help in practicing.' In other works a pianoforte accompaniment *ad libitum* is added, which sometimes (cf. Op. 42/2 and Op. 44) gives more than a mere piano score. From these it is but a step to the indispensable obbligato accompaniment of Op. 27 and Op. 30. In these two works Brahms was not concerned with achieving a special tone color in the accompaniment. He expressly says 'pianoforte *or* organ,' and at the first performance of Op. 27 in Vienna he even supported the organ with strings. Such indifference to questions of color can be paralleled elsewhere among the compositions of the second period. It underwent a characteristic change, however, in later years.

To Brahms's third period belong the following works: Seven Songs, Op. 62, for mixed choir (composed Summer, 1874); Two Motets, Op. 74, for mixed choir (No. 1 comp. 1877, No. 2 probably 1860-65); Six Songs and Romances, Op. 93*a*, for mixed choir (1883-4); Five-part songs for mixed choir (1887-8), Op. 104; *Fest- und Gedenksprüche* (Festival and Commemoration Pieces), Op. 109, for eight-part mixed choir (1886-8), Three Motets, Op. 110, for four-part or eight-part mixed choir (Summer, 1889); several canons, among them *Mir lächelt kein Frühling* (The Spring Smiles no Longer) (before 1881); *Wann?* (When?), for soprano and contralto (before 1885); the folk songs *Wach auf* (second version) and *Dort in den Weiden* (both arranged about 1873); *Kleine Hochzeitskantate* (Little Wedding Cantata), for four voices and pianoforte (Summer, 1874); and *Tafellied* (Table Song), for mixed choir and piano, Op. 93*b* (Summer, 1884).

A glance at this list will give rise to the comment that Brahms in his maturity practically confined himself to the mixed choir, and published nothing for male or female choirs exclusively. At the height of his powers he avoided a uniformly high or low tonal color. His efforts were directed towards achieving a carefully calculated equilibrium between male and female voices, in keeping with the equable mood of these works. Further, in his third period, apart from the great compositions for choir and orchestra, Brahms concentrated on *a cappella* work. The not very satisfactory combination of choir and organ or pianoforte accompaniment, characteristic of some works of the second period, recurs only in two small 'occasional' pieces. Here maturity was a time of clarification.

The influence of the music of the past is no less potent in the third than in the preceding period. Examination of the choral song, *Vergangen ist mir Glück und Heil* (Dame Fortune Smiles no More on Me), Op. 62/7, will reveal this influence, which was apparent also in the chorus for men's voices, *Ich schwing mein Horn ins Jammertal* (I Blow my Horn to Sorrow's Vale), Op. 41/1. In the majority of the compositions of this period, however, the personal note of the composer is also very plainly manifested. While some of the compositions of the second period are not free from a certain eclecticism, Brahms, in this third period, though employing the elements of an older style, succeeded in creating works characterized by immediate vitality and great expressiveness.

In this connection it is highly instructive to compare the

two Motets of Op. 74. The second, *O Heiland, reiss die Himmel auf* (O Saviour, Rend the Heav'ns in Twain), composed probably between the years 1860 and 1865, and therefore a product of the second period, presents a series of choral variations in the old style. The *canto firmo* is entrusted to the soprano in the first and second verses, to the tenor in the third, and in the fourth to the bass. Strict counterpoint is provided by the other voices. The fifth verse elaborates portions of the *canto firmo* and culminates in old-style choral coloraturas at the word 'Amen.' Obviously this is a work in which Brahms all but effaced his own personality in his reliance on the methods of the earlier masters.

Quite otherwise is it with the first Motet, composed more than a decade afterwards: *Warum ist das Licht gegeben den Mühseligen?* (Wherefore is Light Bestowed on the Broken-Hearted?). The first movement of this Motet, with its peculiar rondo-like structure, is reminiscent of a piece by Johann Hermann Schein, dating from the year 1623 (*Siehe, nach Trost war mir sehr bange*). A canon for four voices comprises the second movement, and the last consists of a chorale. Nevertheless, the hand of the modern master is unmistakable. The very choice of the texts clearly expresses the personality of the composer who, true Christian that he was, collected them himself from the Old and New Testaments, as he did in the case of his *Requiem* and a number of later compositions. The whole content of the work is typical of the composer, proceeding from a despairing lament at the beginning to quiet resignation at the close; typical too is the ever-recurring question in the first movement: *Warum, warum?* (Wherefore, Wherefore?)—portraying the doubt which gnaws at the heart of the grief-stricken, and again we find the 'real Brahms' in the bold melodies and powerful harmonies. The free use of archaic elements has resulted here in the production of a perfectly complete new creation.

The same thing is true of the *Fest- und Gedenksprüche*, Op. 109, and the Motets, Op. 110. Both works employ the two-choir arrangement, to which the music of the sixteenth and seventeenth centuries owes such impressive effects. Old texts are set to music in both works, and the music embodies choral coloraturas and little tone pictures of the Baroque school. Nevertheless, Brahms's mature style is as evident in these works, composed at the outset of his last period, as in the Fourth Symphony, which was itself a work cast in an archaic mold. We need only to consider the exceptionally terse and compact construction of each piece, and the grave, almost pessimistic character of the texts in the Motets, Op. 110.* The most retrospective piece in this work is No. 2, *Ach arme Welt* (Ah Shallow World). It inclines towards the Dorian mode, and contents itself with a strophic arrangement with variations, and thus, in its simplicity, does full justice to the naive and unaffected poetry of the text.

No. 1, on the other hand, *Ich aber bin elend* (O God, I Am Humble), shows at its very outset a turn of melody which, with its sudden octave leap, clearly reveals the master of the nineteenth century. The continually recurring invocations of the second chorus, *Herr, Herr Gott* (Lord, Lord God), after b. 17, are somewhat reminiscent of the *Warum, warum?* in Op. 74/1. Meanwhile the first chorus glorifies the mercy of God in the style of old Catholic Psalm recitations. As in this Motet, so in Op. 110/3, *Wenn wir in höchsten Nöten sein,* an organic fusion of styles is apparent with the composer's personal note predominant. The two

---

* On a separate leaf Brahms jotted down the texts of the Motets *Ach arme Welt* (Ah Shallow World) and *Wenn wir in höchsten Nöten sein* (When We Are Troubled Through and Through). Between them is another text, which Brahms apparently noted for some future musical setting, a project never fulfilled. It is Heinrich von Laufenberg's *Ich wollt' dass ich daheime wär',* a song full of the longing for death and entirely in keeping with the other texts of Op. 110. Brahms may have discarded it because of the very old German in which it was written (the song dates from between 1400 and 1450), which he felt it was impossible to put into modern German without completely altering the wording.

sharply outlined main themes, which simultaneously symbolize the antithesis of distress and consolation, the animated
polyphony, whose aim is entirely expressive, make this
chorus one of the greatest of Brahms's motets. It is a composition which amply repays the enormous labor involved
in mastering it, technically and intellectually.

Only an artist who belonged wholly to his own age, and
was yet deeply rooted in the past, could have compiled texts
from the Bible so appropriate to the present day as are the
words of the *Fest- und Gedenksprüche*. With their admoni-
tions, their words of praise, and their promises they form a
fit utterance for the German nation, and furnish yet another
proof of the composer's true patriotism. The profound pessimism of Op. 110 is wholly lacking here. The work is steeped
in solemn joy and radiant serenity, and is therefore the ideal
prologue for any ceremony. In its style it resembles the first
and third motets of Op. 110. The archaic idiom is reinforced
by the power and ardor and tenderness of the composer.

The folk song, as was to be expected, also plays a certain
role in the compositions of the period of maturity. Folk-
song features are most clearly pronounced in Op. 62, especially in No. 1, *Rosmarin,* and No. 2, *Von alten Liebes-
liedern* (Of Old Love Songs); less clearly in Op. 93a and
Op. 104. What has already been said of the songs for solo
voice and pianoforte is equally true of the choruses: in the
second half of his third period, Brahms's attitude to the
folk song is less naive than of old; the personal note is far
too insistent. The first piece of Op. 93a, *Der bucklichte
Fiedler* (The Hump-Backed Fiddler), has a good deal of the
folk song in its general tone, but it is not composed in
strophes, and introduces, with the shrill fifths at the word
'Walpurgisnacht' (Walpurgis night), a touch of modern realism. The following chorus, *Das Mädchen* (The Maiden), was
written also as a song for solo voice and pianoforte. It has
already been pointed out, in discussing this arrangement,
that at the outset the piece presents a Serbian feature in the

alternation of 3/4 and 4/4 time and the retention of the B minor key; at the climax, however (bar 37 *et seq.*), the composer casts all national trappings to the winds, and sings in regular 2/4 time, on an exulting B major, of the maiden's preparation for the arrival of her lover. The chorus Op. 104/4, *Verlorene Jugend* (Lost Youth), which is based on a Bohemian folk-song text, reveals similar features. In the canon in minor key, at first divided between contralto and soprano, and then between first bass and soprano, one is inclined to recognize a certain Slavic character. The yearning passion of the two sections in the major key is, however, not Czech, but pure Brahms.

Completely Brahmsian are all those pieces in which the requirements of the text do not impart a folk-song or national flavor to the music. We see the composer as a true romantic in the intimately tender Op. 62/3, *Waldesnacht* (Night in the Forest). Again, Goethe's *Beherzigung* (Reflection), Op. 93a/6, breathes a spirit of wild and defiant strength. Who but Brahms, in the nineteenth century, could have created in a canon form a work of art so concise, so expressive, and yet so absolutely faithful to the poem! The piece is genuine Goethe, genuine Brahms, and incidentally a genuine canon. The choruses of Op. 104, like the motets of Op. 110, breathe a spirit of farewell and resignation. The mood of the two nocturnes, *Nachtwache* (Night Watch), Nos. 1 and 2, is rapt and inspired. This music is all feeling and expression and mood, its outlines are never very clearly drawn. The contralto and bass, with their darker tone, are doubled, while the lighter voices of soprano and tenor are employed singly. By these means the color effects of both pieces are heightened, that of the first producing an almost ethereal impression. In the last chorus of this work, No. 5, *Im Herbst* (In the Autumn), Brahms has achieved a very dark tone color. The piece was originally written in A—and only when the very unusual depth of the parts began to involve the executants in difficulties did he decide to transpose the whole composition a third upwards, to C. The profoundly earnest, grief-stricken character of the whole is, however, preserved in the higher key.

The two choruses with pianoforte accompaniment are pieces for special occasions, in which the hand of the master is apparent for all their carefree, joyous spirit. This is especially true of the *Tafellied,* which from the delicate, somewhat rococo gaiety of the opening, passes in the final *tutti* to powerful, almost crude, jubilation. The composer was not too well pleased with Gottfried Keller's words for the *Kleine Hochzeitskantate,* as he flatly told the poet in a letter. Nevertheless, the broad humor of the poem is well reproduced in the music, and many points in the little minuet—for example, the exaggerated descriptiveness at the word 'Himmelshöhen' (heav'n above)—betray Brahms's never-failing delight in pleasantry.

In his last period Brahms wrote no new choral works. He contented himself with collecting his canons for female voices, composed at various times, and publishing them as his Op. 113. And here we have a remarkable example of the tendency, characteristic of the composer's last period, to theoretical ventures. He scored the canons in a peculiarly abbreviated manner, which was quite unprecedented, and to the best of my knowledge has never been imitated, and— as he jestingly wrote—'was prouder of this invention than of the canons themselves.'

XXI

LARGE CHORAL WORKS

WORKS FOR CHORUS AND ORCHESTRA

A survey of the works for chorus and orchestra will lead to generalizations similar to those made in the case of the smaller choral works. In his first period Brahms did not use this form; the second period frequently reveals the influence of alien models, and only in his maturity did Brahms reach the summit of his powers in this particular field. Within the comparatively short space of fourteen years (1868-82) the composer completed seven great choral works, finally bidding this form farewell at the age of fifty. Composition for chorus and orchestra, as also the symphonic form, was neglected by the older Brahms.

To the second period belongs the *Ave Maria,* Op. 12, for female chorus and orchestral or organ accompaniment (composed in the autumn of 1858), the *Begräbnisgesang* (Burial Song), Op. 13, for mixed choir and wind instruments (Autumn, 1858), and the Songs, for female choir, accompanied by two horns and harp, Op. 17 (February 1860). These works reveal once more Brahms's preference for a female choir. This is not to be explained by the mere external circumstances of his work with the ladies' choir in Hamburg, for Op. 12 was begun before that period. We must assume rather that the young Brahms cherished a particular fondness for this form cultivated by Schumann, Mendelssohn, Gade, and others, by reason of its delightful and melodious character. Further, by the arrangement of the instrumental accompaniment he endeavored to achieve particular tonal effects. In the orchestral part of the *Begräbnisgesang* not only are the melodious string instruments lacking (even the 'cello and bass parts, originally included in the score, were finally struck out), but also the soft flutes and blaring trumpets. Oboes, clarinets, bassoons, horns, trombones, tuba, and kettledrums provide the somber, dirge-like accompaniment. More novel still is the tone color in the female choruses Op. 17. Brahms supports the voices in this work with horns and harp, thereby obtaining a highly romantic combination of tone. Only in the first of his choral works, the *Ave Maria,* Op. 12, can a certain indifference be detected in the arrangement of the accompanying instruments. Brahms had originally had the organ in mind, as in Op. 27 and Op. 30, and later he arranged the organ part in a somewhat schematic fashion for small orchestra.

In some other respect also the *Ave Maria* has the qualities of an experimental study. It is full of a tender but somewhat impersonal charm, rarely met with in the composer's other creations. It would be difficult indeed to detect the hand of the North German in the gently rocking rhythm of this piece, with its hint of popular Italian music, were it not for certain characteristic passages, such as the strange harmonies shortly before the close. Brahms was far more inspired by Michael Weisse's powerful German poem, the *Begräbnisgesang,* written in the middle of the sixteenth century, than by the Latin text of the *Ave Maria* from the Catholic Liturgy. The former piece, composed in the style of Bach and based on a Protestant hymn, is a work of simple, yet overwhelming magnificence. For the first time Brahms's imagination was kindled by the eternal theme of death and resurrection, and even in this early work one finds something of the expressiveness of the *Requiem,* the *Vier ernste Gesänge,* and certain of the motets. In the *Begräbnisgesang* all is straightforward, yet monumental: at the opposite pole to sentimental lamentation. The unusual accentuation of the words, the ruthlessly monotonous melodies of the first and third parts, the somber, harsh, sometimes shrill effect of the accompanying wind instruments, give the composition a character and a charm all its own.

Among the choruses of Op. 17, the song of lament No. 4, *Gesang aus Fingal* (Song from Fingal), is perhaps the most immediately arresting. To this chorus may be applied the dictum of W. Lübke, who said of the sadder songs of Brahms that the composer 'weeps the great, heavy tears of men . . . which none had shed since Bach and Beethoven.' (Comp. Billroth's letter to Brahms, 16 October 1874.) As in the chorus *Darthulas Grabesgesang,* written a little later, Brahms recaptured with amazing success the somber Nordic mood of Ossian's poems. The peculiar color of the two low horns and harp, and the measured lament, almost like a funeral march, of the main section, are the very antithesis of the traditional conception of a female chorus. The first piece of this work, however, *Es tönt ein voller Harfenklang* (I Hear a Harp), Op. 17, of which the opening horn notes recall Nature's own music, is tranquil and composed. The third piece of this work, *Der Gärtner* (The Gardener), is strangely reminiscent of Mendelssohn's setting of the same text. Unconsciously, of course, the opening and the climax (*Grüss ich dich tausendmal* (And greet thee thousand-fold)) remind us of the older master's duo. Even the vocal setting is similar; Mendelssohn wrote for two sopranos, Brahms for two sopranos and contralto. In his second period Brahms found inspiration not only in the art of bygone centuries, but also in that of the immediate past.

The Cantata *Rinaldo,* Op. 50, after Goethe, for tenor solo, male chorus, and orchestra, was composed for the most part in the summer of 1863, although the final chorus was not completed until 1868. Its whole structure proclaims it a work of the second period. The text deals with one of the most popular subjects of the seventeenth and eighteenth centuries. No lesser musicians than Lully, Handel, Gluck, and Haydn—to say nothing of a host of minor composers— have set to music the story of the hero Rinaldo, who falls a victim to the charms of the beautiful enchantress Armida, and is only with difficulty rescued by his devoted friends and recalled to the path of duty. It was the purely human interest of this tale that had attracted Goethe: the agony of the lover who tries to free himself from the bonds of an unworthy passion. There is, however, nothing of the opera libretto about Goethe's text. He did not hesitate to let Armida appear and take a decisive part in the action without speaking a single word. In the absence of stage directions the reader learns of Armida's presence only from the speeches of Rinaldo and his friends. So, too, with other dramatic crises in the poem, such as the presentation of the magic diamond mirror, which first shows Rinaldo how low he has fallen. And since the somewhat weak and passive character of Rinaldo himself hardly makes him a dynamic figure in the poem, the whole text must be accounted one of Goethe's most problematical works. Brahms, however, was enthralled rather than repelled by this problematical quality. The romantic composer was attracted by the possibilities offered by the description of the love spell, the effect of the diamond mirror, or even the sea voyage. The spiritual problem, too, arrested him, no less than the magnificent language of the poem. But he had no more idea than the poet of writing an opera or a work of an operatic character. This must be kept in mind if we are properly to understand *Rinaldo*. It is a sequence of delightful pieces for orchestra, chorus, and solo, linked together by some sort of action. Actual intellectual or musical unity is neither achieved nor attempted. The detail, however—and it is the detail that really matters in this work—is often extremely beautiful. It will suffice to mention the orchestral introduction, in which Armida's spell, Rinaldo's longing, and his friends' pleading are impressively portrayed; Rinaldo's splendid aria; the mysterious apparition of the magic mirror; and above all, the magnificent sweep of the final chorus, in which Brahms seems now and again to speak with the voice of Weber. *Rinaldo* is a mine of gems of the first water; but it was only in his next choral work, the *Requiem,* that Brahms succeeded in setting such gems in an imperishable diadem.

The composer's greatest choral work, *Ein Deutsches Requiem* (*A German Requiem,* usually known as Brahms's *Requiem*), Op. 45, for solo voices, chorus, and orchestra, occupied him at intervals for upwards of ten years. It is not impossible that the master found the title, as early as 1856, in a sketchbook left by Schumann, which contained the outlines of works never completed; though Brahms himself had no recollection in later years of having done so. The second movement, which was originally intended to form part of the projected Symphony in D minor (the later Pianoforte Concerto, Op. 15), was composed between the years 1857-9. In the autumn of 1861 Brahms had arranged the text for a cantata in four movements. The work remained in this preparatory stage for four years, until 1865, when Brahms took it up again after his mother's death. By August 1866 movements one, two, three, four, six, and seven were completed. The fifth was composed in May 1868.

In many respects the *Requiem* occupies a unique position among the works of the master. The score is not only the most extensive which Brahms has left us, it is also one of the most precious. Despite all his dependence on the art of the past, here the master decisively strikes into new paths. This becomes at once apparent if we compare the text of the *Requiem* with the customary requiem text set to music by Mozart, Cherubini, Berlioz, Verdi, and others. The difference resides not merely in the fact that these masters faithfully adhered to the Latin words prescribed by the Roman Catholic Liturgy, whereas Brahms chose his own texts from the German Bible; far more essential are the differences in the content and tendency of the two texts. The Latin requiem is a prayer for the peace of the *dead*, threatened with the horrors of the Last Judgment; Brahms's *Requiem,* on the contrary, utters words of consolation, designed to reconcile the *living* with the idea of suffering and death. In the liturgical text whole sentences are filled with the darkest menace; in Brahms's *Requiem* each of the seven sections closes in a mood of cheerful confidence or loving promise.

The idea of writing a *Missa pro Defunctis* in German goes back further than Brahms or Schumann. In 1636 Heinrich Schütz wrote a *Teutsche Begräbniss-Missa* under the title *Musikalische Exequien*. In a later age, among other composers, Henkel, Moralt, and Franz Schubert (erroneously attributed to his brother Ferdinand), reverted to the idea. None of these works, however, which are more or less closely related to the Latin liturgical text, is so nearly akin to the poetry of Brahms's composition as J. S. Bach's Cantata No. 106, entitled *Actus Tragicus*. Bach was about the same age as the composer of the *Requiem* when he wrote this magnificent cantata. He too had compiled the text himself, chiefly from the Bible, or from old Church hymns, scrupulously avoiding those accretions of contemporary 'Pietism' which so often disfigure his later compositions. Above all, the idea underlying the *Actus Tragicus* is akin to that of the *Requiem*. Bach too seeks to reconcile mankind with the thought of death, and by the promise of bliss to rob the end of its terrors. There is, however, one very marked difference between the older work and the new. Bach alludes to the mercy and aid of the Redeemer, who leads the souls of the departed to a better world beyond the grave, while in Brahms's work all mention of the name of Christ is expressly avoided.* Although the work of the North German composer is firmly rooted in the Christian faith, it is wholly removed from dogma in the narrower sense. It is, indeed, addressed to all who believe, irrespective of creed.

The *Requiem* was begun at the transitional stage between youth and maturity, and the music as a whole bears the

* In the English translation in common use, the name of Christ is introduced in the second movement. This means a deviation from Brahms's original intentions.

imprint of both. The desire for larger and ever larger forms is characteristic of youth; and in obedience to it one movement was expanded into a cantata in four movements, and this latter into an oratorio in six, and finally seven parts. This tendency to increase the dimensions and scope of his works can be observed in many of Brahms's earlier instrumental compositions (cf. Trio in B major, first version). The essential thing about the *Requiem*, however, is the fact that the composer has completely mastered the form which his youthful temperament had led him to enlarge again and again. The symmetry and perfect equilibrium of all its parts stamp the work as a product of Brahms's complete maturity, and this perfect fulfilment of his self-imposed task reveals the composer at the very height of his powers. Most of the movements of the *Requiem* are in three parts, and this tripartite symmetry gives the whole work of seven movements its special stamp. Not only do the first and last movements correspond to each other, but the second and sixth, and the third and fifth. The central point, however, is the graceful fourth movement, which is, as it were, the gentle trio of the work. The connection between the two outer movements is most clearly defined. It lies not only in the correspondence of the words, but even more in the fact that Brahms, with unobtrusive art, passed towards the end of the seventh movement into the close of the first. In the sixth movement the content of the second appears, but repeated, as it were, on another and a higher plane. But while in this second movement the weird dance of death at the opening gives place to a veritable hymn of joy, the mournful, groping uncertainty which opens the sixth movement passes into a vision of the Last Judgment (characteristically stripped by Brahms of all its terrors), to conclude in a mighty double fugue of Handelian strength and glory. Lastly, the third and fifth movements stand to each other in the same relation as lamentation and deliverance. Both pieces begin with solo voices; but while the man's voice at the opening of the third move-

ment first suggests grief and even despair, to gain confidence
and hope in God's mercy only at the very end of the movement, the fifth movement, opened by a woman's voice, is
from the first note to the last conceived in a mood of maternal consolation. It testifies to the mature artist's unerring
sense of form that after the enormously successful first performance of the six-part *Requiem* in the cathedral of
Bremen, he himself recognized the absolute necessity of adding yet another movement, the present fifth; and it is characteristic of the composer's reserve in all matters of personal
feeling that this movement, devoted as it is to the idealiza-
tion of true mother love, was not begun until Brahms stood
at a certain distance from the terrible day of his own mother's death.

In the orchestration, as well as in the form, there are certain points which suggest the youth of the composer, while
others indicate his maturity. If we glance at the first movement, we shall see that Brahms has doubled the dark-toned
violas and 'cellos by dividing them, and has altogether omitted the bright-sounding violins, clarinets, and trumpets.
With the profoundest musical insight he has chosen a tonal
color in keeping with the spirit of the movement, and preserved it unaltered throughout the piece. A contrast is provided by the funeral march of the second movement, where
the violins and violas, used in the higher position, are divided into several sections. The direction *con sordino* robs
the instruments of any brilliance, and gives the movement
the quality of sinister gaiety desired by the composer. In
both movements the original 'stops' (we purposely employ
this organist's term) are retained from beginning to end.
This is the instrumentation of a Bach, which Brahms had
ample opportunity of learning during his study of the
'Thomaskantor's' works; it is also the technique of Brahms's
early works, of his Second Serenade, of the choruses for female voices with horns and harp accompaniment, and of the
Begräbnisgesang. It is noteworthy that in the *Requiem*

[313]

Brahms handles it with consummate skill, and—for instance, by means of the harp, or even the kettledrum—obtains color effects which he never surpassed in any of his later compositions. On the other hand, the *Requiem* is not lacking in the technique of Brahms's mature style of orchestration. In the symphonies and overtures of a later period the composer generally employs the full orchestra. In so doing he succeeds in avoiding all heaviness of tone by allowing the melodies to wander from one instrument to another, thus distributing the longer melodies among the different interpreters. A glance at the passage between letters D and E in the third movement of the *Requiem* ('He passeth away like a shadow') will reveal an instance of this technique.

Naturally, the art of contrapuntal writing, with which Brahms had made himself thoroughly familiar by the study of the older masters, is exemplified in the *Requiem;* witness several passages in the second movement, the fugue built up over a mighty organ-point at the close of the third movement, and the great double fugue in the sixth. But Brahms reveals himself even more significantly in those pieces in which the fitful, twilight tone, wavering between darkness and light, or the delicate tenderness of his own personal note is heard. Unsurpassable is the resigned, emotional melancholy of the first, fifth, and seventh movements, the spectral gaiety at the opening of the second, and the calm transfiguration in which the jubilation of this movement closes. Another master would have thundered out the words, 'Joy everlasting upon their heads shall be.' But Brahms, shortly after the *fortissimo* is reached, sinks into the *piano,* and even into the *pianissimo.* For him the last climax of joy is silent rapture.

After *Rinaldo* and the *Requiem,* Brahms wrote no more choral works on the same scale. Thenceforth he generally avoided the larger vocal compositions in several movements. He preferred slighter forms; but these are enormously effective in their profound and concise expressiveness. This is clearly illustrated by the first of these compositions, the *Rhapsody,* Op. 53, for contralto, male chorus, and orchestra, composed in the autumn of 1869. Like *Rinaldo,* it is based upon a somewhat problematical text of Goethe's; and yet how simple and clear is the later work, how effective its construction, how beautifully finished the whole! Whoever reads the three stanzas taken by Brahms from Goethe's *Harzreise im Winter* will be surprised by the unwonted freedom of the form which the poet has chosen for the portrayal of a misanthrope cut off from all human society, and the final invocation to the 'Father of Love.' In Brahms's setting, however, the first and most rhapsodic of the three stanzas, with the prominence of the orchestra and the recitative-like solo, provides the necessary introduction to the second, which takes the form of an aria in three sections. These first two stanzas find their solution and fulfilment in the profound emotion of the third, where the chorus supports the solo voice for the first time. Logically and lucidly the little drama is unfolded until love is invoked in the transfigured and genuinely Brahmsian close. It should be noted that the intense emotion of this music is as far as possible removed from sickly sentimentality. It is a great and simple work of art; and it is no mere chance that the famous interpreters of Gluck's *Orpheus*—above all Amalie Joachim—are precisely those who have shone in the solo part of the *Rhapsody.* Here we encounter for the first time, in a choral work by Brahms, that Hellenic spirit which was to appear so clearly in the artist's later compositions.

Interesting sketches have been preserved of the *Rhapsody,* as of the *Requiem,* which in their main features are in line with the composer's other drafts of vocal works. They show that, when the sketches were hastily jotted down, the upper voice and the bass were noted and he sometimes added to the bass figures indicating the harmonies, but that as a rule he sketched a proper pianoforte score, with middle parts complete. But even the bare outline sketches generally correspond pretty closely to the completed version; it was seldom that any alteration was made, unless Brahms lost the thread in the sketch itself. Thus, in the sketch of the *Poco Andante* of the *Rhapsody* the first 16 bars are practically identical with those of the printed pianoforte score. Suddenly the text breaks off; and then the middle voice of the piano part. As far as the eye can tell the sketch has miscarried, and actually these bars were left out of the finished version. The bold leaps which are a feature of the printed version at this point (b. 17-22 of the *Poco Andante*) were penciled in the sketch as an afterthought.

The *Schicksalslied* (Song of Destiny), Op. 54, for chorus and orchestra, dates back in its earliest stages (as A. Dietrich informs us) to 1868. It was completed three years later, in May 1871. Not the least of reasons for the long period occupied by the composition of a comparatively short work was the difficulty Brahms experienced in finding a suitable ending. Hölderlin's poem describes the bliss of the immortal gods, and as a contrast the despair of suffering mankind. The *Requiem*, the *Rhapsody*, and many another instrumental work reveal a like antithesis of light and darkness. But in all these compositions Brahms—quite in the spirit of Beethoven—struggles from darkness to light, from fear and sorrow to redemption and joy. In the text of the *Schicksalslied*, however, the course is reversed. The poem opens with a description of the blest immortals, and closes with the despair of mankind. This cheerless conclusion was deeply repugnant to Brahms, greatly as the wonderful poem—inspired with the very breath of antiquity—may have attracted him, by its forceful expression and beautiful diction. He adopted the expedient of repeating the luminous orchestral prelude at the end of the work, thus closing on a note of reconciliation. Later he even contemplated repeating the text of the beginning. Hermann Levi, however, who made the acquaintance of the *Schicksalslied* before its completion, dissuaded Brahms from adopting this course, and so the work, as it stands, closes with the original epilogue. This instrumental passage rounds off both the inner content and the external form of the work, and ranks among the master's most moving inspirations. Even Brahms did not often write melodies so simply inspired, so broadly flowing. The voice part, in the frame of the orchestral setting, follows the poem, consisting of two clearly defined sections. A luminous clarity prevails in the music dedicated to the gods. At its climax ('light as fingers that play to us heavenly music') the composition sinks from *forte* into a rapt *piano,* as at the end of the second movement of the *Requiem.* In strong contrast to the first half of the work is the darkly passionate second section of the voice part, where the racing semiquavers of the strings, the menacing passages in unison, and the wild outcries of the chorus, are overpoweringly realistic. Especially impressive are the words sharply hurled forth by the choir: 'As water from boulder to boulder is hurtled,' followed by the pause interpolated in the *fortissimo,* and the sudden *piano* at 'to aimless wand'ring condemned.' Brahms repeated this part of the text, probably in response to considerations of form, since the description of human suffering is only half as long as that of divine bliss. Above all, however, the repetition gave him the opportunity of a second and even mightier and more terrific outburst. The vocal part ends on a note of sorrowful resignation, and the effect is now overwhelming when the message of salvation is heard in the C major Adagio of the instrumental epilogue, uniting the lot of men and gods in one reconciling bond.

To celebrate the victory of the English armies over the French at Dettingen in 1743, Handel wrote one of his most brilliant works, the *Dettingen Te Deum.* This splendid composition was one of Brahms's favorites, and when he became artistic director of the *Gesellschaft der Musikfreunde* in Vienna in 1872, he placed it in the forefront of the first concert. The score he used on this occasion is literally strewn with his own markings, betraying the exceptional pains spent on preparing the work for performance. But he had already paid tribute to the *Dettingen Te Deum* in an original work. This is the *Triumphlied* (Song of Triumph), Op. 55, for eight-part chorus, baritone solo, and orchestra, which he composed in 1870-71 to celebrate Germany's victory over France and the foundation of the German Empire. The stylistic dependence of this powerful work, now jubilant, now full of pathos, on Handel is unmistakable. It may be seen in the polyphonic, motet-like treatment of the two four-part choruses, the introduction of a *canto firmo* into the second movement, and above all in the radiant, vital brilliance of the whole work. Yet in the *Triumphlied*, as in the *Requiem*, Brahms goes a step further than his model. Handel used an English text, not the Latin of the Liturgy; but his text is little more than a free paraphrase of the original. Brahms, on the contrary, as was his wont, himself compiled the text of his *Te Deum* from the Bible. His chief source was the 19th chapter of Revelation, in which is celebrated the triumph over Babylon. From this passage Brahms took the noble words of glorification, but to his regret he was obliged to omit a few rather too drastic expressions, in which the Evangelist exulted over the downfall of the detested Babel of sin. He consoled himself by writing the beginning of the ticklish passage in his own copy over an expressive melody for wind (first movement, b. 70 *et seq.*) and by always drawing his friends' attention to the original text.

The first movement of the *Triumphlied* is perhaps the most brilliant of the whole work. Its principal theme is based on the melody *God Save the King*, which was the German as well as the English national anthem. Shortly before the final climax a *tranquillo* passage reveals the gentle and reflective Brahms—one might almost say, the *true* Brahms. The second movement also contains, after 'Oh, be joyful,' a passage of a more subjective character. To the rocking triplets of the chorus there is added the hymn *Nun danket alle Gott* (Now Thank We All Our God), played by the wind instruments. It is a passage of wonderful poetical fervor. In the third movement a baritone solo part is added as a further means of expression, and a mysterious and fantastic passage contributes a fresh emotional element. These motives of contrast seem only to enhance the brilliant effect of the pealing, Handelian, final Hallelujah.

Among Brahms's works for chorus and orchestra are two arrangements of compositions not his own, written in the early 'seventies. Both are adaptations of Schubert's songs for solo voice and piano. To the *Gruppe aus dem Tartarus* (arranged before 1871, published in 1934 by O. E. Deutsch) Brahms gave a peculiar setting for one-part male chorus and full orchestra. Schubert's solo part is left absolutely intact, and is sung by the tenors and basses in unison. The accompaniment, however, is effectively distributed over a large orchestra. Without being overloaded, it provides the magnificent song with the necessary background, and the effective climax at the close is beautifully expressed in the instrumentation.

This arrangement was first performed on 8 December 1871, at a concert of the Vienna *Akademischer Gesangverein.* On the same evening an arrangement of Schubert's *An Schwager Kronos,* by Brahms, was performed with a male chorus in unison. This, as well as the songs *Memnon* and *Geheimes,* Brahms had orchestrated in 1862 for his friend Stockhausen. (An arrangement of the song *Greisengesang,* which was in the possession of H. Levi, has been lost.) We have reason to be grateful to W. H. Hadow for having published these interesting scores for the first time, in 1933. The instrumental clothing given by Brahms to Schubert's songs is transparent. For *Memnon* and *An Schwager Kronos* he used—except for four horns—only the normal classic orchestra; for *Geheimes* only strings and one horn. In its lucidity and economy the orchestration clearly shows the features of Brahms's Serenades, which were only a little earlier in date.

In 1873, Brahms arranged another Schubert work, *Ellen's*

Second Song, Op. 52/2 (published in 1906), from Sir Walter Scott's *Lady of the Lake,* for soprano, female chorus in three parts, four horns, and two bassoons. Again Brahms preserved Schubert's vocal part untouched, and gave it to the soprano. The dreamy, hushed hunting calls of the accompaniment are most effectively rendered by a wind sextet. Further, Brahms heightened the coloring of Schubert's work by adding a female chorus in three parts which softly accompanies the solo soprano as she sings the lovely melody. In spite of their artistic value, Brahms attached but little importance to these arrangements. He never thought of publishing them himself, and when they were performed his name was not printed on the program.

With the *Triumphlied* Brahms bade a long farewell to the works for chorus and orchestra, a form to which he did not return until the early 'eighties. In the interval his style became still simpler, more compact and lucid, and even more intolerant of irrelevancies.

The *Nänie,* Op. 82, for chorus and orchestra, was begun in 1880 and finished in the summer of the following year. Schiller's noble lament was set to music by Brahms in memory of the painter Anselm Feuerbach, who died in the January of 1880, and the work was dedicated to his friend's stepmother. His attention may first have been directed to the text by a performance of Hermann Goetz's *Nänie,* which took place at a concert of the *Gesellschaft der Musikfreunde* on 14 February 1880, shortly after Feuerbach's death. The work of Goetz, who was acquainted with Brahms, may have been unconsciously present in the latter's mind when he began the composition of *Nänie.* For the compositions of Brahms and Goetz have more in common than the use of chorus and orchestra alone. Far more significant is the warm and gleaming F sharp major and the slowly upward-flowing melody with which each work greets the climax of the poem, when the divine Thetis rises with her sisters from the sea. Similarly, at the passage 'Yet a sad song is sweet,' the time-signature changes in each work from 4/4 to 6/4. Other small points of resemblance might be mentioned, and yet no two works could be more different. Goetz has chosen for his *Nänie* a loose form, consisting of many small sections, akin to the old madrigal. In the short composition, time-signature, key, and tempo are varied so frequently that an impression is given of a series of disconnected pieces, and a feeling of restlessness prevails, somewhat inconsistent with the austere dignity of Schiller's poem. Brahms's *Nänie,* on the other hand, is written in the simple, monumental form *a b a.* The first and third parts are in the same key, the same time-signature, and the same tempo, and to a certain extent embody the same thematic material. The F sharp major middle section alone introduces a certain element of contrast, with its still deeper and more radiant coloring.

As in form, the two compositions differ in mood. The general tone of Goetz's *Nänie* is gloomy, and minor keys prevail. Brahms, however, portrays death as a kindly genius, in whose arms those weary of life on earth find sweet repose. In his work the spirit of antiquity is reincarnate; death is conceived as surrounded by youth and beauty, flowers and wine. The impressions received on his first two journeys to Italy and from the neo-classic paintings of Anselm Feuerbach are enshrined in this work; moreover, that greater clarity and repose of mind appear which characterized Brahms in his later years. It is therefore comprehensible that the three movements should be composed in the major key, and that a spirit of perfect harmony, tranquil and serene, should reign over the whole work. As in the *Schicksalslied,* a moving orchestral prelude ushers in the entry of the chorus. It is repeated, in briefer form, at the opening of the third part. The far-ranging oboe melody in this Prelude is matched by the melody of the chorus. It rises to a sweet intensity at the mention of Adonis (b. 65 *et seq.*), war-like accents hail the name of Achilles (b. 74 *et seq.*), and yet the fundamental content is unaltered. Only when there is the sea-goddess

Thetis referred to does Brahms strike a warmer, richer note. In particular, the passage 'See how the gods all are weeping' (b. 97 *et seq.*), with its strange octave leaps, is charged with the deepest feeling. This noble composition closes with a delicate repetition of the choral opening. The spirit of consolation pervading the *Nänie* is preserved until the very end, for which Brahms chose not the last line of Schiller's poem, 'For the ignoble goes silent and mute to the grave,' but the preceding line, 'Yet a sad song is sweet, and sung by a loved one is glorious.'

Brahms's last composition for chorus and orchestra, the *Gesang der Parzen* (Song of the Fates), Op. 89, was composed in the summer of 1882. This powerful work is, if possible, even more succinct and compressed than the preceding compositions. Including the purely instrumental passages, the setting of the text of seven stanzas does not exceed 176 bars. In keeping with the compactness of the structure, Brahms has even avoided the fugato passages which play so important a part in his earlier choral works. The homophony of this composition is interrupted only by little imitative passages. In keeping with its oppressively heavy gait, Brahms employs an exceptionally large and darkly colored body of sound. The chorus is in six parts, and as in the *a cappella* choruses, Op. 104, the lower parts of the male and female voices, the contralto and bass, are doubled. The wood wind is reinforced by the contra bassoon, the brass by three trombones and a bass tuba.

The text of this work is once again an antique theme treated by a German poet. Goethe's *Gesang der Parzen,* however, is far removed from the gentle serenity of the *Nänie.* It is more akin to the *Schicksalslied,* where human frailty is compared with the bliss of the gods. But whereas in the older work suffering mankind still rebels against the might of Destiny, in the later work the terrible decrees of Fate are inevitably fulfilled. Sorrow itself is stricken dumb before the savage majesty with which Ananke reveals herself. Naturally the structure of such a compressed work is closely knit and easily comprehensible. It is the small Rondo form *a b a c a,* where a principal subject in the minor, interrupted by two episodes in the major, is twice repeated. As in the earlier works, the *Gesang der Parzen* opens with a short and effective instrumental introduction—a D minor movement, full of violent modulations. In the first section the vocal part is marked by unhasting yet irresistible power. The lower voices alternate with the higher, and sometimes with the whole chorus, while a drum motive provides an effective background, and by its very monotony produces an impression of irresistible force. At b. 72 the second part begins, with a gentle, almost dance-like, theme. The entry of the key of F major seems to herald the advent of kindlier moods. But this one ray of light is deceptive. At the words 'From deepest abysses,' a new gloomy minor passage enters and paves the way for the return of the main section, whereupon the beginning of the vocal part is repeated in slightly altered form. It would have been quite possible, it was indeed almost imperatively necessary, to conclude at this point. But the master of the *Schicksalslied* was unable to end on a note of such unrelieved hardness. He felt impelled to add a passage of milder and more human tones in order to give the composition a more consoling character. Thus a second episode makes its appearance, in its expression somewhat reminiscent of the *Nänie.* The agonized words of the poem are sung to gently transfigured, quietly resigned melodies. The work closes with a final echo of the beginning. While the violins return to the opening melody, the choir softly chants the epilogue 'So sing the three sisters . . .' and the music dies away in a dreamy, mysterious *pianissimo.* The whole of Brahms is in this brief composition; the master of tragic power and of recollected serenity, all too soon overcast, the dispenser of mild and blessed consolation, and finally the Brahms of vague and ethereal moods and broken dreams.

[323]

PART THREE

THE MAN AND THE ARTIST

XXII

THE MAN AND THE ARTIST

B RAHMS had not a firm, self-contained, homogeneous character. A discord, a conflict of opposing forces, pervaded his whole existence, coloring his life and his work alike. Two powers fought in him, which we may roughly call an 'urge to freedom' and a 'desire for subjection.'

The seeds of this discord already existed in the character of Brahms's father. He came of a respectable, sedentary family of craftsmen and tradespeople, who may be described as prototypes of bourgeois simplicity. Johann Jakob Brahms, however, had artistic blood in his veins. He strove to get away from home, away from the pursuits of his forebears. This drove him from the narrowness of provincial life to the capital, and he longed for the imagined freedom of a musical career. To be sure, we must not exaggerate Johann Jakob's desire for independence. As soon as he had reached his goal, and become a musician, his one ambition was to find a situation in an orchestra. He married, set up house, and brought several children into the world. And when his first wife died he remarried after a short interval. Jakob Brahms's restless nature, however, still expressed itself in a certain passion for making financial experiments. At one time he started rearing rabbits and chickens; at another he opened a small shop, and he even planned to emigrate to America.

If in Johann Jakob, with his modest talent, these opposing forces were still to some extent compatible, they created insurmountable difficulties for the genius Johannes Brahms. The desire for bourgeois respectability and bourgeois comfort which he had inherited from generations of forefathers was hardly less in the son than in the father. The urge for independence and the impatience of all restraint, however, which Brahms may have inherited also from his romantic mother, assumed far greater proportions in the son. Any reconciliation of these diverging tendencies, which made Brahms partly a petty bourgeois, partly a genius, was inconceivable.

The simplicity that Brahms displayed in all matters of daily life may be regarded as an inheritance from his forefathers. Even when a famous man, he lived in a modest dwelling, dressed with greatest economy, ate in the cheapest restaurants, and took a pride in spending little on his food. He had no extravagant tastes, and he devoted only comparatively small sums of money to his passion for collecting original manuscripts by great masters.

Nevertheless, Brahms was anything but a cynic or an ascetic. He loved to eat well and to drink well, and when he was invited to his friends' homes he was easily persuaded to exchange his ordinary plain fare for culinary delights on a higher plane.*

Similar in origin was the pedantic love of order which Brahms displayed in everything connected with his work and his intellectual needs. He boasted that he could always instantly lay his hand on those books he valued—for ex-

---

* In this connection it is interesting to read the diary of Frau von Miller in which are recorded the menus of the dinners she gave to Brahms. By the courtesy of Frau Ribartz-Hemala I had the opportunity to look over this delightful document. I found there, for example, the following menu for a Sunday dinner (20 February 1892): Brain consommé, lobster salad, filet de bœuf garnished with vegetables, ham cooked in Madeira wine, hazel grouse, ice cream, pastry, champagne, coffee. Brahms must have been well satisfied with such a large menu, as his kind hostess continued on the same line (always offering beside soup and some sort of fish three different kinds of meat), while she once scrupulously noted that Brahms hadn't seemed content with a certain plum cake.

ample, the Bible—even in the dark. His manuscripts are covered with rapidly written script, which is, however, clearly and methodically arranged, and even his sketches can easily be deciphered. He was no less orderly in his reading: with him it was a matter of course to correct, with pedantic conscientiousness, every mistake he found in a printed book or music work.

Further, in all questions of money the bourgeois vein is apparent in Brahms. His letters to his publisher show remarkable commercial astuteness, and he insisted on being paid enormous fees for his works.

Most bourgeois of all was his ambition to occupy a permanent post, which would make it possible for him to settle down in his own home. The existence of a wandering virtuoso was abhorrent to him. He dreamed of a position as conductor that would keep him in one place, assure him a secure income, and enable him to marry and found a family. For Brahms this was by no means a vague desire. It took a very definite shape; where he had spent his childhood and youth, where he felt at home, there Brahms wanted to live. Had the fairy godmother of fiction stood before him, promising to fulfil a single wish, the master would not have hesitated for a moment before asking for the conductorship of the Hamburg Philharmonic Orchestra.

But all these traits of Brahms's character were opposed by others, which were directly antithetical, hence the peculiar duality of his character.

Brahms's love of order stopped short at his own person. He was accustomed to wander through the streets of Vienna in garments which were anything but the ideal of bourgeois respectability. His trousers were always pulled up too far, his clothes were hopelessly creased, an enormous safety pin held a plaid in place on his shoulders, and he always carried his hat in his hand instead of on his head. The cupboards containing his clothes and linen were in the most terrible confusion, which was a constant source of grief to his last landlady, Frau Truxa. His neglectfulness was not confined to these superficialities. Brahms never attended to a matter which must have often occupied the mind of one who had from his youth kept his eyes fixed upon death: the drawing up of his will. He left his last will and testament half finished, and in a legally invalid form, although it was practically completed six years before his death. The meticulous love of order in everything that directly or indirectly concerned his art was balanced on the other hand by a definite carelessness and indifference in everyday affairs.

Once he had earned his money, Brahms, oddly enough, was as careless with it as he had been conscientious in its making. He left the management of his considerable fortune to his publisher Simrock, and was not in the least unhappy when his friend had to tell him that he had lost substantial sums belonging to Brahms in some Stock Exchange speculation. He left whole bundles of bank notes lying uncounted in his closet, and hardly ever took the trouble to check on his bank balance.

Even more peculiar was Brahms's behavior in connection with obtaining a permanent post. Various cities tried to secure his services as conductor; Cologne made him three offers. Usually, however, he found some pretext for refusing, for he could not make up his mind to sacrifice his personal liberty. In Detmold, however, and later in Vienna, he did accept especially tempting offers after long hesitation. But even then he could not get used to the yoke, or the less enjoyable contacts with the workaday aspects of art; and in each instance he was glad when a pretext occurred for retiring from these positions. Yet his unpleasant experiences as a young man in Detmold, and later on in Vienna, did not prevent him from believing with undiminished confidence that a position in his native city would bring happiness. The short-sightedness of his fellow citizens saved him from realizing how unfounded were his hopes. In Hamburg he was persistently neglected, and thus he was spared the last and bitterest experience of failing in his beloved native city to suppress his vague desires and impulses, and transform himself from an 'outsider' of genius into a useful member of bourgeois society.

But Brahms never admitted to himself that, when all was said and done, it really did not matter to him whether he was elected in Hamburg, or defeated by another candidate. He who accepted with stoical calm the public lack of understanding for his work regarded his disappointment in respect of Hamburg the one real defeat of his life. On this he laid the blame for the fact that he had to go through life as a 'vagabond,' was unable to settle down in a home of his own, and there lead a happy, peaceful life with wife and children.

It has already been noted that Brahms attributed even his attitude towards marriage to external events, and especially to the grievous wrong done him at Hamburg. Again and again he declared that he had been unable to marry in his youth because he had not an adequate position and an assured income; but also because the sympathy of a loving wife in his fight against the hostility of the public would have shamed and hindered him far more than it would have strengthened him. This corresponds only to a certain extent with the external facts. For it was not long before Brahms was earning a quite respectable income, and after the success of his *Requiem* he was counted among the most highly esteemed German composers of his time. In a deeper sense, however, Brahms's explanation would seem to be justified. For that part of his nature which longed for bondage, a marriage was conceivable only on the basis of a fixed monthly income and the social esteem paid to the holder of a prominent position. The artist in Brahms might have been able to disregard such considerations had there not been, on his side, far greater obstacles to marriage. Yet the composer was anything but a misogynist. He paid tribute to the charms of the fair sex by unconditional worship. And when physical beauty was coupled with intelligence and musical talent—

he was especially fascinated by a beautiful voice—he was only too ready to fall in love. He did so not once only, but again and again in the course of his life. And not only the passionate handsome youth, but also the mature artist, and even the master on the verge of old age, had reason to be confident that his love would be returned. Nevertheless, he never formed a permanent connection; he always shrank from the last decisive step. The thought of sacrificing his personal liberty, his freedom from restraint, of adapting himself and surrendering part of his own being for the value of a new and higher unity, was entirely abhorrent to Brahms. Dimly he felt that he would be acting in defiance of his aim in life if he, who had dedicated himself wholly to art, were to belong to another. There is some significance in a story Lienau tells in his Memoirs. He once accompanied Brahms home from a concert and the conversation turned upon marriage. Brahms finally pointed to his house and exclaimed: 'Look, now I go upstairs and enter my room, and there I am quite alone and undisturbed. Oh, this is wonderful!'

Hitschmann and Schauffler have undertaken, with the help of the methods of psychoanalysis, to explain Brahms's attitude towards marriage as the result of an 'Oedipus complex.' This is supposed to have appeared in an unnaturally strong attachment to his mother, and a feeling of rivalry towards his father, which would have made Brahms incapable of physical passion when spiritual ties bound him to a woman. The authors adduce, as the main proof of their assertion, the fact that Brahms's deepest love was given to the mother of seven children, to Clara Schumann, who was fourteen years older than he; a woman in whom, of all others, he was bound to see the motherly friend. The assumptions of this theory are, in my opinion, unfounded. Those who read his parents' letters to Brahms, and the son's letters to his father, will find there not the slightest proof of the accuracy of such a conjecture. On the other hand, it is significant that Johannes—in spite of his full understanding of the position of the elderly wife—was inclined rather to take his father's part when called upon by both parents to give judgment on the occasion of the differences between them. Moreover, it would be difficult to picture Clara Schumann as a motherly matron at the time of Brahms's passion for her. Clara was then thirty-five, famous for her physical beauty and charm. If we add to this her magnificent art, and Brahms's sympathy with her in her affliction, we can easily understand how it was that the romantic young man devoted the first and greatest love of his life to this exquisite woman. The maturer master, however, had no time for 'motherly women.' He felt drawn towards beautiful girls, and women who were not only much younger than he, but who also conceived the greatest admiration for his art. Brahms's disinclination to marry, therefore, can hardly be explained by the theory of an 'unnaturally strong attachment' to his mother.

However this may be, we can at all events be sure that the renunciation of marriage was anything but easy for the composer. He had always longed for the comfort of a home, and further, he had ardently wished for children, in whom he hoped to see his own gifts more strongly and purely developed. As this was denied him, he bestowed his affection on the children of others. During his summer holidays Brahms quickly formed friendships with the young people of the village, and even in Italy he scraped up his knowledge of the foreign language in order to converse with the children. A great help in his advances were the sweets which he used to keep in his pockets for any little friend. Thus Hermine Spies wrote to Klaus Groth: 'How I used to respect and admire him when he distributed Christmas sweets among the poor children who stood with longing eyes and mouths before a pastry cook's window, and when he stroked their often none too clean cheeks. How splendid it is when the greatest artist is also the most human man!' Brahms felt all the more drawn towards children, for he himself, like many a great artist, had much of the child in his nature. At the age of twenty, just when the blossoming friendship with the Schumanns was growing into an imperishable experience, he asked his mother to send his tin soldiers to Düsseldorf.[1] Even in his last years, when he visited the little prodigy, the violinist Bronislav Huberman, his attention was so held by the fascinations of a stamp album that the fourteen-year-old boy had to spend over an hour initiating him into the secrets of his collection.[2]

The description of Brahms's life has shown what an influence the abandonment of his hopes and dreams had on the development of his character. In his youth Brahms, though modest and shy, was amiable, frank, and enthusiastic. There was a decisive change after his experience with Clara, and the changes became more and more marked after each disappointment in his career or his personal life. Qualities that slumbered in him, but had rarely appeared, now came boldly to the fore. When, at the end of the 'seventies, Brahms hid his smooth and still boyish face behind a thick, full beard, he seemed to have become a different person. The careless inconsiderateness which had distinguished Brahms even as a young man (and had certainly helped him to achieve many of his artistic aims) increased alarmingly, and was often coupled with rudeness. The reputation that Brahms enjoyed in Vienna in this respect may be judged from the widely circulated anecdote to the effect that the master, on leaving a company in which he had found himself for the first time, took his departure with the words: 'If there is anybody here whom I have forgotten to insult, I beg him to forgive me.'

Thus Brahms clothed himself in an armor of irony and coldness, and this armor was so stout that sometimes even his best friends could not hear the great warm heart of their Johannes beating behind it. When, on the other hand, help, sympathy, and advice were needed, no one was so quickly on the spot as the reserved composer. He who for months left letters unanswered forced himself, in the case of a request for help, to respond immediately. Indeed, the Rhenish singer, Aloisia Schrötter, who had approached him with such a request, wrote to him: 'This is how one must tackle you in order to get a sign of life from you: one must ask a favor of you—that's what I like.' [3]

Brahms helped many fellow musicians to obtain positions: Zellner, Buths, Knorr, Wüllner, and others. Many more had to thank him for loans and gifts of money, which he always kept strictly secret. The help he bestowed on his family was truly magnanimous. Not only the sums he gave, but the manner in which he gave them prove that to give and to aid was one of the most essential elements of his character.

We can thus discern two totally different strata in Brahms's character—irony and reserve, coupled with genuine kindness and readiness to help. The relations of those about him to the artist were determined by their ability to penetrate the uncouth shell. At first Brahms generally evoked timidity and embarrassment; a good judge of men, however, soon discovered the secret of his double nature, and those who gained an insight into the master's true character remained loyally attached to him for life. Many eminent men felt his attraction. The famous violinist Adolf Brodsky (later the principal of the Manchester College of Music) wrote once to Brahms:

When I have been enchanted, touched, and thrilled by your work the whole year through, now in this place, now in that, it is the greatest pleasure of my life to be able to chat with you, their creator, so pleasantly and unconstrainedly. Life holds no greater happiness for me than to love you, dear master, with all the strength of which my soul is capable. Don't laugh at me! [4]

But also on non-musicians Brahms had—in the words of the poet Richard Voss—the effect of 'a great current of strong, life-giving mountain air.' [5] This stimulating effect may have been due mainly to Brahms's intense intellectual life. He was anything but a one-sided musician. The gaps in his education, which were bound to be left by the short period of his schooldays, he filled by untiring private study; and his library gave one an impressive idea of the width of his mental horizon. Religious, philosophical, esthetic, historical and political works, and books relating to the history of art could there be seen side by side with the poetry of all times and all countries. Numerous marginal notes and annotations are proof that Brahms had read these books with real application. This living interest in all questions of art and science brought him into contact with eminent representatives of the various professions. Practical men like Dr. Fellinger and Arthur Faber; the physicians, Billroth and Engelmann; the painters, Anselm Feuerbach, Wilhelm Menzel and Heinrich Klinger; the engraver, Julius Allgeyer; the historian of art, Wilhelm Lübke; the poets, Klaus Groth and Joseph V. Widmann; the literary historian, Erich Schmidt; the philologist, Theodor Wendt; the musical historians, Friedrich Chrysander, Philipp Spitta, Karl Nottebohm, and Eusebius Mandyczewski; and numerous actors, such as E. Robert and Joseph Lewinsky—all these men found in Brahms a warm and untiring interest in all that concerned them; and they, for their part, were stimulating acquaintances. If we add to this list of names the many musicians whose friend Brahms was, we shall see that the master had a special talent for friendship with members of his own sex. It is at this point, however, that the discord in his whole character is once more apparent. Hardly one of the great friendships of his life—and here we are thinking of Joachim, Levi, Billroth, and Bülow—persisted untroubled. Although in each of these cases there are special circumstances to be taken into account, the explanation of Brahms's behavior is always to be found in his aversion to ties of any kind. He was invariably ready for cheerful and easy company, or for a matter-of-fact exchange of ideas. But, as he avoided marriage, so he withdrew from the claims of a really close friendship that threatened to encroach on his own life.

The master's personality was thus determined by the conflict of two opposing principles. One would be tempted to call this life, thus riven by inner dissension, an unhappy one, had not triumphant success been his in the region of his highest endeavors: in his art. Here, too, the same principles prevailed which we may see at work in his life, and which may best be described by the words 'fantasy' and 'obedience to law.'

Brahms's art was derived from the romantics. Schubert, Schumann, and the late Beethoven were the patron saints of his first creative period. The young man adored Jean Paul Richter and Novalis, called himself, after the well-known character in E. T. A. Hoffmann's tale, 'Johannes Kreisler, junior' (see page 23), and wrote melodies which were incomparably tender, sweet, and pensive. Later on these traits became less obvious; always, however, Brahms loved the vague twilight moods and unreal, ghostly backgrounds. Further, his profound affection for the German folk song and the folk music of other countries proved him a true romantic. We find the romantic pianoforte piece, and above all the romantic song, constantly recurring in his creative work.

However, even in the works of the young Brahms a force asserted itself in opposition to his fantasy, his extravagance of feeling, and his romantic enthusiasm. This force found expression in the striving for clearly articulated structure and established form.

The compositions written by Liszt about this time, which are, from the standpoint of musical form, extremely free in their construction, were abhorrent to Brahms. For his own work he felt that obedience to law and strict articulation were indispensable, and he felt this the more strongly as he grew older. It is characteristic of him that where he confined himself within the strictest formal bounds his imagination soared to its most magnificent heights. The composer never surrendered to the first inspiration. Only after he had 'taken it out walking' for some time, and had passed it through the crucible of mind and spirit, did he put it into writing. This explains why he wrote his works only when some time had elapsed since the external events that had inspired them (cf. the *Requiem,* second String Sextet, etc.), and also why his few extant sketches show such astonishing similarity to the finished works. These traits are constant elements in the classic writers, and one can often see them at work in Hadyn, Mozart, and the younger Beethoven, whose compositions Brahms took as his models in many respects. In Brahms we find the rare, even unique, case of an artist who belonged heart and soul to the romantic movement, yet who at the same time turned quite as naturally towards the classic style. It is in his finest works that heart and mind, inspiration and elaboration, freedom and restraint are most perfectly balanced. That even the aging master was able to achieve this balance may partly be due to the influence of his adopted home, Vienna. The romantic fervor, the romantic tenderness which had filled Brahms in his youth drew ever fresh nourishment from the city on the Blue Danube, and all that was tender and enthusiastic in his art found an echo in the imperial city.

The fact that Brahms, who belonged to the romantic period, absorbed numerous elements of the classic style into his work reveals yet another characteristic feature: his love of the past. It is true that in Brahms's daring melodies, his complicated harmonies, his varied polyrhythmics, and his occasional experiments in form, we find many traits prophetic of the future. On the whole, however, Brahms made less use of modern license than of the restrictions to which his adherence to the principles of the past committed him. His antiquarian interests and tendencies went far deeper than in any other of the great masters of music. He possessed the works of the most important musical theorists, beginning with Fux, Forkel, and Mattheson, down to the end of the nineteenth century. The great masters of the past were represented in his collection of music by precious original manuscripts, valuable first prints, and often complete editions. He possessed works in every style from the sixteenth to the eighteenth century, many of which he had copied himself in the public libraries. Like a mere craftsman, he—the only creative artist of his eminence to do so—prepared many critical revisions and new editions of the older masters.

The list of works that Brahms edited—many of which were published for the first time—is amazingly long. It includes compositions by Friedemann and Philipp Emanuel Bach, Handel, Couperin, Mozart, Schubert, Chopin, and Schumann. On all these editions Brahms expended the greatest pains. A copy of Chopin's Mazurkas, revised for the collected edition, which has been preserved in the *Gesellschaft der Musikfreunde,* is sprinkled all over with red, blue, and black corrections from Brahms's hand. Further, the composer's correspondence with Clara Schumann and Mandyczewski shows us with what zeal and devotion Brahms prepared the supplementary volume (of hardly seventy pages) for the collected edition of Schumann's works.

Remembering all this, we shall understand how deeply rooted was his predilection for the past. Under these circumstances it was bound to find eloquent expression in his work. As a matter of fact, the threads that connect Brahms's compositions with the music of the past reach not only into the classical period, but much farther back. The medieval Church modes, the masterpieces in canon form of the old Dutch composers, and the style of Palestrina: all celebrate their resurrection in Brahms's works. With fugues, *a cappella* motets, choral preludes, and *bassi ostinati* the composer built a bridge to the art of Bach, and to Handel's oratorios, with his powerful *Triumphlied.*

The musical output of five hundred years is summarized in Brahms's works. But in spite of their unbending rigidity of form, these compositions are anything but servile imitations of preceding models. They are saved from this fate by the modern and progressive note in Brahms's creative work, and by the original personality of the master. A lesser composer would have been oppressed and hampered in his independent creations by the colossal precedents of Bach and Handel. Not so Brahms, who was able to aim at a true creative renaissance of the old masters, in which the rigid forms and laws are filled with a new spirit.

This enables us to understand why Brahms had no individual pupils (with the exception of young Jenner). To explain this only by referring to his impatience and lack of teaching ability would be unjust. All in all, the master's work, with all its individuality, marked a terminus and a conclusion. And so the would-be beginners did not rally round his banner, but around that of the masters who were looking towards the future rather than the past. Not even Max Reger has developed Brahms's tendencies; in reality he only repeats them in his own way, but less successfully.

Brahms's retention of old forms resulted in his being blamed for reactionary views by the radical modern 'New German' school, whose members crowded round Liszt and Wagner. This assertion is symptomatic of the complete lack of understanding on the part of the 'New Germans,' a necessary consequence of the extreme dissimilarity of their artistic aims. Wagner's center of gravity lay in the region of musical drama; the opera was to him the measure of all things. Liszt began as a virtuoso; later in life he became increasingly interested in composition, and wrote 'program music,' in which the musical form was influenced by a poetic content. A further essential element of his compositions is musical color. Liszt, like Wagner, possessed a strong literary talent; they both enlisted it in the service of their ideas, the catchwords of which were 'Away from the past' and 'Reform.' None of the foregoing traits are to be found in Brahms. Theatricality was foreign to his intensely spiritual nature, and he cared as little for virtuosity. He was a magnificent pianist, to whom, however—if only because of his intense shyness—public appearances were repugnant. In 1895 he wrote to Joachim: 'Why should I worry whether the people who after a concert say or write that my playing was inadequate are right or not? I know only too well, unless I am in a particularly good mood, that one has to be accustomed to play before an audience, if one wants to perform in public.'

Brahms cared little for superficial brilliance and sparkling technique, and he endeavored (so far as possible) to withdraw his own personality behind the works he performed. To program music, in Liszt's sense, Brahms was fundamentally opposed. Even if—as sometimes in his pianoforte pieces —he portrayed a poetic content, it was subordinated to purely musical form. Such a shattering of form as we find in Liszt's *Symphonic Poems* was completely beyond the comprehension of Brahms, who regarded musical architecture as the basis of his creations. Moreover, clear and unbroken outlines were infinitely more important to him than musical color. His orchestration is temperate and austere, and far removed from the glowing splendor of color found in the compositions of Berlioz or Wagner. It is characteristic of Brahms that in the domain of painting he felt drawn towards the excellently designed but somewhat colorless pictures of Feuerbach, while he had no feeling whatever for the gorgeous blaze of Makart's improvisations in color. As for any literary activity, Brahms, although he possessed great literary sensitiveness, never thought of expressing in words his views on his art or the principles of his work. His innate reserve forbade him; as did his whole conception of music as an absolute art, which one must not approach indirectly through literature. And while the artists of the 'New German' school assumed the airs of revolutionaries in duty bound to alter and better all things, Brahms looked upon himself as the guardian and preserver of the great traditions.

Thus a great gulf lay between Brahms and the 'New German' school. This became the more apparent inasmuch as two composers who were sworn allies of Wagner's were also living in Vienna. In the domain of song, Hugo Wolf had done very much what Wagner had done for music-drama. The voice in Wolf's songs had to declaim the text as carefully as possible, and he transferred the expression and characterization mainly to the pianoforte part. Anton Bruckner's solemn symphonies, on the other hand, have their source in the South German Catholic mysticism. They are conceived in a grandiose *al fresco* technique, whereby the architectural structure is often shattered by the vastness of the musical conception. To these two masters also Brahms was utterly opposed. For him the voice was all-important in song; the pianoforte part, however richly he may have treated it, was only a sort of accompaniment. His symphonies, in the last resort, like the orchestral compositions of J. S. Bach, originated from chamber music, and excelled through the beautiful structural union of all their parts.

Even though Brahms had many adversaries among contemporary composers, he was never overlooked or underrated. His fame constantly increased after the performance of the *Requiem*. Not only in Austria and Germany, but also in Switzerland, Holland, England, and America, the number of his adherents was continually multiplying. All those groups who believed in the progress of art, and yet held fast in love and veneration to the past, rallied round Brahms. They felt that it was to him that various branches of musical art, to which innumerable lovers of music were devotedly attached, owed a sort of renaissance, while the 'New Germans' had little understanding for them. Chamber music, and all music that can be performed at home, underwent a revival, thanks to Brahms; while to choral music and Protestant Church music he gave fresh vitality.

Iron self-control and·discipline enabled Brahms to achieve the things which have assured him of immortality. He never took things easily; with relentless severity and self-criticism he examined everything he wrote. No unfinished or indifferent work left his hand. His whole strength and energy were given to composition; thereby his life suffered. Dominated by the conflict between bourgeois respectability and genius, it followed a discordant and somewhat disappointing course. In his art, however, Brahms succeeded in uniting the apparently irreconcilable. Freedom and bondage, fantasy and discipline, progress and loyalty to tradition are combined in Brahms's work in one splendid organic whole, which has a character all its own, through the harsh vigor, the stern melancholy, the delicate fervor, and suppressed gaiety of the master's nature.

UNPUBLISHED LETTERS REFERRED TO:

1. Letter from Christiane Brahms, 28 October 1853.
2. According to personal information furnished by Professor B. Huberman.
3. Letter from Aloisia Schrötter, 4 August 1859.
4. Letter from Adolf Brodsky, 13 February 1891.
5. Letter from Richard Voss (undated).

APPENDIX

BRAHMS WRITES LETTERS

B RAHMS liked to stress his lack of talent for writing letters. Again and again he declared that the very sight of notepaper waiting to be used by him filled him with inhibitions, and that the invention of the post card was one of the greatest of blessings for him. He shrank from the task of expressing in words anything of real importance to him, and complaints like the following written to Elisabeth von Herzogenberg abound in his correspondence: 'Usually I blunder over what I try to express in writing—if I don't, the blunder is sure to occur on the part of him who reads.'

Posterity does not agree with the composer on this point. It is true that Brahms's letters do not reveal the literary and poetic gifts of a Schumann or a Mendelssohn; that, unlike so many letters written by romantic composers, they are certainly not little works of art, delightful in themselves apart from their biographical significance. Nevertheless they should by no means be overlooked, for they are most revealing, both in what the composer says and what he leaves unsaid. In these letters the two-sided Brahms becomes strikingly alive. We witness his grim humor, his craving for a settled existence, and his poignant awareness of not belonging anywhere, no less than his inmost gentleness, his enthusiasm for great composers, his fairness in business dealings, and his staunch loyalty to his friends.

As the greatest part of the Brahms correspondence has so far not been made available to the English reader, an attempt has been made to present herewith a selection of characteristic letters, which may help to round off the picture of Brahms gained in the preceding pages. The correspondence between Brahms and Clara Schumann has been purposely omitted in this connection, as it is available in an excellent English translation and should be read in its entirety by the student of Brahms.[1]

A beginning is made with some letters by young Brahms. At an early age he was not so reluctant to express himself in writing as he became later and these letters therefore have a charm not to be found in the subsequent correspondence. Escaping from the narrowness of his existence at Hamburg, Brahms discovered a new world, in the center of which stood his new friends, Joachim and Schumann.

Brahms tells Joachim of his first visit to the Schumanns:

Düsseldorf, September 1853

BELOVED FRIEND,

You will have received a letter from the Schumanns telling you of my being here. I need not, I think, tell you at length how inexpressibly happy their reception, kind beyond expectation, has made me. Their praise made me so cheerful and strong that I can hardly wait for the time when at last I can settle down to undisturbed working and composing.

What shall I tell you about Schumann; shall I burst into encomiums of his genius and character, or shall I lament that folks still sin badly in misjudging a good man and a divine artist so freely and respecting him so little?

And I myself, for how long did I commit this fault? It is only since I left Hamburg and particularly during my stay at Mehlem [2] that I got to know and admire Schumann's works. I should like to ask pardon from him.

---

1. The only other set of Brahms letters available in an English translation is the correspondence between Brahms and the Herzogenbergs. This work has been out of print for many years; besides, the highlights of this correspondence are not Brahms's but Elisabeth von Herzogenberg's letters.

2. See p. 35.

To go to Leipzig as Wehner [3] urges me to do in every letter does not, frankly speaking, appeal to me. I am afraid of that gigantic office, and I also believe I can now use my time to better advantage by diligently continuing my studies rather than by trying to get the most practical results out of my music.

It would be heavenly if during your visit to Düsseldorf you could for once go with me to Mehlem. You just can't imagine how I enjoyed it there; and all of it would please you as well.

I long for you as though years had passed since our last meeting.[4] I have so much, such an immense amount of what is beautiful to tell you about. Write me that you are soon coming to your

JOHANNES

Brahms looks up to Joachim as a creative artist:
Excerpts from two letters to Joachim

Düsseldorf, 1 April 1854

DEAR PRESENT TIMER,[5]

What you write about the [bad] reception of your Overture [at Leipzig] was quite unexpected by me. I had dreamed of immense acclamation and encores and of its traveling through the whole of Germany in the shortest possible time. One should not venture to experience sublimer and purer emotions than the public. You can see from my case that if one dreams merely the same dreams as the public and puts them into music, one gets some applause. The eagle soars upwards in loneliness, but rooks flock together; may God

---

3. See p. 34.
4. In reality only a few weeks.
5. Brahms refers with the word *Gegenwärtler* (Present Timer) to Joachim's inimical attitude towards the 'New German school' and Wagner's *Kunstwerk der Zukunft* (Art of the Future).

grant that my wings grow thoroughly and that I belong at last to the other kind. . . Your

JOHANNES

Düsseldorf, 16 February 1855

MY DEAR FELLOW,

What can I write or say later about your splendid Variations [Op. 10]? What else than that they are just what I expected and as your Overtures promised? Your music affects me just as Beethoven's does. When I got to know a new symphony or overture, it absorbed me completely for a long time. Everything else just formed arabesques round the beautiful great picture. It is just the same for me with your new works, the *Hamlet, Heinrich,* and *Demetrius* overtures, and now with this new splendor. How often have I felt an urge to write to you after looking long with increasing wonder at one of your works, but I couldn't do it, and even now I can only say that more and more I admire and love it all. This full and warm love has, in fact, developed in me only after long gazing in wonder at them. The Variations are perhaps not so entirely your own as the Overtures, but probably nobody has wielded Beethoven's pen so powerfully. . . I beg you, do look at the immense crescendo from your Opus 1 to now! Where will it lead to? Probably beyond the seventh heaven! I wish you realized only the half of how much your works absorb me and with what love and hopefulness I think of you. . .

With the best greetings,

Your JOHANNES

In his rapturous praise, and, as we see it today, overrating of Joachim's music, young Brahms was undoubtedly sincere. For years afterwards he believed that Joachim would give the world his best as a composer, and he was therefore vehemently opposed to his friend's ever-increasing concert activities, especially his regular visits to England. Eventually he could no longer close his eyes to the fact that Joachim's strenuous life as a virtuoso and teacher made creative work impossible. This meant a grave disappointment to Brahms, and may also have contributed to the gradual cooling off of his relation to Joachim.

Brahms celebrates his twenty-second birthday at Clara Schumann's house:

To Julius Otto Grimm

Düsseldorf, 8 May 1855

Accept my warmest thanks for your friendly thought; you have made me very happy. If only you had been here to see how wonderfully and mysteriously the big white cake [sent by you] suddenly appeared on the scene! I first supposed that it was a girl sweetheart who sent it, but today I found out how the cake got here. If only you had been here to spend this splendidly jolly day with us! In the morning I received many beautiful flowers covering a portrait of my mother and sister, such good likenesses that I wanted to kiss them. Then there was a photograph of dear Schumann . . . then the works of Dante and Ariosto. At 3 P.M. Joachim arrived, and with him a big parcel of bloaters, some [lead] soldiers, etc., with letters from loved ones in Hamburg. Seldom have I been so merry and joyful as I was yesterday. We are having a lot of music now and magnificently done, Bach, Beethoven, Schumann—we never can have enough. Just think, our revered master [Schumann] thought of my birthday and sent me the MS. of his *Braut von Messina* with a most affectionate inscription. . . We think of you, mainly when we play music, drink, read or go for walks—and what else is there to do?

Sincerely,

Your JOHANNES BRAHMS

[348]

The letter shows how much Brahms felt at home in Clara Schumann's house, and how his whole being expanded in this congenial atmosphere. This time he sounded especially carefree, because the news from Endenich about Schumann was most reassuring. Unfortunately the joy of Clara and Johannes was not long-lived, for Schumann's condition deteriorated rapidly.

Brahms describes Schumann's passing to Julius Otto Grimm:

[Heidelberg, September 1856]

MY DEAR JULIUS,

. . . I shall probably never again experience anything so moving as the meeting between Robert and Clara. He lay first for some time with closed eyes, and she knelt before him with greater calmness than one would think possible. But later on he recognized her, and he did so again next day. Once he clearly wished to embrace her and flung his arm round her. Of course he was past being able to talk any more, one could only make out single words, perhaps in imagination. But even that was bound to make her happy. He often refused the wine offered to him, but he sucked it from her finger sometimes so eagerly and long, and with such fervor that one knew for certain that he recognized her finger. Midday Tuesday Joachim arrived from Heidelberg, and this kept us somewhat longer in Bonn, otherwise we should have arrived before he passed away. As it was, we were half an hour late. We felt like you did on reading about it; we should have breathed with relief at his deliverance, and we could not believe it. . . He looked calm in death. What a blessing this was! . . . I wish I could write you just what I feel but this is impossible, and if I only set down the crude facts, you can imagine for yourself how sad, how beautiful, how touching this death was. We (Joachim, Clara, and I) have put in order the papers Schumann left behind. . . With every day one thus spends with him one gets to love and admire the man more and more. I shall again and again plunge into them. . . Next time I'll write more and more calmly. . . Frau Clara is as well as can be expected, though not as one could wish.

Sincerely yours,

J. BRAHMS

With Schumann's death and the subsequent crisis in the relationship with Clara, Brahms's youth in the real sense of the word came to an end. The following letters show him wandering around, trying to get a foothold in Detmold, and Hamburg, and finally in Vienna.

Brahms describes his life at Detmold to Joachim:

[Detmold], 5 December [1857]

DEAREST JOSEPH,

. . . The recreations of their Excellencies leave me no time to think of myself. So I am glad that they occupy me thoroughly and that I can derive advantages from a great deal I have so far missed. What a small amount of practical knowledge I have! The choir rehearsals have shown me many weak spots; they won't be a waste of time for me. My stuff is written far too unpractically. I have studied a lot of things with them, and fortunately from the outset with sufficient assurance. . . Bargheer [6] is, as you may imagine, most pleasant to me here. Otherwise there is a complete lack of musical friends, except for a few ladies. I don't want to discourse to you at length on the pleasant and less pleasant experiences I have had here. I even refrain from talking to myself about them; it's better so. But I live most comfortably (in the room where you stayed) and with Kiel [7] I hit it off somewhat better than not at all. . . How is life in Hanover? It's really just as if I had emigrated, as though I had already

6. See p. 56.
7. See p. 65.

become quite rusty as a Detmold conductor. Don't let us leave such long gaps between our letters; it pains me. With all my love your

JOHANNES

Brahms writes to his dear trio [8] *at Göttingen:*

Monday morning [Detmold, Autumn 1858]

Best thanks, my dears, for the beautiful letters and in particular for the long discussions of my things. I could only have wished that your review of my works hadn't warbled and tootled as pleasantly as they are supposed to sound. The few remarks to the contrary are clearly correct, and I am ashamed that they were needed. But I wrote and dispatched too hurriedly and absent-mindedly. The *Brautlied* [9] [Bridal Song] is disgracefully common and dull, though the poem could be beautifully set to music. But it is really unfair. A poor composer sits sadly alone in his room and his head swims with things that should not concern him, and then a critic sits down between two beautiful girls [10] . . . and I don't care to depict the rest.

Thank goodness, my time is half over; the Princess has already told me so with sighs. She is the only person I care about, except Bargheer. Your study of harmony, dear ladies, seems to me to be rather scanty. It seems that Ise [11] has still got to stuff the rules into your mouths like pills. You should remember that the thing only works the other way round. One learns only what one gets out of the teacher. I at least have picked up what I know through question and an-

8. Julius Otto Grimm, his wife Pine, and their common friend, Agathe von Siebold. Apparently Brahms made it a habit to send notes to Agathe through the Grimms.
9. An unfinished work for soprano solo and women's chorus on words by Uhland.
10. Frau Grimm and Agathe.
11. Ise was Grimm's nickname.

swer. . . Now, my dear couple, let me remain behind a little and stroll about with Agathe. That old and cherished custom must not be given up.

Sincerely,

Your JOHANNES

Returning to Hamburg, Brahms does not feel quite at home there any more:

To Joseph Joachim

Hamburg, 18 June 1859

DEAREST JOSEPH,

I was most delighted to see your handwriting, unluckily now so rare. I too can only reply by letter. Frau Musica is rather ungracious; I can't send you a friendly greeting from her. . . I have to complain that I am living here just as in a kitchen [12] . . . and that I can no longer enjoy a walk, or even take one, as I used to when a boy,[13] since I have grown unaccustomed to the big city. You can imagine that it would create difficulties on account of my parents, if I were to live here by myself. So I shall have to leave merely out of delicacy, and yet I should really like to make my home here, I am a regular son of Hamburg. . . I have often made big plans to entice you to this place. There are lovely rooms here outside the gates, so beautiful that I often look longingly at them.[14] However, I am content to let things take their course from day to day (only not so far as concerns your arrival). . . I 'also am busy teaching. One girl always plays better than the other, and some even play still worse.

Sincerely,

Your JOHANNES

12. With as little privacy as a servant.
13. Brahms often composed while walking.
14. It was such a room that Brahms rented from Frau Dr. Rösing in 1861.

First impressions of Vienna, tinged with homesickness:

To Julius Otto Grimm

[Vienna, November 1862]

DEAR FRIEND,

. . . Well, so it goes. I have made a move and am living here ten paces from the Prater [15] and can drink my wine where Beethoven used to drink his. It is also quite cheerful and pleasant here, since it can't be better.[16] To wander through the Black Forest with a wife, as you did, is of course not only jollier but also more beautiful. . .

Your friend

JOHANNES BR.

To Adolf Schubring [17]

[Vienna] [26] March 1863

GREATLY ESTEEMED FRIEND,

. . . I have spent the whole winter here, very much at a loose end, but rather enjoyably and cheerfully. I regret above all things that I didn't know Vienna before. The gaiety of the town, the beauty of the surroundings, the sympathetic and vivacious public, how stimulating all these are to the artist! In addition we have in particular the sacred memory of the great musicians whose lives and work are brought daily to our minds. In the case of Schubert especially one has the impression of his being still alive. Again and again one meets people who talk of him as of a good friend; again and again one comes across new works, the existence of which was unknown and which are so untouched that one can scrape the very writing-sand off them. . .[18] I am suffering

15. A huge park near the Danube.
16. I.e. since I can't be in Hamburg.
17. Adolf Schubring, a judge by profession, was an enthusiastic music friend and music critic.
18. This is to be taken literally. Brahms carefully removed the sand from Schubert's manuscripts and lovingly preserved it in a special box.

in a somewhat old-fashioned way from homesickness and so, when the spring is at its best, I shall probably leave and visit my old mother. . .

Sincerely,

Your Johs. Brahms

Brahms congratulates Joachim on his engagement to Amalie Weiss:

[Vienna 24] February 1863

You lucky dog! What else can I write but some such exclamation? If I set down my wishes, they might appear almost too solemn and serious. Nobody will appreciate your good fortune more than I do just now, when your letter found me in just the mood to be deeply affected. For I cannot leave off wondering whether I, who had better be on my guard against other dreams, am to enjoy everything here except the One, or to go home to have just this one thing, namely the being at home, and give up everything else. Now you break in on these thoughts and boldly pluck for yourself the finest and ripest apples of Paradise. . . May things proceed according to my most heartfelt wishes, and I shall look forward to the time when in your home, as in that of many a faithless friend, I can bend over a cradle and forget to ponder while watching a dear smiling baby's face. . . Take my best wishes and don't stop loving your

Johannes

Brahms about Schubert:

To Adolf Schubring

[Hamburg, 19 June 1863]

My Dear Friend,

. . . My love for Schubert is of a very serious kind, probably because it is not just a fleeting infatuation. Where else is there a genius like his, that soars with such boldness and

[354]

certainty to the sky where we see the very greatest enthroned? He impresses me as a child of the gods, who plays with Jove's thunder, and occasionally handles it in an unusual manner. But he does play in a region and at a height to which the others can by no means attain. . .

Heartiest greetings from your

JOHS. BRAHMS

Brahms considers the town of Dessau on his search for a position:

To Adolf Schubring

[Baden-Baden, 25 June 1865]

DEAR FRIEND,

. . . Since 1 May I have been at Baden-Baden. . . Should you go south for once, let me persuade you to come here. Not only will you give me the greatest pleasure, but you yourself will experience it, pleasure in the natural surroundings and the people here. I also wish that Frau Schumann could make your acquaintance. That would bring you life-long happiness. . .

But I had almost forgotten to write to you about the post of conductor. It now looks as though I may get rid of my involuntary vagabondage. Dessau is not the only place that gives me a bit of a nod. Going by the map, the locality doesn't seem too pleasant, and the neighborhood, of which you boast, is not at all to my liking. What else is there to be said about it? Should one be addressed as Conductor No. 2? Does one have to accept for life? Does one get decent things to bite? Isn't it possible that your theatre is as unbearable as your concerts certainly are not? Yet I am by no means uninterested in such proposals and should be grateful if you would write me more about them. . .

Greetings to your family and yourself

from your

JOHS. BRAHMS

Brahms is reluctant to accept Joachim's invitation to a joint concert tour:

[Lichtental, 10 October 1866]

BELOVED FRIEND,

It may sound like a dissonance to you that I didn't write a single word in answer to your letter. And yet I was so over-joyed, almost touched indeed, to see your handwriting once more. If only the word 'concert' were not spoiling my taste for what is best. But that doesn't sound any better, you'll say. Let it sound like that for the time being; in writing I should modulate too extensively and confusedly. Perhaps the discord can be better resolved in conversation.

Altogether I am not keen on concerts, but this is true of concerts with you for quite a different reason. I cannot say more than that it would be a real delight for me to feel at home in my virtuoso get-up. Now you have grown right up to the sky as a virtuoso, and I have my own ideas and do not like strumming in your company, etc., etc.

Meanwhile do not regard as indifference what was only confusion and do not believe that in my thoughts I join my friends as reluctantly and tardily as I do with my pen. I do look forward to your arrival and, as far as possible, to our little trip. . .

Your JOHANNES

A humorous appeal to Julius Allgeyer [19] to look for something Brahms might have left at his friend's house: [20]

[Vienna] January 1869

DEAR FRIEND,

Methinks I have already failed once in my contention that the attic of thy house still shelters some property of mine. But I cannot refrain from once more advancing this claim,

19. See p. 90.
20. Brahms humorously used a very old-fashioned, Biblical German in this letter, which seemed to ask for the use of the pronoun 'thou' in the translation.

and by no means as mere guesswork. The request is hereby made that thou shalt forthwith prepare to start without delay, climb up to said attic, and look round. Take up old broken crockery and dusty covers, open boxes and cupboards and see whether they are hiding books or clothes. Should'st thou find boots or flimsy summer garments that bring tears of compassion for the friend who wore such wretched things, just throw such moldy stuff into your neighbor's garret.

Carry downstairs and carefully pack up anything that can be used again and address it to my father: Hamburg, Anscharplatz, 5. But if thou would'st dispute the existence of the treasure, or gladden a distant friend with a letter, write to me at Musikhandlung Gotthardt, Vienna. . . Write a good deal more, for in this Carnival-solitude one longs to hear from people and friends.

The pen is bad, the ink little better. Fare thee well. My greetings at home, in the town [of Karlsruhe] and wheresoever thou wilt. Above all remain kind to

Thy

JOHS. BRAHMS

Confronted by suggestions for an opera-libretto from All-geyer, Brahms always finds something wrong with them:

MY DEAR FRIEND, [Vienna, January 1869]

Unfortunately I can make no deduction from the huge sum of my bad manners. I received your kind letter in due time and have nothing whatever against a poet [21] whom I don't know, and a lot in his favour, if you like him. But— I have little courage and inclination to reach into the wide blue sky to snatch at opera libretti by some new poet or

21. Strangely enough, the poet referred to was Joseph V. Widmann, who was to become one of Brahms's dearest friends.

other. If I could go to Winterthur [22] in the spring, I certainly would not fail to have a thorough talk with Widmann. By the by, I am not too much encouraged by your liking for his *Iphigenia* and his finding subjects in Celtic myths. I would rather that his *Stolen Veil* [23] were not inspired by Musaeus and went straight to one's heart. But this is all by the way. Men like myself stand so far removed, not only from the theatre but from all other practical activities, that it is above all desirable for the second partner in such an undertaking to be versed in the usual routine. As a kind remembrance your consignment does not leave my nearest drawer—but I haven't looked much at it!

Greet everybody heartily. I promise solemnly to become a better correspondent. In sincere friendship,

Your

J. BRAHMS

[Vienna] April 1870

DEAR FRIEND,

I shall not fail to ask you as urgently as possible not to give up looking about [for libretti] on my behalf. A man like myself is of very little use in the world. The sort of thing that one could make a decent job of—myself, for example, as a conductor and ultimately as the writer of operas or oratorios—doesn't turn up at the right time. Anyhow do send me the book of *Uthal.* . .[24] I am now pondering over the Jewish liberation from Babylon, though an oratorio would be less acceptable to me than an opera, but I cannot find a satisfactory ending (possibly a reference to Christ). The only thing I can arrive at after much hard thinking is always a 'No.' For instance [Kleist's] *Käthchen von Heilbronn*

22. Widmann was living at Winterthur at that time.
23. *Iphigenia in Delphi* and *Der geraubte Schleier* (The Stolen Veil) are dramas by Widmann.
24. Libretto composed by Méhul.

has often attracted me, and now when I have a decent libretto of it in front of me, all I have learned from it is not to use any text at all, where we, so to speak, only obscure the music of the words by cloaking it with our music.

Greetings at home and in the town and let me hear from you from time to time—if only spasmodically—about what you are reading on my behalf.

Yours

JOHANNES BRAHMS

Brahms gives his publisher, Simrock, a very objective report on the first performance of his 'Rinaldo':

[Vienna], March 1869

DEAR MR. SIMROCK,

. . . I am sure you will want to hear about the first performance and I will tell you all about it at once. First of all, I found it rather amusing and felt no misgivings. The performance was really of a quality that I shall not easily experience again. . . The choir (300 young people) was excellent and the orchestra, after all, was the opera orchestra.

For you, it's the public and the critics that are probably the most important—but on this point there is, as usual, nothing very brilliant to be said. *Rinaldo* was not soundly hissed as my *Requiem* was last year, but I don't think I can call it a success. And this time the critical bigwigs listened and really wrote quite a lot. It is an old experience that people always have definite expectations and are always being served up by us with something quite different. Thus everybody expected this time a crescendo of the *Requiem*, and certainly beautiful, exciting voluptuous goings-on *à la* Venusberg, on account of Armida, &c. That I was recalled more than three times cannot be claimed by me as a proof of success. Therefore I ask you to think matters over once more [before publishing the work]. After all there is quite

a lot of it, and that it gave pleasure to me and a few enthusiasts does not mean much. . . Friendly greetings to you and
your ladies,

Your

J. BRAHMS

Brahms is reluctant to write a sequel to his 'Lullaby':

To Fritz Simrock

[Vienna], April 1869

DEAR MR. SIMROCK,

. . . I am glad, to be sure, that your dear wife has once
more found out why you are married. But as regards the
trifle [Lullaby] you ask for, I have by degrees supplied
enough samples of this article, and I would rather participate
in another capacity in this matter, which, after all, can be
considered from other standpoints. I am afraid this is a terribly long-winded sigh. But I really should have to find some
amusing words to set if I am once more to help rocking other
people's children to sleep. . . But now Addio, greetings to
your dear wife and the Miss,

Your devoted

J. BRAHMS

Brahms tries to curb his publisher's enthusiasm:

To Fritz Simrock

Vienna, February 1870

DEAR FRIEND,

Stop putting pressure on your composers; it might prove
to be as dangerous as it is generally useless. After all,
composing cannot be turned out like spinning or sewing.
Some respected fellow workers (Bach, Mozart, Schubert)
have pampered the world terribly. But if we can't imitate
them in writing beautifully, we should certainly beware of
matching their speed in writing. It would also be unjust to

[360]

put all the blame on idleness alone. Many factors co-operate in making writing harder for my contemporaries, and especially for me. If, incidentally, they would use us poets for some other purpose, they would see that we are of thoroughly and naturally industrious dispositions. But I shall soon be able to give up looking for a 'job.' A contract with you 'for life'! [25] In such a case the advantage would most probably be on my side. Anyway I should be the one to accept such a suggestion without hesitation—therefore I'd rather not do it.

By the way I have no time; otherwise I should love to have a chat on the difficulty of composing and how irresponsible publishers are. . . Before long you'll hear more from your

J. BRAHMS

Brahms's aversion to professional journalism:

At Brahms's suggestion, Allgeyer tried his hand at writing articles on their common friend, the painter Anselm Feuerbach. In the autumn of 1872 he sent one of these to Brahms, who had it published in the magazine *Oesterreichische Wochenschrift für Wissenschaft und Kunst,* and wrote to the author:

[Vienna, 1872-3]

DEAR FRIEND,

I have sent you twelve copies of your admirable article, although the bookseller thought that Levi [26] had already ordered some. Again it gave me the greatest pleasure. One notices particularly when a writer is not a newspaper hack— that is an abomination enough to kill the stoutest heart. I think it cannot be merely my warm feelings for you and Feuerbach that make your words so stimulating to me; others also will realize that a fresher breeze blows from here than from any journalistic desk, and that you have a finer, wider,

25. Simrock's suggestion.
26. Hermann Levi, the great conductor, a common friend of Brahms and Allgeyer (see p. 90).

and clearer point of view. Many will enjoy your sincere, clear, and masterly writing.

Yours,

Joh. Br.

Brahms talks to Otto Dessoff of letter-writing and of his stay at Lichtental:

June 1878

I take a freshly cut pen [27] to have one excuse the less— first, to tell you that I am passionately fond of reading letters from wise, good, and dear people (such as you are), that I even have a secret passion for writing letters, but it is very secret indeed and completely evaporates in front of the note-paper. Never in my life have I written a letter easily or comfortably. Furthermore I must send a greeting to the Villa Becker.[28] Many a happy hour have I spent there in writing much decent music, tunes both sad and gay—which had no influence on the happiness of the hours. . . Now have a good time in this pasture, it is well kept and by no means overgrazed. Leave something behind for me when I come in the autumn. . . Feeling an immense respect for myself and my perseverance,[29] I send the heartiest wishes to you and your hostess as well as to Mrs. Schumann,

Your

J. B.

Brahms's attachment to the Villa Becker was reciprocated by the owner of the house. Dessoff wrote to Brahms: 'Mother Becker sends her greetings and feels as happy as a queen looking for-

27. Brahms preferred quill pens to metal ones.
28. Dessoff was staying and composing at Villa Becker, Lichtental, as Brahms had done before him.
29. The letter, from which only an excerpt is reproduced, was unusually long and dealt mainly with Dessoff's compositions.

ward to your arrival. She confessed to me, she would have cried if you were not coming.'

Brahms vents his dislike of the stage and the work connected with it:

The letter is addressed to Mrs. Wüllner who had written to Brahms that her husband, Franz Wüllner, had been forced by very unpleasant intrigues to resign from his position as court conductor at the Dresden Opera.

[7 May 1882]

DEAR MRS. WÜLLNER,

Pray forgive my keeping silence for so long in spite of all my sympathy. Your letter brought me no unexpected news and your husband can tell you how long I had anticipated something of the kind. If there can be any redeeming feature in connection with such experiences, it is to be found here in the fact that the brutality with which these people acted has made all fair-minded persons express their sympathy with your husband loudly and emphatically, instead of doing so, as usual, only softly and inaudibly. I don't know whether I should say it—but again, like last time,[30] I cannot suppress the wish that your husband should give up his philandering with the stage. A decent and excellent man is at any rate not being pampered, but there [in theatrical circles] he is deliberately asking for the most unjust blows. . .

With kindest greetings to you and him,

Your

J. BRAHMS

Brahms comments on musical conditions in North Germany:

Hans von Bülow had been invited to take over the concerts at Bremen and had accepted on condition that half of them should still be conducted by Karl Reinthaler, who had been in charge

30. When Wüllner suffered a similar fate at the Court Opera of Munich.

of them for twenty-nine years. When informing Brahms, Bülow
observed that Reinthaler, to whom Brahms was indebted for the
first complete performance of his *Requiem,* had more on his
artistic conscience than Brahms knew or cared to believe, whereupon the composer answered:

ESTEEMED FRIEND,   [Between 17 and 28 March 1887]

I am truly glad about your, as I believe, right decision
and your noble action. Let us hope that it will help to give
Reinthaler's life a reasonably pleasant sunset. It may well
be that Reinthaler has more on his conscience—not indeed
than I know or believe—but than I care to mention or discuss. Yes, I concede you this more critical aspect of his activity during the past ten years and should like just to add that
everybody in Bremen has contributed to that [deterioration
of the musical standard] to the utmost of his ability. There
still remain some twenty years during which I can testify
from my own experience that he worked most honorably,
unselfishly, and diligently—and in conflict with what stupidity, indifference, brutality, and foolishness!—and quite
single-handed in this daily fight! How do you think Richard
Strauss, for instance, would shape after being interned in
Bremen for thirty years? . . .

Today but sincere wishes and best congratulations to the
first half-dozen jobs.
                                    Your
                                            J. BRAHMS

*Brahms's reaction to Simrock's purchase of his early compo-
sitions from Breitkopf & Härtel:*

MY GOOD SIMROCK,   1 April 1888

You expect me to congratulate you? But I don't know what
to say, because I don't understand the whole matter, and
what I should like to say or ask seems all indelicate and presumptuous to me. I can't help your over-estimating me im-
mensely. Certainly I haven't contributed towards it through

[364]

my behavior and language. . . Your sympathy touches me,
but I think it exceedingly unwise of you to buy Härtel's
things at goodness knows what high prices, music that cost
them approximately a hundred Louis d'or [31] and which in
the near future won't be worth powder and shot. That I
shall not give my new works to any other publisher I need
hardly promise after our experiences.[32] My wish so to do is
based, as I hope you believe, on very childish and hazy ideas.
You must allow me just a tiny bit of liking for the Peters
edition. I know every argument against it—but it would give
a composer much pleasure if his scores or the *Liebeslieder*
for instance could be bought with greater ease,[33] for certainly
the galleries in the theatre have a better public than the
boxes. But to prove my sympathy to you or rather my commiseration with your great sympathy, I suggest or propose
truly and seriously that henceforth I receive no honorarium,
but that you place a certain sum to my credit, which I can
claim in case of need, but which is simply canceled by my
decease. You know my financial position (better than I do)
and are aware that I can live very well without receiving any
further fees. And live well I will, so far as a man of my
stamp, which is very different from Wagner's,[34] cares to.
After my death, however, I should really leave everything to
you, so that you would get a trifle out of the deal with
Härtel. Well, if I must send them, here are my congratulations, but I wash my hands with carbolic and so forth! And
so, with all my sympathy and heartfelt commiseration,

Your most devoted

J. B.

Written on the first of April. I wish it were an April fool
joke!

31. Brahms refers to the negligible honorarium formerly paid to him.
32. Simrock mostly had his way, even when Brahms felt like giving a
    work to another publisher, such as Peters.
33. Brahms means: at lower prices.
34. Wagner had a penchant for luxurious living.

*Brahms's letter to Heinrich v. Herzogenberg after the death
of the 'wonderful Frau Liesel':*

Vienna, January 1893

BELOVED FRIEND,

I cannot write to you, much though I am with you in my
thoughts. It is useless to try to express to you what absorbs
me wholly and fervently. And you will be sitting mutely in
your grief, you will have no words to utter and will not wish
to hear any.

With anxiety, however, and with the very deepest sympathy do I think of you and I cannot refrain from asking
questions. You know how inexpressibly much I have lost
with your beloved wife, and can therefore imagine with
what emotion I think of you, who were as close to her as
human beings ever can be. When you are again able to
think of yourself and others, let me know how you are and
how and where you plan to live now.

How good would it be for me, if only I could sit silently
near you, to press your hand and think, together with you,
of the dear and glorious one!

Your friend,

J. BRAHMS

How well Brahms, in spite of his reserve, succeeded in expressing his deep-felt emotion! A similar note is struck in a letter to
Julius O. Grimm, after the death of his wife. Here the mood is
one of peculiar gentleness, as the event necessarily brought to
Brahms's mind the unforgettable days spent at Göttingen with
the Grimms and Agathe v. Siebold.

[Vienna, April 1896]

BELOVED FRIEND,

The thought of you does not let go of me! But beautiful
and dear though everything is that reminds me of you and

[366]

your dear wife, how greatly are these thoughts now shrouded in melancholy! It is distressing that two who were so long and closely united must thus be sundered. Maybe your love for her will find serious comfort in the fact that *she* does not now have to share *your* grief and that in your children you have the gracious consolation of seeing her live on. How gladly do I think of your daughter being with you, and with what love will she try fondly to resemble her mother. Perhaps it may also soothe you a little to know how deep a love attaches all your friends to you and how very dear her memory is to us all. Receive my heartfelt greetings in old and true friendship!

Your

J. BRAHMS

Brahms's reaction to the loss of 20,000 marks:

Simrock, who used to invest Brahms's money, lost 20,000 marks for him and proposed to refund the money. Brahms refused this indignantly:

5 April 1895

DEAR FRIEND,

Do not make a useless fuss over the famous bankruptcy—I mean if you were [going to replace [35]] the loss to me—ridiculous! Of course I haven't bothered a moment about the matter, except when I wrote you. Only one thing would have made me angry—if it had been my fault, if it had been my wish to buy those shares. You don't misunderstand me, I hope! I should be ashamed and very vexed if I had wanted to make money that way. But if a good friend makes a mistake, I am sorrier for him than for myself—nay, sorry for him alone, because I think of money merely while I am talking about it. . .

Best greetings to all,

from your J. BRAHMS

35. Brahms actually omits these words to show how utterly repulsive Simrock's suggestion of refunding the money is to him.

Brahms about the prospect of Clara Schumann's death:

In April 1896, after Clara Schumann had suffered an apoplectic stroke, Joachim wrote to Brahms: 'God be thanked, today there was better news of Frau Schumann. I am dizzy at the thought of losing her, and yet one has to get used to the idea.' Brahms answered:

10 April 1890

MY DEAR FRIEND,

. . . I cannot term sad what your letter mentions. I have often thought that Frau Schumann might outlive all her children and me too, but I never wished that for her. The idea of losing her cannot frighten us any more, not even my lonely self, for whom there are far too few living in this world. And when she has gone from us, will not our faces light up with joy at the remembrance of her, of this glorious woman, whose great qualities we have been permitted to enjoy through a long life, only to love and admire her more and more? In this way only shall we grieve for her.

Greeting you with all my heart,

Your J. BR.

APPENDIX II

BRAHMS AS A READER AND COLLECTOR

RARELY has the honorary title of Doctor of Philosophy been bestowed upon an artist with such justification as in the case of Johannes Brahms. The University of Breslau named him *doctor honoris causa* in 1879, paying tribute to Brahms the composer; though doubtless unwittingly, the faculty honored simultaneously a man who merited the distinction for the exceptional breadth and profundity of his culture. For Brahms, whose regular schooling had ceased in his fifteenth year, strove from his earliest youth with uncommon fervor to deepen and extend his knowledge. By his thirst for information and his never-flagging industry, this son of a poor musician became an authority esteemed not only by fellow artists but among men of science as well. It was no mere chance that Brahms's circle of friends and acquaintances included scholars like Spitta, Nottebohm, Pohl, Chrysander, Jahn, and Mandyczewski, the music historian, as well as Wendt the philologist and the famous physicians, Billroth and Engelmann.

This hunger for knowledge manifested itself very early. As a schoolboy Brahms always used his pocket-money for a subscription to the circulating library; and when, in his teens, he played dance-music in little pubs and taverns, he would set a book before him on the music-rack, eagerly reading while his fingers mechanically performed the long-familiar tunes. He made diligent use of the library of his teacher, Marxsen. Here for the first time he had the run of a valuable and well-ordered collection of books and music which he studied with the greatest care, copying out in full anything—such as Beethoven symphonies—that particularly interested him. Later on he ransacked the Schumanns' library, as he himself wrote, with great delight *(mit grosser Wonne)*; and he gladly undertook the task of arranging its books and music in order to become acquainted with their contents. During his summer visits to Thun, in 1886-88, he would wander over to his friend Widmann in Bern with a large leather traveling-bag in which to abduct as many books as possible from the home of that widely cultured writer. In the last years of his life, too, he was a frequent visitor to public libraries. Time and again, in Hamburg, Einsiedeln, Berlin, Vienna, and other cities, he read or copied whatever particularly enthralled him.

In view of the excellent education he thus achieved, it is not surprising that Brahms now and again undertook some piece of work that had no direct connection with his own creative activity: the realization of the continuo in Handel's thirteen chamber duets and two trios, the editing of Couperin's piano works as well as of a supplemental volume to Clara Schumann's edition of her husband's works, the revision of Mozart's *Requiem* wherein he acutely distinguished between the composer's handwriting and Süssmayer's attempts at imitating it. Brahms's analysis was so convincing that it was included in the Collected Edition of Mozart's works. He also edited a sonata for two pianos by W. Friedemann Bach, two violin sonatas by C. Ph. Emanuel Bach and almost three dozen dances for the Collected Edition of Schubert's works. Typical of the wide musicological knowledge Brahms gradually acquired in his attitude on the authenticity of the supposed Bach "Passion According to Saint Luke. "Although the work appeared to be in Bach's own hand, Brahms quite definitely denied the genuineness of the authorship, thus setting himself in opposition to the view of Philipp Spitta, the foremost Bach authority. Today Brahms's standpoint is generally accepted by Bach scholars.

Brahms's interest and learning come to a focus, as it were,

in his own collections. His books and his music are like bits of himself. But although he had a passion for acquiring musical and literary works, ancient and modern, collecting was for him always a means, never an end. Nothing that failed to advance or enrich his experience did he consider worth keeping. Thus his collections—most of their contents conveyed by his last will to the Gesellschaft der Musikfreunde in Vienna (cf., p.177) —enable us to look deep into his mental life.

A true child of his time, Brahms learned as a youth the romantic poetry of the Germans; we find in his library works of Eichendorff, Arnim, Novalis, Hölderlin, Mörike, and his favorite poets, Jean Paul Richter and E.T.A. Hoffmann. Of romantic origin also is Brahms's strong predilection for folk-art. From that sturdy collection *The People's Sayings (Wie das Volk spricht)* and a particularly rich assemblage of old German popular books *(Die schöne Magelone, Dr. Faust, Siegfried, etc.)* , to the great folk-song collections of Herder, Arnim-Brentano *(Des Knaben Wunderhorn)*, the Edda, old English, Scottish, and Danish ballads, and the folk-song collections, with music, of Erk-Böhme, Kretchmar-Zuccalmaglio, Arnold, there is here an abundance of works of popular art from a great variety of nations. Classical literature Brahms experienced later, though in hardly less quantity, than the romantic. Besides works of the "Storm and Stress" period, Herder, Lessing, Goethe, Schiller are fully represented in his collection. He possessed in addition a copy, read almost to pieces, of the Schiller-Goethe letters, as well as Goethe's correspondence with the composer and outstanding choral conductor, C.F. Zelter. Of the older German poets there are, among others, the works of the medieval poet Gottfried of Strassburg and Goedecke's anthology of 16th-century verse.

Brahms was anything but a linguist. Various well-worn French and Italian grammars in his library bear witness to his strenuous efforts to master those languages. Nor did the Italian translations of German classics, presented to him (after their journey to Italy together) by his friend Billroth in the hope of inducting Brahms pleasantly and easily into the secrets of the foreign tongue, achieve their purpose. Brahms's disinclination to desert German-speaking territory (the trips to Italy excepted), and more particularly his opposition to receiving the honorary doctor's degree from Cambridge University (where he would have had to make a personal appearance), were doubtless connected with this weakness. Nonetheless he took the greatest interest in world literature, reading good translations instead of the originals. The ancient classics are represented by the works of Aeschylus, Apuleius, Catullus, Herodotus, Homer, Ovid, Plautus, Plutarch, Sophocles; Romance literature by Boccaccio, Cervantes, Dante, Gozzi, Ariosto, Camoëns, Lesage, and Molière: English by Shakespeare, Buckle, Byron, Emerson, Thomas Moore, and Sterne.

Just as he especially delighted in the literature of bygone days, so also he read history with particular pleasure. The history of civilization, and more especially of art, were favorite subjects, and in these fields he possessed the best works of his time: Grimm's *Life of Michelangelo,* Burckhardt's *Culture of the Renaissance* and *Cicerone,* Lübke's *History of Architecture* and *History of the Renaissance in France,* Wölfflin's *Renaissance and Baroque.* Some indications of Brahm's connection with the artists of his own day are also to be found: Anselm von Feuerbach's *Legacy* and Allgeyer's Feuerbach biography, Adolph Menzel's illustrations to the works of Frederick the Great, and Max Klinger's *Amor and Psyche* etchings, dedicated to Brahms, as well as his *Brahms Fantasies.*

Brahms also followed political developments in Germany with lively concern; his library contained Bismarck's letters, books on the War of 1870, Treitschke's *Historical and Political Essays,* Exner's *On Politics,* and other volumes of the sort. Through his friends Billroth and Engelmann he even came in touch with the medical profession, which explains the pres-

[372]

ence of the former's *Surgical Letters* and the latter's *Experiments on the Microscopic Changes in Muscle-Contraction.* In addition to so much serious matter in this varied collection of books, there is a good representation of light and humorous literature. Brahms owned more than twenty volumes of the satirical magazine *Kladderadatsch,* a short anthology of Wilhelm Busch, the popular humorist, and a manuscript copy of his notorious *Judith and Holofernes* (a travesty on Hebbel's *Judith*), whose title-page proudly notes that the passages suppressed by the censor are here included.

Brahms's music books are naturally of particular interest to us. First and foremost there are the older theoretical works of Adlung, Forkel, Fux, Gerber, Hiller, Keller, Kirnberger, Marpurg, Mattheson, Scheibe, Walter, and others, which Brahms began assembling as a very young man. Then came the great musicological and critical works of his own contemporaries: Jahn's *Mozart,* Chrysander's *Händel,* Spitta's *Bach,* and Pohl's *Haydn;* Nottebohm's *Beethoveniana* and thematic catalogs of Schubert and Beethoven, Köchel's Mozart catalog, Dommer's *Dictionary* and *History of Music,* and Hanslick's critical writings.

The quantity of music Brahms collected is immense. Its foundation-stones are complete editions of Bach, Handel, Schütz, Chopin, Schumann, and Mendelssohn, to which were added a number of magnificent first editions of works of Johann Sebastian and Carl Philipp Emanuel Bach, Domenico Scarlatti, and Gluck. Scarcely to be counted are the works of Mozart, Haydn, Beethoven, and Schubert among Brahms's holdings, some of them also in valuable first editions. So numerous were these—especially insofar as Beethoven and Mozart—that he suffered no loss in not acquiring the monumental complete editions of these composers. Brahms was particularly fond of the little pocket chamber-music scores published by Heckel in Mannheim, which had been given him by Clara Schumann and Joseph Joachim; numerous marginal notes in his own hand show how carefully he used them. Among his contemporaries, his friends are naturally very well represented. But the presence in his library of compositions of Joachim, Herzogenberg, Dvořák, Bruch, Goldmark, Reinthaler, Gräde-ner, has in a way less to do with Brahms's musical convictions than with the circumstances of his life. Yet works by composers outside of Brahms's own circle also found their way into his collection. Of Bizet's compositions which Brahms greatly admired, he owned eight volumes comprising all the operas, but he also collected works by Liszt, partly for piano, partly for orchestra. Of Wagner's music we find a magnificent luxury edition of the *Rheingold* score with a friendly dedication from the composer to Brahms (cf. p.83), the *Tannhäuser* score printed from Wagner's beautiful holograph and presented to Brahms by Peter Cornelius, as well as *Lohengrin* and *Flying Dutchman*. Bruckner is represented by symphonies Nos. 7 and 8 and the *Te Deum;* Hugo Wolf by the Mörike songs. Of Berlioz he owned four compositions, among them the score to *La Damnation de Faust* which Hans von Bülow had given him as "a small sign of homage." Cherubini is included with his opera *Médée,* Boieldieu with *La Dame Blanche,* an opera, incidentally, whose German edition Brahms had instigated. César Franck sent his symphonic poem *Rédemption* and Grieg his String Quartet, Op.27, both with courteous dedications.

While some of these works may not have kindled Brahms's interest, he wholeheartedly enjoyed and thoroughly studied the older music which he acquired, eagerly awaiting the appearance of each new volume in the various collected editions. Haydn's works, which he greatly admired, were unfortunately not yet available in a complete edition. Brahms owned much of his output, including the miniature score of the string quartets published by Heckel. He entered in the text all deviations from the several autographs available to him. He carefully studied the *Catalogue thématique et chronologique des quatuors complets de Joseph Haydn* published by Trautwein,

[374]

Berlin, and added all the information available to him regarding the original manuscripts and dates of publication,
thus producing quite a respectable *catalogue raisonné* of these
works.

Not less fervent was Brahms's interest in the music of pre-
'classical times. He owned and cherished organ works by Bux-
tehude as well as Georg Muffat's *Apparatus musico-organis-
ticus,* in its original 1680 edition. Of Domenico Scarlatti's
sonatas he owned no less than three different editions: the
rare original print of thirty Sonatas published in Madrid; the
Czerny edition of 200 Sonatas; and a large handwritten set of
over 300 Sonatas in seven volumes whose provenance, in all
likelihood, was the imposing collection of Abbate Santini in
Rome. To these seven volumes Brahms made a careful thematic catalog.

Unquestionably the autographs form the most precious
part of Brahms's collection (cf p.177) . The jewel among these
is the score of Mozart's great G-minor Symphony which
Brahms received from the Landgravine Anna of Hesse as a
token of thanks for the dedication of his Piano Quintet. Of
particular value also are the daintily-penned scores of Haydn's
six "Sun Quartets" (Op. 20) and two unique sheets bearing
Beethoven's song "Ich liebe dich so wie du mich" and a Schubert Andante for piano in D minor (later transposed to G
minor and used in the E-flat major piano sonata) . Brahms
owned more than sixty sheets of Beethoven sketches, among
them some for the *Egmont* Overture, the Ninth Symphony,
and the Piano Sonata, Op. 106. There is also a complete score
of the *Missa Solemnis* written by a copyist, but exhibiting
numerous corrections and additions by the composer. Of original Schubert manuscripts he possessed a number of songs,
among them the "Wanderer," several fragments and sketches,
and twenty-four pages with various dances. Schumann,
Brahms's intimate friend, is represented by larger works, such
as the first version of the D-minor Symphony, the Overture to

Schiller's *Bride of Messina,* the orchestral suite *Overture, Scherzo and Finale,* the "Davidsbündler" dances, the piano score of "Scenes from Goethe's *Faust,*" and the original finale to the G-minor Piano Sonata. Among smaller compositions of other masters there are Berlioz's *La mort d'Ophélie,* Chopin's E-minor Mazurka and A-flat major Prelude, Mendelssohn's motet *In the midst of life we are in death,* the closing scene of Johann Strauss's *Ritter Pazman,* and the concert ending of Wagner's prelude to *Tristan und Isolde.* Last but not least, there are forty of Brahms's own manuscripts, among them the *Liebeslieder* waltzes, the C-minor Piano Trio, the Double Concerto, the G-major String Quintet, the Clarinet Quintet, the Cello Sonata in F major, and others.

Brahms was a diligent copyist, reproducing by his own hand poetry which he used later for song-texts as well as music he deemed worthy of study. He had one notebook with manuscript copies of canons by Caldara, Cherubini, Haydn, Mozart, and others. Works by older composers appear in Brahms's hand as well, among them Bach, Cesti, Cherubini, Frescobaldi, Giovanni Gabrieli, Gallus, Hassler, Lasso, Mattheson, Praetorius, Schütz, and more. This interesting part of Brahms's library also contains a great many transcriptions of folk-songs.

His collections engage our attention not only for the variety of their contents but also for Brahms's extensive marginal notes—delightful glimpses into the nature and the idiosyncrasies of the man. A highly conscientious reader, he always corrected typographical errors and mistakes in grammar. With scholarly care he would compare the modern editions of the classics with the best sources—autographs and first editions, noting all differences or inaccuracies. Naturally he painstakingly hunted for the errors in the printed editions of his own works. He kept corrected copies of all his compositions, and these provided the most important basis for the critical edition of his complete works.

He had a passion for ferreting out parallel fifths and octaves in the works of great composers. Whatever his keen critical eyes espied, he scrupulously registered for purposes of study, starting with Lasso and progressing up to Schumann and Liszt, thus getting well over a hundred items for his collection. Here are a few out of the many examples he so noted:*

Sometimes Brahms's marginal entries are spontaneous outbursts of a lively temperament. At one point in the *Butterflies*, verses by the Swiss poet Spitteler, he wrote "Beautiful" *(Schön)*. On the other hand, at a sugary passage in Suess's *Progress of Mankind* he says: "a better example might have

*Cf., H. Schenker: *Johannes Brahms, Oktaven und Quinten*. Wien 1933.

been chosen. Sentimental" *(hätte wohl etwas Besseres als Beispiel gewähit werden können. Sentimentale)* As a youth— quite in the Romantic spirit—he had copied out passages that particularly appealed to him. The notebook containing these entries, together with the *Fine Thoughts about Music,* was published in 1909 by the German Brahms Society. In riper years Brahms lacked the leisure to carry on these time-consuming quotations; but the necessity also fell away, for now he could afford to acquire any books that appealed to him for his library. He adopted the simpler method of marking the passages that pleased him, and there is an immense number of these highly characteristic underscorings.

Naturally only a few examples can be given here. In Arnim's *Raphael and his Women Neighbors* Brahms underlines: "The artist must limit himself in order not to dissipate his efforts" *(Der Künstler muss sich beschränken um nicht zerstreut zu werden).* Equally expressive of Brahms's self-discipline is the marked passage in Vischer's commentary to Goethe's *Faust:* "Certainly: without the mood, no poetry. But the poet (and artist) must not be too soft, must not always wait for the mood just to come. He must, like any other workman, force himself on many a long day to work in the hope that in the course of progress the beginning will improve. Even the poet has to exert his will if something is to be accomplished" *(Gewiss: ohne Stimmung keine Poesie. Aber der Dichter [und Künstler] darf auch nicht zu weich sein, nicht immer warten, dass die Stimmung eben komme. Er muss doch wie ein anderer Arbeiter auch gar manchen lieben Tag sich zur Arbeit zwingen in der Hoffnung, dass im Fortgang der Anfang sich verbessere. Auch der Poet braucht eben Willensakte wenn etwas fertig werden soll).* There is surely a sorrowful autobiographical significance to be seen in the passage from Reichel's *Day of Judgment* which Brahms has marked with several exclamation marks: "Suffering raged in his soul, which only he can feel who is condemned to sorrow over the failure of his ex-

[378]

istence" *(In seiner Seele wühlten Schmerzen, die nur der ver-mag zu fühlen, der verdammt ist zu trauern über ein verfehl-tes Dasein).*

But with Brahms's native humor, tragedy had its satirical relief. He always marked jokes, funny and coarse, and what-ever curiosities he ran across in his books, and it is scarcely surprising that the highly-spiced treasury of *The People's Say-ings,* with its crude expressions, was full of such marginal markings. Similarly it was but natural that, in his copy of the Koran, the misogynist Brahms should have approvingly marked all those passages referring to the inferiority of women.

Brahms was a perfectionist and a venerator of learning. He would work away for years at his compositions, altering, im-proving, pouring them from one mold into another, until he had succeeded in giving them the perfect form. If he compiled a list of the parallel fifths and octaves he found in great com-positions, it was not for the petty joy of discovering little shortcomings, but because he was bent on discovering in what cases these "forbidden" progressions were possible, even nec-essary. The words underlined by Brahms in Goethe's *Theory of Color* were for him a sort of confession of faith: "We are only original because we know nothing" *(Wir sind nur origi-nell, weil wir nichts wissen).*

Many such threads link Brahms the collector with Brahms the composer, clearly showing that his passion for collecting sprang from the very nature of his artistic personality.

July, 1981

BIBLIOGRAPHY

G. Adler: *Handbuch der Musikgeschichte.* Berlin 1930.

'Johannes Brahms.' *Musical Quarterly,* April 1933.

W. Altmann: 'Bach-Zitate in der Violoncello-Sonate op. 38 von Brahms.' *Die Musik,* 1912.

H. Antcliffe: 'Brahms.' *Bell's Miniature Series of Musicians,* London 1905.

R. C. Bagar: *Brahms on Records.* New York 1942.

O. von Balassa: *Die Brahms-Freundin Ottilie Ebner.* Wien 1932.

R. Barth: *Johannes Brahms und seine Musik.* Hamburg 1904.

W. Blume: *Brahms in der Meininger Tradition.* Stuttgart (1933).

J. Brahms: Collected Edition of his works, edition of the 'Gesellschaft der Musikfreunde,' revised by E. Mandyczewski and H. Gál. Leipzig 1926-28.

Correspondence, published by the 'Deutsche Brahms-Gesellschaft,' 16 volumes. Berlin 1907-22

Volumes 1 and 2 (Letters to and from Mr. and Mrs Herzogenberg) translated by H. Brayant. London 1909.

F. Brand: *Das Wesen der Kammermusik von Brahms.* Berlin 1937.

'Das neue Brahms Trio.' *Die Musik,* February 1939.

Ph. Browne: *Brahms: The Symphonies.* London 1933.

E. Bücken: 'Ein neuaufgefundenes Jugendwerk von Johannes Brahms.' *Die Musik,* October 1937.

M. von Bülow: *Hans v. Bülow, Briefe und Schriften.* Leipzig, 1895-1908.

J. N. Burk: *Clara Schumann.* New York 1940.

F. Callomon: 'Some Unpublished Brahms Correspondence.' *Musical Quarterly,* January 1943.

H. C. Colles: *Brahms.* London 1920.

The Chamber Music of Brahms. London 1933.

H. Deiters: *Johannes Brahms: A Biographical Sketch,* translated by R. Newmarch. London 1880.

O. E. Deutsch: 'The First Editions of Brahms.' *Music Review,* 1940.

A. Dietrich and J. V. Widmann: *Recollections of Johannes Brahms* (translated by Dora E. Hecht). London 1899.

H. S. Drinker: *Texts of the vocal works of Johannes Brahms*. New York 1945.

The Chamber Music of Johannes Brahms. Philadelphia 1932.

S. H. Drinker: 'Brahms's Music for Women.' *Music Clubs Magazine*, January 1940.

A. von Ehrmann: *Johannes Brahms, Weg, Werk und Welt*. Leipzig 1933.

Johannes Brahms, Thematisches Verzeichnis. Leipzig 1933.

A. Einstein: 'Briefe von Brahms an E. Frank.' *Zeitschrift für Musikwissenschaft*, 1922.

J. L. Erb: *Brahms*. London 1925.

G. Ernest: *Johannes Brahms*. Berlin 1930.

E. Evans: *Historical, Descriptive and Analytical Account of the Entire Works of Johannes Brahms*. Four volumes. London 1912-38.

R. Fellinger: *Klänge um Brahms*. Berlin 1933.

M. Friedlaender: 'Brahms' Volkslieder.' *Jahrbuch Peters*, 1902.

Brahms' Lieder (translated by C. Leonard Leese). London 1928.

Neue Volkslieder von Brahms. Berlin 1926.

J. A. Fuller-Maitland: *Johannes Brahms*. London 1911.

K. Geiringer: 'Brahms als Musikhistoriker.' *Die Musik*, 1933.

'Johannes Brahms im Briefwechsel mit E. Mandyczewski.' *Zeitschrift für Musikwissenschaft*, 1933.

'Ein zweites Schatzkästlein des jungen Kreisler.' *Zeitschrift für Musik*, 1933.

'Brahms as a Reader and Collector.' *Musical Quarterly*, 1933.

'Brahms and Wagner.' *Musical Quarterly*, 1936.

'Brahms' Mutter.' *Schweizerische Musikzeitung*, 1936.

'Brahms and Chrysander.' *Monthly Musical Record*, 1937/38.

R. Gerber: *Johannes Brahms*. Potsdam 1938.

C. A. T. Gottlieb-Billroth: *Billroth und Brahms im Briefwechsel*. Wien 1935.

C. Gray: 'Johannes Brahms' in H. J. Voss: *The Heritage of Music*. London 1927.

W. H. Hadow: *Studies in Modern Music*, 2nd series. London 1926.

J. A. G. Harrison: *Brahms and his Four Symphonies*. London 1939.

Sir G. Henschel: *Personal Recollections of Johannes Brahms*. Boston 1907.

Musings and Memories of a Musician. London 1918.

R. Hernried: *Johannes Brahms*. Leipzig 1934.

R. Hill: *Brahms*. London 1933.

E. Hitschmann: *Johannes Brahms und die Frauen*. Wien 1933.

R. Hohenemser: 'Brahms und die Volksmusik.' *Die Musik*, 1903.

BIBLIOGRAPHY

W. Hübbe: *Brahms in Hamburg.* Hamburg 1902.

C. Huschke: *J. Brahms als Pianist, Dirigent und Lehrer.* Karlsruhe 1936.

Die Frauen um Brahms. Karlsruhe 1937.

W. Hutschenruyter: *Johannes Brahms.* The Hague 1928.

G. Jenner: *Johannes Brahms als Mensch, Lehrer und Künstler.* Marburg 1905.

'Zur Entstehung des Dmoll-Klavierkonzertes von Brahms.', *Die Musik,* 1912.

J. Joachim: *Letters from and to J. Joachim,* selected and translated by Nora Bickley. London.

M. Kalbeck: *Johannes Brahms.* Berlin 1904-14.

Brahms als Lyriker. Wien 1921.

J. Karpath: *Begegnung mit dem Genius.* Wien 1934.

L. Koch: *Brahms in Ungarn.* Budapest 1933.

M. Komorn: *Johannes Brahms als Chordirigent in Wien und seine Nachfolger.* Wien 1928.

'Brahms as Choral Conductor.' *Musical Quarterly,* 1933.

C. Krebs: *Des jungen Kreislers Schatzkästlein.* Berlin 1909.

P. Landormy: *Brahms.* Paris 1921.

E. M. Lee: *Brahms the Man and his Music.* London 1915.

Brahms's Orchestral Works. London 1931.

R. Lienau: *Erinnerungen an Johannes Brahms.* Berlin 1934.

B. Litzmann: *Clara Schumann.* Leipzig 1902-8.

English translation (abridged) by G. E. Hadow. London 1913.

Letters of Clara Schumann and Johannes Brahms. New York 1927.

V. Luithlen: 'Studie zu Johannes Brahms' Werken in Variationenform. *Studien zur Musikwissenschaft,* 1927.

E. Mandyczewski: 'Die Bibliothek Brahms'.' *Musikbuch aus Oesterreich,* 1904.

F. H. Martens: *Brahms.* New York 1925.

D. G. Mason: *From Grieg to Brahms.* New York 1927.

The Chamber Music of Brahms. New York 1933.

F. May: *Johannes Brahms.* London 1905.

E. Michelmann: *Agathe von Siebold.* Göttingen 1930.

P. Mies: *Stilmomente und Ausdrucksstilformen im Brahms' schen Lied.* Leipzig 1923.

'Aus Brahms' Werkstatt.' *Simrock-Jahrbuch,* 1928.

'Der kritische Rat der Freunde und die Veröffentlichung der Werke bei Brahms.' *Simrock-Jahrbuch,* 1929.

Johannes Brahms. Leipzig 1930.

H. Miesner: *Klaus Groth und die Musik. Erinnerungen an Brahms.* Heide 1933.

V. von Miller zu Aichholz: *Brahms-Bilderbuch.* Wien 1905.

A. Moser: *Joseph Joachim.* Berlin 1908-10.

J. Müller-Blattau: *Johannes Brahms.* Potsdam 1933.
'Der junge Brahms.' *Die Musik,* 1933.

W. Murdoch: *Brahms, with an Analytical Study of the Complete Pianoforte Works.* London 1933.

W. Nagel: *Die Klaviersonaten von J. Brahms.* Stuttgart 1915.
Johannes Brahms. Stuttgart 1923.

W. Niemann: *Brahms* (translated by Catherine Allison Philipps). London 1929.

G. Ophüls: *Brahms-Texte.* Berlin 1898.
Erinnerungen an Johannes Brahms. Berlin 1921.

A. Orel: 'Skizzen zu Brahms' Haydn Variationen.' *Zeitschrift für Musikwissenschaft,* 1923.
'Johannes Brahms und Julius Allgeyer.' *Simrock-Jahrbuch,* 1928.

W. Pauli: *Brahms.* Berlin 1907.

R. von Perger: *Johannes Brahms.* Leipzig (without year).

J. Pulver: *Johannes Brahms.* New York 1926.

H. Riemann: 'Johannes Brahms und die Theorie der Musik.' *Programmbuch zum 1. deutschen Brahms-Fest,* 1909.

R. H. Schauffler: *The Unknown Brahms.* New York 1933.

H. Schenker: *Johannes Brahms, Oktaven und Quinten.* Wien 1933.

A. Schering: 'Johannes Brahms und seine Stellung in der Musikgeschichte des 19. Jahrhunderts.' *Jahrbuch Peters,* 1932.

W. Schramm: *Brahms in Detmold.* Leipzig 1933.

E. Schumann: *The Schumanns and Johannes Brahms.* New York 1927.

N. Simrock: *Verzeichnis aller im Druck erschienenen Werke von Johannes Brahms.* Berlin 1908.

E. Smyth: Brahms as I Remember Him.' *Radio Times,* 5 May 1933.

R. Specht: *Johannes Brahms* (translated by Eric Blom). London 1930.

M. Spies: *Hermine Spies.* Leipzig 1905.

Ph. Spitta: *Johannes Brahms* translated by Mrs. Bell. New York 1901.

C. V. Stanford: *Brahms.* New York 1912.
Studies and Memories. London 1908.

K. Stephenson: *Johannes Brahms' Heimatbekenntnis.* Hamburg 1933.

S. Stojowski: 'Recollections of Brahms.' *Musical Quarterly* 1933.

A. Sturke: *Der Stil in Brahms' Werken.* Würzburg 1932.

W. A. Thomas-San Galli: *Johannes Brahms.* München 1922.

D. F. Tovey: 'The Chamber Music of Brahms.' *Cobbett's Cyclopedic Survey of Chamber Music.* London 1929.

[384]

V. Urbantschitsch: 'Die Entwicklung der Sonatenform bei Brahms. *Studien zur Musikwissenschaft,* 1927.

J. V. Widmann: *Johannes Brahms in Erinnerungen.* Berlin 1898. *Sizilien und andere Gegenden Italiens.* Frauenfeld 1912.

VOCAL WORKS OF JOHANNES BRAHMS
in new English translations by Henry S. Drinker
AVAILABLE THROUGH THE
Association of American Choruses, Westminster Choir College,
Princeton, New Jersey

Solo Songs with Piano accompaniment, 3 volumes
Forty-nine Folk songs for voice and piano (seven of them with little choruses)
Fourteen Children's Folk songs
Liebeslieder, Op. 52
Neue Liebeslieder, Op. 65
Vineta, for women's chorus (original version)
Es geht ein Wehen, for women's chorus (original version)
In stiller Nacht, for women's chorus (original version of *Todtenklage*)
Dein Herzlein mild, for women's chorus
Grausam erweiset, Töne lindernder Klang, for women's chorus
Fourteen Canons for 3 and 4 voices, for women's chorus
Seven of the part songs from Op. 44, for women's chorus
Six of the *Marienlieder,* Op. 22, for women's chorus (original version)
Seven Folk songs for women's chorus
Fourteen Folk songs for mixed chorus
Geistliches Lied, Op. 30
Vineta, Op. 42. No. 2 (for mixed chorus)
Requiem, Op. 45
Rinaldo, Op: 50
Rhapsody, Op. 53
Schicksalslied, Op. 54
Nänie, Op. 82
Gesang der Parzen, Op. 89
Five mixed choruses, Op. 104
Motets, Op. 110

SUPPLEMENTARY BIBLIOGRAPHY

M. Alley and J. Alley: *A Passionate Friendship: Clara Schumann and Brahms* (translated by M. Savill) . London 1956.

K. Blum: *Hundert Jahre Ein deutsches Requiem von Johannes Brahms.* Tutzing 1971.

J. Brahms: *Intermezzi, Op. 119, Nr. 2 und 3: Faksimile des Autographs* (mit einem Nachwort von F.G. Zeileis) . Tutzing 1975.
  Opus 24, Opus 23, Opus 18, Opus 90 (facsimiles of holograph Mss. in the Library of Congress, Washington, D.C.) . New York 1976.

H.J. Busch: "Die Orgelwerke von Johannes Brahms." *Ars Organi*, 1963.

J. Chissell: *Brahms.* London 1971.

E. Crass: *Johannes Brahms: sein Leben in Bilden. Leipzig* 1957.

K. Dale: *Brahms: a Biography with a Survey of Books, Editions and Recordings.* Hamden 1970.

P. Dedel: *Johannes Brahms: a Guide to his Autographs in Facsimile.* Ann Arbor 1978.

E.S. Derr: "Brahms's Four-Hand Transcriptions of his Works for Various Ensembles." *Detroit International Brahms Congress*, April 1980.

O.E. Deutsch: "Die Brotarbeiten des jungen Brahms." *Österreichische Musikzeitschrift*, 1960.

S. Drinker: *Brahms and his Women's Choruses.* Merion 1952.

I. Fellinger: "Brahms Sonate für Pianoforte und Violine, Op. 78: ein Beitrag zum Schaffenprozess des Meisters." *Die Musikforschung*, 1965.
  "Brahms und die Musik vergangener Epochen," in *Die Ausbreitung des Historismus über die Musik* (hrsg. v. W. Wiora) . Regensburg 1969.
  "Das Brahms-Bild der *Allgemeinen Musikalischen Zeitung* (1863 bis 1882)'," in *Beiträge zur Geschichte der Musikkritik* (hrsg. v. H. Becker) . Regensburg 1965.
  "Grundzüge Brahmsscher Musikauffassung," in *Beiträge zur Geschichte der Musikanschauung im 19. Jahrhundert* (hrsg. v. W. Salmen) . Regensburg 1965.
  Über die Dynamik in der Musik von Johannes Brahms. Berlin 1961.

J.A. Fuller-Maitland: *Brahms.* Port Washington 1972. (Reprint of 1911 edition)

W. Furtwängler: *Johannes Brahms, Anton Bruckner.* Stuttgart 1952.

H. Gál: *Johannes Brahms: his Work and Personality* (translated by Joseph Stein) . New York 1963.

K. Geiringer and I. Geiringer: "The Brahms Library in the Gesellschaft der Musikfreunde, Wien." *Notes* 1973.

K. Giebeler: *Die Lieder von Johannes Brahms:* Münster/Westfalen 1969.

F. Grasberger: *Johannes Brahms: Variationen um sein Wesen.* Wien 1952. *Das kleine Brahmsbuch.* Salzburg 1973.

J.A.G. Harrison: *Brahms and his Four Symphonies.* New York 1971. (Reprint of the 1939 edition)

M. Harrison: *The Lieder of Brahms.* London 1972.

S. Helms: *Die Melodiebildung in den Liedern von Johannes Brahms und ihr Verhältnis zu Volksliedern und volkstümlichen Weisen.* Nordhorn 1968.

R. Heuberger: *Erinnerungen an Johannes Brahms: Tagebuchnotizen aus den Jahren 1875 bis 1897* (edited by K. Hofmann) . Tutzing 1971.

K. Hofmann: *Die Bibliothek von Johannes Brahms: Bücher- und Musikalienverz.* Hamburg 1974.

Die Erstdrucke der Werke von Johannes Brahms: Bibliographie mit Wiedergabe von 209 Titelblättern. Tutzing 1975.

J. Horton: *Brahms Orchestral Music.* Seattle 1969.

B. Jacobson: *The Music of Johannes Brahms.* London 1977.

C. Jacobsen: *Das Verhältnis von Sprache und Musik in Ausgewählten Liedern von Johannes Brahms, dargestellt an Parallelvertonungen.* Hamburg 1975.

B. James: *Brahms: a Critical Study.* New York 1972.

I. Keys: *Brahms Chamber Music.* London 1974.

S. Kross: *Die Chorwerke von Johannes Brahms.* Berlin 1963.

"Rhythmik und Sprachbehandlung bei Brahms," In *Bericht über den Internationalen Musikwissenschaftlichen Kongress.* Kassel 1962.

"Zur Frage der Brahmsschen Volksliedbearbeitungen." *Die Musikforschung,* 1958.

P. Latham: *Brahms.* London 1966.

K. Laux: *Der Einsame: Johannes Brahms, Leben und Werk.* Graz 1944.

D.M. McCorkle, ed.: *Variations on a Theme of Haydn: for Orchestra, Op. 56A and for Two Pianos, Op. 56B.* New York 1976.

D.G. Mason: *The Chamber Music of Brahms.* Ann Arbor 1950. (Reprint, with corrections, of the 1933 edition)

[387]

P. Mast: "Brahm's Collection of Octaves and Fifths," in *Music Forum*, vol. 5, forthcoming, Columbia University Press.

W. Morik: *Johannes Brahms und sein Verhältnis zum deutschen Volkslied.* Tutzing 1965.

H.A. Neunzig: *Brahms: der Komponist des deutschen Bürgertums: eine Biographie.* Wien 1976.

Johannes Brahms in Selbstzeufinissen und Bilddokumenten. Reinbek 1973.

A. Orel: *Johannes Brahms: ein Meister und sein Weg.* Wien 1950.

Johannes Brahms und Julius Allgeyer: eine Künstlerfreundschaft in Briefen. Tutzing 1964.

W. Rehberg: *Johannes Brahms: sein Leben und Werk.* Zürich 1947.

W. Reich: *Johannes Brahms in Documenten zu Leben und Werk.* Zürich 1975.

C. Rostrand: *Brahms.* Two volumes. Paris 1954-55.

E. Sams: *Brahms Songs.* Seattle 1972.

A. Schönberg: "Brahms the Progressive," in *Style and Idea.* New York 1950.

W. Siegmund-Schultze: *Johannes Brahms: eine Biographie.* Lipzig 1966.

N. Simrock: *Thematic Catalog of the Collected Works of Brahms* (enlarged edition, edited with a foreword by Joseph Braunstein). New York 1956.

The N. Simrock Thematic Catalog of the Works of Johannes Brahms (with new introduction, including addenda and corrigenda by D.M. McCorkle). New York 1973.

K. Stehmer: *Musikalische Formung in soziologischem Bezug, dargestellt an der instrumentalen Kammermusik von Johannes Brahms.* Kiel 1968.

K. Stephenson, ed.: *Johannes Brahms in seiner Familie: der Briefwechsel.* Hamburg 1973.

Johannes Brahms und Fritz Simrock: Weg einer Freundschaft: Briefe des Verlëgers an den Komponisten. Hamburg 1961.

Y. Tiénot: *Brahms: son vrai visage.* Paris 1968.

J.F. Weber: *Brahms Lieder: a Discography.* New York 1970.

J. Webster: "Schubert's Sonata Form and Brahms's First Maturity." *19th Century Music*, 1978.

J. Wetschky: *Die Kanontechnik in der Instrumentalmusik von Johannes Brahms.* Regensburg 1967.

W. Wiora: *Die Rheinisch-bergischen Melodien bei Zuccalmaglio und Brahms: alte Liedweisen in romantischer Färbung.* Bad Godesberg 1953.

Other titles of interest

THE DA CAPO OPERA MANUAL
Nicholas Ivor Martin
752 pp.
80807-2 $24.50

**THE ART AND TIMES
OF THE GUITAR**
An Illustrated History
Frederic V. Grunfeld
340 pp., 200 photos
80336-4 $14.95

**THE ART OF ACCOMPANYING
AND COACHING**
Kurt Adler
260 pp., 21 illus.
80027-6 $15.95

CHARLES IVES REMEMBERED
An Oral History
Vivian Perlis
256 pp., 80 illus.
80576-6 $13.95

**THE COMPANION TO
20th-CENTURY MUSIC**
Norman Lebrecht
440 pp., 151 illus.
80734-3 $16.95

**THE COMPLETE OPERAS
OF MOZART**
Charles Osborne
349 pp., 23 photos
80190-6 $14.95

**THE COMPLETE OPERAS
OF PUCCINI**
Charles Osborne
282 pp., 16 photos
80200-7 $14.95

**THE COMPLETE OPERAS OF
RICHARD STRAUSS**
Charles Osborne
248 pp., 19 illus.
80459-X $13.95

**THE COMPLETE OPERAS
OF RICHARD WAGNER**
Charles Osborne
304 pp., 25 illus.
80522-7 $13.95

**THE COMPLETE OPERAS
OF VERDI**
Charles Osborne
458 pp.
80072-1 $14.95